Dictionary of ECONOMICS and BUSINESS

By ERWIN ESSER NEMMERS

About the Author

Received his A.B. from Marquette University; his A.M. in economics from the University of Chicago; and his Ph.D. in economics from the University of Wisconsin. He also holds the LL.B. from the Harvard Law School, the S.J.D. from the University of Wisconsin, and the C.P.A. from the State of Wisconsin. He is a member of the Wisconsin, Illinois, Federal, and United States Supreme Court bars. He is the author of *Hobson and Underconsumption* (1956), *Managerial Economics: Text and Cases* (1962), *Cases in Finance* (1964), *Business Research: Text and Cases* (1966) and *Basic Managerial Finance* (1970). Many of his studies have appeared in scholarly journals. Dr. Nemmers is Professor of Management, Graduate School of Management, at Northwestern University and is associated in various capacities with several industrial companies. Dr. Nemmers was previously on the faculty of the University of Wisconsin (both Madison and Milwaukee) and at Milton College.

Dictionary of ECONOMICS and BUSINESS

By

ERWIN ESSER NEMMERS

Professor of Management
Graduate School of Management
Northwestern University

1976

LITTLEFIELD, ADAMS & CO.

Totowa, New Jersey

First Edition 1959
Second Edition 1966
Third Edition 1974
Reprinted 1976

Library of Congress Cataloging in Publication Data

Nemmers, Erwin Esser, 1916–
Dictionary of Economics and Business

(A Littlefield, Adams Quality Paperback No. 33)
1. Economics—Dictionaries. I. Title.

HB61.N45 1973 330'.03 73–22090
ISBN 0-8226-0033-1

PRINTED IN THE UNITED STATES OF AMERICA

Aids in Using the Dictionary

This dictionary lists terms under their abbreviations. Thus American Federation of Labor is under AFL, since one can find the latter given the former, but not vice versa.

This dictionary is designed to include the terms commonly used in courses in the following subjects:

- accounting
- administration
- business cycles
- business law
- business and government
- business organization
- econometrics
- economics
- economic theory
- finance
- insurance
- international economics
- investments
- labor problems
- management science
- marketing
- money and banking
- operation research
- personnel management
- production
- public finance
- public utilities
- real estate
- securities
- statistics
- taxation
- transportation

This dictionary distinguishes between: SEE, which refers only to the alphabetical location of the term; SAME AS, which identifies two different terms as having the same meaning; CF. (COMPARE), which identifies related terms. Italicized words are defined elsewhere in the dictionary.

One violation of alphabetizing occurs when there are a number of specific types of a general term. These are listed immediately after the general term. Thus, *accounts, types of,* follows immediately after *account* rather than in the place where *accounts, types of* should alphabetically appear.

AAA Agricultural Adjustment Act. A 1933 federal law intended to aid farmers by raising the prices of crops and livestock through controlling their production. The law of 1933 was declared unconstitutional but a revised law of 1938 is constitutional. It provides for: (1) soil conservation, (2) research laboratories, (3) *parity prices* and marketing quotas, and (4) loans by Commodity Credit Corporation. The abbreviation also stands for Agricultural Adjustment Administration, an agency of the Department of Agriculture, administering the law.

abandonment. (1) The relinquishment or surrender of rights, interests, or property by one person to another either expressly or by implication. (2) Fire insurance policies now have an "abandonment clause" which forbids the owner to abandon fire-damaged property, and requires him to take good care of it until an adjustment is made with the insurer. (3) In transportation, the refusal by the consignee to receive freight so damaged as to be worthless.

abatement. (1) Extinguishing all or part of a claim. A tax abatement is really a cancellation of the tax claim. (2) Legal steps to terminate a nuisance.

ability to pay tax theory. The most common principle on which the tax burden is based. Income, property, or consumption can be used as a basis for measuring ability to pay. Theoretically ability to pay is measured by sacrifice (loss of utility). Cf. *benefit tax theory; diffusion tax theory; sacrifice tax theory.*

ab initio. Latin for "from the beginning." In law, used particularly with reference to the question of illegality as to whether a sale, contract, etc., is to be set aside from its inception or from the time of action by a party.

abrasion of coin. The loss of weight sustained by money as it passes from hand to hand while in circulation.

absenteeism rate. The number of days of lost time in relation to the number of possible working days is referred to as the absenteeism rate. The most frequently used formula is $A = L/F$, where A = absenteeism rate, L = number of days of lost time, and F = number of possible working days.

absentee ownership. Separation of the place of residence of owners from the location of the property from which they derive income. E.g., residing in Paris and owning a plantation in Brazil.

absolute advantage. The advantage which one region or country enjoys over others when that region or country has lower costs of production of a particular commodity due to natural advantages, lower labor costs, or some other superiority. In the early development of the principle of *comparative advantage,* differences in real costs, such as labor, were used to explain the origin of advantage. Absolute advantage then became a special case of real costs of production of a commodity that were lower in one country than in another. In a modern statement of the principle in terms of differences in cost or price ratios, when price levels and exchange rates are in equilibrium absolute and comparative advantages are assimilated and appear as a lower price of a commodity in one country than in another. Cf. *comparative advantage.*

absolute income hypothesis. The argument that current consumption is largely a function of the current (absolute) level of income. Identified with Keynes. Cf. *past income hypothesis, life-cycle income hypothesis, permanent income hypothesis* and *relative income hypothesis.*

absolute priority. The right of senior creditors and stockholders to be paid in full before any junior issues receive anything. For example, if there are $500,000 in assets, $100,000 in bonds, $500,000 in preferred stock, and $500,000 in common stock, the bondholders are paid in full, the preferred stockholders get 80 cents on the dollar, and the common stockholders nothing. Cf. *relative priority.*

absorption. In transportation, the assumption by one carrier of switching or other special charges of another carrier of the same shipment without increasing the rate to the shipper.

absorption costing. A product costing method which adds fixed *manufacturing overhead* to the cost of units produced and inventoried. Cf. *direct costing.*

abstinence theory of interest. An explanation of interest as the price paid by the borrower to the lender for the latter's abstaining from consumption of part of current income. Cf. *agio theory of interest, liquidity preference theory of interest, loanable funds theory of interest, marginal productivity theory of interest, time preference theory of interest.*

abstract of title. A document containing the history of a particular piece of land, giving a summary of all transactions, including claims, suits, liens, mortgages, deeds, etc., which evidence or affect title to the land. There may also be some valid claims which are not in the abstract because they are not required to be recorded.

accelerated depreciation. Depreciation at a faster rate than usual. In recent years used to refer to *tax amortization certificates* which upon government consent allow writing off an asset in five years for income tax purposes regardless of its life. Also recently used to describe *sum of the years digits method of depreciation, constant percentage of declining balance method of depreciation* and *double declining balance method of depreciation.*

acceleration. In finance, a provision that upon default of a bond, all future payments may be declared due immediately at the option of the creditor.

acceleration coefficient. The amount of extra capacity needed to produce an additional unit of output. Cf. *acceleration principle.*

acceleration premium. The increasing *rate* of pay allowed workmen with increasing production. Ordinarily used in connection with *piecework* or *incentive pay* systems, and made possible by the decrease in overhead charges per unit of production that results from the increased production.

acceleration principle. In business cycle theory, the principle that changes in demand for *finished* goods and services (consumption) *tend* to give rise to much greater changes in the demand for those *producers'* goods (investment) which are used to make the consumer goods. The acceleration coefficient is the ratio of change in investment to the accompanying change in consumption. Cf. *induced investment.*

acceptance. (1) The formal act of the drawee of a *bill of exchange* (the one upon whom the bill is drawn) making the obligation his own by writing on the face of the bill the word "accepted" and his signature. (2) More generally, the concurrence by one party in the offer of another.

acceptance supra protest. The agreement of one other than the debtor named to pay a protested document. Cf. *protest.*

accepted bill. See *acceptance.*

accession. Where goods that are not *fungible* are mixed, accession may take place. Literally it means "adding to," and the legal doctrine is concerned with the rules governing the rights of a party to recover such goods that have been mixed with or added to goods of another party.

accession rate. In personnel management, the ratio of the number of employees added to the payroll in a month to the average working force in the month.

accessorial services. In transportation, the services in addition to actual transportation which a carrier furnishes as part of the applicable rate. E.g., sorting, packing, precooling, etc.

accident frequency rate. The number of disabling injuries suffered by employees per 1,000,000 man-hours of work on an annual basis. The proportion is:

$$\frac{\text{A.F.R.}}{\text{1,000,000 man-hours}} = \frac{\text{Disabling injuries/year}}{\text{Man-hours/year}}$$

accident insurance. A contract for payment of a certain sum in the event of injury or death by accident. In the case of injury, payment of a certain sum per week for a limited number of weeks is made, usually including medical expenses. Usually classed as a special type of life insurance.

accident severity rate. The number of days lost from disabling injuries or death per 1,000,000 man-hours of work, with 6,000 days charged for death. The proportion is:

$$\frac{\text{A.S.R.}}{\text{1,000,000 man-hours}} = \frac{\text{Days lost by accident/year}}{\text{Man-hours/year}}$$

accommodation indorsement. The placing of one's name on a negotiable instrument for the benefit of another person, with the intention of lending the credit of your name to the document so that it will circulate more freely. An accommodation indorser thus becomes for practical purposes a surety for the party at whose request he placed his name on the paper.

accommodation line. In insurance, policies written by an agent or broker and accepted by the insurer because of the satisfactory character of the account in general even though the individual policy would not be accepted by strict underwriting standards.

accommodation paper. See *accommodation indorsement.*

accord and satisfaction. An agreement between parties changing the terms of an original contract. Both the accord (the change) and the satisfaction (performance of the contract as changed) must take place before the old obligation is satisfied, unless the parties expressly state that the new contract is to replace the old.

account. (1) In accounting, a ledger sheet showing the entries of debits (left-hand side) and credits (right-hand side) of a particular type of asset, liability, ownership, income, or expense. (2) In colloquial language, a customer is referred to as an "account."

accounts, types of. See the following specific terms:

balance sheet account
closed account
closing account
controlling account
income statement account
mixed account
nominal account
open account
profit-and-loss account
real account
realization account
subsidiary account
summary account
suspense account

accountant. One responsible for maintaining and analyzing the records of a business. He may be designated a Certified Public Accountant (C.P.A.), a Chartered Account (C.A.) the English equivalent of the American C.P.A. or a Public Accountant (P.A.).

account balance. The difference between the footings of the debit and the credit sides of an account.

accounting. The principles and techniques in establishing, maintaining, and analyzing the records of the transactions of a business, government, or other unit.

accounting method of return (in capital budgeting). The ratio of the increase in future average annual net income from an investment to the cost of that investment. Cf. *present value method, yield method.*

accounting price. Same as *shadow price.*

account payable. A debt, owed by an enterprise, which arises in the normal course of business dealings and has not been replaced by a note payable of a debtor. For example, bills for materials received but not yet paid. Cf. *account receivable.*

account receivable. A debt, owing to an enterprise, which arises in the normal course of business dealings and is not supported by negotiable paper. For example, the charge accounts of a department store. But income due from investments (unless investments are the business itself) is not usually shown in accounts receivable. Cf. *account payable.*

accounts receivable financing. The use of *accounts receivable* to obtain *working capital* either through a loan secured by such accounts or through *factoring* them.

accounts receivable insurance. Insurance indemnifying the insured for inability to collect accounts receivable because of damage to or destruction of records supporting the accounts receivable. Cf. *credit insurance.*

accounts receivable turnover. The ratio of credit sales of a period to average (daily) amounts of accounts receivable outstanding. Cf. *collection period.*

accredited list. In warehousing, a list of customers to whom the public warehouseman can make distribution of *spot stock* without further authority from the storer.

accretion. In law, the addition to lands by the natural action of waters. Thus an island formed in a nonnavigable river belongs to the owner of the shore on that side of the main channel.

accrual basis. In accounting, a system of allocating revenue and expense items not on the basis of when the cash is received or paid out, but on the basis of when the revenue is earned or the expense incurred. Cf. *cash basis.*

accrued income (or expense). Income that has been earned during a particular period (such as profit on a sale made) but not yet received in cash. Conversely for an expense.

accrued interest. Interest which has been earned but is not yet paid or payable.

accruing. In accounting, the allocation of income and/or expense, which has been earned or incurred but not yet collected or paid out, to the accounting period in which the income is earned or the expense incurred. Cf. *deferring.*

accumulated dividend. A dividend on *cumulative preferred stock* which has not been paid on the date due.

accumulation. (1) The difference between the face value and the cost of a bond purchased at a discount is called the accumulation in determining *bond yield.* (2) In insurance, the percentage addition to the benefits of a policy as a result of continuous renewal of the policy.

accumulation unit. In *variable annuities,* the payments into the fund (the periodic purchase price) are recorded in accumulation units analogous to shares of stock and the value of these units changes as the market values of the equities owned by the fund change. Payment to the *annuitant* is then made in annuity units whose value changes with the market value of the equities.

accuracy. The degree of conformity of a calculation or measurement to the true value. Cf. *precision.*

acid test ratio. Same as *quick asset ratio.*

acknowledgment. (1) In law, an admission or confirmation by a person before an officer of the court or state (usually a notary public) that an act (usually a signature) is the person's own act. This is done to make certain of the identity of the party signing a document. (2) In business, the name of the document accepting an offer to contract made by another party. The other party's offer is called a purchase order.

acquired surplus. In general, surplus arising from changes of the capital structure of one or more businesses. More narrowly, surplus arising from the purchase of one business by another business. Recapitalization surplus arises from changing the par or stated values of various classes of stock. Reorganization surplus arises from bankruptcy proceedings and a changing of par or stated values of stock.

acquisition. A generic term covering all forms of acquiring another firm, such as *consolidation, holding company, merger,* purchase of assets by cash or stock.

acquittance. In law, a written agreement to release one from the payment of money. At common law, an acquittance did not require a *seal* but a *release* did.

acre foot. The volume of water required to cover one acre of land to a depth of one foot, or 325,851 gallons.

across the board. In collective bargaining, "across the board" increases in wages refer to a flat percentage or fixed-amount-per-hour increase for each job classification.

action. In law, the proceeding in a court is called an action.

active life reserve. In accident and sickness insurance, the type of reserve established where a level premium is charged but the claim rate increases with age.

active trade balance. Same as a *favorable balance of trade.*

activity analysis. The application of *linear programming* methods to *general equilibrium theory.*

act of bankruptcy. In law, permitting one of the six acts defined by statute as constituting bankruptcy. Cf *bankruptcy* for these six conditions.

act of God. In law, any event beyond human cause or not subject to human foresight. The doctrine is concerned with liability for loss or damage and its application varies from situation to situation.

act of pais. In law, an act performed outside of court and hence not a matter of the record in court.

activity accounting. Same as *responsibility accounting.*

actual rate of growth. That ratio of the increase in national income to the total national income. See explanation under *Harrod-Domar model.* Cf. *natural rate of growth* and *warranted rate of growth.*

actuary. A mathematician who calculates (1) insurance risks on the basis of experience tables; and (2) premiums based on such risks, with allowance for interest on reserves set aside from the premium, and other factors such as office expenses of the insurer.

Adamson Act. Federal law passed in 1916 granting the basic eight-hour day on the railroads and providing procedures for settling railroad labor disputes. Averted a general railroad strike. Declared constitutional in 1917.

adaptive forecasting. An extension of *exponential smoothing* for forecasting seasonal behavior. The coefficients of the fitted function are revised after each observation of new data.

ad damnum clause. The clause in the plaintiff's complaint which sets forth the amount of damages claimed and makes demand therefor.

ademption. The elimination or reduction of a *legacy* in a will by the action of the *testator* in disposing before death of the specific asset bequeathed or by making advances while living to the legatee with the intention of reducing thereby the legatee's share in the estate. Distinguish *lapsed legacy.* Cf. *advancement.*

additional extended coverage. An indorsement on insurance policies covering dwellings, providing insurance against water damage from plumbing and heating systems, vandalism and malicious mischief, glass breakage, ice, snow and freezing, and the falling of trees.

additional insured. Persons covered by an insurance policy in addition to the insured person named in the policy. The most common example is the clause in an automobile liability policy extending coverage to persons driving the car with the consent of the owner.

additive predicting equation. A predicting equation in which the dependent variable is a function of a constant and several independent variables with a plus (or minus) sign between the terms. Thus $Y = a + bX + cZ$. Cf. *multiplicative predicting equation.*

adjective law. The rules of law pertaining to procedure, in contrast to substantive law which deals with rights and duties.

adjustable currency. Same as *elastic currency.*

adjustable policy. Same as *reporting policy.*

adjusting entry. In accounting, an entry bringing an income or expense account "up to date" because of the accruing or deferring of an item in that account. A *closing entry* is then made to transfer the balance of the account into a summary account (profit-and-loss account). In the next accounting period a reversing entry (if needed) prevents duplication of the expense or income which was accrued or deferred by the aforementioned adjusting entry.

adjustment bonds. Bonds arising out of the reorganization of a corporation. Also called reorganization bonds.

adjustment equation. In *econometrics,* an equation that describes the process that occurs once an economic system or a particular market is in disequilibrium. Cf. *behavorial equation, definitional equation, final equation, reduced form equation, restraint equation,* and *structural equation.*

ad litem. Latin, "for the litigation or lawsuit." See *guardian ad litem.*

administered price. A price set by a producer for his product with the intent of letting that price determine the quantity which is bought in the market rather than adjusting the price to move a given amount of output. Many *producers' goods* are marketed in this manner.

administrative budget. In *macroeconomics*, a governmental budget that excludes transfers into and out of trust funds and records taxes when received rather than when incurred. Cf. *national income accounts budget.*

administrative protection. The use of rules and regulations relating to customs procedure, sometimes in a harassing manner, so as to control imports. Delays in assessing customs duties, high valuation, meticulous enforcement of documentary rules, etc., may be so used. See also *protectionism.*

administrative revenues. Revenues obtained by the various departments and agencies of public administration in the course of performing their functions or services.

administrator. A person appointed by a probate court to manage the estate of a person who died without a will, or who did not name an executor in his will, or who named an executor but the executor has died, become incompetent, or declined to act as executor. The term is also used in a general sense to designate one who is appointed by the court to manage certain affairs, e.g., of a defunct corporation. Cf. *executor.*

administrator's bond. A bond required of court-appointed administrators of estates and other matters to protect those benefitting from the estate against failure to perform duties.

admiralty. That body of legal rules concerned with relations on the high seas. For example, the law governing the collision of ships at sea, loss of cargo, etc.

admission temporaire. The duty-free admission into a country of goods, particularly raw materials, for processing and later export.

admitted assets. In insurance, those *assets* of the insurer which are recognized by the regulating state as qualifying in the determination of various financial standards which the insurer must by law maintain.

admitted company. In insurance, an insurer incorporated under the laws of one state may be admitted to do business in other states by properly qualifying.

ad valorem. According to value and not according to weight or units. Cf. *ad valorem tariff, specific tariff.*

ad valorem tariff. A tariff based on value and not weight, size, or units.

advance. (1) A loan. (2) With reference to the Federal Reserve Banks, a *rediscount* is technically different from an advance. The advance is the transfer of funds by the Federal Reserve Bank to a member bank on the basis of a note secured by specific collateral. A rediscount is the sale and indorsement of eligible paper by the member bank to the Federal Reserve Bank for the funds transferred.

advance bill. A *bill of exchange* drawn before shipment of goods.

advancement. In law, a gift made during lifetime by one who dies without a will and to be taken into account as a reduction of the share of inheritance. Cf. *ademption.*

adverse examination. Same as *discovery.*

adverse possession. Open and continuous possession of another's property which after a period of time set by statute (usually twenty years) establishes ownership in the party possessing adversely.

advertising. Any paid form of presentation of goods, services, or ideas to a group under open sponsorship of the advertiser.

affidavit. A written statement made under oath, signed before a notary public or any other officer appointed by law to administer oaths, and then signed by that officer as witness.

affreightment. The agreement under which a transportation means is hired for carrying freight.

AFL American Federation of Labor. Organized in 1881 as a federation on a national basis of local unions organized originally on trade or craft lines. Today it also grants charters to industrial or vertical unions. Each local retains the right to govern its own affairs. In 1955, the AFL merged with the CIO. Cf. *CIO, Congress of Industrial Organizations.*

AFL-CIO (American Federation of Labor-Congress of Industrial Organizations). These two bodies merged in 1955. See the separate terms, *AFL* and *CIO.*

after-acquired property clause. A clause in a mortgage providing that any property acquired by the borrower after the date of the loan and mortgage will automatically become additional security for the loan.

after market. The term describing the market for a security after it has been initially sold by the issuer through underwriters.

age change. See *annuity age change* and *insurance age change.*

agency. A category in law concerned with the relationships of one party (the principal) in authorizing another party (the agent) to act for him in dealings with third parties. See *general agent, special agent.*

agency selling. In securities, the sale by a broker as *agent* for a selling stockholder or an issuing corporation. Not a true underwriting but sometimes called a *best efforts* underwriting.

agency shop. The employment situation in which all employees in a bargaining unit must pay "dues" to the union even though not required to join the union membership. A variety of *closed shop.* Usually carried out by the "work permit" device: all employees must carry a permit to work issued by the union. Cf. *closed shop, open shop, preferential shop,* and *union shop.*

agent. One who acts for another. There are two primary types of agent: *special agent* and *general agent.*

agent, types of. See the following specific terms:

application agent	*general agent*
del credere agent	*special agent*
exclusive agent	*survey agent*

agent middleman. One who negotiates purchases or sales between producers and retailers without himself taking title to the goods. Eight categories are recognized: (1) agency coöperatives, (2) auction companies, (3) commission houses, (4) export-import agents, (5) manufacturers' agents, (6) merchandise brokers, (7) purchasing agents, and (8) selling agents.

agent's lien. The right of an *agent* to keep possession of property of his *principal* for unpaid commissions.

aggregate demand. The total quantity of goods and services demanded in a period of time, including both *consumer goods* and *producers' goods.* Hence the total of *consumption* and *investment.*

aggregate indemnity. In insurance, the maximum amount that the insurer will pay under the policy for losses sustained by the insured.

aggregate liability. In insurance, the maximum amount that the insurer will pay for liabilities assumed under a policy.

aggregate of intermediates clause. The clause of the Interstate Commerce Act (Sec. 4 of Part 1) which prohibits a through rate higher than the sum of intermediate rates except by Commission order.

aggregation problem. In *econometrics,* the problem stemming from the fact that the sum of functions of a given form need not be a function of that same form. This is more likely to occur in summing nonlinear functions than in summing linear functions and arises from the fact that the coefficients of the individual functions being summated may have different *variances.*

aggregative economics. Same as *macroeconomics.*

aggregative index number. There are many different types, but the common characteristic is the ratio of the summation of the actual prices of different products in the later period divided by the summation of the actual prices of the same products in the base period. This ratio is then multiplied by 100. Different methods of weighting are used for different types of this index number. Cf. *average of relatives index number.*

aging of accounts. Arranging the accounts (such as receivables or payables) in chronological order and grouping the accounts by intervals, such as accounts less than 30 days old, 30 to 60 days old, etc.

agio theory of interest. An explanation of interest as the result of postponement of present consumption to future consumption and the payment of an agio (premium) for the postponement. Cf. *abstinence theory of interest, liquidity preference theory of interest, loanable funds theory of interest, marginal productivity theory of interest, time preference theory of interest.*

agreed amount clause. In insurance, a policy provision that the insured will carry a stated or determinable amount of insurance coverage. Default in this regard by the insured brings into effect the *coinsurance, average* or *contribution provisions.*

agricultural cooperative. A form of cooperative selling. The organizations formed are chiefly for the purpose of effecting the unified sale of a product produced by many small farmers.

agricultural credit banks. See *FCA, Farm Credit Administration.*

agricultural parity. See *parity price.*

air rights. The rights of the owner of real estate to the air space above his land. Such rights may be sold separately from the land (surface) rights by the owner. Cf. *mineral rights.*

Aldrich-Vreeland Act. Act of Congress in 1908, following the panic of 1907, authorizing associations of national banks to issue bank notes on the security of commercial paper and state and municipal bonds. Replaced in 1914 by the Federal Reserve Act.

aleatory contract. A contract dealing with uncertainties, e.g., an insurance annuity contract.

algorithm. A systematized procedure for solving a problem such as the optimal assignment of jobs to machines by use of a *Monte Carlo technique.*

alien corporation. A corporation chartered in a foreign country. Cf. *foreign corporation.*

all-commodity rate. In transportation, a rate (usually a carload rate) applicable regardless of the nature of the commodities shipped.

all-loss insurance. Same as *all-risk insurance.*

allocation. (1) In accounting, allocation is the spreading of an income or expense but not necessarily on a "time" basis. For example, allocation of an expenditure between current expense and capital accounts. (2) In economic theory, the process of selecting one use for a resource or income rather than an alternative use.

allonge. A paper attached to and made a part of a negotiable instrument in order to permit additional indorsements.

allotment. (1) In governmental accounting, that part of an *appropriation* set aside to cover expenditures and *encumbrances* for a stated period or purpose. (2) An English term referring to a small tract of land rented to a laborer for cultivation.

allowed time. Time that a worker is allowed for rest, care of tools, etc., without wage deduction.

alloy. The mixture of baser metals used in coining gold and silver in order to give coins greater hardness and enable them better to resist wear.

all-risk insurance. A policy insuring against loss caused by all perils except those specifically excluded, in contrast to the ordinary policy which names the perils covered.

alternation ranking rating. In personnel management, a system of rating individuals in which the rater is directed to cross out those he does not know well enough to rank. Using the remaining names, the rater places the one having the largest number of favorable attributes at the top of one scale and the one with the least at the top of another scale. Both names are then eliminated and the process repeated with the remaining names.

alternative rate. In transportation, the lower of two or more rates applicable to the same shipment.

alternative use cost. Same as *opportunity cost.*

amalgamation. A general term covering many speicfic types of integration of two or more businesses, e.g., merger, consolidation, majority or controlling stock holdings, etc.

American experience table of mortality. Statistical expression of the probability of survival or death at the different age levels, based on data collected from an unselected large number of insured persons. The data for the table were accumulated in 1895. Since then the life span has greatly lengthened and the table is seriously in error. A new table called the Commissioners' Standard Ordinary (CSO) Mortality Table adopted in 1941 uses mortality experience from 1931 to 1940. Cf. *national fraternal congress table of mortality.*

amicus curiae. Latin for "friend of the court." In law, those who are interested in the general proposition of law involved in a case, but are not parties to the case, may seek to be heard by the court as friends of the court.

amortization. A reduction in a debt or fund by periodic payments covering interest and part of principal, distinguished from (1) depreciation, which is an allocation of the original cost of an asset computed from physical wear and tear as well as the passage of time, and (2) depletion, which is a reduction in the book value of a resource (such as minerals) resulting from conversion into a salable product.

amortization fund. The sum of money accumulated periodically for the payment of a debt.

amortization quota. The funds currently removed from income to provide for amortization.

amortized loan. A loan requiring periodic payments, part of which reduce the principal of the loan.

amortized mortgage. Same as *direct-reduction mortgage.*

amortized value. In finance, certain bonds bought at a premium may be carried on financial statements at their amortized value rather than current market value in the case of banks, insurance companies, and similar institutions. This amortized value is the cost amount of the bond less that part of the premium allocable to time expired from the date of acquisition to the present, using the total period from acquisition to maturity as the basis for allocation.

amplitude. The distance from the highest to the lowest points of a curve.

analog model. A model, one property of which is used to represent another property in reality. The slide rule is an analogue in which quantities are represented by distances in proportion to the logarithms of the quantities. Cf. *iconic model, econometric model* and *mathematical model.*

analysis of distribution by value. Analyzing a line of products by plotting a cumulative *frequency distribution* of the annual dollar sales of each item in a product line. Used to estimate *cycle stock* and *safety stock* in an inventory.

analysis of variance. (1) In statistics, a method of computing the degree of significance in the variations of a particular characteristic among comparable groups or classes of data. (2) In accounting, the analysis of deviations from standard costs when the *standard cost method of cost accounting* is used.

analytic schedule. Same as *Dean schedule.*

anarchism. The theory which denies the justice and expediency of both government and private property. It holds that human beings can be made so perfect that no government will be necessary. Meanwhile violence is advocated to bring about this perfection of humans.

ancillary. In law, a document or proceeding which is subordinate to or related to a principal document or proceeding. Thus, if a person's estate is being probated in the state of his residence at death, ancillary proceedings will handle any real estate he owed at death in another state.

annual return. The rate of return on the purchase price of a security represented by the interest coupons alone without any allowance for the difference between the purchase price and the sum received as principal at maturity. Cf. *yield to maturity.*

annual statement. The annual report by a corporation after the close of its *fiscal year.* This report includes the *balance sheet* as of the end of the year and the *profit-and-loss statement* (income statement) for the year. Usually both statements appear on a comparative basis, i.e., showing the preceeding year's figures in adjacent columns.

annual wage. An agreement by an employer guaranteeing to furnish a full year's employment at the established wage rates. Usually figured at 2,000 hours of work per 52 weeks (50 weeks of 40 hours each), with 52 pay checks to the year.

annuitant. The person during whose life an *annuity* is payable and usually the one to whom the annuity is payable, although occasionally another recipient is designated.

annuity. An allowance or income received in one or more payments annually, typically from life insurance companies, retirement systems, and others. Annuities are for a stated time or for life.

annuity, types of. See the following specific terms:

annuity certain
apportionable annuity
cash refund annuity
contingent annuity
deferred annuity
equity annuity
group annuity
immediate annuity
installment refund life annuity
joint and survivor annuity
last survivor annuity
life annuity
life annuity certain
refund annuity
retirement annuity
reversionary anuity
straight life annuity
survivorship annuity
variable annuity

annuity age change. The date of the last previous birthday is used as the date determining age for premiums and payments in the case of an annuity, but in life insurance the one-year period starting one-half year before and ending one-half year after the birthday is used.

annuity bond. Bond without maturity date, that is, perpetually paying interest. Cf. *consols, rentes.*

annuity certain. An *annuity* providing a stated income for a stated period regardless of the life or death of the *annuitant.*

annuity insurance. An insurance contract providing for payment of a stipulated sum annually or periodically to a party called "the annuitant" for life or for a stated period.

annuity method of depreciation. Taking the initial cost of a capital asset, deducting the expected salvage value at the time it is discarded, and assuming a rate of interest, the straight-line portion of cost plus interest on the undepreciated balance is charged to each period.

annuity unit. In *variable annuities,* the payments made to the annuitant are computed in annuity units analogous to shares of stock whose value changes with the market value of the equities held by the fund from which payments are made.

antedate. Dating an instrument back from the day it is made, as if it had gone into effect at an earlier time. E.g., a check written on January 15 is dated January 10.

ante-nuptial agreement. See *jointure.*

anticipation rate. The rate allowed in addition to the cash discount for payment in advance of the cash discount date or the rate allowed for payment before the due date where no cash discount is stated.

anticipation stock. In inventory analysis, a buffer supply to meet seasonal variations, plant shutdowns, vacations, or responses to special sales campaigns. Distinguished from *safety stock* (to reduce normal outages due to demand variation and replenishment time) and *lot-size stock* (to reduce costs by taking quantity discounts and offsetting order costs and carrying costs). Cf *cycle stock.*

anticipation warrant. A short-term promise to pay, usually issued by a government in anticipation of later revenue.

anticipatory breach. A statement by either party to a contract that he will not live up to the contract's terms. This entitles the party who is wronged to do either of two things: (1) treat the contract as broken and sue immediately for damages or (2) ignore the statement and wait for performance as scheduled and sue if it is not then performed.

antidilution provision. In finance, part of the terms of an *option, warrant, convertible debenture* or other security with exercise rights at a stated price in the future, designed to provide adjustment of the stated price to preserve its relative position at the time of issuance in the event more shares or rights are issued in the future, particularly if such issuance is at a lower price than the stated price of the security being protected against *dilution.*

antidumping duty. A tariff designed to prevent imports of goods for sale at a price in the importing country lower than the price in the country of origin of the goods.

Antiracketeering Act. Act of Congress in 1934 making it a crime to delay, rob, extort, or interfere with the movement of articles in interstate commerce.

antitrust laws. Legislation directed to the elimination of monopoly and restraint of trade through the prohibition of specific practices deemed to lead to such results. In the United States, the legislation began with the *Sherman Antitrust Act* of 1890 and the principal subsequent laws are: *Clayton Act* and Federal Trade Commission Act both of 1914, *Webb-Pomerene Act* of 1918, *Robinson-Patman Act* of 1936, and *Miller-Tydings Act* of 1937, *Kefauver-Celler Act* of 1950, and *McGuire Act* of 1952.

any-quantity rate. In transportation, a rate applicable to any quantity of a commodity shipped.

aon. "All or none." Used to identify a lot of goods which cannot be broken.

appeal. In law, a petition carrying a decided case from a lower court to a higher court for re-examination. More narrowly, an appeal is the petition which is used in a case which the higher court must re-examine and a *certiorari* is the petition in a case which the higher court may in its discretion re-examine.

appeal bond. A *bond* required of an appellant to assure payment of costs and damages if the appeal is lost.

application agent. In insurance, an *agent* without the right to write (issue) policies who must submit the application and survey to the company for action.

applied economics. Utilizing the knowledge of economic principles obtained from pure economics to find means of effecting specific objectives.

apportionable annuity. An annuity providing for a prorated and fractional payment for the period from the date of the last premium payment to the date of the death of the annuitant.

apportioned tax. A tax whose proceeds are distributed to different units of government.

apportionment clause. In insurance, the clause providing that where more than one policy covers the same property and one policy provides coverage for the type of loss suffered (e.g., wind damage under an extended coverage fire policy) but the other policy does not (e.g., standard fire policy), the insurer providing coverage will pay only that proportion of the loss that the face of that policy bears to the total face amount of all insurance covering the same property. Cf. *contribution clause*.

appraise. Literally, "I set a price upon," or "I value," for a sale, tax levy, or other purpose.

appraisal clause. In insurance, the clause stating that the insurer has the right to demand an appraisal of the loss or damage.

appraisal surplus. Same as *appreciation surplus.*

appreciation. An increase in the market value of an asset over its accepted value at some time in the past. Ordinarily appreciation is not recognized until it is realized (e.g., by a sale). Cf. *depreciation.*

appreciation surplus. The addition to *net worth* appearing in *surplus* as the result of a revaluation upwards of the value at which assets are shown on the books of an enterprise.

apprentice. One who is bound by a contract to work for another person or firm in order to learn a trade, usually for a specified period and sometimes subject to state approval of the terms of the contract which is called an Indenture of Apprenticeship.

appropriated surplus. That part of the surplus of a corporation which has been set aside by the board of directors for a specific purpose other than to recognize an existing liability. The appropriation can be reversed by the board.

appropriation. (1) A legislative act authorizing the spending of a certain amount of money or incurring of liabilities by a governmental agency for a specific purpose. Distinguish *fund.* In the case of the federal government all appropriation bills must by the Constitution originate in the House of Representatives. (2) Sometimes used in a related sense for internal management of a business.

arbitrage. Consists of buying and selling the same commodity or foreign exchange at the same time, but in two or more different markets, to take advantage of differences in the prices of the commodity or foreign currency in the markets. In finance, arbitrage also applies between two different securities which have a close relationship, such as convertibility of one security into the other or between the securities of a holding company and a subsidiary.

arbitrary. In transportation, (1) a fixed amount which a carrier agrees to accept in dividing joint rates, (2) a fixed amount added to or deducted from the rate from or to one station to make a rate from or to another station.

arbitration. A method of settling disputes. The contending parties present their differences to a third impartial party who is given the power to make a decision binding on both sides. Arbitration is compulsory when the law requires that disputes be settled by this method. It is voluntary when both parties are at liberty to make use of it by an agreement among themselves. Cf. *conciliation, mediation.*

arbitration clause. A clause in agreements providing that if the parties cannot agree, an umpire is to be selected as provided in the clause and the umpire's decision is binding. It is frequently found in labor agreements and insurance policies.

arbitration of exchange. The use by a person in one country of a bill of exchange purchased in a third country, for payment of a debt in a second country. The bill so bought and used is payable in the money of the second country. The practice can be profitable because the prices of the second country's currency may be different in the first and third countries.

arc elasticity. See *elasticity of demand and supply, arc.*

area sample. The selection of part of the data from the universe on a geographic basis for use in estimating the characteristics of the universe.

area-wide bargaining. Negotiation of a collective bargaining agreement between a union and more than one employer within a given geographical area.

arithmetic mean. This value is obtained by adding all the individual values of a series of items and dividing by the number of items. Cf. *geometric, harmonic* and *quadratic mean.*

arithmetic progression. A succession of terms which increases or decreases by a constant difference, e.g., 1, 2, 3, or 7, 5, 3, 1, – 1, – 3, etc. Cf. *geometric progression.*

Armstrong investigation. In insurance, the 1905 study of insurance practices by a committee in New York resulting in many significant changes in policy provisions and regulations by many states.

arrangement. In law, the term applied to the plan resulting from a *receivership* proceeding under Chapter XI of the Bankruptcy Act.

array. An orderly arrangement of values according to magnitude, usually from the smallest to the largest.

arrival notice. A document notifying the consignee of the arrival of freight at its destination.

arson clause. In insurance, the clause voiding a policy if the insured or someone under his direction sets a fire. The clause does not reach fires resulting from negligence nor fires started by the arson of others.

articles of incorporation. The basic document specifying a corporation's name, period of existence, purpose and powers, authorized number of shares, classes of stock and other conditions. Prepared by the proposed corporation and filed with the state which will issue the *corporation charter*.

ask. The price named by a willing seller. Cf. *bid*.

aski system. An exchange control system under which payment for imported goods is made in marked funds usable only to purchase goods of the importing country. The term is the abbreviation of the German for "foreigners' special accounts for domestic payments."

assented bonds. Bonds deposited by the owner with a trustee or intermediary pursuant to the owner's agreement to accept voluntarily a change in securities of a corporation.

assented stock. Stock deposited by the owner with a trustee or intermediary pursuant to the owner's agreement to accept voluntarily a change in securities of a corporation.

assessable insurance. An insurance contract in which the policyholder is liable for an additional premium payment if losses are unexpectedly large.

assessable policy. See *assessable insurance*.

assessable stock. Stock which is subject to assessment, that is, the stockholder may have to pay more than his original investment if affairs of the corporation so require. Cf. *double liability*.

assessed valuation. The value fixed upon privately owned property by public officials, usually as a basis for computing taxes.

assessment. (1) The official valuation of income or property for the purpose of taxation. Also called assessed valuation. (2) A levy by firms, the government, or a corporation upon stockholders or citizens.

assessment bond. Same as *special assessment bonds*.

assessment insurance. A form of mutual insurance where the policyholders are assessed whenever there is a loss.

asset. Anything of value that is owned.

assets, types of. See the following specific terms:

admitted assets	*inadmitted assets*
capital assets	*intangible assets*
current assets	*liquid assets*
deferred assets	*net operating assets*
earning assets	*operating assets*
fixed assets	*quick assets*
frozen assets	*tangible assets*
hidden assets	*wasting assets*

asset and liability statement. Same as *balance sheet*.

asset dividend. In finance, a dividend paid to stock holders in the form of an asset, usually a product of the company, such as bottles of whiskey.

asset turnover ratio. The ratio of sales to *net operating assets.*

assignee. The one to whom rights under a contract are transferred by *assignment*. Cf. *assignor*.

assigned risk. In insurance, when a person desiring insurance is rejected by a number of underwriters, he can, under some state laws, apply for assignment to an insurer drawn from a pool. Such assignment frequently carries a higher premium on the ground that such risk selection is adverse.

assignment. The transfer of rights under a contract by one party to a third party without the consent of the other party to the contract. Cf. *novation.*

assignment for the benefit of creditors. The voluntary transfer by a debtor of his assets to another person to distribute among the creditors of the one making the assignment. This in itself is an *act of bankruptcy.*

assignor. The one who transfers rights under a contract to another (the *assignee*) by an *assignment.*

assize. French for "a session." In law, a term or period during which a court is in session.

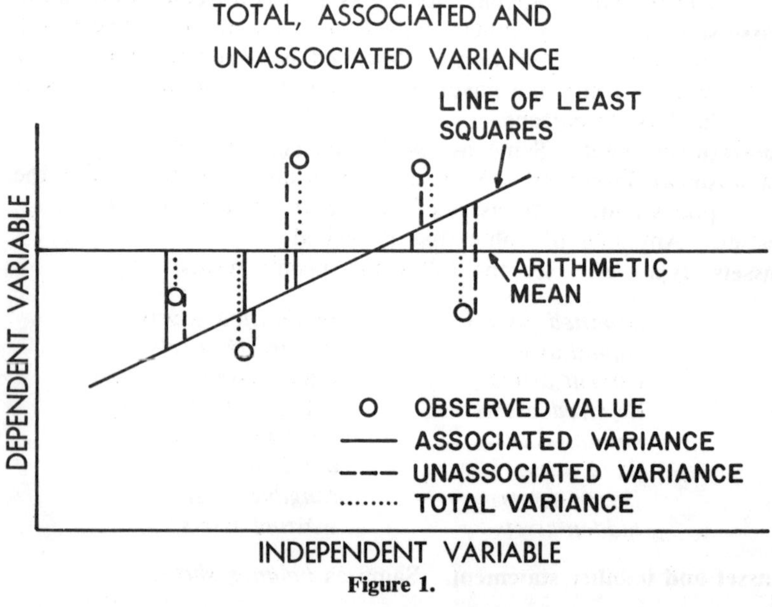

Figure 1.

associated variance. The sum of the squares of that part of the deviation of a variable from its *arithmetic mean* represented by the distance from the line of *least squares* to the arithmetic mean divided by the number of items. Cf. *unassociated variance* and *variance.*

associated variation. The *associated variance* times the number of items. Hence, the sum of the squares of that part of the deviation of a variable from its *arithmetic mean* represented by the distance from the line of *least squares* to the arithmetic mean. Cf *unassociated variation* and *variation.*

assumed bonds. Bonds of the original debtor which have been made the liability of a second debtor who voluntarily assumed them.

assumed liability. A liability of the first party that has, by agreement or by operation of law incident to a transaction, been assumed by a second party. The first party is released from further liability only if the original claimant (third party) so consents. In the event of such consent, there is a *novation.*

assumpsit. A type of action at common law for money damages resulting from a breach of contract. Literally the word means "he has undertaken."

assumption of risk rule. Common law principle that an injured workman cannot recover from his employer where the injury results from a risk inherent in the occupation or known beforehand. The principle has been negatived by *workmen's compensation laws.*

assurance. Same as *insurance.*

assured. Same as *insured.*

attachment. A legal document authorizing the sheriff to seize a debtor's property for nonpayment of a debt. The sale of the property may follow and any excess of funds from the sale over the amount of the debt is turned over to the debtor.

attachment bond. A *bond* required of one seeking to attach the property of another in a lawsuit given to cover any loss that may result to the one whose property is attached if the one attaching should lose his case.

attested copy. Same as *certified copy.*

attestation clause. In a *contract* or *will,* the clause providing for the signatures of witnesses (as contrasted to the signatures of the parties).

at the market. An order to a broker to sell immediately for the best price possible.

attorney in fact. A person acting as an *agent* for another. Cf.

power of attorney.

attorney's lien. The right of an attorney to keep possession of property of a client for money he has advanced or for unpaid services.

attractive nuisance. In law, a dangerous situation particularly attractive to children. Failure to take steps to eliminate the danger imposes liability on the owner or occupant of the property if injuries occur.

attribute. A characteristic which is analyzed by qualitative classification (such as present or absent) but without an attempt to quantify the differences between classes. Cf. *variable.*

attribution. Particularly in taxation of foreign activities where income of the foreign activity is "attributed" to the U.S. owner as if it had been received and taxed accordingly but with credit for any foreign income tax paid.

auction. Offering an article to the highest of several bidders. Different types exist, for example, there may be a reservation by the seller to reject bids he considers inadequate. An auction at law (as in a foreclosure) usually has an *upset price,* that is, a minimum bid which must be met or the auction is cancelled. Cf. *Dutch auction.*

audit. The process of verifying the accounting records of an enterprise or governmental unit. The audit involves checking against the original documents giving rise to the transactions which are recorded, confirming by direct inquiry to creditors and debtors the balances due them or owed by them, verifying the existence and value of physical assets, and other testing to uncover errors or fraud.

Austrian school. Otherwise referred to as the marginal utility school, the Austrian school of thought established by Carl Menger, Eugene von Bohm-Bawerk, and Friedrich Wieser in 19th century Austria has as its distinguishing characteristic the theory that value depends upon utility and, more particularly, on the utility of the marginal unit.

Austrian theory of capital. The proposition that capital is created when the original *factors of production* are embodied in goods and is destroyed when the services of such goods are finally realized.

authentication. A certification (statement by one charged with the duty of keeping records) that the document authenticated is genuine or a true copy of the original.

authoritarian states. States in which government authority has been extended to many phases of human conduct and government does not require approval by the people. Sometimes a distinction is attempted from "totalitarian" which is taken to mean "all phases of human conduct." Cf. *communism, fascism.*

authorized capital. Same as *authorized issue.*

authorized issue. The total number of shares of capital stock which a charter permits a corporation to sell. Also means the total number of bonds which may be sold under a given mortgage. Additional shares after the original amount is exhausted are authorized by charter amendment.

authorized stock. Same as *authorized issue.*

autocorrelation. The situation in which one value of a variable in a time series is related to an earlier variable in that series and successive values of that series. Cf. *serial correlation, Durbin-Watson test,* and *von Neumann ratio.*

automatic cover. In insurance, a provision extending coverage for a stated period and in a given amount for newly acquired assets or increased values.

automatic currency. See *elastic currency.*

automatic premium loan clause. A provision in a *life insurance* contract stating that if a premium is not paid, it will be automatically taken from any available cash surrender value of the policy in order to keep the policy in force.

automatic reinstatement clause. In insurance, a clause providing for the reinstatement of the full *face value* of the policy after a loss has been paid. Without this clause, the face amount of the policy is reduced by any losses paid.

automatic stabilizers. Same as *built-in stabilizers.*

automatic standard. A monetary standard (best example is gold standard) where the amount and value of money is not consciously managed but is the result of the working of demand and supply for the precious metal or foreign currency which follows upon differences in trading volume between countries.

automobile liability insurance. Indemnity insurance covering the liability for personal injury or property damage to others arising from the operation of an automobile. Damage to the car of the holder of the liability policy is not covered by liability insurance but by *collision insurance.*

autonomous investment. New investment caused by events independent of changes in the interest rate or the level of consumption or national income. Cf. *induced investment.*

autonomous tariff. A tariff set by legislative action and not established by treaty. Cf. *conventional tariff*.

autonomous variable. In statistics, a variable determined by non-economic factors such as political action if the area being analyzed is economic.

avail. (1) The remaining balance after deduction of debts or expenses. Used with regard to estates, auctions, etc. (2) The net proceeds of a loan after the discount has been deducted in advance.

available stock. In inventory analysis, the algebraic sum of stock on hand and stock on order less unfilled consumption demand.

average. (1) In statistics, one of many measures of central tendency of a number of items. (2) In admiralty law and certain *marine insurance*, there are two kinds of average: (a) particular average (also called simple average) claims arising from accidental causes, and (b) general average, claims arising from risks of navigation in protecting the venture. Particular average losses are borne solely by the owner of the thing damaged, general average losses are borne proportionately by all parties benefited by the protective acts.

average (in statistics), types of. See the following specific terms:

arithmetic mean	*mode*
geometric mean	*quadratic mean*
harmonic mean	*simple average*
median	*weighted average*

average age of receivables. The weighted average age of receivables computed by summing the products of the number of days from date of each unpaid invoice to date of computation times the dollar amount of each invoice. This sum divided by the dollar total of receivables gives the average age.

average agreement demurrage. In transportation, an agreement between a shipper and a carrier providing that the shipper is to be charged for cars held beyond a stated period and credited for cars released within the period, with demurrage chargeable on the net balance of debits, usually monthly. Cf. *reciprocal demurrage*.

average collection period. The ratio of (1) the total accounts receivable at any date multiplied by 365 to (2) net credit sales for the year. Tests the quality of accounts receivable. Other methods of averaging may be used. Cf. *collection period*.

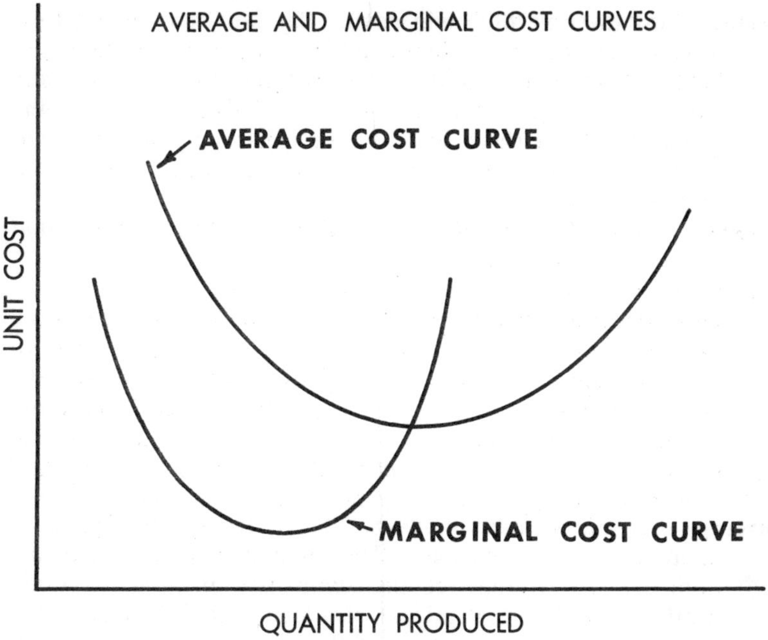

Figure 2.

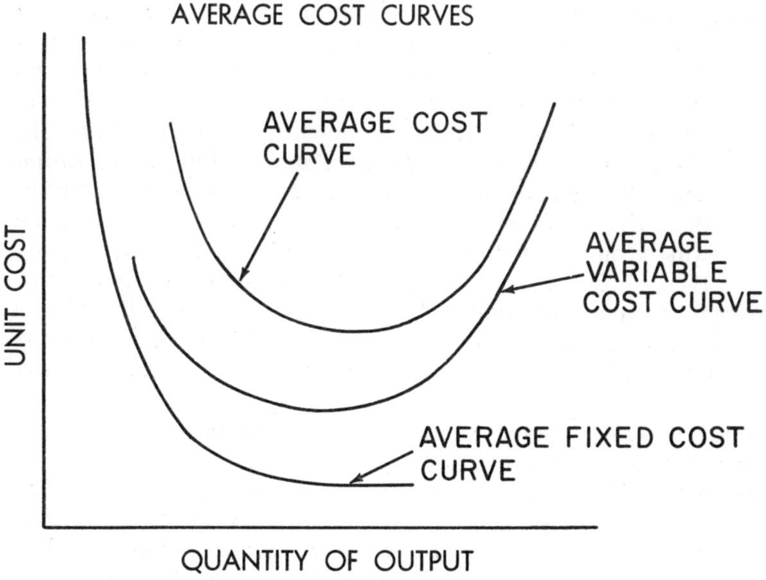

Figure 3.

average cost (average total unit cost). The total costs divided by the number of units produced at the point under consideration. With dollars of cost on the *y* axis and units produced on the *x* axis, the average cost curve will be U-shaped because of the spreading of overhead and because a particular size of plant is involved. Cf. *average fixed cost, average variable cost* and *marginal cost.*

average cost method of inventory valuation. See *cost method (average) of inventory valuation.*

average cost pricing. Same as *full cost pricing.*

average distribution clause. Same as *pro rata distribution clause.*

average fixed cost. The total of those costs of a business that do not vary with the amount of business done, divided by the number of units produced at the point under consideration.

average (mean) deviation. The sum of the deviations (ignoring signs) of the items of a distribution from the median (or arithmetic mean) divided by the number of items.

average of relatives index numbers. There are as many types as there are types of averages. The common characteristic is the ratio of the average of the summation of price relatives (rather than of actual prices) of a later period divided by the summation of price relatives of the base period. This ratio is then multiplied by 100. Cf. *aggregative index number.*

average output curve. Holding some *factors of production* fixed (such as the plant size) and permitting one or more factors of production to vary in physical units (such as labor and materials), the average output curve traces the ratio of total output in units divided by the units of the variable factor for different quantities of the variable factor. With average output per unit of the variable factor on the *y* axis and quantity of the variable factor on the *x* axis, the average output curve will be an inverted u, first because of the less efficient use, then efficient use, and finally inefficient use of the fixed factor.

average revenue (per unit). The total revenue from the sale of a given quantity of the same good divided by the number of units sold. Thus average revenue per unit is equal to price per unit.

average revenue curve. Same as *demand curve.*

average total unit cost. Same as *average cost.*

average variable cost. The total of those costs of a business that vary with the amount of business done, divided by the number of units produced at the point under consideration. With dollars on the *y* axis and units produced on the *x* axis, the average variable cost curve will be U-shaped because with any given plant (or fixed cost) variable ingredients are used more efficiently as the designed capacity is approached from either a larger or smaller volume of production.

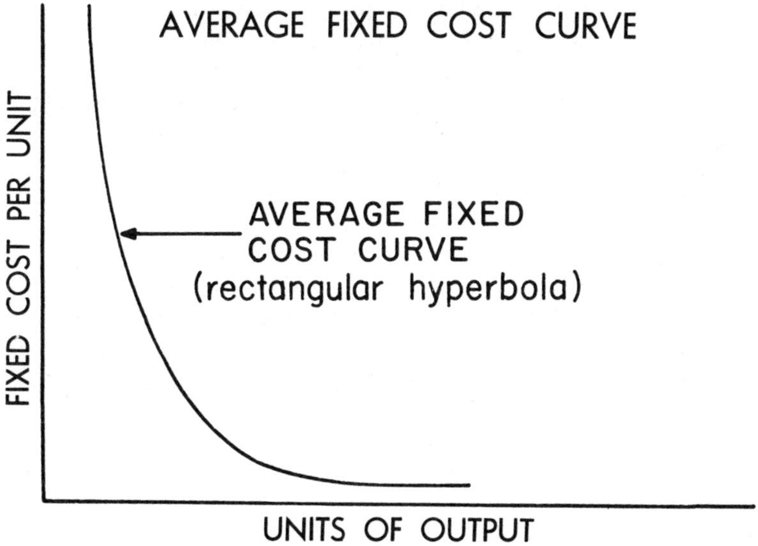

Figure 4.

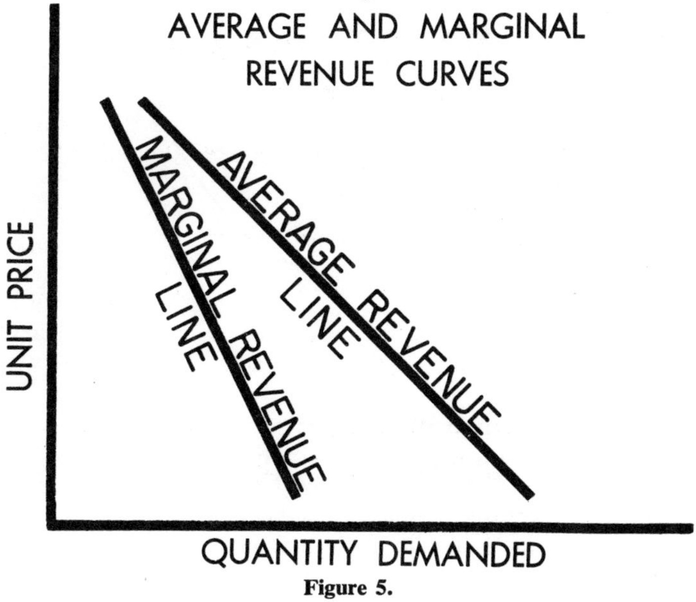

Figure 5.

averaging down. In the stock market, the practice of buying the same dollar amount of shares as the market price is falling in order to lower the average price paid for the shares held.

averaging up. In the stock market, the practice of *selling short* the same dollar amount of shares as the market price is rising so that prices can fall only part way back towards the original starting price and there will be a net profit if the shares are brought to *cover* before the original prices are reached again.

award. (1) The decision of an arbitrator. (2) The sale of goods at an auction to the highest bidder. (3) In foreign trade and taxation, the compensation paid an informer who gives information of a customs or tax violation.

axia. Unchartered, voluntary form of credit union found only in larger cities and limited to a single foreign-born group. Indorsed notes and shares are used as security for loans.

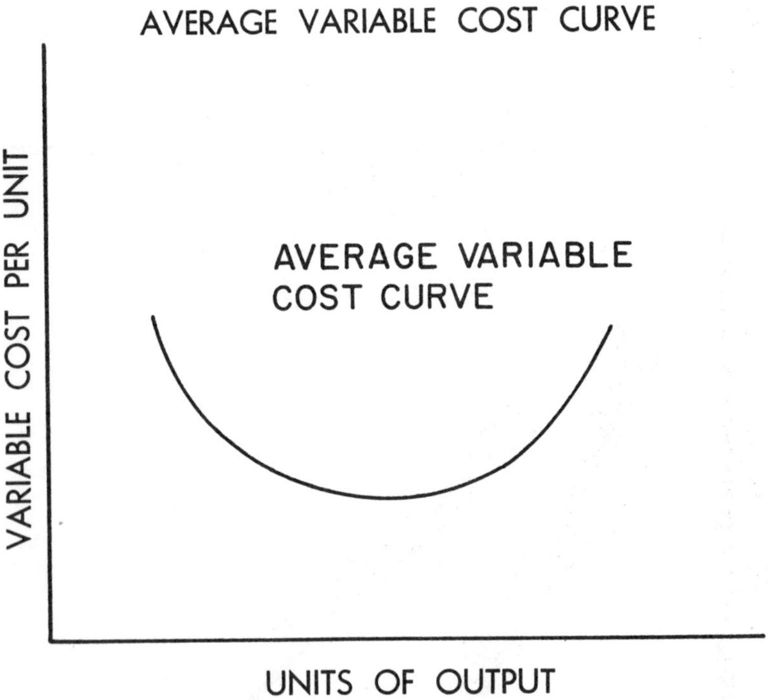

Figure 6.

back bill. A statement of unpaid charges.

back casting. The reverse of forecasting. Testing a relationship between economic variables by applying the values (in prior years) of the independent variables to the formula or relationship involved to arrive at the values of the dependent variable indicated by the formula, for the purpose of examining the exactness of the fit of values established by the formula to the observed values.

back haul. The carrying of goods away from the destination at the start of the trip or beyond the destination at the finish to meet connections, etc.

back log. Used particularly to refer to the total unfilled orders on hand at any one time.

back order. A supplier entering an order for goods not on hand to be filled when the goods become available.

back pay. The difference between wages already paid an employee and higher wages granted retroactively by agreement, arbitration, or legal enforcement.

back spread. In *arbitrage,* the *spread* is the amount of difference between the prices in two markets when the difference exceeds the normal differential. The back spread is the difference when it is less than normal. "Normal" difference between the two markets is the cost of freight, insurance in transit, etc., for moving goods.

back tracking. Same as *bumping.*

backward shifting. See *shifting.*

Bacon-Davis Act. A federal law of 1931 providing that the Secretary of Labor can set wage rates on public construction projects to conform to rates currently paid for similar work in the area. Cf. *Walsh-Healy Act.*

BAE Bureau of Agricultural Economics. Federal bureau in Department of Agriculture, created in 1938 to formulate overall plans relating to agricultural production, distribution, land utilization, and conservation in their broadest aspects.

bail. In law, a bond or money deposited with a court to assure the appearance of a person.

bailee. See *bailment.*

bailee's lien. The right of a *bailee* to keep possession of the bailed property for payment of charges for services performed on the bailed property.

bailment. The relationship created when one party (the bailor) turns over possession of goods to another party (the bailee) but keeps the ownership of the goods. May be for hire or gratuitous. Similar to a lease, except that a lease applies to realty and a bailment to personal property. However, it is possible to lease personal property. This differs from bailment in that the *ownership* is also parted with for the period of the lease. A bailment differs similarly from a *conditional sale*.

bailor. See *bailment*.

bail-out rule. Prior to the 1954 Internal Revenue Code, the stockholders of a corporation could arrange a non-taxable preferred stock dividend on common stock. The stockholders could then sell the preferred to an outsider who redeemed the preferred stock with the corporation. The original stockholder paid a tax only at the *capital gain* rate.

balanced budget. A budget is balanced when receipts attributable to a particular period equal or exceed expenditures attributable to that period. Income or expense attributable to more than one period is allocated to the several periods.

balanced budget multiplier. The concept that when the budget of a government is balanced, taxes result in reduction of consumption by less than the tax (since not all of the money would have been spent). Thus when the taxes are spent by the government more is spent than would have been spent had there been no tax.

balanced budget theorem. The proposition that since the difference between the expenditures *multiplier* and the tax multiplier is 1, any increase in government expenditures that is fully paid for by increased taxes will increase the national income by the amount of the budget increase. Stated otherwise, this is due to the fact that under a balanced budget, the amount of the increase in government expenditures exceeds by the amount of idle funds reached by the increase in taxes that part of the increase in taxes drawn from funds that would otherwise have been spent in consumption.

balance of payments. A statement of international transactions which give rise to money payments between countries, covering: (1) current accounts including trade and services, (2) capital accounts including short term and long term items, (3) gold and silver movements and (4) unilateral transfers by gifts of governments and individuals. The total receipts of the particular country and total payments by that country must balance if gifts, loans and accounts payable are included.

balance of payments, equilibrium. The balance of payments is said to be in equilibrium when, at the existing exchange rate, there is no continued flow in one direction of short term capital or gold. A deficit is said to exist when there is a continued outflow, a surplus when there is a continued inflow, of these items. For a gold-producing country an outflow of gold is in effect a merchandise export, not an indication of a deficit.

balance of trade. A statement of the value of merchandise exports and imports. Usually the merchandise is the largest component of the balance of payments. The general balance of trade of a country includes the value of merchandise exports to and imports from all other countries. A "favorable" balance refers to a net export surplus, an "unfavorable" balance to a net import surplus.

balance sheet. A report as of a given date listing the assets of any organization together with a list of creditors' claims (liabilities), the difference reflecting the equity of the owners, commonly called the net worth of the organization.

balance sheet account. Same as *real account.*

balance sheet equation. The equation stating that the total of assets equals the total of liabilities plus net worth (ownership).

balloon. In finance, the lump sum payable at the end of a term loan or long period loan where only part of the principal amount has been repaid in the scheduled repayments over the life of the loan.

bank. An institution for lending, borrowing, issuing, or caring for money. The essential economic characteristic of a bank is the creation of credit. A bank may be either incorporated or unincorporated (private). Charters are granted by the state or federal governments.

banks, types of. See the following specific terms.

Bank for Cooperatives
Bank for International Settlements
bank of issue
branch banking
central bank
central reserve city bank
chain banking
commercial bank
correspondent bank
country bank
Export-Import Bank
Federal Land Bank
Federal Reserve Bank
group banking
industrial bank
International Bank for Reconstruction and Development
member bank
Morris Plan bank
mutual savings bank
national bank
pet bank
private bank
reserve city bank
savings bank
state bank
unit bank
wildcat bank

bankable bill. A note or *bill of exchange* readily accepted by a bank.

bank acceptance. A *bill of exchange* which has been accepted by a bank; that is, the bank has agreed to make payment on the due date.

bank call. The periodic demand for balance sheets as of a given date made on banks by the state or federal supervising authority.

bank charter. A document of incorporation issued by the state or federal government giving a group of individuals the right to establish a bank.

bank check. A *bill of exchange* drawn on a bank.

bank clearings. The total of checks presented to a clearinghouse for collection.

bank credit. (1) Bank credit is the ability of a bank to create money by lending money (creating deposits) in return for a note or other form of obligation. Such a note can be rediscounted at a Federal Reserve Bank and the lending bank will then receive government money. (2) From the viewpoint of the individual, the money which the bank owes him or will lend him.

bank currency. Same as *bank note.*

bank debits. The total of checks and other documents charged to deposit accounts. When collected for a given area and period, bank debits are used as an index of the volume of business transactions.

bank deposit. The relationship of creditor and debtor in which the one making the deposit is the creditor and the bank is the debtor.

bank deposit, types of. See the following specific terms:

demand deposit
derivative deposit
primary deposit
secondary deposit
time deposit

bank discount. Discounting a note in banking terms means that the banker subtracts the interest at an assumed rate from the face of the note and gives the borrower the balance as a credit. Occasionally when a document is transferred, more than the face value may be paid because of the high rate of interest carried by the note. This is still called a discount.

bank draft. A *bill of exchange* drawn by a bank on another bank.

banker's bill of exchange. A *bill of exchange* drawn upon a bank rather than an individual or business firm. When the bank accepts the bill of exchange it becomes a bank acceptance.

Bank for International Settlements. The bank established in 1930 under Swiss charter to administer reparations payments and in a limited way to engage in general banking.

Bank Holding Company Act. Passed by Congress in 1956, the principal provisions require prior approval by the Board of Governors of the Federal Reserve System before establishment of new bank-holding companies or acquisition of 5 per cent or more of the voting shares of any bank by an existing holding company.

bank holiday. Temporary closing of banks for a period of time in order to stop excessive withdrawal of bank funds by depositors and the consequent hoarding of these funds. All banks in the U.S. were closed from March 5 to March 9, 1933, in this way.

bank line. A *line of credit* offered by a bank to a borrower.

Bank Merger Act. Legislation in 1960 applying the limitations of the *Bank Holding Company Act* of 1956 to bank mergers.

"banking school" principle. A principle developed in England in the nineteenth century maintaining that under a purely metalic currency a gain or loss of gold from abroad would not automatically result in a corresponding increase or decrease of currency in circulation and thus influence the price level, but might instead change the amount of gold in hoards. The banking school also maintained that under a mixed currency of gold and convertible paper notes, the amount of paper notes in circulation was adequately adjusted to the needs of business by the processes of competitive banking. Cf. *"currency school" principle.*

bank money. Deposits (promises by a bank to pay) created by a bank when it is required to have on hand in reserves only a fraction of its total deposits.

bank note. Paper currency issued by a bank with its promise to pay the bearer on demand the amount stated. In the United States, bank notes are issued only by the Federal Reserve System.

bank of issue. A bank issuing notes intended to circulate as currency.

bank post remittance. A foreign bill of exchange whose proceeds are forwarded to the payee of the bill.

bank rate. (1) The rate at which the central bank stands ready to discount eligible paper. In the United States this is the Federal Reserve rediscount rate. Eligible paper could be classified and thus different rates might develop. (2) Colloquially, the rate a bank charges its customers on loans.

bank reserves. The assets of a bank from which it will meet claims of depositors to withdraw.

bank reserves, types of. See the following specific terms:

excess bank reserves	*primary bank reserves*
free reserves	*required bank reserves*
legal bank reserves	*secondary bank reserves*
net borrowed reserves	*working bank reserves*

bank run. Abnormal withdrawal of deposits from a bank due to fear.

bankruptcy. A legal method by which a debtor may be relieved of his financial obligations. A court, through a trustee, takes the debtor's property and distributes it among his creditors in proportion to their respective claims against him. Bankruptcy is subject to federal law and may be voluntary or involuntary. There are six acts, any one of which constitutes bankruptcy: (1) making a general assignment for creditors, (2) admitting in writing inability to pay debts, (3) concealing or conveying property with intent to defraud creditors; and the following three acts if done while insolvent: (4) preferring one creditor, (5) failing to discharge a lien within 30 days, or (6) permitting a receiver to take over while unable to meet debts as they mature.

Banks for Cooperatives. A system of twelve banks scattered over the United States under the supervision of the Farm Credit Administration (FCA) to extend credit to farmer cooperatives.

bank statements. A financial report required from time to time by the supervising authorities, showing the financial condition of the bank. A short report must also be published in a local paper.

bargaining agent. A union chosen by the employees of the appropriate *bargaining unit* to act as their representative and certified as such by the National Labor Relations Board.

bargaining theory of wages. A generalization that wage rates will fall within two limits, the upper limit being break-even production from the viewpoint of the capitalist and the lower limit being the subsistence level of living for workers. The exact point between the limits is determined by the relative bargaining power of the two groups. Cf. *lump of labor theory of wages, marginal productivity theory of wages, residual theory of wages, subsistence theory of wages, wage fund theory of wages.*

bargaining unit. In collective bargaining, the bargaining unit is a group of employees with sufficiently identical interests so that they can be classed as a unit for purposes of negotiating a labor contract. There may be one or more such units in the case of one employer or plant. Cf. *craft union, industrial union.*

bargain money. Same as *earnest money.*

barometer stock. On the stock market, a term applied to a widely held stock of a leading company whose price movement is taken to reflect general market conditions.

barometric forecasting. The method of forecasting which employs *economic indicators* which lead the economy.

barratry. (1) In foreign trade, any unlawful dealing with a vessel or her cargo by the master or crew. (2) In law, inciting quarrels or litigation.

barter. An exchange of goods or services made without the use of money.

barter agreement. An agreement between two countries providing for the exchange of given quantities or values of specified commodities. Cf. *clearing agreement.*

barter terms of trade. See *terms of trade.*

base pay. The wage determined by the *base rate.* Excludes overtime, bonuses, and premiums.

base price. The price used as a starting point. To this price additions may be made for freight, extra services, packaging, etc., or deductions may be made.

base rate. With reference to wages, the rate of pay for a stated output or stated period of labor. Output beyond the minimum or time beyond the period may be paid at a premium rate.

base stock. The desired level of average inventory. Also called *normal* or *standard* stock.

base stock method of inventory. Valuing the relatively fixed and permanent quantity of inventory at a fixed price (usually an historically low point) with the remainder of the inventory valued by another method.

base surplus plan. A pricing scheme (where the product is capable of several uses with each use commanding a different price) giving the producer a fixed price for the amount produced in a base period and a lower price for any surplus. Cf. *use plan.*

basic limit. In insurance, the limit of liability for which the basic premium rate is quoted.

basic yield. The return per year which would be produced by an investment which carried no risk of default.

basing point. In transportation, a point to and from which are computed rates to be used in constructing *through rates* between other points lying beyond the basing point.

basing-point rate. In transportation, the rate to certain competitive centers designated as "basing points." For points not so designated, the *local rate* from the nearest basing point is added to the rate to the nearest basing point, even though the distance is less to that point from the point of origin than from the basing point.

basing-point pricing. A pricing method under which prices are quoted to include transportation from one given point (single basing-point system) or from more than one point (multiple basing-point system) regardless of the point from which actual shipment is made. In the first method the buyer pays freight from the given point regardless of whether shipment is from that or some other point. Under the second method the buyer pays the lowest of the alternative prices, regardless of whether shipment is made from the lowest basing point or some other point. Cf. *delivered price, f.o.b. pricing, mill base system,* and *zone pricing.*

basing rate. A rate used only for the construction of other rates.

basis book. A book of tables used to convert bond prices expressed in terms of yield to maturity (a rate) into the price of the bond in dollars. Thus a $1,000 *face value* bond due in ten years with a 2.5% interest rate coupon quoted on a 2.2% (yield to maturity basis) is shown by the table to be equal to a price of $1026.80. *Municipal bonds* are customarily quoted on the yield to maturity basis.

basis point. In government securities, one one-hundredth of one per cent (or of one unit) change in the yield (or price) of the security. Because government securities move less in absolute dollar amounts than other securities, though relatively the movement in their price may be more significant, the term basis point has come into use as a shorthand method of referring to absolute changes that would be more cumbersome to express in customary terms.

basis price. The price of a bond expressed in terms of yield to its maturity. Thus a $1,000 *face value* bond due in ten years with a 2.5% interest rate coupon is quoted on a 2.2% basis price when the money price sought for the bond is $1026.80.

bathtub theorem. Using the analogy of a bathtub, the total stock of goods (water in the tub) is equal to production (faucet flow) less consumption (drain flow). The rate of accumulation is the excess of inflow over outflow.

Bayes criterion. The proposition that when we know of no reason for probabilities to be different, we should assume them equal. Also called *Leplace criterion.* Cf. *Hurwicz criterion,* and *regret criterion.*

Bayes theorem. If a given probability is established that a particular event will occur (such as the correct size plant to build for different product mixes) and later additional evidence (such as a subjective judgment as to the probability curve for the sales of each type of product) is established, the plant most likely to be adequate can be determined by combining these probabilities.

bearer bonds. Bonds payable to the person having possession of them. Such bonds do not require indorsement to transfer ownership, but only the transfer of possession.

"bearer paper." In dealing with negotiable instruments, an instrument is called "bearer paper" when it is payable to bearer, i.e., the person having possession of it. Ownership of such a document is transferred by delivery, no indorsement being needed. If the person who originally issued the paper placed it in bearer form, it cannot thereafter receive a *special indorsement.* Cf. *"order paper."*

bear market. A market in which prices are falling or expected to fall. Cf. *bull market.*

bear raiding. Driving the price of a stock down by a series of *short sales* in order to buy in at the lower price to cover. Regulations now control this possibility by requiring that a short sale be at a price one-eighth higher than the last sale and also that the prior sale shall not have been a short sale.

"bears." Speculators who hope to profit by a fall in the price of stocks, bonds, or commodities. To achieve this they sell something for future delivery that they do not now own ("sell it short") in the hope of buying and delivering when the price has fallen. Cf. *bulls.*

Bedaux point system. An incentive wage plan under which the employee receives a premium of 75% of the "points" in excess of 60 per hour, a "point" being defined as a unit of measurement of human effort consisting of that useful work which the average employee at normal speed can accomplish in one minute, with allowance for rest. Cf. *Emerson, Gantt, Halsey, Merrick, Rowan, and Taylor plans.*

behavioral equation. In *econometrics,* an equation stating economic behavior of individuals or of an economy. Such behavior is stated as a functional relationship (such as expenditures on shoes depend on income and population) rather than as an identity (such as quantity of a good demanded equals quantity supplied in equilibrium) or definition (such as income equals consumption plus savings when savings is unconsumed income). Cf. *adjustment equation, definitional equation, final equation, reduced form equation, restraint equation,* and *structural equation.*

belt-line railroad. A railroad that circles a major terminal and shuttles cars from one railroad line to another.

bench mark. (1) In statistics an actual measurement distinguished from a value computed by *extrapolation* or *interpolation.* (2) In law and public utilities, a permanently marked point of reference established by a survey.

bench warrant. A writ issued by a judge sitting on the bench and calling for immediate apprehension of the party named.

beneficiary. The person to whom a policy is made payable, or one who is to receive the benefits from a trust fund, or one who is to receive the benefits of any other type of contract. Where the beneficiary has given no consideration for his rights he is called a donee beneficiary, but where he has given consideration he is called a creditor beneficiary.

benefit-cost ratio. Particularly as to public projects, the ratio of the discounted value of future benefits from a project to the cost of a project (initial investment plus discounted future maintenance costs).

benefit tax theory. A tax theory which argues that the burden of a certain tax should correspond to the services which the government renders in connection with the tax payment. Cf. *ability to pay tax theory, diffusion tax theory, sacrifice tax theory.*

Benelux. An arrangement between Belgium, the Netherlands and Luxemburg for the purpose of eliminating trade restrictions between these countries. This has now been replaced by *EEC, European Economic Community.*

Benson-Brannan plan. See *Brannan-Benson plan.*

bequest. In law, technically the distribution of personal property by *will.* The distribution of real property is by *devise.*

Bergson criterion. In *welfare economics,* whether a change in the economy is an improvement is to be determined by a set of explicit value judgments from which an analyst can work. Such value judgments would be determined by an authority, such as government. Cf. *Kaldor criterion, Paretian optimality,* and *Scitovsky double criterion.*

Bernouillian utility. The hypothesis that the utility of money can be approximated by using the logarithm of the number of units of money a person has as the measure of the utility of money.

best efforts. In securities' *underwriting,* an agreement by an *investment banker* to apply his best efforts to selling an issue of securities but with the right to turn back unsold securities.

best evidence rule. In law, the requirement that only the best evidence is admissible. Thus a copy is not admissible when the original is available. Cf. *secondary evidence rule.*

beta coefficient. The *coefficient of regression* (the slope of the regression line) when the variables are stated in units of their own standard deviation.

bid. The price named by a willing buyer. Cf. *ask, competitive bidding, open bid, sealed bid.*

bid bond. A *bond* sometimes required for all bidders to cover any loss if the successful bidder fails to enter a contract and the job must be rebid.

big board. A popular term referring to the board showing the current prices of securities listed on the New York Stock Exchange.

bilateral contract. A contract in which the acceptance is a promise to perform rather than the actual performance. The offer which is thus accepted is also a promise.

bilateralism. An international economic policy having as its object the achievement of particular *balances of trade* between two countries by means of discriminatory tariff, exchange, or other controls. The initiative is usually taken by the country having an "unfavorable" balance of trade. Extensive bilateralism results in a shift of international trade away from channels that would result from the principle of *comparative advantage.* Cf. *multilateralism.*

bilateral mistake. In law, a mistake by both parties to a contract. In general, a contract can be set aside on this basis. Cf. *unilateral mistake.*

bilateral monopoly. The situation in which there is only one buyer and only one seller.

bill broker. One who negotiates the purchase or sale of *negotiable* paper.

bill of credit. The promissory note of a government designed to circulate as money. The term derives from the United States Constitution which forbids states to issue such documents.

bill of exchange. An unconditional written order by one party (the drawer) on a second party (the drawee) ordering him to pay a third party (the payee) or one designated by him on the bill a stated sum of money on demand or at some future date.

bill of exchange, types of. See the following specific terms:

accepted bill	*due bill*
accommodation paper	*external bill*
advance bill	*finance bill*
banker's bill	*foreign bill*
blank bill	*inland bill*
clean bill	*investment bill*
commercial bill	*payment bill*
credit bill	*prime bill*
demand bill	*sight bill*
documentary bill	*time bill*
domestic bill	*trade bill*

bill of lading. A document issued by the carrier to the shipper as a receipt and as a contract governing transportation and delivery of goods. The original copy carries title to the goods if made negotiable (as shown by the terms "bearer" or "to order of"). B/L is the abbreviation. Cf. *order bill of lading, straight bill of lading, through bill of lading.*

bill of materials. A list of all the parts or ingredients needed to produce a good, together with quantity and prices of each part needed.

bill of particulars. In law, a listing of the breakdown of a total figure to show the individual items which compose it.

bill of sale. A contract transferring the listed property from one party to another.

bills-only doctrine. (1) in monetary policy, the practice of limiting *open market operations* to Treasury bills (maturity less than one year). (2) In banking theory, the doctrine that if a bank lends only on bills (inventory or receivables), the bank will be both flexible and liquid.

bimetallism. A monetary system under which both gold and silver coins are used as standard money. Both metals have free coinage and unlimited legal tender, and a stated ratio of exchange is maintained between them (the "mint ratio") by the government.

bimodal. A *frequency distribution* with two *modes.*

binder. In insurance, a temporary agreement covering the insured if loss occurs before the policy is actually issued. Cf. *cover note.*

binomial distribution. The distribution of the probable occurrences of mutually exclusive events (such as black or white) in a given number of independent trials in which each event has a random or equal likelihood. The formula is:

$$P = \left(\frac{n}{x}\right) \Pi^x (1-\Pi)^{n-x}$$

where n = size of sample, x = basic probability of the event (0.5 for a coin), Π is the constant 3.14159 and $\left(\frac{n}{x}\right)$ is $n!/x!$.

BIR. Bureau of Internal Revenue. See *IRS.*

birth rate. The number of births per 1,000 persons. Cf. *net reproduction rate.*

bits. Information statistics are generally written in terms of the logarithm with the base 2 and in this form the value is called "bits."

bivariate analysis. The analysis of values of two variables, e.g., determination of the *coefficient of correlation.* Cf. *univariate analysis* and *multivariate analysis.*

black list. (1) In labor, a list of individuals who have been objectionable to an employer because they are known to be union members or are considered agitators. The list is passed on from one employer to another. Use of the list to discriminate in employment is illegal under the National Labor Relations Act. (2) In international trade, a list of individuals and firms of another country with whom the domestic country forbids commerce by its nationals.

black market. A generic term describing transactions in violation of price control and ration laws. Cf. *gray market.*

Bland-Allison Act. Passed by Congress in 1878. The act directed the Secretary of the Treasury to purchase each month from two to four million dollars worth of silver bullion and coin it into standard dollars at the ratio of sixteen weight-units of silver to one unit of gold.

blank bill. A bill of exchange with the payee's name not appearing.

blank check. A *check* signed by the *drawer* but left blank as to the payee, the amount of the check, or some other particular to be filled in when a determination has been made by the one to whom the check is entrusted.

blanket bond. (1) A bond usually secured by a mortgage on a number of pieces of property, each of which may have other and prior mortgages. (2) A bond indemnifying an employer for loss due to infidelity or non-performance of duty by any employee.

blanket coverage. In insurance, a policy whose face amount (limit of maximum recovery) applies to each of the several perils and is not divided so that only part of the face amount is applicable to a particular peril. Cf. *divided coverage*.

blanket mortgage. A mortgage covering all the fixed assets of a borrower rather than specifically named assets.

blanket policy. In insurance, a policy which covers more than one type of property in one location, or one or more types of property at more than one location. For the rules applicable to the situation where a blanket policy and a specific policy both cover a loss, see *Cromie, Kinne, Page,* and *Reading rules.*

blanket position bond. In insurance, a bond protecting the insured from loss due to dishonesty of employees. The limit of liability of the insured is the face amount of the bond times the number of dishonest employees involved.

blanket rate. (1) In transportation, (a) a rate which applies from and/or to a group of points, e.g., if the same rate applied to all shipments of a given good from all points on the Atlantic coast to all points on the Pacific coast; (b) a special rate for several different articles moving in one shipment. (2) In insurance, the rate applied when there is more than one property or subject of insurance.

blank endorsement. The placing of one's name on a negotiable instrument without any qualification. Also called general indorsement.

blank stock. Stock whose terms need not be set forth in the articles of incorporation but may be established by the board of directors at the time of issue.

blind figure. A bookkeeping and accounting term to describe a figure indistinctly or carelessly written so that it may be taken for another one, as a three for an eight or a two for a seven, etc.

blind selling. A marketing arrangement under which the buyer is forced to accept merchandise without examining it or before completion in order to continue to carry products of the seller. The practice had been common between movie producers and operators and is now illegal.

block. (1) A large amount of stock sold as a unit. (2) Any group with similar economic interests; in this sense the term is usually spelled "bloc."

blocked account. (1) A bank balance or other credit whose use is restricted or prohibited by the government of the country where the account is located, usually with reference to its transfer to other countries. (2) The term is used analogously with reference to governmental restrictions on the spending of accounts within a country as an inflationary control.

blocked currency (or exchange). Currency and bank deposits whose use is restricted by the government of the country where the currency or deposit is located, usually with reference to its transfer to other countries.

block-grant. A British system for the distribution of governmental aids to local governments according to needs as measured by a composite index.

block meter rate. In public utilities, a scale of charges requiring the payment of different (lower) rates for each successive block (or group) of service used. Cf. *step rate schedule.*

block policy. In insurance, a policy covering all the property of an *insured* against many types of risk. The policy usually covers the insured's property off his own premises and the property of others on the premises of the insured.

block rate schedule. Same as *block meter rate.*

BLS. Bureau of Labor Statistics. Established in the Department of Labor in 1913 with the duty of distributing information on subjects connected with labor, especially its relation to capital, the hours of labor, and earnings in various fields. BLS publishes several price indices.

blue chip. A stock market term for the stock of a listed company whose products and financial record are of high quality.

blue list. A daily listing of *municipal bonds* offered for sale by dealers. Called "blue list" because it is printed on blue-colored paper.

blue sky laws. State laws governing securities. So called because they are designed to protect investors from purchasing a piece of the "blue sky" (worthless securities). Different in principle from the current Federal legislation which is directed only at disclosure. Blue sky laws may also extend to determination of the legitimacy of the proposed financing.

board lot. The trading unit on a stock exchange. The unit on the New York Stock Exchange is ordinarily 100 shares. Also called a *round lot.*

Board of Governors of Federal Reserve System. The governing body of the Federal Reserve System, consisting of seven members whose terms are fourteen years each, with one expiring every other year. Their office is in Washington, D.C.

Board of Trade (Chicago). The leading commodity exchange in Chicago, allowing trade according to recognized rules, primarily in grains.

body execution. In law, (1) the seizure of a person by order of a court, or (2) the imprisonment of a *judgment debtor* who has refused to pay a judgment. In the latter case, the procedure is governed by statute which usually limits this remedy to cases of a judgment for tort liability, requires the *judgment creditor* to pay the room and board of the defendant during the time he is in jail, and provides for the release of the defendant if he signs a pauper's oath.

boiler room. A stock market term for high pressure selling of speculative stocks done by many salesmen each in a small cubicle and working with telephones to contact possible buyers.

bolshevism. A term widely used to describe the present social and political system in the Union of Soviet Socialist Republics, i.e., Russia. It is also used to describe any proposal that embodies ideas similar to those existing in Russia. The word itself means "majority," referring to the majority in the Socialist party before the revolution; the minority were called Mensheviks. Later on the Bolsheviki split into the predominant Stalinist group and the opposing Trotzkyist group. Cf. *communism.*

bond. (1) A written promise to pay the holder a sum of money at a certain time (more than one year after issue) at a stated rate of interest. A debt due in less than one year from date of issue is usually called a note. (2) In suretyship, the obligation of a guarantor to pay a second party upon default by a third party in the performance the third party owes to the second party.

bonds, types of. See the following specific terms as to bonds (promises to pay a debt):

adjustment bond
annuity bond
assented bond
assessment bond
assumed bond
bearer bond
blanket bond
bottomry bond
callable bond
chattel mortgage bond
collateral trust bond
consolidated bond
consolidated mortgage bond
continued bond
convertible bond
coupon bond
currency bond
debenture bond
discount bond
divisional bond
dollar bond
double barreled bond
equipment trust bond
extended bond
extension bond
flat bond
full faith and credit bond
general mortgage bond
general obligation bond
general tax bond
gold bond
government bond
guaranteed bond
income bond
indorsed bond
installment bond
interchangeable bond
interest bond
interim bond
irredeemable bond
joint and several bond
junior bond
leasehold mortgage bond
limited tax bond
mortgage bond
municipal bond
open-end mortgage bond
optional bond
outstanding bond
overlying bond
participating bond
passive bond
perpetual bond
profit-sharing bond
real estate mortgage bond
redeemable bond
refunding bond
refunding mortgage bond
registered bond
registered coupon bond
reorganization bond
revenue bond
serial bond
series bond
sinking fund bond
special assessment bond
stabilized bond
subordinate bond
surety bond
tax-anticipation bond
term bond
terminal bond
treasury bond
underlying bond
unified bond
unlimited tax bond

See the following specific terms as to bonds (indemnity and suretyship):

administrator's bond
appeal bond
attachment bond
bid bond
blanket bond
blanket position bond
contract bond
executor's bond
fidelity bond
fiduciary bond
fixed penalty bond
guaranty bond
indemnity bond
judgment bond
name bond
open covenant bond
penalty bond
performance bond
personal bond
position bond
removal bond
replevin bond
schedule bond
surety bond

bonded goods. Goods stored in a warehouse by an owner who has furnished bond to pay duty or taxes due.

bonded warehouse. (1) A warehouse of which the government requires a bond and license to insure against loss of internal revenue taxes (liquor and tobacco) or customs duties. (2) A public warehouse bonded and licensed for storage of agricultural commodities under the U. S. Warehouse Act of 1916. (3) Other warehouses which insure customers against loss are not properly referred to as "bonded."

bond fund. In government accounting, a fund established to account for bond sale proceeds.

bondholders. The holders or owners of the bonds of a corporation or government. They are lenders or creditors.

bond ratio. The total face value of bonds of a corporation divided by the total face value of bonds, preferred stock, common stock, reserve, and surplus.

bonification. The return of a tax paid but later found to be not due, as with an excise tax paid on goods later exported.

bonus. (1) In its strict sense, any method used to increase the laborer's production by giving him extra pay for more than the standard quantity of work. (2) More generally compensation in addition to the regular wage regardless of any relation to the individual's productivity.

bonus stock. Stock given as a premium in connection with the sale of other stock.

book credit. Unsecured promises to pay (for goods) held by the seller constitute book credit to the buyers.

book profit. An unrealized profit such as the excess of an inventory with a market value higher than that at which it is carried on the books.

book value. (1) The value of an outstanding share of stock of a corporation at any one time, determined by adding the par (or stated) value of the stock outstanding to the surplus applicable to that class of stock and dividing by the number of shares of that class outstanding. (2) The valuation at which assets are carried on the books, e.g., cost less reserve for depreciation.

book value method (in capital budgeting). Same as *accounting method of return (in capital budgeting).*

boom. An outburst of some form of business activity, usually speculative. It may be in stocks, bonds, real estate, or anything else of value. The price of the "boomed" goods usually rises very rapidly.

"boot." (1) In finance, the "boot" is the common stock sold as a "bonus" with other corporate securities. (2) In taxation, the cash or other consideration used to balance an approximately equal exchange of two commodities, e.g., one machine plus $100 for another machine.

bordereau. Particularly in insurance, a digest of the transactions between an agent and his company or an insurer and the reinsurer.

borrowing rate in capital budgeting. The rate which an investor must pay in the market for funds. This rate is usually (but not always) above the rate the investor can secure for lending funds to the market. Cf. *lending rate in capital budgeting.*

Boston interest. Ordinary interest computed by using a 30 day month rather than the exact number of days in a month. Cf. *New York interest.*

Boston trustee. An individual who undertakes to act as a professional trustee.

bottleneck inflation. A rise in the *price level* (or fall in real income) without an increase in *aggregate demand* or in the money supply which occurs when the structure of demand (types of goods demanded by an economy) changes more rapidly than resources can be shifted. Illustrated by the situation immediately after the end of World War II. Cf. *cost-push inflation* and *demand-pull inflation.*

bottom line. Colloquial term for *net profit* or earnings which appears at the bottom line of a *profit and loss statement.*

bottomry. A combination of money lending on the security of a ship and insurance of the ship so that if the ship is lost, the lender cannot recover the money lent. Cf. *respondentia.*

bottomry bond. Bond secured by the mortgage of a ship.

bounty. (1) A premium given to exporters by the government for the encouragement of some particular industry. (2) A price paid for the killing of animals or birds considered economically harmful, such as a bounty on timber wolves, crows, hawks, etc.

bourgeois. (1) That group of people who are in the upper middle class. (2) In Marxian theory, everyone who exploits labor. Cf. *proletariat.*

bourse. The French word for an exchange such as a stock or commodity exchange.

box diagram. See *contract curve.*

boycott. Refusing to have any commercial dealings with someone. Used particularly by labor unions against their employers, or by any group against some offending employer, group or government. The term derives from Capt. Boycott, a British trader living in Ireland with whom the Irish would do no business. Cf. *primary boycott* and *secondary boycott.*

branch banking. A system in which the same banking corporation has a number of different locations, but all part of the same corporation. The term is sometimes used to include banks which are integrated through holding companies, but this is confusing the term with *group banking* and *chain banking.*

brand. In ordinary usage, the same as a *trade-mark* placed on packages, casks, or other things.

brand, types of. See the following specific terms:

dealer's brand
house brand
local brand
manufacturer's brand
national brand
private brand

Brannan-Benson plan. A program for dealing with the surplus of agricultural products under which the government purchases at *parity price* (or another high price) and resells at the lower free market price. Benson and Brannan were Secretaries of Agriculture under Presidents Truman and Eisenhower. Cf. *ever-normal granary.*

brassage. The charge made by a government for coining metals. This amount covers only the cost of coinage. Any profit is called *seignorage.*

breach of contract. Breaking the terms of a contract by nonperformance or by some overt act contrary to the agreement. See *damages for breach of contract.*

break bulk point. In transportation, the point at which part or all of the contents of a car are unloaded.

break-even point. There are three break-even points: *cash break-even point, financial break-even point,* and *profit break-even point.* When only the term "break-even point" is used, profit break-even point is the one intended. The formula is $BE = FC/$ (1 — variable cost ratio), where *FC* is the fixed cost in dollars for any output and the variable cost ratio is the ratio of variable costs in dollars to sales in dollars for any output.

breaking point (rate). In transportation, a point from which rates are made or at which a rate is divided.

Bretton Woods Agreement. Agreement reached by an international conference at Bretton Woods, N.H., in 1944, for the establishment of an *International Bank for Reconstruction and Development* and an *International Monetary Fund.*

bridge rate. In transportation, a rate applicable near the borderline between freight zones to "bridge" a difference in rates of the two zones.

bridge supplement. A supplement amending an effective tariff and an issued but not yet effective tariff which is to succeed the effective tariff. In short, it "bridges" the gap between an old and new tariff which arises from the fact that the law requires a 30-day period for tariff changes.

brief. A written argument prepared by attorneys for submission to the judge or administrative agency hearing a legal matter.

broad market. (1) A market situation in which a wide variety of items are being bought and sold. (2) A market situation in which price or geographical limits are broad. Cf. *narrow market.*

broken lot. Goods offered for sale in smaller numbers than usually constitute the unit of sale. Cf. *job lot.*

broker. An agent of a buyer or a seller who buys or sells stocks, bonds, commodities, or services, usually on a commission basis.

broker, types of. See the following specific terms:

bill broker
broker's broker
commission broker
floor broker
investment broker
money broker
odd-lot broker
outside broker
pawn broker
stockbroker
two-dollar broker

brokerage. The fee or commission received by a broker upon execution of a transaction. The fee may be a flat amount or a percentage.

broker's broker. A *dealer,* i.e., one who buys or sells for his own account.

brokers' loan. Borrowings made by members of stock exchanges (brokers) to enable them to carry securities purchased for their customers on margin.

brokers' market. A market in which the public is not active but members of an exchange are trading with each other.

Brotherhoods (Railway). Generally the four big railway unions consisting of the Locomotive Engineers, Firemen, Conductors, and Brakemen.

bucket shop. The illegal practice of some brokers in accepting orders to buy or sell without executing such orders. Such a broker hopes to profit by pocketing the loss which a customer may experience upon closing out the transaction. If the customer closes out at a profit, the broker pays that profit. The illegality lies in an agent's dealing with his principal without disclosing that fact.

budget. (1) A detailed plan of future receipts and expenditures for successive periods of time so that profits are maximized and, in the case of government, funds may be efficiently gathered and spent. (2) More generally, any plan pertaining to one or more of the financial aspects of a business.

budget, types of. See the following specific terms:

administrative budget
balanced budget
capital budget
cash budget
continuous budget
financial budget
fixed budget
flexible budget
multiple budget
national income accounts budget
pro forma budget
project budget
sales budget
static budget
Swedish budget
variable budget

budget line. (Applied to labor.) Using a map of *indifference curves* for a worker with income on the *y* axis and leisure on the *x* axis, a straight line connecting one point on the *x* axis and one point on the *y* axis shows all the combinations of leisure and income that the worker can have (the wage rate remaining constant). This is called the budget line. Any other good could be substituted on the *x* axis to get a budget line for that good.

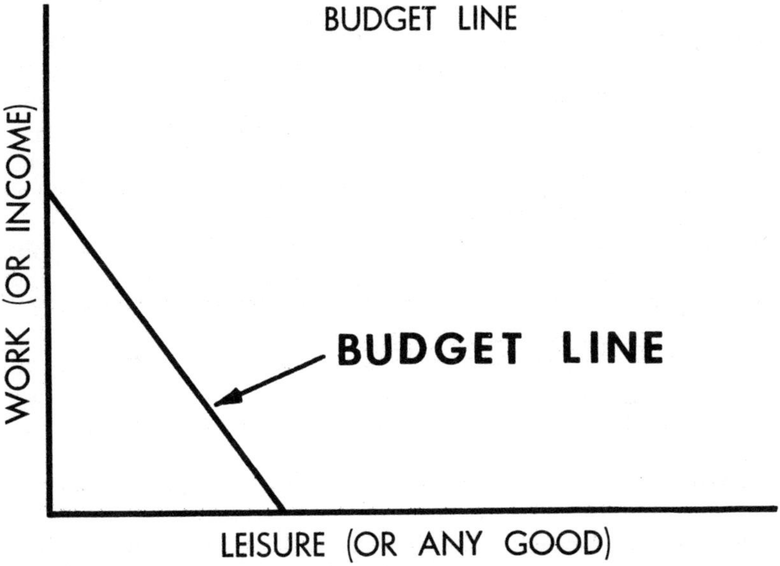

Figure 7.

buffer stock plan. Same as *ever normal granary.*

building and loan associations. Cooperative or quasi-cooperative institutions engaged in financing through mortgage loans the building and purchase of homes with money invested by stockholders.

building cycle. Cycles of maximum and minimum activity have been established for various industries separately from the general business cycle. One of the most definitely verified cycles is that of the building industry as 19 to 20 years in length, as measured by the volume of construction.

built-in stabilizers. Countercyclical factors which automatically come into play when the business cycle rises or falls, e.g., the income tax. When the cycle is rising, the volume of taxes collected rises (even though tax rates stay the same) and has a deterrent effect on further price rises. Vice versa when prices fall.

bulk-line costs or pricing. Setting prices high enough to draw forth the bulk of the production desired from the industry. The government followed such a policy in World War I in setting the price for war contracts.

bulk sale. The sale of all or substantially all the assets of a business. Such a sale has required procedures for the protection of the creditors of the seller.

bulk sales law. See *bulk sale.*

bullion. Bars of precious metal, either pure or mixed with alloy. These bars may be shipped from place to place instead of money, or they may be sent to the mints to be made into coin.

bullionism. (1) This term refers to the monetary policy of mercantilism which called for direct regulation of transactions in foreign exchange and in precious metals in order to maintain a favorable balance in the home country. Cf. *mercantilism.* (2) Followers of the monetary theories of the Bullion Report (England, 1810). Cf. *"currency school" principle.*

bull market. A market in which prices are rising or expected to rise. Cf. *bear market.*

bulls. A slang term applied to speculators who hope to profit by a rise in the price of stocks, bonds, or commodities, and hence purchase the items and hold them for later sale. Cf. *bears.*

bumping. Securing another man's position through the exercise of seniority.

bunch map. A visual and geometric technique for testing whether *multicollinearity* exists between more than two variables. On the first graph, observations of the first two variables, x and y, are plotted against each other and a trend line fitted. On a second graph, observations of the first and third variables, x and z are plotted against each other and a trend line fitted. Then the deviations of the y and z observations from the trend or *regression line* on each of the first two graphs are plotted on a third graph of four quadrants, using the x value common to each y and z observation. If a linear pattern develops, multicollinearity exists.

burden. In accounting, same as *overhead.*

Bureau of Standards. An agency of the government in Washington which tests the quality of goods that the government buys and develops standards or specifications for products. The bureau is equipped with an array of apparatus used to test hundreds of different products.

business agent. A term particularly applied in labor unions and referring to the full-time employee of the union who acts for the union in its business relations.

business barometer. A device attempting to measure the general level of business by an average of index numbers each measuring a different phenomenon.

business cycle. Rhythmic changes which take place in business conditions over a period of time. The phases of the cycle are called prosperity (peak, upswing, expansion), crisis (downturn), depression (trough, downswing, contraction), and recovery (upturn, revival). Various explanations for the business cycle have been developed. In analyzing cyclical statistics a number of different cycles have been found, each named after the man who developed knowledge of it. Thus the Kitchin cycle is about 40 months, the Juglar cycle is from 8 to 14 years, the Spiethoff cycle about 20 to 30 years and the Kondratieff cycle (long wave) about 50 years. See also *building cycle, inventory cycle.*

business cycle, theories of. See the following specific terms:

endogenous theory
exogenous theory
innovation theory
inventory theory
interaction of multiplier and accelerator theory
monetary theory
overinvestment-oversaving theory
psychological theory
underconsumption theory
weather theory

business insurance. Insurance on the life of a business executive or valued employee, the policy being payable to the employing company.

business interruption insurance. Same as *use and occupancy insurance.*

business risk. In finance, the risk of default or variability of return arising from the type of business conducted.

business sector. See *sector accounts.*

business tort. An injury by one person to another, usually arising not out of contract but out of certain "business" relations. For example, illegal restraint of trade, violation of trade-mark, etc., are business torts.

business transfer payments. In national income accounting, transfers by business for which no return is received. Principally corporate gifts to nonprofit institutions and consumer bad debts. *Net national product* less *indirect business taxes,* business transfer payments, and current *surplus* of government enterprises less subsidies establishes *national income.*

business trust. Same as *Massachusetts trust.*

buyers' market. A condition of the market in which there is an abundance of goods available and hence buyers can afford to be selective and may be able to force down the price that had previously prevailed. Cf. *sellers' market.*

buyers' monopoly. The market situation in which a single purchaser or group is able to dictate or influence the price at which a commodity will be sold. More accurately referred to as *monopsony* or *oligopsony.*

buyers' surplus. The difference between what a buyer actually has paid for a good and what he would have been willing to pay.

buying long. Buying stocks, bonds, or commodities outright with the expectation of holding them for a rise in price and then selling. Cf. *selling short.*

buying on margin. See *margin.*

buying to minimum inventory. The policy of adding to inventory of a specific good only when the inventory has fallen to a stated minimum.

by-bidder. One making fictitious bids to boost the price.

by-laws. Rules, supplementary to the articles of incorporation, which a corporation adopts for its internal government.

by-product. The residue arising at various stages in production of a principal commodity, e.g., by-products of the meat packing industry are glue, bone, hair, etc.

by-product method of cost accounting. A system of allocating costs between a principal product or products and a by-product or by-products. The main feature of the system is the initial costing of the by-product at the point where it first appears separately on some arbitrary basis (usually zero cost), and charging all other costs up to this point to the main product or products. Net proceeds of by-products are usually considered to be reductions of the cost of the main product.

CAB Civil Aeronautics Board. A federal board of five members appointed by the President. Its purpose is to establish safety rules, issue *certificates of convenience and necessity,* set rates, and regulate air carriers.

cable transfer. A transfer of funds by cable to avoid delay. Usually used in foreign exchange.

CACM. Central American Common Market. An association of Costa Rica, El Salvador, Guatemala, Honduras and Niagara to remove internal trade barriers and to establish a common tariff for imports into the association. Cf. *EEC. European Economic Community, EFTA. European Free Trade Association, CARIFTA. Caribbean Free Trade Association, LAFTA. Latin American Free Trade Association.*

cadastre. The tax inventory and assessment of real property in a given district.

caeteris paribus. Latin for "other things being equal." The usual assumption in economic theory under which only a few phenomena are permitted to vary at one time to facilitate tracing the effects of the variations. Cf. *mutatis mutandis*.

c.a.f. cost and freight. The price quoted is with freight paid to destination but not insured. Cf. *c.i.f.*

call. (1) An option permitting its holder (who has paid a fee for the option) to call for a certain commodity or security at a fixed price in a stated quantity within a stated period. The broker is paid to bring the buyer and seller together. The buyer of this right to call expects the price of the commodity or security to rise so that he can call for it at a profit. If the price falls the option will not be exercised. The reverse transaction is a *put*. (2) A demand by a corporation for payment against stock subscribed but not fully paid. (3) Notice by a corporation that it will redeem securities on a given date.

callable. The right of a corporation or government to call bonds or notes for payment before they are due. Preferred stock may also be callable.

callable bond. A bond subject to recall, at the option of the borrower, prior to the maturity date. Ordinarily the particular bonds to be recalled are determined by lot. Also referred to as a *redeemable bond*.

callable preferred stock. Preferred stock which can be called in for payment at a price stated on the certificate by the corporation at its option.

call-in pay. (1) Generally used in the same sense as *reporting pay*. (2) May also be used to describe additional payment when a worker is "called in" outside his regular working hours.

call loan. See *call money*.

call money. Money loaned under an agreement that the lender may call for payment or the borrower tender repayment at any time, usually on 24 hours notice.

call premium. The amount over *par* or *face value* payable by the issuer of the security upon calling a security in for payment or redemption.

call price. Same as *redemption price*.

cambist. (1) One who buys and sells *bills of exchange* and *foreign exchange*. (2) The books or lists containing information as to rates of exchange and currencies.

Cambridge equation. See *cash balance equation*.

Cambridge school. The school of economic thought following the Englishman, Alfred Marshall (1842-1924). See *Marshallian school.*

cameralism. The German and Austrian form of *mercantilism.* Attention was devoted more to fiscal problems of the country as a whole rather than to foreign trade alone.

canons of taxation. The principles advanced by Adam Smith that taxes (1) should be in proportion to revenue received, (2) should be certain and not arbitrary, (3) should be levied at a time convenient for taxpayers, and (4) should cost as little as possible to collect.

capacity cost. Same as *fixed cost.*

capacity factor. In public utilities, the ratio of the average load to the installed capacity of the equipment which supplies the load. Cf. *diversity factor, load factor, utilization factor.*

capias. Latin for *you may take.* A writ issued by a civil court for the purpose of seizing a person or property.

capital. (1) In accounting, the amount invested in a business. (2) In economic theory, there are several meanings. "Capital" may be used to mean (a) "capital goods," i.e., the tools of production, (b) the money available for investment, or invested, (c) the discounted value of the future income to be received from an investment, (d) the real or money value of total assets. (3) In law, "capital" means "capital stock."

capital, types of. See the following specific terms: *authorized capital, circulating capital, equity capital, fixed capital, invested capital, paid-in capital, subscribed capital, working capital.*

capital assets. In the income tax, a capital asset is an item not ordinarily bought and sold in the course of one's business. A profit on the sale of a capital asset is a capital gain and may be subject to different tax rates than an ordinary gain.

capital budget (governmental). In an effort to apply private accounting techniques, expenditures and receipts of government are apportioned to the different accounting periods to which they are attributable. Thus the ordinary governmental budget is in reality a *cash budget* and the capital budget is in reality a profit-and-loss statement. Cf. *Swedish budget.*

capital budget (private business). A period by period statement of beginning capital assets, planned acquisitions and disposals, and the resultant ending capital assets together with the sources and disposition of funds so involved.

capital budgeting. The analysis of investment projects to determine the *rate of return* of the investment and the *cost of* *capital* required to undertake the investment so as to compare the proposed investment with other opportunities and to arrive at a decision under all the circumstances whether to make the investment commitment. Differences in risks are important in the computation.

capital coefficient. The coefficient of capital when income or output is a function of capital. Thus if Y or $O = cK$, then c is the capital coefficient where Y, O and K are, respectively, income, output, and quantity of capital. Hence, the capital coefficient is the reciprocal of *capital productivity,* which is K/O.

capital consumption allowance. The deduction from *gross national product* to arrive at *net national product.* The deduction includes (1) depreciation, (2) casualty losses of capital assets, and (3) capital goods bought and consumed in the same period.

capital-deposit ratio. Same as *deposit ratio.*

capital expenditure. The amount paid for a fixed asset.

capital gain (or loss). In income tax law, the gain (or loss) realized upon disposition of an asset held primarily for investment purposes (such as the depreciable assets of a business) and not for resale in the ordinary course of business.

capital gains tax. A provision in the income tax that profits from the sale of capital assets are taxed at separate (lower) rates than the usually applicable rate.

capital goods. Same as *producers' goods.*

capitalism. An economic system which permits private ownership of the means of production. However, such a definition would also apply to other forms of economic organization. The distinguishing facts in modern times are (1) large amounts of capital used in production, (2) relatively great freedom of economic activity, and (3) in recent times, the great importance of the corporate form of business.

capitalism, state. The state as the owner of the chief means of production. Some claim that Russia today is an example of this form rather than of communism.

capitalist. The term usually applied to anyone who furnishes or obtains the capital or funds with which to establish and conduct a business. Also applied to people whose main sources of income are from return on property or investments.

capitalistic production. Same as *roundabout production.*

capitalization. In finance, the total of bonds and the par value of stock outstanding. In the case of *no-par stock,* the number of shares is used because the dollar amount of *stated value* has little significance. Sometimes the term excludes bonds and is then used to refer to *net worth.* Cf. *capital structure.*

capitalization of income. The process of taking the net income of a business and dividing this figure by the appropriate *capitalization rate* to establish the value of the business.

capitalization of taxes. See *tax capitalization.*

capitalization rate. The rate of earning appropriate to apply to the net income of a business to establish its value.

capitalized value. The money valuation set upon the assets of a business by dividing the annual profits by an assumed rate of earning which is usually the current rate for similar risks.

capital levy. A tax on capital, not on income from the capital. This method has been used in Europe but not so far in America unless inheritance taxes are considered capital levies.

capital loss. See *capital gain (or loss).*

capital market. The market for long-term investment funds. Thus primarily investment bankers, savings banks, insurance companies, pension funds, and trust companies are involved. Cf. *money market.*

capital net worth. The total assets of a business less the liabilities.

capital-output ratio. The quantity of capital divided by the quantity of output. This ratio is usually denoted as σ. Same as *capital productivity ratio.*

capital productivity ratio. The capital productivity ratio (usually denoted by σ) is the quantity of capital divided by the quantity of output (for a firm, an industry or an economy).

capital ratio. In *capital budgeting,* the ratio of the total investment fund (in dollars) to the particular investment (in dollars) being analyzed.

capital stock. The shares of ownership of a corporation. Such shares may have a *par value* or *no par value.*

capital stock, types of. See *stock, types of.*

capital stock tax. A tax on the stock of a corporation usually computed as a percentage of par value or assigned value. A special form of capital stock tax was the declared value capital stock tax which was combined with an excess profits tax.

capital structure. In finance, the total of bonds (or long term money) and ownership interests in a corporation, i.e., the stock accounts and surplus. Cf. *capitalization* and *financial* *structure.*

capital surplus. Surplus which arises from "capital" transactions and not from usual business profits, e.g., surplus from writing down the par value of capital stock.

capital turnover. Same as *investment turnover.*

capitation tax. Same as *head tax.*

captive shop. As a result of vertical integration of a firm (ownership by one producer of all the means of production from raw material to finished product), the factories in such a firm are called captive shops as opposed to factories that produce for more than one customer

cardinal utility theory. The proposition that economic analysis should proceed from absolute levels of pleasure measurements. Cf. *ordinal utility theory* and *von Neumann-Morgenstern utility index.*

CARIFTA. Caribbean Free Trade Association. In 1968 most of the island countries of the Caribbean formed to remove internal trade barriers and establish a common tariff for imports from outside the association. Cf. *EEC. European Economic Community, EFTA. European Free Trade Association, CACM. Central American Common Market, LAFTA. Latin American Free Trade Association.*

carload and less than carload lot or rate. See *l.c.l.*

carloadings. The number of railroad freight cars loaded in a period. Used as an index of business activity.

carload minimum weight. The least weight at which a shipment will be handled at carload rate.

car mile. Refers to the movement of a loaded freight car one mile. A more effective means of measuring volume of traffic than, for example, the train mile. Cf. *passenger mile.*

car (railroad), types of. See the following specific terms:

consolidated car
foreign car
home car
merchandise car
package car
peddler car
pool car
station-order car
trap car

carrier's lien. The right of one furnishing transportation services to keep possession of the property of a shipper or passenger for unpaid charges.

carry back (or carry forward). The income tax law contains provisions permitting *operating losses* or *capital losses* to be carried back or carried forward to preceding or following years to be used to offset the other year's profits or *capital gains*.

carrying charge. The addition to the regular price for goods to cover interest and other charges made for installment credit.

cartel. An agreement, often in writing among manufacturers, dealers, etc., of various countries which restricts prices, quantities, territories, etc., of goods, e.g., the nitrate cartel divided the world markets between its members and set prices for these markets.

cascaded systems. Multistorage operations where the input to each stage is the output of the preceding stage, causing interdependences among stages.

case law. The body of law established by prior decisions of courts and not resting on statutes or enactments of a legislature.

cash balance equation (exchange form). In monetary theory, the cash balance equation is $P = M/KT$ where $P =$ average price level of T below, $M =$ quantity of money, $T =$ total business transactions, $K =$ the fraction of receipts held in idle cash and hence $= 1/V$ in the *Fisher equation.* Also called Cambridge equation. Another form of the equation is the income approach rather than the exchange approach above. Cf. *income equation.*

CASH BREAK-EVEN POINT

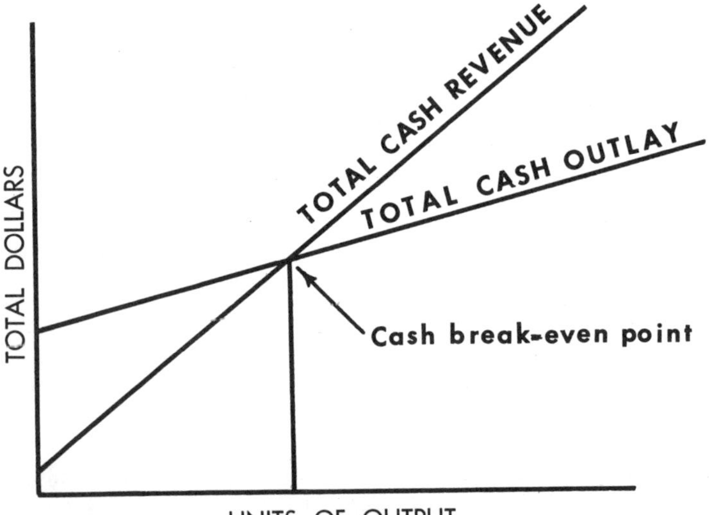

Figure 8.

cash basis. In income taxation, a system of recognizing income and expense items only at the time cash is received or paid out. Cf. *accrual basis.*

cash basis delivery. In the stock market, the sale of a security with delivery of cash payment and of the security due on the day of the transaction. Cf. *delayed delivery* and *regular way delivery.*

cashbook. A record of all cash transactions of an organization in one book, as distinguished from one separate book for cash receipts and another for cash payments.

cash break-even point. Assuming a plant organized for a given ideal volume of output, if units of output are put on the x axis and total dollars on the y axis, the cash break-even point is the intersection of the total cash revenue curve with the cash outlay curve. Cf. *financial break-even point.*

cash budget. A period by period statement of opening cash on hand, expected cash receipts, expected cash disbursements and resulting expected cash balance at the end of each period.

cash cycle. The time lapse between purchase of materials and collection of account receivable for finished product sold.

cash discount. A discount allowed for payment of a debt in advance of a due date. For example, 2/10, net 30 means 2% discount if paid within 10 days, net price if paid after 10 but before 30 days.

cash flow. The *net profits* of a business plus the charges of the accounting period for *depreciation, depletion, amortization,* and extraordinary charges to reserves not paid in cash. This is the cash generated in a period if all other accounts do not change. In addition, decreases in assets, increases in liabilities and new capital added are sources of cash while increases in assets and decreases in liabilities and net worth are applications of cash.

cashier's check. A *check* drawn by a cashier on the bank at which he is cashier.

cash or spot market. The sale of goods such as wheat, corn, or any other commodity for cash and immediate delivery.

cash position. The ratio of cash on hand and in banks to bank loans. Other ratios carry this name, e.g., ratio of cash to total assets.

cash position ratio. The ratio of cash and marketable securities to current liabilities.

cash refund annuity. An annuity policy that provides for the payment in one cash sum at the death of the annuitant of the difference between the total the annuitant received and the price paid for the annuity.

cash reserve. (1) The amount of cash kept by a bank to meet the demand created by cashing checks, bank drafts, bank notes, and its other obligations. (2) In ordinary business, the amount of cash maintained from day to day.

cash statement. A classified summary of cash receipts and disbursements.

cash surrender value. In life insurance, the amount which the insurer will pay upon cancellation of the policy before death. This value increases with the age of the policy but is somewhat less than the legal reserve held against the policy by the insurer.

cash to daily purchases ratio. The ratio of cash to average daily purchases. Used as a test of the liquidity position of a firm.

casualty insurance. All insurance except (1) life (including personal accident), (2) marine, and sometimes (3) fire.

catastrophe reinsurance. An agreement by an insurer with one engaging in *reinsurance* that losses above a stated amount that result from catastrophe will be borne by the reinsurer rather than by the insurer.

catch crop. A crop which fills in the rotation of other crops or grows between the rows of other crops.

causa mortis. Latin for "in contemplation of death." Used particularly with regard to gifts and attempts to evade the *estate* or *inheritance taxes.*

cause of action. In law, a claim enforceable by a court. Same as *right of action.*

caveat emptor. Latin, meaning *let the buyer beware,* or buying at one's own risk. The doctrine means that a buyer is subject to all risks of a transaction except what constitutes fraud and certain implied warranties.

caveat venditor. Latin, meaning *let the seller beware.* Not a legal doctrine but the popular opposite of caveat emptor used particularly in financial circles.

CCC Commodity Credit Corporation. A corporation organized by the United States government with $100 million capital appropriated by Congress for the purpose of performing functions incidental to the farm price support program. Activities include lending on security of commodities, buying and selling, storing and transporting the commodities.

CEA Commodity Exchange Administration. An agency within the Department of Agriculture which has control of all commodity exchanges in the United States. Cf. *Commodity Exchange Act.*

cease and desist orders. Decrees issued pursuant to a statute (for example, Federal Trade Act, Interstate Commerce Act, etc.) which provides for the issuance of an order by the administrative agency to cease and desist from certain illegal practices.

ceiling price. The maximum price allowed by law.

central bank. The dominant bank of a country such as the Bank of England, the Federal Reserve Banks of the United States, etc. Distinguished presently from other banks by its function in currency-issuing, discounting for banks, open-market operations and holding of reserves for other banks. Usually this bank, has official or semi-official status in the government of the country.

central limit theorem. In statistics, the theorem that the distribution of sample means approaches a *normal distribution* as the number of samples increases.

central reserve city bank. In the Federal Reserve System, a former classification for a member bank located in New York or Chicago. See *Federal Reserve System.*

central traffic control. A traffic system in which the central operator has control over far removed trains, switches, and automatic signals.

certainty equivalent. That certain return which equates to higher but uncertain return.

certificate of beneficial interest. The term applied to a share in a *Massachusetts trust.*

certificate of convenience and necessity. A term used in the public utility and transportation field. E.g., a firm that wants to build a new electric light plant or open a new bus or truck line must secure from the Public Utilities Commission of the state (or in the case of interstate commerce, the Interstate Commerce Commission) a certificate granting permission on the ground that the public needs this new service and will be convenienced by it.

certificate of deposit. A document issued by a bank when the depositor agrees to leave funds for a specified period such as a year. Thus this is a time deposit and not a demand deposit and the depositor may receive interest.

certificate of incorporation. See *corporation charter.*

certificate of indebtedness. (1) In banking, same as *certificate of deposit.* (2) As a government security, same as *Treasury* *certificate.*

certificate of insurance. A written statement that there is an insurance policy covering a named insured against a stated risk and giving the essential terms of the policy. Used as proof of insurance in connection with loans, legal requirements, and similar matters.

certificate of manufacture. In foreign trade, a statement signed by an exporter that goods ordered by the importer have been finished and set aside for shipment. This document is used with a *letter of credit* for the benefit of the exporter.

certificate of origin. A document certifying the place of origin of imported goods.

certificate of participation. A certificate issued instead of shares of stock to show a proportionate interest in an unincorporated business or in the ownership of debt of a corporation.

certificate of registry. A statement by the registration authority of a country that a named ship is registered under that flag, who the owners are, the tonnage, etc.

certification. (1) In labor, the formal declaration by a national or state labor board that a given union is the bargaining agent for a group of employees is called "certification." (2) In general, a written statement by one in authority attesting to the facts set forth in the statement.

certified check. The certification (indorsement) of a check by a bank warrants: (1) that the signature of the drawer is genuine, (2) that the account has sufficient money to cover the check and that such money has been set aside, and (3) that there are no legal defects in the case of parties whose signatures are on the check at the time it is certified.

certified copy. A copy of a document which is attested by an official as a true copy of the original. The certifying officer in the case of a corporation is the secretary. Others frequently certifying are the secretary of state, clerks of court and registers of deeds.

certified public accountant. The title conferred by a state upon an accountant who meets the requirements of state law for the public practice of accounting. Others can do bookkeeping but only persons licensed as certified public accountants may use that title.

certiorari (petition for a writ of certiorari). In American law, a petition to a higher court asking it to review the decision of a lower court, the review being not a matter of right but in the discretion of the higher court. If the petition is allowed, a writ of *certiorari* is issued directing the lower court to certify the record and transmit it to a higher court. Cf. *appeal.*

cession. In insurance, the amount transferred (ceded) as reinsurance by an *insurer* to the *reinsurer.*

cestui que trust. The beneficiary of a trust, the one for whose benefit the trustee manages the property held in trust.

ceteris paribus. Same as *caeteris paribus.*

chain banking. Control of a group of banks through a holding company or other organization. Cf. *branch banking.*

chain discount. A series of discounts taken on a base lessened successively by the amount of the preceding discount. For example, a chain discount of 40, 10, and 2 on 100 equals 47.08% discount.

chain index. *Link relative index numbers* "chained" back to the original base by a process of successive multiplication. For example, let 1870 = base year, 100. If 1875 is 132% of 1870 (link) × 100 = 132 (chain); if 1880 is 145% of 1875 (link) × 132 = 191 (chain).

chain of title. The series of conveyances, probate proceedings, court decrees, etc., by which the present owner of real estate has title (ownership) of real estate. The starting point of such a chain is a patent (deed) from the government to the first owner.

chain promotion. If an employer follows the practice of filling vacancies in higher level jobs from his own workers, an opening on a higher level will result in a series of promotions, or a chain of promotions, with each worker stepping up a level in the chain.

chain store. One of a group of retailing establishments (in U.S. census, four or more stores) of essentially similar type and with a substantial degree of uniformity in management all under one central ownership. Cf. *voluntary chain store.*

chairman of the board. In corporations, the chairman of the board of directors may limit himself to being chairman of meeting of the board or he may be the top-ranking officer. The articles of incorporation or by-laws determine the scope of his authority.

champerty and maintenance. Unlawful intermeddling in a law suit by one not genuinely concerned, usually through furnishing funds for the purpose of creating litigation.

chancery. A legal term for a court of *equity* as opposed to a court of *common law*. The chief judge of such a court is called a chancellor. Those directed by the court to conduct detailed hearings are called masters in chancery.

Chandler Act. Passed by Congress in 1938, this act revised the federal law on financial reorganization of corporations, including bankruptcy.

change-over cost. The sum of setup cost and tear-down cost of a job.

charge. In accounting, the same as *debit*.

charge account. A debt to be paid at a future date. Used by retailers and others to describe the class of customers permitted to purchase merchandise on *open account* as distinguished from cash or from *installment account* customers.

charges forward. Same as *f.o.b.*

charging what the traffic will bear. A vague concept referring to the situation in which the price *elasticity of demand* for a product is thought to be relatively inelastic and hence price is raised to the point when the elasticity of demand begins to increase sharply.

charter. A document issued by a legislature or legislative authority and granting rights and privileges while imposing duties. Most commonly, the term is used to refer to the articles of a corporation.

charter agreement. The contract between the owner of transportation and the party using the transportation. This may be an outright lease or simply an agreement by the owner to furnish transportation.

chartered accountant. See *accountant*.

charter party. Same as *charter agreement*.

charts. A pictorial method of presenting data, e.g., (1) Bar chart: showing quantities as rectangles or bars with the vertical distance proportional to the quantities represented. (2) Pie chart: use of circular figure (a pie) to represent the whole and "slices" to represent segments. (3) Band chart: the same as a bar chart but with horizontal bars.

chattel. Ordinarily, any property or right, except real estate rights other than leases.

chattel mortgage. A conveyance of personal property as security for the payment of a debt.

chattel mortgage bonds. The bonds of a business which are secured by a mortgage on its movable property. Cf. *equipment trust certificates.*

chattel real. A nonfreehold interest in real property. The principal types are leases regardless of their length and estates at will.

cheap money. (1) The condition where the purchasing power of money is low, i.e., the general price level is high. (2) The prevalence of low interest rates making for easier borrowing. Cf. *dear money.*

check. A written order by a depositor directing his bank to pay a sum of money. A *bill of exchange* drawn on a bank.

check, types of. See the following specific terms:

bank check
blank check
cashier's check
certified check
counter check
memorandum check
negotiable check
personal check
registered check
traveler's check
voucher check

check book money. Demand deposits of a bank circulating in the form of checks. Also called deposit currency.

check-off clause. A clause in a labor contract providing that the employer will deduct union dues from the wages of union members and remit such dues directly to the union. The money for the dues never reaches the hands of the employee. The check-off may exist under either the *open shop* or the *closed shop.*

child labor amendment. A proposed amendment to the U.S. Constitution giving Congress the power to regulate child labor. Passed by Congress but not yet ratified by the required number of states. The effect of such an amendment has, however, been achieved under court construction of the interstate commerce clause.

Chinese auction. A less common term for *Dutch auction.*

chi-square test. The ratio of the product of the number of *degrees of freedom* plus one times the *variance* of a sample (S^2) divided by the variance of the universe (σ^2): $\chi^2 = \frac{NS^2}{\sigma^2}$.

The value so computed (χ^2) is then compared to the critical value of χ^2 in a table for the appropriate degrees of freedom and level of probability desired to determine the likelihood of getting such a value of χ^2 in either direction. Thus, a comparison of theoretical frequencies computed from the *normal curve* with observed frequencies. Chi-square (χ^2) is the sum of the difference between a series of observed frequencies and corresponding theoretical frequencies. One use is to test the goodness of fit of a normal curve to observed data.

chose in action. Any right which a person has to recover money or property from another in legal proceedings.

churning. In the stock market, creating a large number of transactions by *wash sales* or otherwise for the purpose of giving the impression of an active market.

c.i.f. Cost, insurance, and freight to point of destination included in price quoted. Cf. *f.o.b., zone pricing.*

CIO Congress of Industrial Organizations. A federation of industrial unions (and some craft unions) originally established in 1935 as a committee within the AFL, called the Committee for Industrial Organization; later became an independent body, because of disagreement on the *industrial union* question. Then in 1955, the CIO merged with the AFL. Cf. *AFL,* American Federation of Labor.

circular combination. A combination of firms based in part on horizontal (same type product) and in part on vertical lines (one firm making a product that is used by the next firm in its work). Distinguish *horizontal combination, vertical combination.*

circular letter of credit. A *letter of credit* not addressed to any specific person or bank.

circular note. Same as *circular letter of credit.*

circular trust. Same as *circular combination.*

circulating capital. Same as *working capital.*

civil authority clause. In fire insurance, the clause providing that losses caused by firemen and other authorities in trying to deal with fires and other risks are included within the coverage of the policy.

civil law. The term civil law is used in two senses: (1) the law of European countries based on codes or Roman law, as opposed to the common law of English-speaking countries, (2) all the law outside the field of criminal law. Cf. *common law.*

claim-jumping. In mining, the filing of duplicating claims to land already claimed in the hope the earlier claims may prove invalid.

Class A and B Stock. During recent years it has been the practice of some corporations to issue common stock in two general classes, A and B, with the holders of only one class having voting power or with one class having preferences. Also called classified common stock.

class gift. In law, a gift (or legacy) to a class of persons such as "my children" without naming them individually.

classical economics. Generally used to refer to the economic ideas of the English economists from 1775 to 1850, including principally Adam Smith, David Ricardo, T. R. Malthus, and John S. Mill. The fundamental concern of the school is the explanation of how the economy is continually working toward an equilibrium in terms of the principal economic groups of that time: landlords, laborers, and capitalists.

classification rating. In transportation, the class to which a commodity is assigned for purposes of applying class rates.

classification territory. The division of the country into zones for the application of uniform classes and rules within the zone. There are three railroad classification territories: (1) official (the northeast), (2) southern, and (3) western.

classified common stock. Same as *Class A and B stock.*

classified directors. A system of electing a percentage of the board of directors (usually one-third) each year for a period more than one year (usually three years) so that any attempted take-over of a corporation will be slowed.

classified risk. In life insurance, the scaling of premiums to compensate for substandard health or other risks. More commonly called substandard risk. Cf. *numerical rating system.*

classified tax. Separation of property or the object being taxed into groups for different tax treatment, usually different tax rates for each group.

class interval. In statistics, when items are classified into groups by magnitude, the difference between the values of the upper limit of the group and lower limit is the class interval.

class price. The price established for a group of buyers of the same commodity, with other prices established for different groups of buyers of that commodity. In effect, *price discrimination* based on the ignorance of buyers.

class rate. In transportation, a rate applicable to the numbered or lettered groups of classes of commodities contained in the classification columns of freight-rate tariffs.

class struggle. A concept developed by Karl Marx referring to the innate antagonism of different economic and social interests, the existence of which he believed he had demonstrated, particularly between the owners of capital (the bourgeoisie) and the non-owning workers (the proletariat), both as functional social classes.

Clayton Antitrust Act. A supplement, enacted by Congress in 1914, to the Sherman Antitrust Act of 1890. The act makes an effort to define some specific types of restraints on trade and excludes labor unions from liability under the antitrust laws. Specifically forbidden are: (1) *interlocking directorates* lessening competition, (2) *holding companies* lessening competition, (3) *tying contracts,* and (4) *price discrimination.*

clean bill. A *bill of exchange* without documents attached.

clean bill of lading. A *bill of lading* without notations of defects in the goods received by the carrier or similar qualifications.

clean hands doctrine. A rule of *equity* that a party seeking the aid of a court must himself be free of taint or he will get no aid.

clean-up provision. In bank loans, an agreement by the borrower that at least once a year, he will have repaid all bank loans and be "out of the bank" for a stated period, usually thirty days.

clearance loan. A loan to clear or pay for stocks received by a broker who must pay for delivery of the stocks before he can pledge them for a loan. The clearance loan is repaid by the proceeds of the later pledge loan.

clearance papers. The papers given by the collector of a port to the captain of a ship when it is ready for sea. All port charges must have been paid and the cargo fully accounted for to the customs official before clearance papers are released.

clearing agreement. In essence a method of divorcing the exchange markets of two countries while still permitting commercial intercourse. Importers in each country pay into a special office, usually the central bank, all sums due for imports. Each clearing office at stated intervals then pays exporters for goods shipped.

clearing checks. The return of checks to the bank on which drawn for payment.

clearing house. An agency established by banks or brokers to reduce the labor of paying and receiving funds due one another. Each member's *net* credit or debit to another member for a trading period (usually one business day) is settled by transfers of *net* balances to or from accounts maintained in the agency by members.

clearings. Checks and other documents presented by a bank for collection at the clearing house.

clearing the market. In securities and commodities, the satisfying of all buyers or sellers by moving the price.

clearing title. The process of removing clouds on the title of real estate, that is, questions about proper transfer, payment of taxes and liens, etc. The process may be voluntary, for example, by people who have technical claims surrendering such claims. Or it may be legal or compulsory by a court action to *quiet title*.

Clifford trust. The transfer of the income of property to another for a minimum period of 10 years through the use of a trustee. After the elapse of the period, the property reverts to the original owner. The income during the period of the trust is taxable to the *beneficiary* of the trust and not to the *grantor*. Named Clifford after the grantor who prevailed against the government in the case establishing the rule which has since been incorporated into the Internal Revenue Code by legislation.

close corporation. A corporation whose stock is owned by a few people.

closed account. An account in which a closing entry has been made transferring the balance in the account to another account. See *closing entry*.

closed contract. In insurance, a policy under which rates and policy provisions cannot be changed by the insurer without the consent of the insured.

closed economy. An economic system which is not free to interact with other economic systems. Cf. *open economy*.

closed-end investment trust. An investment company whose number of shares of stock is limited. A shareholder sells to another person in order to liquidate his holdings. Cf. *open-end investment company*.

closed-end mortgage. A mortgage which does not permit additional borrowing.

closed indent. An importer's purchase order to an exporter which must be filled with goods from a specified manufacturer or firm. Cf. *open indent.*

closed model. In *econometrics*, a model in which the values of the *exogenous variables* change but the interaction of the values of the *endogenous variables* produces future values of the endogenous variables and feedback is a characteristic. Cf. *open model.*

closed shop. A business firm within which all employees hired must be union members at the time of hiring and so continue during employment. Declared illegal by *Taft-Hartley Act* amending the *Wagner Act.* Cf. *agency shop, open shop, preference shop,* and *union shop.*

closed stock. In merchandising, the sale only of complete sets or without assurance that replacements will be available.

closed system. (1) A theoretical device for analysis by which some factors are excluded or controlled while other factors are varied. The method is adapted from the natural sciences. (2) A theoretical device in which a country is considered as isolated from the rest of the world for purposes of analysis.

closed trade. In securities and commodities, a completed speculative trade, e.g., a *short sale* that has been *covered.* Before the covering, the trade is an *open trade.*

closed union. A labor union which limits its membership by making entrance conditions artificially difficult. Cf. *open union.*

closed union shop. A business firm in which only union members are employed and in which the union sharply restricts its membership and usually circumscribes the employer's right to discharge. Cf. *closed shop, open shop, preferential union shop, union shop.*

closing account. In accounting, an account in which various *ledger* accounts are merged for summary and ultimate transfer to a final statement.

closing agreement. Any final or definitive agreement. Used particularly to refer to final settlement of income tax liability, and to real estate deals.

closing entry. An entry which transfers the balance of a *nominal account* to a summary account such as the *profit-and-loss* at the end of a fiscal period. The resulting debit or credit balance in the profit-and-loss account is closed to surplus on the balance sheet.

closing of transfer book. In corporations, setting a date after which changes of stock ownership for purposes of dividends and voting at meetings will not be accepted for a period to avoid confusion at dividend and meeting times.

closing price. The price at which the last sale on an organized market is made on a particular day.

cloud on title. Real estate which has claims outstanding against it by people other than the apparent owner is said to have a cloud on its title.

Cobb-Douglas function. The production function developed by Cobb and Douglas using the annual data for American manufacturing for 1900 to 1922. The equation developed is $P = 1.01\ L.^{0.75}C^{0.25}$ where P is output, L is labor input and C is capital input. This particular function assumes that the exponents of L and C should add up to 1 or that there are constant *returns to scale.* The function states that a 1% increase in labor input will (other things remaining the same) result in a .75% increase in output and similarly a 1% increase in capital will result in a .25% increase in output. The function also excludes from consideration the impact of variations in management as *factors of production.*

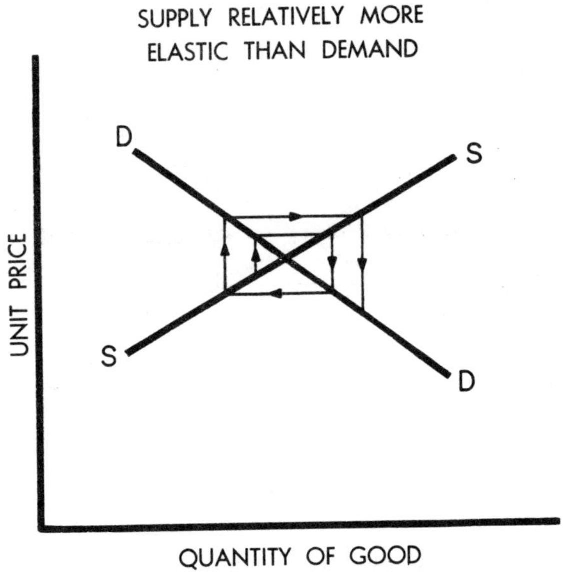

Figure 9.

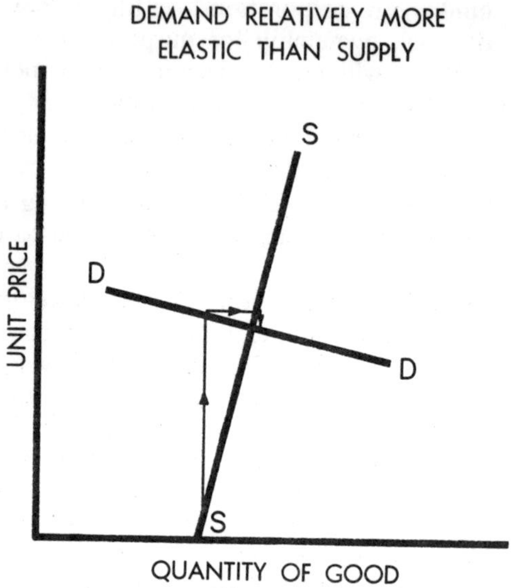

Figure 10.

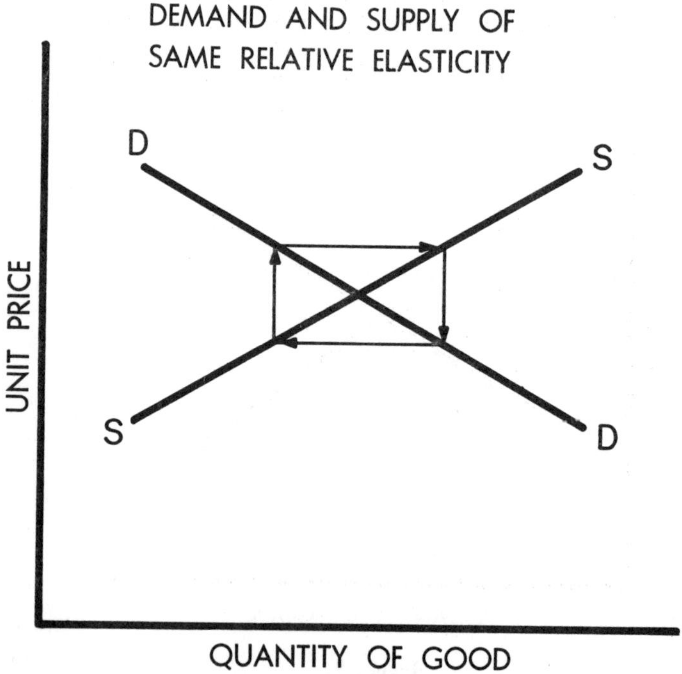

Figure 11.

cobweb theorem or problem. Using the illustration of a farmer, the essence of the problem is that in determining quantity to be produced in a given year, the farmer projects last year's price to this year and, failing to take into account similar plans by other farmers, produces for that price. This results in over- or underproduction for that price. Depending on the elasticities of the demand and supply curves involved, this process if carried on over a number of years may or may not lead to equilibrium. The word "cobweb" comes from the visual appearance of the graphing of the problem. See figures 9, 10 and 11.

c.o.d. Collect on delivery; also cash on delivery.

codes of fair competition. A set of rules providing for the manner in which competitive businesses shall be conducted so that excessive or predatory competition may be avoided. (1) Originally developed under National Industrial Recovery Act of 1934 which was declared unconstitutional. (2) Some states have enacted legislation on the subject under this term. (3) Codes developed in trade practice conferences conductd by various industries.

codicil. A supplementary document making an addition to or change in a will. It must conform to the same formalities of execution (witnesses) as the will.

coefficient of acceleration. See *acceleration principle.*

coefficient of alienation. In statistics, the complement of the *coefficient of determination,* namely, $1 - r^2$. The *unassociated variance* divided by the total *variance.*

coefficient of association. The per cent reduction in error in estimating one variable by use of the relationship of that variable to another variable(s) when the relationship is determined by correlation analysis. The formula is $A = 1 - \sqrt{1-r^2}$ where r^2 *is the coefficient of determination.* While the *coefficient of determination* gives the per cent of variation (the sum of squares of the deviation from the arithmetic mean) explained, the coefficient of association gives the per cent reduction in error (in terms of the unsquared deviation).

coefficient of autocorrelation. See *Durbin-Watson test* and *von Neumann ratio.*

coefficient of correlation (simple). The degree of association between two variables. The symbol for the coefficient of correlation is r. This in turn is the square root of r^2 (*the coefficient of determination*) which is the ratio of (1) the *variance* of the *dependent variable* explained by the *independent vari-*

able to (2) the total variance of the dependent variable. The variance of the dependent variable explained by the independent variable is the sum of the squares of the deviations of each value of the dependent variable (computed by substitution of the independent variable in the equation of the *regression line* of the two variables) from the *arithmetic mean* of the observed values of the dependent variable. Also the geometric mean of the slopes of the two *regression lines* when an independent variable and a dependent variable are plotted on a scatter diagram and one *regression line* is fitted minimizing the sum of the squares of the horizontal deviations and another regression line is fitted minimizing the sum of the squares of the vertical deviations.

coefficient of determination. The ratio of the *associated variance* due to the *independent variable* to the total *variance* of the *dependent variable*. The symbol for the ratio is r^2.

coefficient of dispersion. Same as *relative quartile deviation*.

coefficient of elasticity. See the various definitions under the heading *elasticity*.

coefficient of expectations. The percentage of the change in the prior period's output which is expected to constitute the change in output in the present period.

coefficient of multiple correlation. The degree of association between a *dependent variable* and two or more *independent variables*. The symbol for the coefficient of multiple correlation is R. This in turn is the square root of R^2 (the coefficient of multiple determination) which is (1) the ratio of the *variance* of the dependent variable explained by the independent variables to (2) the total variance of the dependent variable. The variance of the dependent variable explained by the independent variables is the sum of the squares of the deviations of each value of the dependent variable (computed by substitution of the independent variables in the equation of the *regression line*) from the *arithmetic mean* of the observed values of the dependent variable.

coefficient of nondetermination. The term for ratio of the *non-associated variance* to total *variance*. Hence 1 — coefficient of determination.

coefficient of optimism. See *optimism criterion*.

coefficient of partial determination. In *multiple correlation*, the ratio of the *associated variance* of one *independent variable* to the total *variance* with the effect of the other independent variables held statistically constant.

coefficient of partial correlation. The square root of the *coefficient of partial determination.*

coefficient of quartile deviation. Same as *relative quartile deviation.*

coefficient of regression. The slope of a *regression line.* Hence the average number of units increase or decrease in the dependent variable associated with a unit increase of the independent variable. Cf. *beta coefficient.*

coefficient of skewness. Same as *relative skewness.*

coefficient of variation. In statistics, the measure of relative dispersion of data. The *standard deviation* divided by the *arithmetic mean* gives the coefficient of variation.

cognovit note. A note containing a clause authorizing the holder to appear in court without notice to the maker and have judgment entered against the maker. Literally, cognovit is Latin for *he has confessed.*

coinage. The process of manufacturing metal money. Called gratuitous if no charge is made; *brassage* is the charge for the cost of the coinage itself, *seigniorage* is the charge higher than the cost yielding the mint a profit.

coinsurance clause. A provision in an insurance policy specifying that the liability of the insurance company is limited to that proportion of the loss which the amount of insurance bears to a given percentage of the value of the property at the time of loss but in no event more than the face amount of the insurance or the total of the loss. For example, under an 80% coinsurance clause with $40,000 insurance on property valued at $100,000 and a loss of $10,000, the insurance company would pay $5,000; under a 60% coinsurance clause, $6,667; under a 40% coinsurance clause, $10,000.

collapsible corporation. Under income tax law, a corporation formed to avoid income tax particularly by holding an asset and distributing it in kind to shareholders who will then sell it and no double taxation will occur.

collateral loan. A loan secured by the pledge of specific property. The pledge may be made by a document or by transferring possession of the property to the lender.

collateral note. A note secured by specific property such as stocks, bonds, drafts, etc.

collateral security. Collateral is property, usually in the form of documents of title, given as security. For example, bonds, notes, etc.

collateral trust bonds. Bonds of one corporation secured by its holdings of stocks, bonds, and/or notes of another corporation.

collateral trust certificate. A security issued by a trustee pursuant to an agreement under which the trustee holds stocks and bonds of a number of companies for the benefit of the holders of the collateral trust certificate.

collection items. In banking, checks drawn on banks other than the bank in which they have been deposited and in the process of collection.

collection period. The average number of days needed to collect an *account receivable.* To compute, divide average daily credit sales into accounts receivable outstanding. Cf. *average collection period* and *accounts receivable turnover.*

collective bargaining. Bargaining by a committee or union representing individual employees before an employer or group of employers to arrive at agreements regarding wages, hours, or conditions of employment.

collectivism. A theory or policy advocating common ownership of all means of production, but which might permit individuals to own their homes, clothes, food, etc.

collision insurance. Insurance protecting the party insured against loss which he may suffer to his own property in a collision. In contrast, the loss to the other party for which one may be liable is covered by *liability insurance.*

colorable title. A claim to ownership supported by some facts or circumstances tending to support the claim.

column rate. In transportation, a *commodity rate* published as a fixed percentage of class rates. The term is derived from grouping commodity rates in a tariff book by "columns."

combination. The bringing together of several companies in a united effort to eliminate or control competition and/or effect economies. The generic term covering: *cartel, holding company, merger, pool, syndicate, trust.*

combination policy. In insurance, a policy combining the coverage of several risks ordinarily handled in separate policies.

combination rate: In transportation, a rate made by combining two or more rates published in different tariffs. A combination rate is used when no *joint rate* exists.

combination through rate. In transportation, a *through rate* made by combining two or more rates published in different tariffs. Cf. *joint combination rate.*

combined entry (compound entry). In accounting, a journal entry for one transaction consisting of two or more debits and one credit, or one debit and two or more credits, or of several debits and several credits.

commerce clause. The clause in the U.S. Constitution which reserves to the federal Congress the regulation of commerce between the states and with foreign countries. Much federal legislation concerning business rests on this clause in Article I, Section 8.

commercial bank. A bank, one of whose main functions is acceptance of deposits and creation of credit through short term loans mainly for business purposes. Cf. *investment banker.*

commercial bill. A *bill of exchange* covering the payment for a shipment of goods.

commercial credit company. A company dealing in specialized financing of dealers and manufacturers, e.g., in financing on the pledge of accounts receivable or installment accounts. More recently, better known as a *sales finance company.*

commercial finance company. Same as *commercial credit company.*

commercial or mercantile credit. The credit which businessmen extend to one another in the distribution of goods. Represented by drafts, trade acceptances, open book accounts, etc.

commercial overhead. Those expenses of a business other than materials, direct labor, manufacturing expense and income taxes. The principal categories are selling, administration, and financial expenses.

commercial paper. (1) Promissory notes, commercial drafts, trade acceptances, and similar documents issued by business firms. (2) In banking, loans arising from transactions covering purchases of goods. Cf. *commodity paper, financial paper.*

commercial paper company or house. A company engaged in the business of buying and selling bills of exchange, drafts, acceptances, notes, and other short term obligations.

commercial set. The four principal documents covering a shipment of goods: *invoice, bill of lading, bill of exchange,* and *certificate of insurance.*

commercial treaty. See *reciprocal trade agreement.*

commission broker. (1) A member of a stock exchange who acts for others in executing buying and selling orders. Cf. *floor trader.* (2) An agent middleman whose remuneration for services rendered is received in the form of a fee or commission.

commission house. An agent middleman handling agricultural products but only for sellers. He does not take title to the goods but does handle possession. He receives shipments without notice and has wide discretion to sell at spot prices.

Commissioners' Standard Ordinary Mortality Table. See *American experience table of mortality.*

commissioners' values. An annual list of securities and the values placed upon them by the National Association of Insurance Commissioners for use by insurance companies in preparing their financial statements.

commission merchant. An agent middleman who buys or sells commodities for another. Usually goods are shipped to him for sale to others or, if purchased from others, are shipped to him for the account of his principal.

commitment fee. The amount (such as ½ or ¼ per cent) paid by a borrower to a lender for a loan in addition to interest on the loan. The fee may be against the total amount of the loan or against the unborrowed balance of a loan commitment or *line of credit* and may be paid once or annually.

commodity clause. The clause of the Interstate Commerce Act (Art. 8 of Sec. 1 of Part 1) which makes it illegal for a railroad to carry any article in interstate commerce except timber and its products if it is directly interested.

commodity cost. In gas, water, and electric utilities, the total of production costs or those costs associated with the product. Cf. *demand costs* and *customer costs.*

commodity dollar. A proposal for stabilization of the purchasing power of money by making the dollar interchangeable with a fixed quantity of one or more standard commodities.

commodity exchange. A group of traders organized for buying and selling commodities such as grains. Sales are made with documents controlling title to the commodities.

Commodity Exchange Act of 1936. Provides for close regulation and control of all commodity exchanges under the supervision of the Commodity Exchange Administration.

commodity paper. Promissory notes, drafts, and similar documents representing loans secured by bills of lading or warehouse receipts covering commodities. Cf. *commercial paper, financial paper.*

commodity price index. An index of wholesale prices. Cf. *cost of living index, consumer price index.*

commodity rate. In transportation, a special rate on a specific commodity (or group of commodities) taking it out of the *class rate* either generally or for certain hauls. Usually the commodity rate is lower than the class rate on the same commodity.

commodity reserve theory. A monetary theory under which money would be convertible into one commodity at a specified rate or the commodity convertible into money at the same rate at the option of the holder of either the money or the commodity. One variation of the theory substitutes a bundle of staple commodities in place of just one commodity.

commodity standard. That monetary system under which money is convertible into a commodity (other than gold or silver) at a specified rate. Cf. *monetary standard, types of.*

commodity theory of money. A theory of money which explains changes in the value of money as due to changes in the demand for and supply of gold and silver in nonmonetary uses. Cf. *quantity theory of money.*

common average. In *marine insurance,* same as *particular average.*

common carrier. A common carrier is a transportation agency operating under a certificate from the government which requires the carrier to serve all people. Distinguish *contract carrier, private carrier, industrial carrier.*

common cost. Same as *joint cost.*

common disaster clause. In insurance or in a will, the clause directing what disposition is to be made in the event the insured (testator) and the beneficiary (legatee) die in a common disaster.

common law. Usages and customs which have come to be sanctioned precedents, but are not reduced to codes. The courts decide what the common law is. Distinguished from statutory law, which is law reduced to codes. Distinguished from equity, which consists of changes in the common law after it had become frozen. Cf. *civil law.*

common-law copyright. All the incidents of common law copyright have now been supplanted by the U. S. Copyright Act except that common law copyright still applies before publication of the work.

common-law defenses. In suits by an employee against an employer for injuries sustained on the job, the common-law defenses of the employer are: (1) *contributory negligence* on the employee's part, (2) *fellow servant* responsibility, and (3) *assumption of risk* by the employee. These defenses are abolished by the *workmen's compensation laws* as to the employer, but they can be claimed by a third party working on the employer's premises.

common-law restraint on trade. Under the *common law,* a number of restraints on trade have been recognized as legal for centuries. These categories continue to be legal until changed by statute. For example, the buyer of a personal service business (e.g., barbershop) may exact the seller's agreement not to compete.

common-law voting. One vote for each stockholder in a corporation, regardless of number of shares held. Cf. *cumulative voting, ordinary voting.*

common market. See *EEC. European Economic Community.*

common stock. Shares in a corporation which have no fixed rate of dividends, and are the last to secure a share in the property when the corporation is dissolved. The shares have voting power in the meetings of the shareholders and may have par value or no par. See *Class A and B Stock.*

common stock ratio. The stated value of common stock plus surplus reserves and surplus divided by the total value of bonds, preferred stock, common stock, surplus reserves, and surplus.

common trust fund. The combination of two or more trust funds for investment purposes to secure greater efficiency in handling, diversity in risks, etc.

communism. An economic system which is based on public ownership of all productive wealth and much consumption wealth. Only wages are paid. What would be profits, rent, and interest belong in theory to the workers with the state as custodian. Russia (USSR) claims to be an example of this system.

Communist Manifesto. A document published in 1848 by Marx and Engels, setting forth certain basic theories of communism, especially the materialistic interpretation of history and the doctrine of *class struggle,* and calling upon the workers of the world to organize and overthrow the capitalistic system.

community property. Derived from the Spanish law and applicable in certain western and southern states (Arizona, California, Idaho, Hawaii, Louisiana, Nevada, New Mexico, Oklahoma, Texas, and Washington), community property law provides that husband and wife are considered as each entitled to one-half of the total earnings of the two during marriage.

commutation (of sentence). See *reprieve.*

commutation rights. In insurance, the right of the beneficiary at his option to receive in one sum the cash value of the remaining payments under an option selected by the insured of a life insurance policy.

commuted value. The present value of future payments when discounted at a given rate of interest.

company. A general term for a business being run in the form of *sole proprietorship, partnership* or *corporation.*

company, types of. See *corporation, types of.*

company town. A community existing primarily because an employer is located in a remote place. The employer often owns the major part of the town's housing and stores.

company union. (1) A labor union under company domination. (2) A labor union for the workers of one company. In this sense, an unaffiliated union.

comparative advantage. A general principle explaining the condition under which mutually profitable trade between two economic regions can arise. A comparative advantage arises when because of different endowments of natural resources, capital, population, etc., the ratios between the production costs of a series of commodities in one country are different from the same ratios in another country. The first country enjoys a comparative advantage in those commodities having the lowest ratios, and trade can be mutually advantageous if it specializes in producing the commodities having the lowest ratios and trades some of them with the second country which acts conversely. Cf. *absolute advantage.*

comparative balance sheet. See *comparative statement.*

comparative costs, law of. See *comparative advantage.*

comparative negligence rule. A statutory principle that when two or more individuals are negligent in an accident, the damages resulting will be apportioned in the same proportion as the negligence of each. Cf. *contributory negligence rule.*

comparative statement. A statement showing the financial reports for two separate periods side by side for purposes of comparison and evaluation.

comparative statics. In economic theory, the comparison of economic equilibrium situations each under different assumptions but without regard to the path of change over time. Cf. *dynamics* and *statics.*

compensated dollar. A proposal for stabilizing the purchasing power of the dollar. The tendency for the dollar to change its value is to be counteracted by changes in the bullion equivalent of the dollar. Cf. *commodity dollar.*

compensating balance. In banking, the balance a borrower from a bank is required by the bank to keep in his account. Typically 15 per cent of the borrowed amount.

compensating depreciation. A depreciation system dealing with the problem of fluctuating prices for the good being depreciated.

compensating expenditures. See explanation under *income leakages.*

compensating payment. That sum of money just offsetting a given change in price or market condition.

compensating tariff. An increase in the tariff on a finished good (e.g., woolens) in order to compensate for an increase in the tariff on a raw material (e.g., wool) used in that commodity. If the tariff were raised on wool to protect farmers, then to maintain the same relative position of manufacturers, an increase in tariff on woolens is required.

compensatory duty. (1) In same sense as *countervailing duty.* (2) A duty on imports to offset the higher domestic cost of production of the same commodities.

compensatory finance. A general theory of government spending that the government budget should be unbalanced by a deficit during depression periods and unbalanced by a surplus during prosperity periods in an effort to secure stable economic conditions. Cf. *fiscal policy, functional finance.*

compensatory principle of bimetallism. The principle applying when the currency of a country is redeemable for fixed amounts of either gold or silver at the option of the currency holder. The principle is that the ratio between gold and silver established by the government will prevail in the free market by withdrawals from the mint or deliveries to the mint, according as the market price of one metal relative to the other is respectively higher or lower than that prevailing in the market for that metal.

competency or competent party. Being of legal age and sound mind, and under no legal handicap.

competition, types of. See the following specific terms: *cutthroat competition, imperfect competition, monopolistic competition, nonprice competition, perfect competition, pure competition,* and *workable competition.*

competitive bidding. The process of preparation of a security issue through the solicitation by the issuing company of the highest bids from competitive groups of investment banking firms and awarding the issue to the highest bidder. Since 1941 the required method for public utility holding companies and their subsidiaries unless exempted by the *SEC*. Cf. *negotiated purchase*.

complaint. In law, the first statement of his case (pleading) by the plaintiff.

complement. In statistics, 1 minus a number gives the complement of the number. Cf. *reciprocal*.

complementary goods. Two or more goods are said to be complementary if an increase in quantity demanded of one accompanies an increase in the quantity demanded of the other. Cf. *substitutional goods*.

complete oligopoly. The situation in which a few sellers dominate the selling side of the market for a product and they act in such a manner as to maximize the joint profits of the group. Cf. *imperfect oligopoly* and *partial oligopoly*.

completed contract accounting. Where the period of production exceeds the annual accounting period, one method is to recognize profit or less only in the period of completion. The alternate method is *percentage of completion accounting*.

composite demand. The total quantity demanded of a given product or service for various uses (where one good is capable of satisfying different wants).

composite rate depreciation. A single depreciation rate to be applied against the total of depreciable assets or a group of such assets; based on an average of the rates applicable to individual items with some weighting of the relative importance of the several items.

composite supply. The total quantity of goods or services which can satisfy one type of want.

composition of creditors. An agreement of all the creditors with each other and the debtor to accept a certain percentage of their claims in full settlement to save the expense and delay of legal proceedings.

compound arbitrage. *Arbitrage* achieved by using four or more markets. Cf. *arbitrage*.

compound duty. Same as *compound tariff*.

compound entry. Same as *combined entry*.

compound interest. Calculation of interest such that interest is computed on interest past due. The past-due interest is added to the original principal to become the principal for the new period.

compound-interest method of depreciation. Taking the initial cost of a capital asset, deducting the expected salvage value at the time it is expected to be discarded and spreading the difference in equal installments per unit of time over the estimated life of the asset but then reducing the depreciation charge for each period by the amount of interest that such a charge would earn from the period of the charge to the time of discard.

compound tariff. Consists either of (1) an ad valorem duty plus a specific duty or (2) a provision that ad valorem or specific duty will apply, whichever is higher. Cf. *ad valorem tariff, specific tariff.*

comprehensive insurance. Same as *all-risk insurance.*

comptroller. The head of an accounting staff, or one whose approval is required for expenditures.

Comptroller General. The head of the General Accounting Office of the United States whose duty is auditing all government agencies to check for unlawful disbursement of funds.

concensus-communications scale. Communication testing by securing opinions to determine their tendency to agree, regardless of the rightness or wrongness of the opinions.

concentration ratio. (1) As used in the census, the percentage of total output of a particular product (or group of products) supplied by those whose sole (or principal) activity is the making of that product (or group of products). Used by analogy in other applications. Cf. *coverage ratio* and *specialization ratio.* (2) As used in distribution analysis, the ratio of the area between the *Lorenz curve* and the diagonal representing equality to the area under the diagonal. The ratio measures the departure of the *Lorenz curve* from complete equality, expressed as a ratio to complete inequality (which would be represented by the full right-angle triangle under the diagonal). Also called Gini coefficient.

concentric chart. In personnel management, a series of concentric circles with the president at the center, all those on the next lower level of management located on the next circle going outward, and so down through the various levels of management. This brings out the fact that the further one moves from the center, the more space is available for larger numbers of personnel and positions on each circle.

conciliation. Settlement of a dispute, often between an employer and his employees, through the cooperation of a third party (called a conciliator) who guides discussion but does not have power to make decisions. Cf. *arbitration, mediation.*

concurrent insurance. Two or more insurance policies covering the same risk as to the same property with substantially the same provisions although the amounts of coverage and policy dates may differ.

condemnation. Used in three senses: (1) The judicial process of seizing property for public use and setting a valuation upon it to reimburse the owner. (2) The elimination of property pursuant to health, safety, and similar laws. (3) The forfeiture of property to the government for violation of law.

conditional acceptance. Same as *counteroffer.*

conditional indorsement. A conditional indorsement is a *special indorsement* plus words of condition. For example, "Pay Smith, but only when one Ford is delivered." Any subsequent taker must be certain the condition has been fulfilled.

conditional sale. A contract for the sale (not a "sale" and not a "contract to sell") of property with title remaining in the seller until the payment under the contract is complete. Possession and risk of loss pass to the buyer. Distinguish *consignment, sale or return, sale on approval. Cf. installment buying.*

condition concurrent. A provision in a contract that two events must occur simultaneously, such as delivery of goods and their payment. A tender of performance by either party and rejection by the other creates liability on the part of the one rejecting.

condition precedent. A provision in a contract that rights and duties shall arise only after the happening of an event. The happening of the event is the condition precedent.

condition subsequent. A provision in a contract that upon the happening of an event, one of the parties is, for example, released from previous duties and rights. The happening of the event is the condition subsequent.

conditional probability. The likelihood that event B will occur, given that event A has occurred.

condominium. A legal rule governing direct ownership of a single unit in a multi-unit structure. The owner holds title to his unit and a common interest with the owners in the underlying land and usually in some common facilities such as staircases.

confession of judgment. A clause in a note or agreement consenting in advance to the entry of judgment upon default without notice of the proceeding.

confidence coefficient. The probability (such as 95 cases out of 100) that the value of a statistical measure (such as the *arithmetic mean*) determined from a given sample of a population will fall within a given range either side of the true value of that measure in the population.

confidence interval. See *confidence limits.*

confidence limits. In the case of a sample from a population, the range either side of the true value in a population that a statistical measure (such as an *arithmetic mean*) of a sample will fall with an established probability (such as 95 cases out of 100).

confirmed letter of credit. A *letter of credit* which guarantees the payment of all credit extended under it.

confiscation. The seizure of private property by a government without payment of adequate compensation to the owner.

confluence analysis. Analysis of the situation in which independent variables are highly correlated with each other so that *standard errors* of *regression coefficients* become inadequate measures.

confusion of goods. The intermingling of the goods of two different owners where the goods are difficult to separate once intermingled.

conglomerate. A company with widely diversified *product lines* which comes about through *merger* of many companies.

connected load. In public utilities, the combined rating of all devices for receiving power on the customers' premises.

connectivity. A relationship is connective if it applies to every pair of elements whether taken in one order or another order.

consent decree. A consent decree involves the admission by the defendant of certain charges in a law suit and the acceptance by the defendant of the remedy proposed by the plaintiff. Such a termination of a lawsuit by agreement is subject to the approval of the court.

conservator. A person appointed by a court to manage the affairs of an incompetent (or in some cases merely one unable to manage his own affairs) or to liquidate a defunct business.

consideration. Contracts must be supported by a consideration which may be defined as a benefit to the promisor or a detriment to the promisee.

consignee. See *consignment.*

consignment. A form of *bailment* in which one party (the consignor) sends goods to another party (the consignee) for sale.

Title does not pass in a consignment unless there is some further action by the consignee indicating a sale. Distinguish *conditional sale, sale or return.* The primary difference between a consignment and a conditional sale is that risk of loss remains in the consignor, but passes to the vendee in a conditional sale unless the parties agree otherwise.

consignor. See *consignment.*

consistent equations. A system of equations such that any two equations have coefficients of which all but the constant terms bear the same ratio to each other.

consol. An interest bearing bond issued by the British government having no maturity date. Cf. *rentes.*

consolidated. Used in two senses: (1) as an abbreviation for a *consolidated bond,* (2) referring to perpetual annuities without expiration date (the British national debt was placed on this basis in the nineteenth century).

consolidated balance sheet. See *consolidated statement.*

consolidated bonds. Bonds issued to replace two or more outstanding issues and thus to bring such indebtedness together in the one issue. Also called unified bond.

consolidated car. A carload of goods assembled by an agency, e.g., freight forwarding agent or public warehouse, from several shippers and consigned to a public warehouse for distribution to any number of consignees.

consolidated mortgage. A mortgage created to replace or unify several mortgages already existing. It may be the unification of several mortgages of one creditor or the unification of the mortgages of several creditors.

consolidated mortgage bonds. Bonds secured by a mortgage on an entire property formed by the consolidation of bonds of several corporations or of several bond issues of the same corporation.

consolidated statements. The financial reports for a group of affiliated corporations or enterprises eliminating intercorporation debts and profits, and showing minority stockholders' interests.

consolidation or fusion. A union of several corporations into a new one, the old ones ceasing to exist. Cf. *merger.*

conspicuous consumption. A term originated by Veblen to describe the phenomenon of consumers buying goods to show their position or status rather than for the other usefulness of the goods.

conspiracy. A combination of two or more persons, designing by concerted action to accomplish some criminal or unlawful purpose, or to accomplish a legitimate purpose by criminal or unlawful means, or sometimes to accomplish a legitimate purpose by legitimate means with the mere fact of concerted action being the illegal factor. Conspiracy is classified by law as either criminal or civil.

constant cost. The situation in which average cost per unit of output remains unchanged as output varies. Cf. *constant cost industry.* Distinguish *decreasing cost* and *increasing cost.*

constant cost industry. An industry where *average total unit cost* remains the same as production volume increases or decreases.

constant-dollar plan. An investment plan under which funds are divided into two parts: a stock fund to purchase diversified common stock and a cash fund to be kept in liquid form. The plan calls for keeping the dollar (market) amount of the stock fund constant by selling on a rise and transferring to the cash fund and vice-versa on a price fall. Cf. *constant-ratio plan, dollar averaging, variable-ratio plan.*

constant dollars. Dollars of constant purchasing power. The regularly reported price of a good divided by a *price index* gives the price in constant dollars.

constant per cent of decreasing balance method of depreciation. Taking the initial cost of a capital asset, deducting the expected salvage value at the time it is expected to be discarded, and spreading the difference by a constant percentage of the undepreciated balance, so that at the end of the expected life the undepreciated balance equals the salvage value. The percentage is determined by the formula $r = 1 - \sqrt[n]{s/c}$ where $r =$ the percentage, $n =$ the number of periods, $s =$ the scrap value and $c =$ the cost or other basis.

constant product curve. Same as *iso-product curve.*

constant-ratio plan. An investment plan under which funds are divided into two parts: a stock fund to purchase diversified common stocks and a cash fund to be held in liquid form. The plan then calls for keeping the dollar (market) amount of the stock fund in a constant ratio to the cash fund by selling on a rise and transferring to the cash fund and vice versa on a price fall. Cf. *constant-dollar plan, dollar averaging and variable-ratio plan.*

constant returns to scale. See *Euler theorem.*

constrained cycle. A *business cycle* whose upward movement is limited by full employment of the *factors of production.* Cf. *free cycle.*

constructive delivery, payment, or receipt. When delivery, payment or receipt has not been made but conduct or a token going as far as possible to show intention to do the act has been performed, the law says there is constructive performance.

constructive mileage. An increase in mileage over actual mileage of a carrier route due to adverse physical conditions over the route. Used for freight charge computing.

constructive total loss clause. In an insurance policy with this clause, goods are protected to full value when cost of salvage and reconditioning would exceed value.

constructive trust. In law, a remedial device applied by a court after it has decided that a wrong has been committed. Goods wrongfully held are said to be held in trust for the rightful owners.

consular invoice. An invoice signed by a consul of the country to which a shipment of goods is destined. Such invoices facilitate customs processes.

consumer credit. Short-term and intermediate term credit to individuals to finance personal activities.

consumer credit controls. The primary controls over consumer credit are the regulation of installment credit (through the size of the down payment and the maximum period for payment of the balance) and the regulation of housing credit (such as through the size of the down payment, maximum loan period, interest rate, and eligibility for special programs).

consumer durable goods. *Consumer goods* having a normal life in use over three years are classified as durable, those having a six-month to three-year life are classified as semidurable and those under a six-month life as nondurable. Cf. *consumer nondurable goods* and *consumer semidurable goods.*

consumer good. A good used directly in satisfying a human want. Consumer goods are classified into durable and nondurable, namely, those whose use extends over a period of time and those whose use is short-lived. Cf. *producers' goods.*

consumer loan companies. The modern term for *personal finance companies.*

consumer nondurable goods. *Consumer goods* having a normal life in use less than six months. Goods with a normal life of six months to three years are semidurable and those with a life over three years, durable. Cf. *consumer durable goods* and *consumer semidurable goods.*

consumer price index. Same as *cost of living index.*

consumers' cooperative. Usually a retailing establishment owned by its patrons. Its major purpose is to reduce the costs of commodities by eliminating the middleman's profits. Ordinarily each member has one vote regardless of the number of shares he owns. Many consumer cooperatives sell at competitive market prices and distribute "profits" in the form of periodic dividends to members on the basis of relative quantities purchased. Cf. *Rochdale plan.*

consumer semidurable goods. *Consumer goods* having a normal life in use over six months but less than three years. If the life is over three years, the goods are consumer durable goods. Cf. *consumer durable goods* and *consumer nondurable goods.*

consumer's surplus. On the assumption that the marginal utility of money remains constant, consumer's surplus represents the gain to those consumers who would be willing to pay more than the market price for particular goods. Cf. *producer's surplus.*

consumption. The final using of goods or services in the satisfaction of human wants.

consumption function. (1) The relation between total consumption expenditure of a country and *national income.* The relationship is such that usually consumption outlays rise as income rises but by a smaller amount. (2) The same relation for an individual between his consumption expenditures and his income.

consumption loan. A loan whose proceeds are used for personal purposes.

consumption tax. A tax on expenditures for consumption goods and services.

contents policy. In insurance, a policy that protects personal property of the insured on specific premises.

contingency reserve. A reserve established (1) to recognize a liability whose amount is uncertain and this is a *liability reserve* or (2) to recognize a prospective loss such as might result from price changes and this is a *surplus reserve.*

contingent annuity. An *annuity* presently established and funded but with payments to commence upon the happening of an uncertain event such as the death of a named person other than the annuitant.

contingent beneficiary. In life insurance, the person who is to receive the proceeds of the policy if the *primary beneficiary* dies before the death of the *insured* person.

contingent liability. A liability or claim which has not materialized at the time a financial statement is prepared but which may or may not become definite at a future date. Uncertainty as to liability is the test, not mere lack of definiteness as to the amount of a known liability.

contingent obligation. An obligation dependent upon other events. E.g., in the case of income bonds, the payment of interest is contingent upon the earning by the corporation of an amount sufficient to pay the interest.

contingent remainder. In law, an interest in property to commence in enjoyment at some time in the future with the person who is to enjoy it undetermined at the present, or the taking of enjoyment dependent on an event which has not yet been resolved. Cf. *vested remainder*.

contingent rent. A rental made dependent upon some variable, such as gross earnings, net earnings, or the volume of traffic.

continued bond. A bond that may be presented for payment at maturity or held by the bondholder at his option for a further definite or indefinite period as the bond provides.

continuous budget. A budget which continuously adds a month or quarter in the future as each present month or quarter expires.

continuous variable. A variable whose values are capable of infinitely small variations. For example, heights and weights of people.

contrabalance. A balance in an account which is the opposite of the "normal" balance of that account. E.g., an accounts receivable account with a credit balance; such a balance is correctly shown as a liability. Asset valuation accounts, such as bad debt reserve, are contrabalances to the asset.

contract. An agreement between two or more competent parties for a legal purpose and supported by a consideration.

contract, types of. See the following specific terms:

aleatory contract
bilateral contract
closed contract
exclusive contract
executed contract
executory contract
full requirements contract
implied contract
open end contract
option (contract)
pignorative contract
subcontract
tying contract
unilateral contract
void contract
voidable contract

contract bond. A bond indemnifying the insured for failure of a contractor to perform. Also called a *performance bond*.

contract broker. On the stock market, a contract broker is one member of the exchange trading for other members. Prior to 1919, the fee for this service was a flat two dollars per 100 shares. Hence the contract broker is called a *two dollar broker.*

contract carrier. A contract carrier is a transportation agency which serves on an individual contract basis. Some states now require them to be licensed. Distinguish from *private carrier, common carrier* and *industrial carrier.*

contract clause. A clause in the U.S. Constitution (Sec. 10 of Art 1) forbidding a state to impair the obligations of contracts.

CONTRACT CURVE

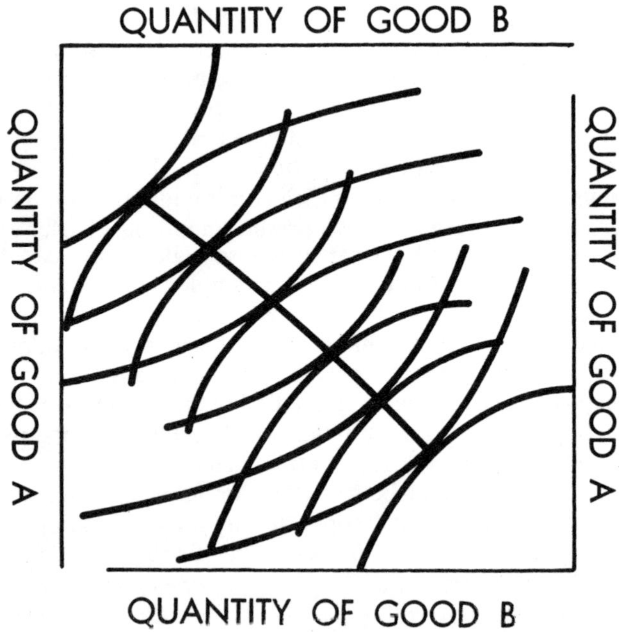

Figure 12.

contract curve. Using a separate *indifference map* for each of two individuals with respect to the same two commodities (one of which may be money), the contract curve is traced by the points of tangency of the two sets of indifference curves when the inverted map of one individual is superimposed on the map of the other individual. Thus the curve connects all possible points of final equilibrium of trading between the two individuals. When the superimposing is done, a "box" is created. Hence the term "box diagram." The opposite sides of this box are the axes for the same good of the two different individuals. Thus the size of the box depends on the quantities of the two goods held by each individual.

contract for deed. Same as *land contract.*

contraction. See *depression.*

contract market. A terminal grain market which qualifies under the Commodity Exchange Act.

contract month. The delivery month for a grain contract. Also, the month when grain is deliverable against future contracts.

contract to sell. An agreement which will later become a sale upon the happening of a missing circumstance which is necessary to the sale, e.g., the present nonexistence of the property involved. Cf. *sale.*

contractual plan. In investment companies, a plan under which the investor agrees to pay the *investment company* a series of periodic payments (typically over a ten-year period) and the company agrees to pay a fixed return at the end of the period but with all or a large part of the sales charge (that would be made if carried to maturity) to be deducted in the event of premature termination of the plan by the investor. Cf. *level charge plan.*

contract wage system. An agreement by a worker to perform a definite job in a stated time without commitment as to further work. Common in colonial America.

contribution. (1) In general a payment for his share of the loss made by one of several individuals having a common liability. (2) In insurance, the rules and policy provisions determining what part of a loss will be born by each insurance company where there are several insurers of the same subject matter. In the absence of contrary contract provisions, the rule of contribution requires the insurers to contribute in proportion to the face of their policies.

contribution clause. In insurance, the clause providing that where more than one policy covers a loss, the insurers share the loss in proportion to the face amounts of the policies. Cf. *Cromie, Page, Kinne* and *Reading rules.* Cf *apportionment clause.*

contribution margin. The excess of sales of a product over the direct costs of manufacture constitutes the contribution of that product to overhead and profits.

contribution profit. Same as *profit contribution* and *contribution* *margin.*

contributory negligence rule. The common law principle that one negligent individual cannot be held liable by another individual who was also negligent in the same accident regardless of the relative degrees of their negligence. The principle has been negatived by *workmen's compensation laws* as between employer and employee. Cf. *comparative negligence.*

controlled economy. A state whose economic affairs are largely regulated by the government. Cf. *planned economy.*

controlling account. A general ledger account which contains a summary of all of the information recorded in detail in the related subsidiary ledger. Column totals of the books of original entry are posted to control accounts whereas the detail in those columns is posted to the subsidiary ledger accounts.

convenience goods. Consumers' goods for which people do not "shop around" or make comparisons between the qualities, prices, etc., offered by different sellers. Cf. *fashion goods, impulse goods, point of purchase good, shopping goods, specialty goods.*

conventional tariff. A system of duties established by commercial treaties. Cf. *autonomous tariff.*

convention value. Same as *commissioners' values.*

conversion. (1) In law, the wrongful exercise of dominion by another over the owner's personal property in derogation of his rights. (2) In finance, see *convertible bonds, convertible stock.*

conversion cost. The sum of labor cost and total manufacturing overhead.

conversion point. The price (adjusted for accrued dividends) at which stock into which a bond is convertible will just equal the current market price of the bond plus accrued interest on the bond.

conversion price. The price stated in a bond or stock at which it can be exchanged at the option of the bondholder or stockholder for another security.

convertible bonds. Bonds which may be converted into stock at the option of the owner.

convertible collision insurance. Automobile *collision insurance* for which the insured pays a lower premium than for regular collision insurance, but upon making his first claim must pay an additional premium. Thereafter losses are paid in full to the limit of the policy. This is an alternate form of *deductible coverage* except that the deduction in deductible coverage applies to every loss.

convertible life insurance. Life insurance, usually *term insurance,* which gives the right to the insured to convert the policy into a permanent form of insurance without evidence of insurability (such as a medical examination).

convertible money (paper). Paper money which can, at the option of the holder, be converted into a standard amount of precious metal.

convertible stock. Preferred stock which may be converted into common stock at the option of the owner.

conveyance. (1) A document or deed transfering title to property. (2) A means of transportation.

cooperative. A type of corporation in which voting is on the basis of one vote for each member regardless of his investment. The purpose is to unite those in similar circumstances, such as consumers or producers, to gain the advantages of large-scale operations. Any "profits" are distributed to the members. The cooperative is exempt from income taxation on the ground that the "profits" are refunding of overpayments by the members.

cooperative, types of. See the following specific terms:

agricultural cooperative
consumers' cooperative
marketing cooperative
producers' cooperative

cooperative insurance. Same as *mutual insurance.*

co-ownership. See *joint tenancy, tenancy by the entirety, tenancy in common.*

copartnership. Same as *partnership.*

copy. An advertising term referring to the part of an advertisement to be set in type or to everything which is to appear in an advertisement. Applies also to radio and TV scripts and radio and TV commercial announcements.

copyright. The exclusive right granted by government to publish and sell copies of literature or art. The initial term in the United States is 28 years, renewable for another 28 years. Cf. *common-law copyright.*

coram nobis. Latin for "before us." In law, a writ of a court directed to bringing a case up for review before the same court that originally decided the case.

corner. (1) To corner is to secure such complete control of a commodity or security that its price can be controlled. (2) More specifically, obtaining more contracts requiring the delivery of commodities or securities than the quantity of such commodities or securities actually in existence.

corn-hog ratio. The ratio obtained by dividing the price of 100 pounds of live hog by the price of a bushel of corn. E.g., if the price of hogs is $10/cwt and the price of corn $1/bu, the ratio is 10. The ratio is useful to farmers in forecasting whether it will be more profitable to sell corn or hogs on the assumption it takes some 11½ bu. of corn to put 100 lb. of meat on a hog.

corn laws. Using "corn" in the general English sense of grain (primarily wheat), the corn laws refer to tariff enactments of England in the eighteenth and first half of the nineteenth centuries.

corporate society. See *vocational groups.*

corporate state. Cf. *fascism.*

corporation. An association of stockholders created under law and regarded as an artificial person by courts. The chief characteristics are (1) limited liability of stockholders, (2) continuity in existence, and (3) easy transferability of ownership interests.

corporation, types of. See the following specific terms:

alien corporation
close corporation
collapsible corporation
de facto corporation
de jure corporation
domestic corporation
eleemosynary corporation
foreign corporation
membership corporation
municipal corporation
nonprofit corporation
nonstock corporation
open corporation
tax haven corporation
thin corporation

corporation charter. A document issued by the state or federal government giving a group of persons the right to act as a legal person in the conduct of an enterprise and specifying at least some of the conditions of operation.

correlation. The coefficient of correlation *(r)* is the measure of the degree of association between two variables. Simple correlation may be calculated in several ways: (1) the square root of the *associated variance* divided by *total variance,* (2) the geometric mean of the slopes of the two *regression lines* (the one minimizing the squares of horizontal deviations on a *scatter diagram* and the other minimizing the squares of the vertical deviations). More than two variables may be associated. The following are examples: (1) simple correlation: the effect of rainfall on growth of crops; (2) multiple correlation: the effect of rainfall and temperature on growth of crops; (3) partial correlation: the effect of either rainfall or temperature on growth of crops when both rainfall and temperature act together but holding one of the two statistically constant while examining the relationship of the other to growth.

correlation, types of. See the following specific terms:

autocorrelation
curvilinear correlation
intercorrelation
joint correlation
multiple correlation
nonlinear correlation
partial correlation
rank correlation
serial correlation
simple correlation
spurious correlation

correlation ratio. The statistic for the degree of association between a quantitative dependent variable and a qualitative independent variable. This ratio is parallel to the coefficient of correlation for two quantitative variables. The number of items are classified for the qualitative variable into groups (such as concrete roads, gravel roads, mud roads). The correlation ratio (η) is then computed:

$$\sqrt{\frac{\Sigma\,[n_o\,(M_o^2)]\;-\;n\,(M_y^2)}{n\,s^2_y}}$$

where n_o = number of items in each qualitative group
n = number of all items
M_o = the arithmetic mean for each qualitative group
M_y = arithmetic mean of the quantitative variable
s^2_y = variance of the quantitative variable

correspondent bank. A bank which acts as agent for another bank or as a point of contact for another bank, particularly with regard to clearance of checks.

cost. (1) In accounting, the outlays and/or obligations incurred in the production of a good or service. (2) In economics, the value of the *factors of production* used in producing a good or service, using the word "produce" in the widest sense. Cf. *expense, expenditure.*

costs, type of. See the following specific terms:

alternative use cost
average fixed cost
average total unit cost
average variable cost

capacity cost
change-over cost
commodity cost
common cost
constant cost
consumer cost
continuous cost
conversion cost
decreasing cost
demand cost
differential cost
direct cost
discretionary cost
economic cost
expired cost
explicit cost
fixed cost
implicit cost
imputed cost
increasing cost
incremental cost
indirect cost
joint cost
long run cost
marginal cost
mixed cost
nominal cost
opportunity cost
out-of-pocket costs
overhead cost
prime cost
product cost
programmed cost
real cost
recurring cost
relevant cost
replacement cost
reproduction cost
semi-variable cost
set-up cost
short-run cost
standby cost
sunk cost
unexpired cost
unit cost
user cost
variable cost

cost accounting. A collective term applied to various methods of allocating costs among various products or among various processes involved in making one product.

cost accounting, methods of. See the following specific terms:
by-product method of cost accounting
job method of cost accounting
process method of cost accounting
standard cost method of cost accounting

cost-benefit ratio. See *benefit-cost ratio.*

cost center. In accounting, the establishment of areas to reflect the scope of responsibility of a supervisor (such as a department or process) and the accumulation of costs under the control of these areas.

cost classification in public utilities. See *customer costs, demand costs, output costs.*

cost curve. A graphical presentation with dollars of cost on the vertical axis and quantity of product on the horizontal axis, the curve connecting the cost of varying quantities of product.

cost function. The statement of cost conditions in equation form with cost as the dependent variable (left-hand side of the equation) and fixed cost as a constant (right-hand side of the equation) and variable costs as coefficients plus dependent variables.

cost ladder. The ranking of producers within an industry by their cost efficiencies. If there is little difference between costs of different firms, supply of the industry will be very elastic. Conversely if there are large differences, supply will be inelastic.

cost method (average) of inventory valuation. Valuing inventory after physical count (or balance from a control account) by multiplying the count by an average cost determined by taking the weighted average of the unit cost of the beginning inventory and the unit cost of those units produced or bought in the fiscal period. Sometimes the "averaging" is done by deducting from the beginning inventory plus purchases a weighted average unit cost for units charged out of the inventory to get the ending inventory.

cost of capital. In *capital budgeting,* the cost to the investor of the funds to be committed to a proposed investment. This cost includes not only the "nominal" rate paid for the funds but the net effect (plus or minus) on the investor's cost of funds if he did not make the investment.

cost of capital theory of rate making. Particularly since the *Hope* case decided by the U. S. Supreme Court in 1944, this theory has crystallized as allowing a public utility to earn a return sufficient to meet bond interest payments and any preferred stock dividends, and to give the common stock the rate of return currently prevailing in the market on similar stocks. Cf. *fair return on fair value, investment cost, original cost, prudent investment cost,* and *reproduction cost theories of rate making.*

cost of goods sold. Determined for any period by subtracting the value of the ending inventory from the total of the value of the beginning inventory plus the cost of goods manufactured during the period. The cost of goods manufactured includes materials, *direct labor,* and *manufacturing overhead* but does not include general and administrative overhead, selling expenses, and other overhead not identified with the manufacturing department.

cost of living index. The weighted average of prices of 296 commodities commonly purchased by consumers, used particularly to adjust wages to compensate for changes in the purchasing power of money. Since 1945 called the Consumer Price Index.

cost of merchandise sold. In accounting, the total cost of the units of merchandise sold during a fiscal period. It is determined by substracting the cost of ending merchandise inventory from the costs of the beginning merchandise inventory plus inventory purchased (or manufactured) during the fiscal period involved.

cost of production theory of value. The proposition that the value of goods is ultimately determined by their cost of production.

cost of reproduction theory of rate making. See *reproduction new cost theory of rate making.*

cost of sales. Same as *cost of merchandise sold.*

cost of service principle. In railroad and utility rate making, establishing the rate on the basis of the cost of the particular service. Sometimes the total costs and sometimes only the variable costs are covered. Cf. *value of service principle.*

cost or market whichever is lower method of inventory valuation. Valuing inventory after physical count (or balance from a control account) on the basis of cost or market price per unit, whichever is lower. The cost price is commonly determined as above under *cost method (average) of inventory,* or below under *first-in, first-out method of inventory.* Market price is determined by current quotations or by averaging *bid* and *ask* quotations.

cost-outlay curve. Same as *iso-outlay curve.*

cost-plus contract. A contract specifying that the selling price is the total of costs to be incurred by the producer plus (1) a stated percentage of such costs as profit, or (2) a flat, invariable amount as profit.

cost-plus pricing. Same as *average cost pricing.*

cost-push inflation. A rise in the *price level* occasioned by the competition between groups in the economy attempting to increase their relative share of the national income. Cf. *bottleneck inflation* and *demand-pull inflation.*

cost schedule. A tabular arrangement showing the cost of each different quantity of production.

cosurety. One of two or more issuing a *surety bond.*

counter check. A receipt signed by a depositor when withdrawing funds from his own bank account.

counterclaim. The right of the defendant in a law suit to seek to reduce the claim of the plaintiff based on some fact growing out of the same transaction as the claim. For example, plaintiff sues for account due on a gas stove. The defendant can counterclaim for defects in the stove. More generally, any counteraction the defendant has against the plaintiff. Cf. *recoupment* and *set-off*.

counteroffer. If the one to whom an offer is extended proposes terms different from those set forth in the original offer and thus rejects the original offer, he in effect makes a counteroffer. An effort to accept an offer conditionally is a counteroffer.

counterpart fund. Under the European Recovery Program, every participating country is required to establish a fund in local currency equal to three-fourths the gift in dollars by the United States, for later release with the consent of the United States for internal improvements.

countersignature. A signature vouching for the authenticity of another signature.

counterspeculation. Action by the government in a controlled economy designed to counteract the power of buyers or sellers to influence price (and thus speculate) by estimating the price that would prevail in the absence of restrictions by sellers or buyers and then guaranteeing that estimated price. The guaranteed price is achieved by government purchases or sales.

countervailing duty. (1) A duty levied by an importing country to offset an export bounty paid by an exporting country. (2) Also used to describe a duty by one country to match a duty imposed by another country.

countervailing power. The proposition that in the current economy there is not much competition but that as a monopoly threatens to grow it is limited by the development of a countervailing power. In short, big business breeds big government and big labor and each is a check on the other. Or big distribution (e.g., national *chain stores*) acts as a check on big manufacturing.

countervailing tariff. An extra tariff imposed by one country to offset the export bounty granted by another country.

country bank. (1) A bank situated in a rural community. (2) In the Federal Reserve System, any bank not located in a reserve city. See *Federal Reserve System* for reserve requirements of country banks.

coupon. (1) A promise to pay interest when due. Usually attached to a bond, and at the due date it is detached and submitted for payment. (2) A trade device redeemable in whole or in part in merchandise.

coupon bonds. Bonds provided with coupons, one for the amount of interest due on each interest date. Upon surrender of the coupon on the maturity date, the bondholder receives the interest payment.

coupon policy. In insurance, a *nonparticipating policy* sold in competition with policies that carry dividends. Attached to the policy are coupons that are redeemable in cash each year.

covariance. For two variables the covariance is $(xy)/n$ where x is the deviation of the values of the X variable from the arithmetic mean of X, and y is the deviation of the values of the Y variable from the arithmetic mean of Y, and n is the number of items.

covenant. (1) An agreement between two or more persons. (2) One of the clauses of such an agreement.

cover. An insurance policy.

coverage. (1) In insurance, the term refers to the amount and extent of risk which the insurer assumes. (2) In finance the term refers to the degrees of safety in earnings of a security's income. Cf. *times interest earned, times preferred dividend, times interest and preferred dividend earned.*

coverage ratio. As used in the census, the percentage of the output of a product that is produced by those firms which are classified in the industry as producing the bulk of that product. Cf. *concentration ratio* and *specialization ratio.*

covering a short. See *short covering.*

cover note. In insurance, a written statement by an agent that the coverage is in effect, pending the issuance of a policy. Distinguished from a *binder* which serves the same purpose but is issued by the company.

craft guild. An organization of the masters in an occupation during the Middle Ages. Cf. *journeyman guild.*

craft union. A union organized on the basis of the same type of work performed by the members, e.g., electricians' union, carpenters' union.

crawling peg standard. That monetary system under which the exchange rates between the currencies of the several countries are periodically adjusted (crawl) according to some indicator of the level and direction of international transactions. Adjustment occurs only when conditions have changed sufficiently. Cf. *monetary standard, types of.*

credit. (1) In the early days of accounting, the credit was an entry in an income account. Today, however, a "credit" is nothing more than an entry in the right side of an account. Cf. *debit.* (2) The ability to secure money, goods or services in the present against the promise to pay for them in the future.

credit, types of. See the following specific terms:

bank credit
book credit
commercial or mercantile credit
consumer credit
investment credit
irrevocable credit
open credit
personal credit
public credit
revocable credit
revolving credit
trade credit

See also *letters of credit, types of*

credit agency. Same as *mercantile agency.*

credit bill. A bill of exchange where the debtor has arranged in advance for credit with the drawee.

credit control, quantitative and qualitative. Central banks exercise control over credit in two ways: (1) quantitative control, which refers to the dollar volume of credit and is controlled, for example, through the rediscount rate and open-market operations (see those terms); and (2) qualitative control, which refers to the type of credit and is controlled, for example, through installment credit regulation, margin regulation (stock market), and selective rediscount rates.

credit instrument. Any written or printed paper by means of which funds are transferred from one person to another. The most common are checks, drafts, money orders, promissory notes, and letters of credit.

credit insurance. Insurance providing that a manufacturer or jobber shall not suffer from losses caused by the insolvency of debtors. The amount paid by the insurance company is the net excess over the normal losses in the business.

credit life insurance. Life insurance on the life of a debtor to assure repayment of a loan or the payment of remaining installments in the event of the death of the debtor.

credit line. The maximum amount which a lender agrees to loan a borrower. Cf. *open credit.*

credit memo(randum). A document given by a supplier to a customer allowing credit to the customer for defective or returned goods.

credit money. (1) Loans created by a bank on the basis of money deposited. Such loans can be in excess of actual money deposited, provided the required reserve is kept against the total deposits including the amount lent. (2) The notes of a bank or government which are not convertible into precious metal.

creditor. One to whom a debt is owed by another (the debtor).

creditor, types of. See the following specific terms:

general creditor
judgment creditor
preferred creditor
secured creditor
unsecured creditor

creditor beneficiary. See *beneficiary.*

creditor nation. A nation which has more money owing it than it owes other nations, due to international trade and finance.

creditors' bill. In law, a proceeding commenced by one or more unpaid creditors petitioning a court of *equity* to appoint a *receiver* to manage the affairs of a debtor who is not meeting his obligations.

creditors' committee. In law, when a firm is in financial difficulty, the creditors may select a committee of representatives to work with the owner in attempting to solve his problems.

credit union. An association whose members usually belong to a specific occupational group, such as employees of a factory, mill, store, or of the state or federal government, created for the purpose of receiving deposits from members and loaning to members. Shares are usually in five dollar denominations. Originated in Germany during the 1800's.

creeping inflation. A slowly rising *price level.* Cf. *hyperinflation.*

crime of 1873. In 1873 the coinage laws were revised and the standard silver dollar was omitted, i.e., silver was demonetized. This was done because very little silver had come to the mint after 1834 since the market value of silver was higher than the price paid by the Treasury. The law was later called the "Crime of '73."

crisis. See *business cycle.*

critical path analysis. See *PERT.*

Cromie rule. In insurance, where there is a loss on two items, both of which are covered by a blanket policy and one by a specific policy as well, the rule requires the blanket policy to pay in full, up to the face of the policy, for any loss on the item covered by it and to contribute for any remaining face amount with the specific policy for the other loss. Cf. *Page, Kinne,* and *Reading rules* for this general situation.

cross-elasticity of demand. See *elasticity of demand, cross.*

cross exchange. See *cross-rate.*

cross-footing. The totaling of the footings of figures or of totals of individual columns to produce a grand total. E.g., in a columnar cash payments book, the totals of the expense distribution columns may be totaled (cross-footed) to produce a total expense.

cross-freight. The situation in which goods are shipped from one part of the country to another for processing and then back to the original point for sale, or where, e.g., some bananas are shipped from New York City to Baltimore for sale and others from Baltimore to New York City for sale.

cross-haul. The hauling of goods from one point to another while the same type of goods are being hauled in the opposite direction.

cross-licensing. An agreement between two or more parties by which any party to the agreement is authorized or licensed to use certain property (usually patents) of any other party to the agreement.

cross order. In the stock market, an order to a broker to buy and sell the same security. If the buy order and sell order are from two different persons, the broker must execute them through the exchange, and may not directly pair them. If the orders are from the same person or collusive where by two persons, it is a *wash sale.* Cf. *matched order.*

cross purchase agreement. An agreement between partners under which the surviving partner(s) will purchase the deceased partner's interest on an agreed basis.

cross-rate. The exchange rate between two currencies computed from the rate of exchange between each of the two and a third currency.

cross sale. On the stock exchange, the transfer by a *floor broker* of a security for which he holds a buy order from one customer and a sell order from another both on the same terms. The transaction is executed at the price of the last sale on the exchange.

cross section data. Observations of the values of economic variables at a given point in time or during a given short-time interval, such observations being classified by geographical area or some other dimension. Cf. *time series data.*

CSO table. See *American Experience table of mortality.*

cum dividend. Latin for "with dividend." Stock sold "cum dividend" is sold with the next dividend which has already been declared but not yet paid, that is, the purchaser of the stock will get the next dividend. Cf. *ex dividend.*

cum rights. Latin for "with rights." Stock sold cum rights is sold with rights of subscription to a current new issue of a corporation. Cf. *ex rights.*

cumulative dividend. A dividend which if not paid annually (or periodically as provided in the stock certificate) will ultimately have to be paid before any common stock dividend can be paid. The arrearage is said to accumulate.

cumulative preferred stock. Preferred stock whose dividends are to continue to accumulate even though they are not earned, or if earned are not declared, and any arrears on this stock must be paid up before any dividend can be paid on non-cumulative stocks. In the event of liquidation, the accumulated dividends may or may not take precedence over inferior stock, depending on the language of the stock.

cumulative probability. The combination of two or more probability distributions by summing the areas under the curve of each distribution.

cumulative voting. In a corporation a method of voting for directors involving the simultaneous election of all directors with each stockholder receiving as many votes as he has voting shares multiplied by the number of directors to be elected. This assures some representation on the board for the minority if they cast all their votes for a limited number of directors. The number of shares needed to elect one director if all such shares are voted for one director is determined by this formula (dropping fractional shares) provided all stockholders vote and vote only for the number of directors who can be elected by the holdings of each group of shareholders:

$$\frac{\text{total number of shares outstanding}}{\text{total number of directors} + 1} + 1$$

Cf. *common law voting, ordinary voting.*

curb market. Originally a group of traders in stock who met in the open on the curb. Today the New York Curb Exchange (renamed American Stock Exchange) is separate from the *New York Stock Exchange* and in general securities listed on either exchange are not listed on the other.

currency. (1) In the narrow sense, legal tender. (2) In the board sense, whatever is used as a medium of exchange, including bank deposits.

currency, types of. See the following specific terms:

adjustable currency	*fiduciary money*
blocked currency	*fractional money*
convertible money	*inconvertible money*
credit money	*irredeemable money*
elastic currency	*managed currency*
fiat money	*mixed currency*

See also *money, types of.*

currency bond. A bond payable in any kind of legal tender.

currency depreciation or devaluation. The term has several meanings. (1) Reducing or eliminating the gold, silver, or other commodity for which the currency can be exchanged. (2) Altering some or all of the ratios of exchange between domestic and foreign currency. (3) Changing the supply of currency without requiring a corresponding change in goods produced.

currency exchange. A business establishment whose sole function is to cash checks, money orders, etc., for a fee.

"currency school" principle. A principle developed in England in the 19th century, maintaining that under a purely metallic currency any loss of gold to foreign countries or the reverse would result automatically in a corresponding decrease or increase in currency in circulation and thus immediately influence the price level. Under a "mixed" currency of gold and convertible paper the same effect would not occur automatically, but would be brought about only by regulation of the quantity of paper money to conform to the quantity of gold. This principle was essentially embodied in Peel's Bank Charter Act of 1844. Cf. *"banking school" principle.*

current assets. Any property which will be converted into cash in the normal operation of business at an early date, usually within one year.

current capital. Same as *working capital.*

current debt. Debt due within one year.

current liability. A liability which will be paid in the normal operation of a business at an early date, usually within one year.

current ratio. Current assets divided by current liabilities. The "normal" ratio for a business is 2:1. Cf. *quick ratio, cash position ratio.*

current yield. The ratio of the current income from an investment to the purchase price or the current price of the investment.

curtesy. The right at common law of a husband to a life interest in all the lands in which his wife at her death had an interest beyond her life, provided the husband had a child by that wife. Cf. *dower,* the similar interest of a wife.

curvilinear correlation. Same as *nonlinear correlation.*

customer cost. In gas, water, and electric utilities, the total of costs associated with the number and location of customers rather than the peak rate of use or the average use of the service. Cf. *demand costs* and *commodity cost.*

customer frontage. A method of measuring the efficiency with which space is used in retailing. Relating sales to number of feet of counter display, etc.

customer rate. In public utilities, the rate based on some index of *customer costs.* Usually combined with another type of rate to compute the total charge. Cf. *demand rate, output rate.*

customer's man. An employee of a member firm of the N.Y. Stock Exchange who is registered with the exchange and authorized to deal with the public.

customs duties. The tax on goods imported into the country. Collected from the importer but, in accordance with the principles of tax shifting, may be shifted in varying proportions forward to the consumer, backward to the exporter, or absorb by the importer. A similar tax may also be applied to the export of goods, though excluded in the United States by the Constitution. Cf. *tariff.*

customs union. An agreement between two or more countries to eliminate customs duties on shipments between themselves and to adopt a uniform policy in regard to shipments between any country in this union and all countries not members of it.

cutback. The sudden reduction or cessation of production.

cutback rate. In transportation, that part of a rate incurred in connection with transit shipments at the transit point.

cutoff rate. In capital budgeting, the *rate of return* at which further investments will not be currently undertaken. Also called *hurdle rate.*

cutthroat competition. Competition such that price falls to the point where the bulk of producers can cover little more than their *variable costs* (those costs they could avoid by closing down).

cybernetics. The study of integrated control systems in which an input-output model uses feedbacks. The classical example is the thermostat controlling space temperature. The furnace produces heat that is measured by the thermostat, which in turn regulates the activity of the furnace.

cycle. See *business cycle.*

cycle stock. That part of inventory which diminishes between replenishment orders. Cf. *anticipation stock, lot-size stock, safety stock.*

cyclically balanced budget. A governmental budget that is balanced over the period of a business cycle but in individual years has surpluses or deficits. Cf. *Swedish budget.*

cyclical unemployment. Unemployment connected with fluctuations in business activity reflected by business cycles.

damages for breach of contract. When one party fails to perform a contract the other party can sue and recover damages. The partics may anticipate this question and may specify the *amount* of damages. This is called liquidated damages. In the absence of such a provision, the party guilty of breach of contract is liable for the difference between the economic position the other party would be in if the contract had been performed and the position he is in as a result of failure of performance.

damnum absque injuria. Latin for "an injury without a wrong." In law, a loss without a remedy provided by law.

damnum emergens. Latin meaning "loss arising". In breach of contract, one element of damages is the actual loss as distinguished from lost profit. Cf. *lucrum cessans.*

data processing. The use of computing machines to sort, classify and perform arithmetic computations on data fed to the machine on cards or magnetic tapes.

date of maturity. The date on which a debt must be paid. Usually applied to those debts evidenced by a written agreement such as a note, bond, etc.

dating. The practice of extending credit for longer than appears on the surface by changing the date from which the usual terms are to be figured.

Dawes plan. The plan advanced in 1924 by Charles Dawes for reparations payments by Germany after World War I, providing for fixed payments for five years and thereafter conditioned on prosperity together with controls over the German economy. The plan was superseded in 1929 by the *Young plan.*

day book. A record book in which all financial transactions are noted without regard to debit or credit. Later the journal entries are made from the daybook. Sales checks, petty cash slips, and other devices have largely replaced the daybook.

day loan. Same as *morning loan*.

day order. In finance, an order to buy or sell on a stock exchange, but the order expires if not executed on the same day. Orders correspondingly limited to a week or month are called week order and month order. Cf. *market order, limit order*.

day rate. Historically, pay by the hour or day rather than by the piece. Today, the minimum hourly rate paid workers on a piece-work system where the worker is not making the standard production rate. When the day rate is due to breakdown or repairs, it is called "down-time rate."

days of grace. See *grace period*.

day work. See *day rate*.

d.b.a. Abbreviation for "doing business as."

dead asset. An asset which has no realizable value of any kind, e.g., worthless notes, bonds, stocks, mortgages, etc.

dead float. Checks and items for collection in process of collection or not yet collected and hence the proceeds not yet available.

deadheading. Returning empty vehicles and/or their crews after completing a shipment.

dead rent. That part of rental paid for land or buildings not being used but held available for future use.

dead stock. Inventory for which there is little or no demand.

dead storage. Goods stored for a considerable period of time and without easy access.

dead time. Unproductive time resulting through no fault of an employee, e.g., breakdown of machinery.

dead weight. The weight of freight-carrying vehicles without a load.

deadweight tonnage (vessel). The number of long tons (2,240 pounds) of cargo, stores, and fuel a vessel can transport. The difference between the tons of water a ship displaces when empty and when loaded to the load line. Cf. *gross tonnage (vessel), net tonnage (vessel), registered tonnage (vessel)*.

dealer. (1) One who purchases goods for resale to final consumers. (2) In securities, one who acts for his own account rather than as an agent for another.

dealer's brand. Same as *house brand*.

Dean schedule. In *insurance,* a system for analyzing relative fire hazards on an objective (experience) basis, covering construction type, occupancy, and similar factors influencing risk. The completed analysis is the base for establishing premium rates.

dear money. (1) The condition where the purchasing power of money is high, i.e., the general price level is low. (2) The prevalence of high interest rates making for more difficult borrowing. Cf. *cheap money*.

death rate. The number of deaths per 1,000 persons in a year. This is the crude death rate. The refined death rate makes corrections for the number of people in each age group.

death sentence. A clause in the Public Utility Holding Company Act of 1935 requiring that all such companies register with the Securities and Exchange Commission and that no more than three levels of corporations are permitted (a parent company, its subsidiary and a sub-subsidiary). All holding companies exceeding these three levels must be dissolved (the death sentence). Cf. *grandfather clause*.

death tax. Same as either *estate tax* or *inheritance tax* or both.

debased currency. (1) A reduction in the weight or fineness or both of the precious metal content of a monetary unit. (2) A monetary system severed from its base which might have been gold or another precious metal. In the case of a small country the base might have been the currency of a large country rather than gold. Cf. *devaluation*.

debenture. Same as *debenture bond*.

debenture bonds. Bonds not secured by any specific property but issued against the general credit of a corporation or government.

debenture stock. Rarely used and refers to an advantage in some respect over another class of stock.

debit. An entry on the left side of an account, bringing about an increase in an asset or a decrease in liability and net worth accounts. In early days, an entry in a disbursing account

debt. Amount owed by one to another. Thus debt and credit are opposite ends of the same transaction.

debt, types of. See the following specific terms:

current debt
fixed debt
floating debt
funded debt
gross national debt
national debt
overlapping public debt
public debt
unfunded debt

debt coverage ratio. The ratio of total assets to total debt of a firm. Sometimes stated as ratio of total debt to total assets.

debt-limit. (1) In the United States, the maximum amount of indebtedness which Congress has fixed by joint resolution, subject to change by majority vote of Congress. (2) A similar limitation is sometimes found in state constitutions, municipal charters, and articles of a private corporation.

debt monetization. The process by which the national debt is used to increase currency in circulation. Essentially this is carried out by the purchase of government bonds by the Federal Reserve System, thus releasing Federal Reserve notes into circulation. These purchases may be effected through member banks.

debt service. The interest and charges currently payable on a debt, including principal payments.

decentralization of industry. Breaking down an existing business into smaller units or expanding through the establishment of separate units. Ordinarily achieved through some geographical separation of units.

decile. One of the nine values that divide a *frequency distribution* into ten parts each containing ten per cent of the total number of items.

decision theory. A recently developed body of knowledge in the social sciences resting on measurements of probabilities which involve determination of the possible strategies available and the probabilities attached to each "state of nature" (situation) that may develop for the purpose of selecting the course of action most likely to attain the defined objective(s). Considerable use is made of probability theory. Cf. *payoff matrix,* and *standard-gamble method.*

decision tree. Probability analysis of alternative possibilities at each stage of decision. Each level of decision presents several alternatives each with its own *expected value* (diagrammed as branches of a tree) and there are several levels of decision (diagrammed as sub-branches of the tree).

declaratory judgment. In law, the interpretation of a statute or document by a court in advance of expected events. Not possible at *common law* but now authorized by statute.

declining industry. An industry in which per capita output in real terms is declining through time. Ultimately the absolute amount of output will decline.

decoupling inventory. The inventory maintained between two operations to make it possible to vary the rate of two operations.

decreasing cost. The situation in which *average total unit cost* of a business decreases over the usual range of output as the volume of business increases. True of railroads and other transport agencies. Cf. *decreasing cost industry.* Distinguish *constant cost* and *increasing cost.*

decreasing cost industry. An industry whose *average total unit cost* decreases as production volume increases over the usual range at production.

decreasing returns. Same as *diminishing marginal productivity, law of.*

decree. A judgment or sentence of a court. Sometimes used in foreign countries to describe an executive order. Originally in English and American law, the decision of a court of equity as opposed to a court of law whose decision was a judgment.

decree nisi. Latin for a decree "unless." A temporary decree which will become final with the mere passage of time if no further action is taken.

dedication. The acts or conduct of a person in giving rights to the public in land or other property he owns. May be done by express grant or implied from conduct indicating such an intention.

deductible coverage. In insurance, a provision that only the loss in excess of a minimum figure is covered. Cf. *full coverage, franchise clause.*

deed. A legal document conveying an interest in land from one party who owns such an interest to another party. The deed must conform to the requirements of the law of the state where the land is located (for example, as to witnesses, acknowledgement before a notary public, etc.). Two types: *warranty deed* and *quit-claim deed.* Deed is also used to describe a written document conveying personal property.

deed, types of. See the following specific terms:

deed of trust
deed poll
indenture deed
quit-claim deed
sheriff's deed
special warranty deed
tax deed
trust deed
warranty deed

deed of trust. The document creating a *trust.*

deed poll. A *deed* by one person conveying property to another individual as opposed to conveying to two or more in which case it is called an *indenture deed.*

deepening of capital. The adoption of more roundabout (but more efficient) methods of production which increase the ratio of the amount of capital employed in producing a given amount of goods. Cf. *widening of capital.*

de facto. Where there has been failure to comply with technical requirements of law, but an intention to achieve the status (as in incorporation) plus conduct assuming the status to exist. Cf. *de jure.*

de facto corporation. A corporation which has failed to comply with some legal requirement as to its organization or existence, but is considered by the law to qualify as a corporation. Cf. *de jure corporation.*

default. Failure to perform a term of a contract at the stipulated time.

defeasance clause. The clause in a mortgage defeating the forfeiture of the property as long as the debtor performs his obligations.

defendant. In law, the party against whom a judicial proceeding is commenced. Cf. *plaintiff.*

deferred annuity. An annuity policy in which payments to the annuitant commence at some date after the purchase date. If there is no contrary provision, upon death of the annuitant in this interval, there is a forfeiture of the purchase price to the insurer. Cf. *retirement annuity.*

deferred asset. Same as *prepaid expense.*

deferred bonds. Bonds on which interest payment has been postponed for a definite period by agreement of debtor and creditor.

deferred expenses. Same as *deferred charge.*

deferred charge. In accounting, a nonrecurring charge not currently payable although it involves a service already partially consumed such as a discount on the company's own bonds sold. The part already "consumed" goes to the profit-and-loss statement, but the deferred part is shown as an asset on the balance sheet. Cf. *prepaid expense.*

deferred credits or income. In accounting, obligations to be liquidated by the future furnishing of services or merchandise rather than cash, e.g., future deliveries on contracts already paid for. Shown as a liability on the balance sheet of the one due to furnish the service.

deferring. In accounting, relieving the expense and/or income accounts of those portions of expenditures and receipts which are not yet actual expense or income, and diverting them to future accounting periods. Cf. *accruing.*

deficiency bill. A legislative act authorizing an additional appropriation when the original appropriation was not sufficient.

deficiency judgment. A judgment in a *foreclosure* action in which the proceeds from the sale of the mortgaged property have not been sufficient to wipe out the debt. Judgment is then given for the amount of the debt which was not satisfied by the proceeds of the sale. If the debtor later gets assets, the creditor can then collect with this judgment.

deficit. A debit balance in the surplus account. The excess of liabilities and capital stock over assets.

deficit financing. (1) Financing which is intended to result in debt as a means of control. Cf. *functional finance* and *compensatory finance.* (2) Financing which results in debt because of a present deficiency in income or over spending.

definitional equation. In *econometrics,* an equation stating alternatives, equilibrium conditions, or a mathematical necessity. Thus, to state that current income equals current consumption plus current savings where current savings is defined as unconsumed current income (alternatives), or to state that quantity of a good demanded equals supplied (equilibrium condition), or to state that quantity of a good purchased equals expenditures on that good (mathematical necessity). Cf. *adjustment equation, behavioral equation, final equation, reduced form equation, restraint equation,* and *structural equation.*

definitive. The term for a permanent certificate or document replacing one temporarily issued.

deflation. A period when purchasing power of the monetary unit is rising. Sometimes defined as a period of generally falling prices and wages. However, in an economy where prices are rising but costs are rising faster (profits are decreasing) there is deflation sometimes described as relative deflation. Cf. *inflation.*

deflationary gap. The difference between the amount of spending theoretically necessary to maintain full employment at current prices and the smaller amount of spending actually taking place.

degeneracy in linear programming. If a constraint line happens to pass through the intersection of two other constraint lines, the problem is said to be degenerate. At such a point two products are manufactured, but three facilities are used to capacity. Computational difficulties are encountered unless one of the constraints is shifted slightly.

degree of freedom. The number of items in a sample less the number of *parameters* in the equation being fitted.

degressive tax. A *progressive tax* where the tax rate increases at a decreasing rate.

de jure. Where there has been full compliance with all technicalities of the law. Cf. *de facto.*

de jure corporation. A corporation which complies with all legal requirements as to its organization and existence. Cf. *de facto corporation.*

delayed delivery. In the stock market, instead of *regular way delivery* (the fourth business day after the transaction) delivery of the security may be delayed to a later date by mutual agreement.

del credere agent. An agent selling on credit at his own risk rather than at the risk of his principal.

delivered price. The price which includes freight charges to the point of delivery to the buyer. Cf. *basing point system, f.o.b. pricing, mill base system,* and *zone pricing.*

delivery receipt. A document signed by the consignee acknowledging receipt of merchandise.

demand. (1) The amount of a good that buyers are ready to buy at each specified price in a given market at a given time. Also called demand schedule. (2) Sometimes used to mean "quantity demanded" at one specified price.

demand, types of. See the following specific terms:

composite demand
derived demand
elastic demand
inelastic demand
joint demand
kinked demand
reciprocal demand

demand bill. A bill of exchange payable immediately (on demand).

demand cost. In gas, water, and electric utilities, the total of the costs imposed by the type of customer equipment. These are influenced more by peak rates of use rather than average rates of use. Cf. *commodity cost* and *customer cost.*

demand curve. Graphical presentation with dollars on the vertical axis and quantity of product on the horizontal axis, the curve connecting the points showing the different quantities of product that buyers will purchase at each different price.

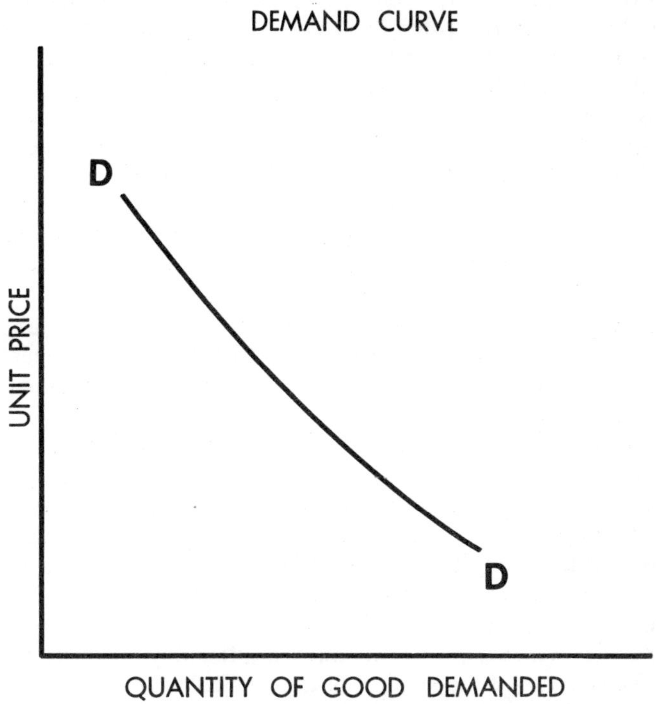

Figure 13.

demand deposit. The right to withdraw at any time (1) the amount of money previously left with a bank or (2) the amount of money loaned by the bank to the customer. The line between a demand deposit and a *time deposit* is drawn at 30 days required notice of withdrawal by the depositor to the bank. All deposits withdrawable on less than 30 days notice are demand deposits.

demand, law of. Subject to exceptions, the greater the amount of a given commodity demanded in a given market at a given time, the lower will be the price at which the entire amount of the commodity offered will be purchased. Also called first law of demand, or first law of purchase.

demand note. A written promise to pay a sum of money on demand.

demand-pull inflation. A rise in the *price level* occasioned by an increase in *aggregate demand* consequent upon an increase in the money supply such as follows upon a budgetary deficit. If this rise in the price level occurs at a time when some of the resources of the economy are idle, it is sometimes called *reflation*. Cf. *bottleneck inflation* and *cost-push inflation*.

demand rate. In public utilities, a rate based on some index of demand (such as number of rooms). Also called readiness-to-serve charge. Usually combined with another type of rate to compute the total charge. Cf. *customer rate, output rate*.

demand schedule. A tabular arrangement showing the quantities of a product that buyers stand ready to purchase at different prices.

demography. Population and its characteristics, such as the number in various age groups, the birth rate, the percentage of each age group married, and the urban-rural ratio of the population.

demonitization. Used in two senses: (1) "Legal" demonitization occurs when a country passes a law removing one type of money from its list of *legal tender*. (2) "Factual" demonitization may occur when the price of the metal as metal goes so high that people melt down the coins made from that metal. Also applicable to non-metallic forms of money.

demonstrative legacy. A gift by will of a particular fund or from specific personal property. Such a gift enjoys priority over a *general legacy* to the extent of the particular asset. Cf. *general legacy, lapsed legacy, residuary legacy,* and *specific legacy*.

demurrage. A penalty charged when freight cars or trucks are held for loading, unloading, or shipping instructions beyond the allowed free time (usually 48 hours). Cf. *average agreement demurrage, reciprocal demurrage*.

demurrer. A claim by a party in a civil or criminal action (lawsuit) that the court has no jurisdiction in the matter, or that there is not cause for a lawsuit against him even if the facts set forth by the other party are assumed to be true.

department store. A retail store which handles a wide variety of lines such as men's and women's clothing, house furnishings, etc., and which is organized into separate departments for purposes of promotion, service, accounting, and control.

dependent variable. A variable which is determined by another factor. For example in a time series of wheat output per year and rainfall per year, wheat output is the dependent variable and rainfall the independent variable. Cf. *independent variable*.

depletion. The reduction in value of a wasting asset (natural resource) through conversion into saleable product. E.g., gas, oil, minerals, etc., are subject to depletion.

depletion reserve. An account recording periodic charges to income to reflect the decrease in value of an asset in the form of a natural resource which is exhausted in obtaining the income.

deponent. In law, one who makes a *deposition.*

deposit. A deposit is a credit admitted by a bank in favor of an individual. When money is "deposited" in a bank it is not just the individual's money there for safekeeping. The money then belongs to the bank and the relationship of the bank and individual is only that of creditor and debtor. The same relationship is created when a bank grants a loan. Distinguish *special* and *specific deposits.*

deposit, types of. See the following specific terms:

demand deposit	*special deposit*
derivative deposit	*specific deposit*
primary deposit	*time or savings deposit*
secondary deposit	

deposit-capital ratio. Same as *deposit ratio.*

deposit currency. Bank credit circulating in the form of checks. Also called "bank money" or "check book money."

deposit function. The practice of a bank to receive the money, checks, notes, and drafts of its customers for deposit.

deposit insurance. Insuring the deposits of individuals and companies in banks against possible loss in case the bank fails or closes. Inaugurated in 1933 and conducted by the Federal Deposit Insurance Corporation (FDIC) for subscribing banks. A similar system applies to savings and loan associations. The current maximum guarantee of a single account is $10,000.

deposition. In law, a written statement given under oath before an authorized official, usually for the purpose of preserving testimony or to avoid travel.

deposit loan. A loan granted by establishing a credit in the deposit account of the borrower.

deposit multiplier. The extent to which a banking system could theoretically expand under a partial reserve requirement. Thus if each individual bank is required to keep 20 per cent of its money deposits on reserve, the bank system could theoretically expand to five times the money deposits through granting loans (deposit credits) and the subsequent circulation of checks. The deposit multiplier in this case is 5. Conversely, as one dollar of money deposits is withdrawn from the system, loans would have to be contracted by five dollars if the system had been fully expanded.

deposit premium. In insurance, the provisional premium left with the *insurer* pending accurate determination of the premium in the case of policies subject to premium adjustments.

deposit ratio. In banking, the ratio of total deposits to total capital accounts. Cf. *risk ratio.*

depreciation. (1) In accounting, the allocation of the cost (purchase price minus salvage) of an asset which will be used up over a long period of time by charging a portion of the cost to each period of expected life. (2) More generally, any drop in value.

depreciation, methods of. See the following specific terms:

annuity method of depreciation
composite rate depreciation
compound interest method of depreciation
constant percent of decreasing balance method of depreciation
double declining balance method of depreciation
labor-hour method of depreciation
production unit method of depreciation
retirement method of depreciation
sinking fund method of depreciation
straight-line method of depreciation
sum of the years digits method of depreciation
unit cost method of depreciation

depreciation of money. (1) The fall in the value of the monetary unit measured in terms of goods and services which the unit will buy compared with a base point in time. (2) Sometimes restricted to change of the metal content of the monetary unit. Cf. *devaluation of money.*

depreciation reserve. An account recording periodic charges to income to reflect the portion of the cost of a long-lived asset recovered. If the amount is kept in cash or a specific asset, it is referred to as a fund. When an asset is disposed of, the account is credited with all the depreciation charges previously made for that asset.

depression. The period of a business cycle when production is lowest, unemployment highest, prices lowest, and pessimism prevalent.

derivative deposit. Deposits arising from loans made by a bank to a customer. Loans may be made by a bank in excess of actual money deposited provided the required legal reserve is maintained against total deposits.

derivative suit. In corporation law, a suit by a stockholder on behalf of the corporation, in which the stockholder alleges that the officers of the corporation have failed to act to protect the interests of the corporation and therefore the particular stockholder is suing on behalf of the corporation.

derived demand. (1) The demand for one product or service because it contributes to another. For example, the demand for brick and clay arises, in part, from the demand for a house. (2) The term is also used in investment discussions as the equivalent of the *acceleration principle.*

descent. The passage of real estate to heirs when there is no *will.* Cf. *devise.*

descriptive labeling. The labeling of consumer goods by quality, size, etc., to aid in judging the price, but without reference to recognized standards or grades. Cf. *grade labeling.*

descriptive statistics. The term used to describe elementary statistical concepts such as *mean*, *variance*, or *standard deviation.*

deseasonalized. Data with the seasonal influence eliminated by dividing the actual data of each period by the *seasonal index* for that period.

design flood. The maximum flood against which a given area is to be protected.

desk jobber. Same as *drop shipper.*

desterilizing gold. The issuance by the Treasury of gold certificates to the Federal Reserve System covering gold previously bought by the Treasury but against which the Treasury had not yet issued gold certificates. Cf. *sterilizing gold.*

detainer. In law, the same as *detinue.*

detinue. A common-law action to recover personal property. Distinguished from *trover* which seeks recovery of damages rather than the property, and from *replevin* which is based not on ownership but on the right to possession.

devaluation. Reduction of the gold or silver content in the monetary unit or, where one currency is quoted in the currency of another country, reducing the number of foreign units which can be had for one unit of the home (devalued) currency.

deviation (in statistics). See these specific terms:

average (or mean) deviation *quartile deviation*

relative average deviation *relative standard deviation*
relative quartile deviation *standard deviation*

devise. In law, the passing of real property by will. cf. *descent.*

dictionary of occupational titles. A standardized list of occupations with a brief description of each job. Prepared by the Department of Labor and used for example, in comparing job rates between various employers for the same type of job.

dictum. See *obiter dictum.*

difference equation. When a dependent variable is stated as a function of independent variables, a difference equation states the difference between two values of the dependent variable as a function of the difference in values of the independndt variables which are associated with the two values of the dependent variable.

differential. In transportation, the difference established between rates from related points of origin, or to related points of destination, or via different routes between the same points.

differential cost. Same as *marginal cost.*

differential duty. A difference in the duty on the same commodity based on the origin of the commodity or some similar fact. Same as *discriminating duty* or *preferential duty.*

differential pricing. Same as *price discrimination.*

differential rate. In transportation, the rate for one route between two points established by deducting or adding a fixed amount to the rate for another route between the same two points. Cf. *standard rate.*

differentiated oligopoly. The situation where the product is sold by only a few sellers and is not standardized, e.g. automobiles. Cf. *undifferentiated oligopoly.*

diffusion index. A measure of the time spread of the movement among *economic indicators.* The percentage of a group of economic indicators that is changing in the same direction at each point in time. Cf. *pressure index.*

diffusion theory of taxation. The theory that all taxes are spread over the whole population by price changes rather than coming to rest on the person who pays the tax. Cf. *ability to pay, benefit* and *sacrifice tax theories.*

dilution. In finance, crudely used to describe the reduction in the proportion of a corporation owned by old shareholders when new shares are sold. More accurately, dilution occurs only when the proceeds of the new shares earn at a lesser rate than the earning rate just before the new shares are issued.

diminishing marginal productivity, law of. The proposition that when successive units of one or more variable factors are applied to a fixed factor in production, output will show three stages: (1) increase at an increasing rate, (2) increase at a decreasing rate of increase, and (3) reach a maximum and thereafter decrease.

diminishing marginal utility, law of. The consumption of each succeeding unit of a good will yield less satisfaction than the preceding unit. Hence total utility will increase at a decreasing rate.

diminishing returns, law of. Same as *diminishing marginal productivity, law of.*

DIMINISHING MARGINAL PRODUCTIVITY

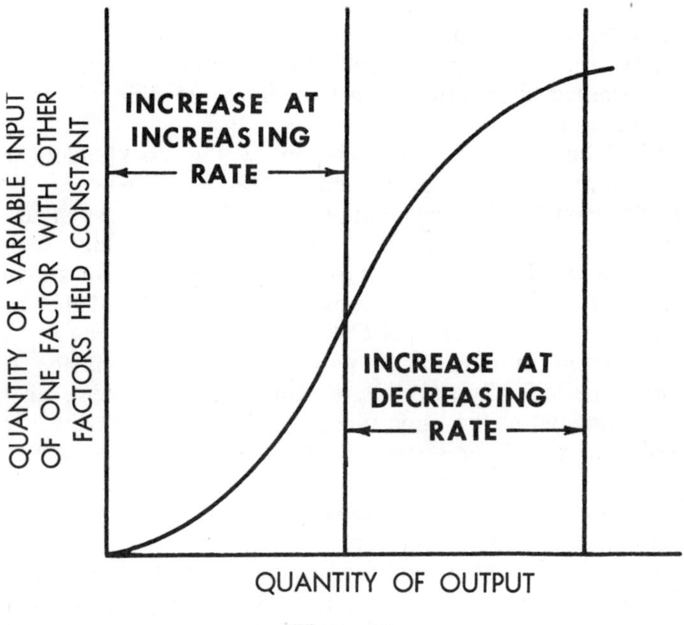

Figure 14.

direct costing. In accounting, the practice of charging the fixed component of manufacturing overhead directly to the *profit and loss account* of the accounting period in which such overhead occurs rather than distributing such overhead over the units produced in that account period. Under the latter method, such of these units as are unsold during this period are shown in the finished goods inventory at a value including the allocable share of such overhead. Cf. *absorption costing.*

direct costs. (1) In accounting, direct costs include material and *direct labor* costs—those expenses which can be "directly" and conveniently identified with units of a finished product. Cf. *overhead cost, indirect cost.* (2) In economics, same as *variable costs.*

directed verdict. In a law suit where reasonable men (the jury) could not disagree as to the facts or inferences to be drawn from them, the judge instructs the jury what the verdict must be or himself gives that verdict.

direct financing. The securing of funds by direct negotiation by the borrower with the investor, rather than through use of an underwriter.

direct labor. In accounting, the amount of wages paid to employees working "directly" on specific products. The amount of such labor put on a specified product can be more exactly determined than other wages such as machine repair. Cf *indirect labor.*

directors, board of. A group chosen by the stockholders of a corporation to manage the enterprise.

direct placement. The negotiation by a borrower, such as an industrial or utility company, directly with the lender, such as a life insurance company or group of companies, for an entire issue of securities. No underwriter is involved and the transaction is exempt from SEC filing.

direct-reduction mortgage. A mortgage under which the borrower periodically pays interest and makes payments against the principal at the same time, and the mortgage debt is thus reduced with interest payable by the borrower only on the unpaid balance.

direct strike. Employees ceasing work because of a grievance against their own employer.

direct tax. A tax which cannot easily be shifted to some one else by the person from whom the government collects the tax. Examples are the personal income tax, poll tax, and inheritance tax.

disability premium waiver insurance. A separate clause in a life insurance contract (for which a special premium is charged) providing that if the insured becomes disabled, no further premiums will be due during the period of disability providing the disability extends beyond a stated period (usually six months).

disagio. The charge for exchanging a depreciated foreign currency.

disbursement. Technically, the payment of cash. Distinguish from *appropriation* which is the authorization to spend and *expenditure* which is the spending or commitment.

discharge in bankruptcy. At the termination of a bankruptcy case in federal court, the debtor receives a discharge, that is, he no longer is liable for debts listed in the proceeding.

discontinuous function. A relationship that changes sharply at specific points. Thus a discount of 10 per cent on shipments up to $1,000 and 15 per cent thereafter creates a discontinuity of the function at $1,000 whether the lower discount is applied to the first $1,000 and thereafter 15 per cent or whether the discount shifts as to the total. In the second case the curve on a graph with total sales in dollars on the *X* axis and total discount in dollars on the *Y* axis has a sharp corner; in the first case, the curve jumps.

discount. A reduction of a principal amount. Often this principal amount is the face value or list price.

discount, types of. See the following specific terms:

bank discount
cash discount
chain discount
functional discount
ordinary discount
quantity discount
trade discount

discount bond. A bond sold for less than face or maturity value. No interest is paid annually, but all interest accrues to the maturity date when it is paid.

discounted cash flow. In *capital budgeting*, a method of analysis emphasizing the time factor in considering receipts and outlays and further emphasizing that receipts are to be considered as after income tax but with depreciation charges "added back." The time factor is recognized in the form of a rate of interest (or discount) applicable to both outlays and receipts. Two methods are common: *yield method* and *present value method*.

discount house. (1) Same as *commercial credit company*. (2) More recently, a retailer dealing in durable *consumer goods* at cut prices.

discovery. In law, a proceeding before the trial in which either party to a lawsuit seeks to determine the evidence that the opposing side will present at the trial so as to be prepared to meet it and thus avoid the problem of being taken by surprise at the trial and requesting an adjournment of the trial to prepare to meet unexpected evidence. Occasionally discovery is used to enable a party to formulate his pleadings. Cf. *interrogatories.*

discrete or discontinuous variable. A variable whose values necessarily are spaced by a definite interval. E.g., the number of people can vary only by units.

discretionary buying power. *Discretionary income* plus personal credit available.

discretionary costs. Same as *programmed costs.*

discretionary income. (1) *Disposable personal income* less payments currently due on commitments previously made. (2) *Disposable personal income* less that part of this income usually spent on necessities.

discretionary trust. (1) Same as *general management trust.* (2) Any trust which permits the *trustee* to use his judgment in administering the purpose of the trust. Cf. *fixed trust.*

discriminating duty. Same as *differential duty.*

discriminant analysis. A technique in which the dependent variable is classificatory rather than numerical. If the variable were numerical, *regression analysis* could be performed. The degree of association between characteristics of the variables is developed.

discrimination. (1) Used in sense of *price discrimination.* (2) In the field of labor relations, the term refers to the *unfair labor practice* of treating nonunion employees differently from union employees.

diseconomies. See (1) *internal economies and diseconomies,* and (2) *external economies and diseconomies.*

disequilibrium. The absence of equilibrium. Simply the negative of the various types of "equilibrium" defined under that term.

disguised unemployment. The situation in which a fall in *aggregate demand* leads to the withdrawal of labor into occupations with a low or zero *marginal productivity.*

dishoarding. Removal from storage and placing in use. Usually applied to money.

dishonor (of an instrument). Failure or refusal to make payment on a note or bill of exchange when due.

disinflation. The deliberate reduction of the general price level by governmental action.

disinvestment. The reduction of total investment, that is, the reduction of the total of *producers' goods*.

dismissal pay. A payment made to a worker by an employer when the worker is being permanently dropped from employment for reasons that are not attributed to misconduct by the worker. Now largely replaced by pensions and *unemployment compensation*.

displacement. The volume or weight of water displaced by a floating ship.

disposable personal income. Personal income available for consumption or investment. *Personal income* less personal income taxes.

dis-saving. Excess of consumption over income thus decreasing total savings.

dissenters' rights. Under the laws of many states these stockholders who do not agree to a *merger* or *consolidation* have the right to be paid out in cash the market value of their shares if they follow specified procedures.

dissolution. As applied to a partnership or corporation, the termination of the business with the assets distributed according to priorities to the creditors and owners.

distress. A common law remedy (now governed by statutes) by which the landlord obtains a distress warrant and can then seize personal property of the tenant for overdue rent. Also extended to seizure for failure to pay taxes.

distress selling. (1) The selling of stocks in a period of recession because of fear of a crash. (2) The selling of assets upon foreclosure or bankruptcy.

distributed lag. The situation in which the economic effect of a change in one variable (such as cost) is transmitted to another variable (such as price) in a number of succeeding periods rather than immediately. The transmission may follow a decreasing or increasing amount in each succeeding period.

distribution. (1) The classification of payments in the form of rent, wages, interest, and profits related to the functions performed by land, labor, capital, and enterprisers. Distribution is the pricing process viewed by the receiver of income rather than the payer of costs. (2) As a synonym for *marketing*.

distribution clause. In property insurance covering several properties, a clause providing for the prorating of the insurance in proportion to the value of one property to the total property. Same as *pro rata distribution clause*.

disturbance term. In *econometrics*, the random error or that part of the *variation* in the *dependent variable* not explained by the *independent variables*. Also, a term introduced into an equation to allow for random shifts in the functions being analyzed.

disutility. The fatigue, pain, or displeasure caused by a good, by acquisition of an income, or by work.

diversifiable risk. Investments whose returns are not systematically related to the market as a whole carry a diversifiable risk. Cf. *nondiversifiable risk*.

diversification. The distribution of investments by an individual or a business or the multiplying of the number and types of products for the purpose of stability through offsetting gains and losses.

diversion. In transportation, a change in routing while goods are in transit.

diversion privilege. The privilege of shipping in carload lots to a diversion point where inspection, grading, and reshipping may be done. The *through rate* plus a small charge is applicable.

diversity factor. In public utilities, the ratio of the noncoincident maximum demands for service of all customers in a group to the maximum demand of that group. Cf. *capacity factor, load factor, utilization factor*.

divided coverage. In insurance, (1) the division of the risk under a policy between two or more insurers, (2) the distribution of varying amounts of insurance in the same policy over various risks. Cf. *blanket coverage, full coverage, deductible coverage*.

divided syndicate. In finance, the *underwriting agreement* is divided when the maximum number of shares each underwriter is liable for is specified. Cf. *undivided syndicate*.

dividend. (1) The earnings or profits which a corporation, upon the order of its board of directors, pays to its stockholders. The dividend may be in cash, property, securities, or any combination of these. Dividends can also, in some states, be declared out of nonearnings, e.g., out of paid-in surplus. (2) Special types of business (e.g., cooperatives and insurance companies) also declare dividends. In this case, the "dividend" is a refund due to overpayment of sales price or premium.

dividend, types of. See the following specific terms:

accumulated dividend
asset dividend
cumulative dividend
extra dividend
Irish dividend
optional dividend
scrip dividend
stock dividend
year-end dividend

dividend options. In life insurance the choices available to a policyholder as to what he wants to do with the dividend. These options are (1) take the dividend in cash, (2) apply it against the next year's premium, (3) use it to buy paid-up additions to the policy at the single premium rate for the then age of the policy holder and (4) let it accumulate at interest, or (5) in the case of some policies, apply it to shorten the period over which premiums are to be paid.

dividend-price ratio. The ratio of the current dividend to the market price of a stock.

dividend yield. The current annual dividend of stock divided by the market price per share.

divisible surplus. In life insurance, the surplus remaining after adequate provision for contingency reserves (discounted present value of death claims that will occur). This surplus is available for dividends to policyholders.

divisional bond. A bond backed by a mortgage on a division or part of a railroad.

division of labor. Separation of work into its many different component operations through specialization.

docketing a judgment. In law, the entry of a judgment in the court files which have an index system showing the names of judgment debtors alphabetically.

documentary bill. A bill of exchange with documents attached, such as a bill of lading.

document of title. A piece of paper signed by the seller or carrier showing that the person named (buyer) has the right of ownership to the thing described in the document, e.g., a deed to land.

dole. Originally a form of poor-relief in England. Now used more generally to refer to relief expenditures and sometimes also to unemployment expenditures.

dollar. The unit of money in the United States. The gold dollar, adopted in 1792, containued 24.75 grains of pure gold. Lowered to 23.2 grains in 1834, but raised to 23.22 grains in 1837. Reduced to 13.71 grains of pure gold or 15.238 grains of standard gold in 1934, but not coined since that date.

dollar, types of. See the following specific terms:

commodity dollar	*silver dollar*
compensated dollar	*stabilized dollar*

dollar averaging. The policy of buying uniform dollar amounts of a security regardless of price changes. Thus more shares are bought when prices are low, fewer when prices are high. Hence the average price per share acquired is always under the (unweighted) average of the market prices at which the shares were bought. Cf. *constant dollar plan, constant ratio plan, variable ratio plan.*

dollar bond. (1) A bond whose price is quoted in dollars rather than yield to maturity. Cf. *basis price.* (2) In international finance, a bond payable in U.S. dollars as contrasted with bonds payable in the currencies of other countries.

dollar cost averaging. Same as *dollar averaging.*

dollar deficit. See *dollar gap.*

dollar exchange. *Bills of exchange* payable in United States dollars. More particularly used to refer to the quantity of such bills outstanding in international trade.

dollar gap. The difference between total dollars due the United States and its citizens from abroad and total dollars due by the United States and its citizens to foreigners.

dollar-gold standard. The pre August 1971 situation in which the U.S. dollar was convertible into gold. Cf. *monetary standard, types of.*

dollar-only standard. The post August 1971 situation in which the U.S. dollar is not convertible into gold. Cf. *monetary standard, types of.*

dollar stock. An English term describing American stocks.

Domar model. See *Harrod-Domar model.*

domestic bill. (1) In law, a draft payable in the same state in which it is drawn. If payable in another state it is a foreign bill. If payable in another country, it is an external bill. (2) In economics, a domestic bill is a draft payable within the country in which it is issued and a foreign bill is one payable in another country.

domestic corporation. A corporation is domestic within the state where it is chartered. In all other states it is a foreign corporation.

domestic system. Following the handicraft system, the domestic system is that stage in economic development where the merchant capitalist puts out the work to be done in the home. Followed by the factory system. Also called the "putting out system." Cf. *household system, handicraft system, factory system.*

domicile. In law, a person can have but one domicile, although he can have many residences. One's domicile is where one intends and acts as if his home were. An old domicile continues until a new one is acquired.

donated stock. Stock given to the corporation by stockholders usually for resale. Originally used as an evasive device because different rules of law applied to the original sale and to the resale.

donated surplus. Surplus created by the gratuitous return by stockholders to the corporation of stock previously sold them or by the contribution of assets such as might be given by a municipality as an inducement to locate.

donee beneficiary. See *beneficiary.*

doomage power. The power of the government to base a tax assessment on any available data where the taxpayer fails or refuses to furnish a return.

double auction market. On the stock market, the process of constant varying of prices by those bidding (buyers) and asking (sellers) in order to make a market. A sale occurs when the highest bidder meets the price of the lowest asker.

double-barreled bond. In municipal finance, a *bond* secured by the pledge of both the taxes of the governmental unit and the revenues of a specific project such as a turnpike.

double declining balance method of depreciation. Spreading the initial cost of a capital asset over time by deducting in each period double the percentage recognized by the straight-line method and applying that double percentage to the undepreciated balance existing at the start of each period. No salvage value is used in the calculation.

double entry. An accounting system requiring two entries, a debit and a credit, to be made for each transaction. Debits record increases of assets and expenses or decreases in liabilities (or ownership). Credits record increases in liabilities (or ownership) and income or decreases in assets. Thus debits must always equal credits.

double factoral terms of trade. See *terms of trade.*

double indemnity. A separate agreement in a life insurance policy for which an additional premium is charged providing for payment of twice the face of the policy if there is accidental death, but excluding suicide and death in war.

double jeopardy. In law, the restriction of the U.S. constitution and state constitutions that a person cannot be tried twice for the same charge but more than one charge may grow out of a set of facts. This rule applies only to criminal matters, but a somewhat parallel doctrine applicable to civil cases is the rule of *res judicata.* The rule of double jeopardy applies only when an accused has been involved in proceedings before a court of competent jurisdiction on a valid indictment. In most states, the point at which jeopardy attaches is when the jury has been selected.

double liability. The provision formerly in many state laws and in federal law until 1937 imposing a liability on stockholders of banks to pay an additional amount (in event of insolvency of the bank) equal to the par value of stock they bought.

double option. The right to buy or sell a certain commodity within a stated period at a stated price, the other party agreeing to accept either a buy or sell order. Hence, a combination of a *put* and a *call.* The other party is convinced that the market will remain stable or is compensating for other commitments. Also called a *straddle* or *spread.*

double rate declining balance method of depreciation. Same as *double declining balance method of depreciation.*

double tax. Used in several senses: (1) taxation of the same property or income by any two governmental bodies, (2) taxation of corporate income in the hands of the corporation and then again in the hands of the stockholders.

dower. The right at common law of a widow to a one-third interest for her life in all lands which her husband owned at any time during his married life. The right is called "inchoate" while the husband is alive. The right can be extinguished if the wife joins in a deed by the husband. Cf. *curtesy,* the similar interest of a husband.

down payment. That part of the purchase price required to be paid in cash by the buyer at the time the purchase agreement is entered.

Dow-Jones averages. There are four stock averages: (1) the Dow-Jones average of the prices of 30 leading industrial stocks, (2) the Dow Jones average of the prices of 20 leading railroad stocks, (3) the Dow-Jones average of the prices of 15 leading public utility stocks, and (4) the Dow-Jones average of the combination of 30 industrials, 20 rails and 15 public utilities. There are five Dow-Jones bond averages: (1) of 10 high-grade railroad bonds, (2) of 10 second-grade railroad bonds, (3) of 10 public utility bonds, (4) of 10 industrial bonds, and (5) of a combination of these 40 bonds.

down-time rate. See *day rate.*

Dow theory. A method of stock-market forecasting begun by Charles Dow in 1897 and based on the movement of the average prices of railroad and industrial securities, separately computed. Three separate price movements are assumed: primary movements (from less than a year to several years), secondary reactions interrupting the primary movement for a period from three weeks to three months, and daily fluctuations. The penetration of high and low points of the preceding secondary reaction, if confirmed by both averages, is taken to indicate further price movement in the same direction. Consideration is also given to daily total transactions.

draft. Same as *bill of exchange.*

draft, types of. See the following specific terms:

bank draft	*sight draft*
overdraft	*time draft*

drawback. (1) A remission of all or part of the duty on imported raw materials used in the production of exports. (2) Same as *rebate.*

drawee. The person against whom a draft is drawn.

drawer. The person who draws a draft against another one.

drawing account. A general account in enterprises recording withdrawals by executives either as salary, profit share, or, in some cases, expense reimbursement.

drop shipper. A middleman who secures orders from buyers and sends the orders to manufacturers or other suppliers who ship directly to the buyers. He usually is responsible for collection of the purchase price.

drummers: In early American history, agents of wholesalers who sought to bring retailers to visit warehouses. Today the term applies to traveling salesmen and in general to promoters.

dry loss. (1) Due to the imposition of a tax, a loss to sellers and consumers combined which is greater than the revenue to the government, leaving a net loss. The principal illustrations would be in a decreasing cost industry. (2) An analogous term is used in international trade.

dry trust. A trust in which the trustee has no duties except to hold property for a period of time.

dual federalism. A constitutional theory that the federal government is limited to the regulation of "commerce" and the states can control "production." Actually, the theory involves only a narrower definition of "commerce." With the *Butler* case in 1936 the doctrine of dual federalism is said to have ended.

duality theorem. In *linear programming,* the theorem that the solution of the problem of the optimal production program (e.g., the most profitable combination of resources) solves the problem of the valuation of the limiting factors of production (e.g., what one value is to be imputed to one unit of each limiting factor).

dual pay system. A wage system permitting workers to choose the more remunerative of two or more methods of computing wages, e.g., in transportation, on the basis of miles traveled or hours worked.

dual union. A union organized in a company already having an established union.

dual unionism. An effort by one union to organize as its members individuals who already belong to another union.

due bill. A written admission of a debt.

due process clause. The fifth amendment to the U. S. Constitution guarantees that no person will be denied by the federal government life, liberty, or property without "due process of law." The fourteenth amendment guarantees the same rights with respect to the powers of the states. Both clauses have been interpreted to have two aspects: (1) procedural due process, guaranteeing fair procedures, and (2) substantive due process, assuring payment for property taken or infringed upon.

dummy directors. Members of a board of directors of a corporation who act only according to the dictates of a controlling group who for one reason or another do not care to act directly as directors.

dummy stockholder. One who holds in his name stock which belongs to another party, and whose identity is thus concealed.

dummy variable. A colloquial term for a "binary variable," that is, a variable each of whose items is assigned either of two values (usually 0 and 1). The purpose is testing in one way or another, such as determining the probability, that the items assigned a value of 0 come from the same universe as the items assigned a value of 1.

dumping. A form of *price discrimination* in which a producer sells in two or more different markets at different prices because of some barrier between the markets and different elasticities of demand in the two markets. Most common in foreign trade. The goods or services are "dumped" at the lower price.

dunnage. Material used to protect freight in cars or vehicles.

duopoly. The situation in which there are only two sellers of a particular commodity. Cf. *duopsony.*

duopsony. The situation in which there are only two buyers of a particular commodity. Cf. *duopoly.*

durable goods. Goods which can be used over and over again. For purposes of classification, some arbitrary "life" periods must be established to distinguish from semi-durable and non-durable goods. Cf. *consumer durable goods.*

Durbin-Watson test. A coefficient of *autocorrelation* is computed from the residuals of (deviations from) a line fitted by the *least squares method.* Using z to designate the residual for any observed value and z_{+1} to indicate the residual of the next observed value, the coefficient of autocorrelation is the ratio of the sum of $z \cdot z_{+1}$ to the sum of z squared. This coefficient is then compared to a table of critical values (at given levels of probability and for the given number of observations). If the coefficient exceeds the critical value, autocorrelation exists. One set of critical values is used for a positive coefficient and another for a negative coefficient. An alternative method of testing for autocorrelation employs the *von Neumann ratio.*

duress. Unlawful force or threat of force such as imprisonment, personal violence, or other injury to a person or his property in order to secure consent to a contract.

Dutch auction. The reverse of the ordinary auction, with the bidding starting at a higher price and then proceeding downward. Used particularly where no one buyer is willing to take all of the lot offered and it is necessary to successively lower the price in order to dispose of the quantity offered for sale.

duty. See *tariff.*

dynamic equilibrium. *Equilibrium* recognizing that variables are changing through time. Several definitions are possible such as: (1) when the rates of change of the essential variables are constant though they need not be equal or offsetting, (2) when the expectations of the various segments of a society are mutually compatible and fulfilled so that current output can always be sold at expected prices. Cf. *equilibrium of firm or industry (partial) long run, equilibrium of firm or industry* *(partial) short run, expectational equilibrium, equilibrium (under monopoly or monopolistic competition), equilibrium (under pure competition), intermediate equilibrium, market equilibrium, momentary equilibrium, neutral equilibrium, normal equilibrium, partial equilibrium, stable equilibrium, static equilibrium, and unstable equilibrium.*

dynamic model. In *econometrics*, a model recognizing time as a variable. The typical dynamic model is *recursive*. Thus the value of an *endogenous variable* is determined not only by *exogenous variables* but by lagged endogenous variables or preceding but current endogenous variables. Cf. *static model.*

dynamic programming. A method of sequential decision making in which the result of the decision in each stage offers the best possible position to exploit the expected range of likely (but unpredictable) outcomes in the next decision-making stages. Cf. *linear programming.*

dynamics. In economic theory, the consideration of the effect of the time dimension on economic situations. Cf. *statics.*

each way. In securities and commodities, a broker charging 1% each way is collecting 1% from each, the buyer and the seller.

eagle. A $10 United States gold coin. The double eagle is $20, the half eagle is $5 and the quarter eagle is $2.50.

earmarked gold. Gold owned by one country stored in another country.

earned income. Under federal income tax laws, the income of an individual from services he has performed, thus excluding income from property, which is considered unearned. The distinction was developed in order to apply different effective income tax rates to the two different classes of income. Not currently in income tax law.

earned premium. In insurance, that part of the insurance premium which is allocable by the insurer to that part of the policy period which has already passed.

earned surplus. Surplus which is accumulated from profits.

earnest money. A sum of money paid by a buyer at the time of entering a contract to indicate the intention and ability of the buyer to carry out the contract. Often the contract provides for forfeiture of this sum if the buyer defaults.

earning assets. In banking, earning assets include securities and loans and discounts but exclude cash and due from other banks. The latter category produces no income.

earnings multiplier. Same as *price-earnings ratio.*

earnings per share. One common measure of the value of common stock. The figure is computed by dividing the net earnings (after interest and prior dividends) by the number of shares of common stock. Cf. (1) as to bonds, *times interest earned,* (2) as to preferred stock, *times preferred dividends earned.*

earnings report. Same as *profit and loss statement.*

earnings statement. Same as *profit-and-loss statement.*

earn out. A type of *merger* agreement in which all or a part of the price received by the acquired company is dependent upon the future earnings of that company.

easement. An interest in land other than the ownership of the land. For example, a right of way over land is an easement and can be possessed by a party who does not have title to that land or adjoining land.

easement appendant. Same as *easement appurtenant.*

easement appurtenant. An *easement* which belongs to the owner of property adjoining the property subject to the easement. This type of easement passes on to new owners of the adjoining property. Cf. *easement in gross.*

easement in gross. An *easement* which belongs to a person even though he owns no property adjoining the property which is subject to the easement. This type of easement is not transferrable. Cf. *easement appurtenant.*

easement of necessity. An *easement* which is implied by law for one whose land is completely surrounded by that of others with no access available by public road. An easement to pass over the land of others is then implied with the easement crossing the land of the last of the surrounding land which once owned the enclosed land.

ease of entry. In economics, the degree of difficulty in entering an industry. The aspects most commonly determining the degree of difficulty are: the minimum scale of operations and the minimum amount of capital needed to compete, the degree of product differentiation achieved by producers presently in the industry, and the significance of legal protection (patents, franchises, etc.) enjoyed by these presently in the industry.

EBIT. Abbreviation for "earnings before interest and taxes."

econometric model. A *mathematical model* (a set of relations among economic variables that is consistent) adjusted so as to employ statistical data to determine the adequacy of the model. Cf. *analogue model, iconic model* and *mathematical* *model.*

econometrics. The study of economic measurements in order to test and develop hypotheses in economic theory.

economic cost. (1) Same as *opportunity cost.* (2) Sometimes more loosely used in the sense of *real cost.*

economic goods. Goods (physical and services) that are scarce and useful.

economic growth. Increasing per capita real income over time. Cf. *stagnation.*

economic indicator. An economic series which has a sufficiently stable relation (of lead, lag, or coincidence) with the average of the general economy or of some other series so that the first series has some value in predicting the course of the economy or the second series.

economic law. A generalization as to the results likely to follow under given economic conditions. E.g., a lowering of the price of shoes, other things remaining the same, will tend to bring in many new buyers so that a larger number of shoes will be sold than otherwise would be the case.

economic lot size. See *optimum lot size.*

economic man. A hypothetical man motivated solely by the principle of maximizing outputs from given and scarce inputs.

economic order quantity. That lot size which minimizes the total cost per unit of output. Also called *optimum lot size.*

economic rent. (1) Whenever in an industry in equilibrium any unit of a factor of production is receiving a greater income than the minimum amount necessary to induce that factor to remain in its present occupation, the surplus of such receipts over that minimum supply price is economic rent. (Boulding). (2) The difference between the current earnings of a resource and what that resource could earn in the next best alternative use (Samuelson, Stigler).

economic royalist. A term of derision to denote persons who consider themselves superior because of their great wealth and income.

economics. (1) The study of the principles governing the allocation of scarce means among competing ends (analytical definition). (2) The study of man's activities in satisfying his wants (descriptive definition). Cf. *applied economics, home economics, mathematical economics, normative economics, positive economics,* and *pure economics.*

economic strike. A strike by workers to enforce economic demands upon an employer. Distinguish *unfair labor practice strike.*

economic warfare. Economic activities designed to harass another country, such as interference with supplies flowing to that country (embargo), putting pressure on those dealing with the country often through the money system, and finally blockading transportation to and from the country.

economy of flexibility. The advantage accruing to a producer with many plants of different sizes in allocating increases or decreases in operations to that plant whose size is such as to handle the total output change of the producer most efficiently.

economy of scale. The reduction in average unit cost associated with the increase in the size of plant or activity up to a point and thereafter an increase in such cost. Cf. *external economies and diseconomies* and *internal economies and diseconomies.*

EEC European Economic Community. An affiliation of nine countries of western Europe for the encouragement of mutual trade through preferential tariff treatment among the members and to establish a common tariff applicable to all imports from outside this Common Market. The latter is what distinguishes EEC from *EFTA.* The countries included (1973) are West Germany, Italy, France, Belgium, the Netherlands, Luxembourg, Denmark, Ireland, and the United Kingdom. Cf. *CACM. Central American Common Market, CARIFTA. Caribbean Free Trade Association, EFTA. European Free Trade Association, LAFTA. Latin American Free Trade Association.*

effective demand. (1) The actual purchases being made as distinguished from those which could be made by persons with ability to buy but no such desire or with desire but no funds. (2) The quantity demanded at the normal price.

effective rate. See *yield to maturity.*

efficiency ratio. The ratio of ends produced (output) to means used (input).

efficient frontier. The set of securities that minimizes the *variance* of a *portfolio.*

EFTA European Free Trade Association. An affiliation of seven countries of western Europe for the encouragement of mutual trade through preferential tariff treatment. Also called the Outer Seven to distinguish from the *EEC (European Economic Community).* It includes Finland, Iceland, Sweden, Norway, Switzerland, Austria, and Portugal. Does not provide for a common tariff applicable to all imports from outside the Association as does the EEC. Cf. *CACM. Central*

American Common Market. CARIFTA. Cariibbean Free Trade Association.

ejectment. In law, the type of action in which the legal rights to the possession of real property are determined.

ejusdem generis. Latin for *of the same kind.* When a series of terms is used which have an apparent common characteristic, an ambiguous term in the series will be construed in whatever meaning places it in the same category as the other terms in the series.

elastic currency. A currency which expands and contracts in proportion to the volume of business is called elastic. In the United States this has been attempted by the Federal Reserve System. Cf. *inelastic currency.*

elasticity of demand and supply, arc. The elasticity of a curve over an arc, i.e., over a certain range of values of price and quantity, as shown for demand and supply by the formula

$$\frac{p_0 + p_1}{q_0 + q_1} \bullet \frac{\Delta q}{\Delta p} \quad \text{or} \quad \frac{\Delta q}{q_0 + q_1} \div \frac{\Delta p}{p_0 + p_1}$$

where p = price (with *o* indicating the first point on the curve and 1 the second)

q = quantity (with *o* indicating the first point on the curve and 1 the second)

Δp = the small difference between p_0 and p_1.

Δq = the corresponding small difference between q_0 and q_1

The result has a minus sign for a demand curve, and a plus sign for a supply curve.

elasticity of demand and supply, cross. The relationship between the relative change in quantity of one product in response to the relative change in price of another commodity. E.g., arc cross elasticity of demand for commodity X in terms of price of commodity Y is shown by the formula

$$\frac{Py_0 + Py_1}{Qx_0 + Qx_1} \bullet \frac{\Delta Qx}{\Delta Py} \quad \text{or} \quad \frac{Qx_0 - Qx_1}{Qx_0 + Qx_1} \bullet \frac{Py_0 + Py_1}{Py_0 - Py_1}$$

where Qx shows quantity of X commodity (with *o* indicating the first point on the curve and *1* the second) and Py shows price of commodity Y.

The result has a minus sign for *complementary goods* and a plus sign for *substitutional goods.*

elasticity of demand and supply, point. The elasticity of a curve at a point as shown, e.g., for demand and supply, by the formula

$$\frac{p}{q} \bullet \frac{dq}{dp}$$

where p = price (at a point)
q = quantity (at that point)
dq = rate of change in quantity
dp = rate of change in price

The result has a minus sign for a demand curve and a plus sign for a supply curve.

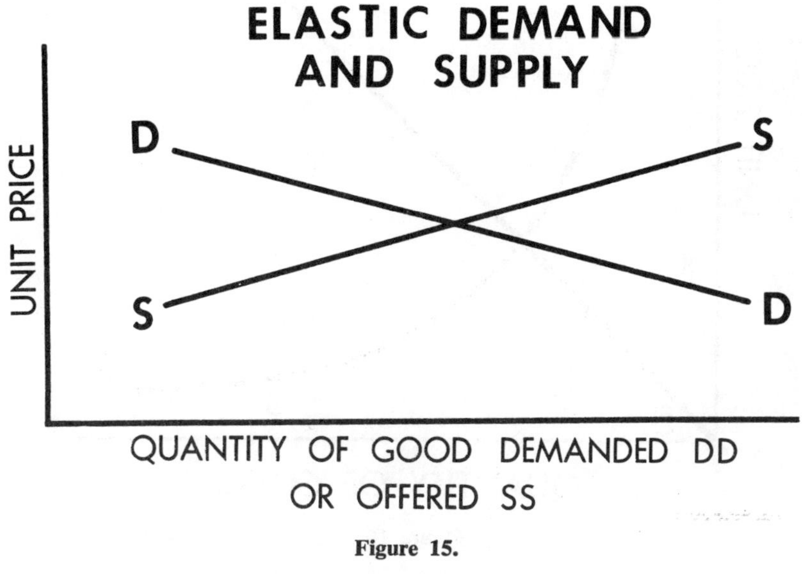

Figure 15.

elasticity of demand and supply, price. A synonym would be "sensitivity to price change." The measurement of a small relative price change as being accompanied by a proportionately smaller, equal, or larger relative change in quantity taken or offered. The result would be an elasticity less than unity, equal to unity, or greater than unity, respectively. The symbol indicating elasticity is the Greek letter η (pronounced "a-tah"), or the Greek letter ϵ (pronounced "epsilon"), or the English letter *E*.

elasticity of demand, income. With all prices constant, income elasticity of demand is the relative change in quantity demanded of a good consumed compared with the relative change in income. Cf. *income effect*.

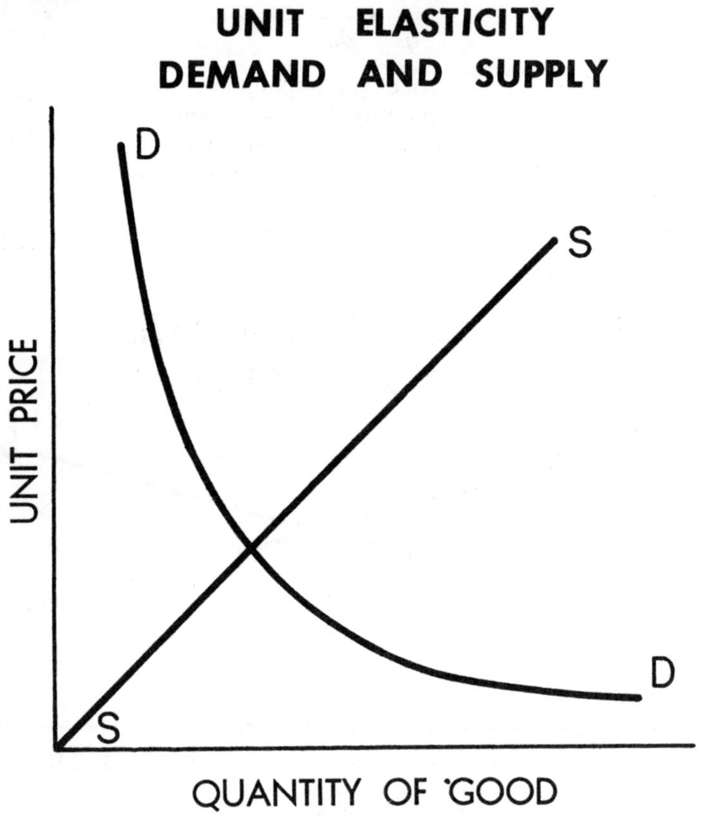

Figure 16.

elasticity of expectations. The ratio of the relative rise in expected future prices of commodity *X* to the relative rise in price in the preceding period (or sometimes compared with a preceding price and not its rise).

elasticity of production. The ratio of the relative change in output to a relative change in input. Relative change is defined as percentage change.

elasticity of substitution. The rate at which one factor of production will be substituted for another in response to a change in their relative prices. Similarly as to the consumer, the rate at which one commodity will be substituted for another in response to a change in their relative prices. In formula form, the elasticity of substitution is:

$$E_s = \frac{\text{per cent change in ratio } \dfrac{\text{quantity demanded of product A}}{\text{quantity demanded of product B}}}{\text{per cent change in ratio } \dfrac{\text{price of product A}}{\text{price of product B}}}$$

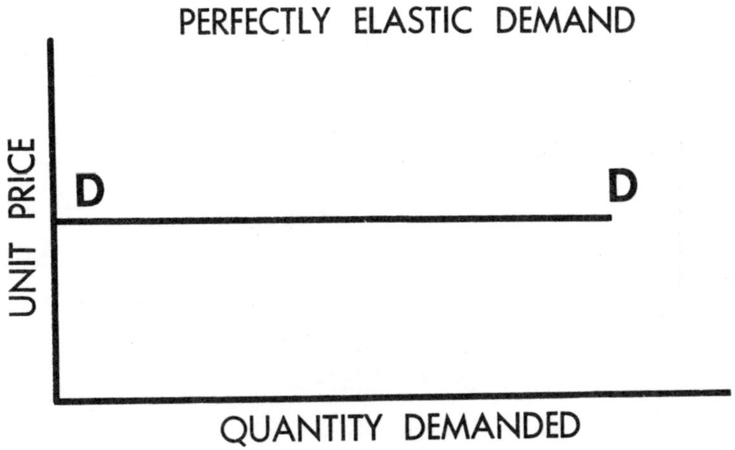

Figure 17.

elasticity, perfect or infinite. Demand or supply elasticity is called perfect or infinite when the quantity taken or offered at a given price is not limited.

elasticity, perfectly inelastic. See *perfectly inelastic demand (or supply).*

elasticity, promotional. A measure of the relative change in consumption of an item as relative expenditures for advertising and/or selling are increased while price and other factors remain constant.

elastic money. See *elastic currency.*

eleemosynary. The technical word for "charitable" or "non-profit."

eleemosynary corporation. A corporation directed to charitable purposes.

eligible bond. See *legal list.*

eligible investment. See *legal list.*

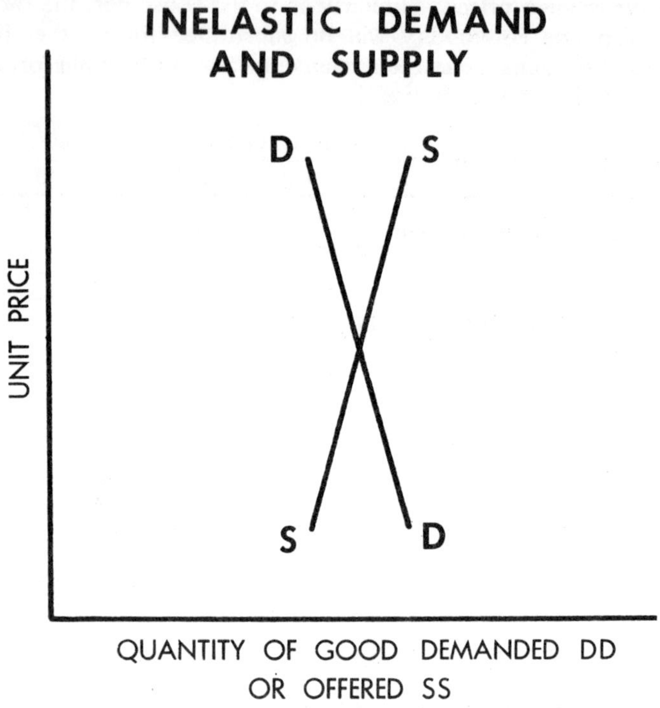

Figure 18.

eligible paper. In banking, such *commercial paper* as will be accepted by a Federal Reserve Bank for rediscount or an advance.

Elkins Act. Federal law of 1903 supplementing the Interstate Commerce Act of 1887 prohibiting rebates and tightening penalty provisions of the law.

emancipation. The legal process by which a parent or child establishes the independence of a child who is under 21 years. Achieved by declared intent of parent, marriage of the child, or actual self-support by the child.

embargo. (1) In transportation, an order restricting, prohibiting, or regulating shipment of freight because of an emergency. (2) In international trade, the prohibition or regulation of import and export of goods and/or services.

embezzlement. Converting the property of another to one's own use after having legally acquired possession of it. Theft is distinguished as illegal acquisition of possession and conversion.

Emerson efficiency plan. An incentive wage plan under which the employee receives a minimum wage for all work up to the standard output plus a percentage of this rate beginning not at the standard output point but at ⅔ of that output, the percentage increasing with the degree to which the employee exceeds the ⅔ point. Cf. *Bedaux, Gantt, Halsey, Merrick, Rowan,* and *Taylor plans.*

eminent domain. The right of the government to take privately owned property for public use. An impartial officer or board makes an appraisal and sets a price which the owner can accept, or if dissatisfied he can appeal to a court. The owner can also challenge the need of the public for the property. The railroads and utilities in the United States and the colleges in some states can also exercise this right.

employee stock repurchase agreement. A plan under which stock in a corporation is sold to employees with an agreement providing for repurchase by the corporation. Many variations are possible.

employers' liability insurance. Same as *workmen's compensation insurance.*

employment multiplier. The reciprocal of the ratio between the men initially employed as a result of additional expenditures to the total increase in employment which also includes the consequent increases in employment caused by the first increase.

enclosures. The fencing of land which had previously lain open. Refers particularly to the English development of large estates by elimination of villagers and tenants. This was widespread before 1645 and again after 1765 (the "first" and "second" enclosures).

encumbrance. A claim against specific property created by the consent of the owner of the property (e.g., a mortgage). The claim enjoys some priority over general creditors of the owner. Transfer of the property by the owner leaves the buyer subject to the rights of the party holding the encumbrance.

encumbrance account. In governmental accounting, a budgetary device to insure that appropriations will not be overexpended. As expenditures are authorized an encumbrance account is established to reduce available appropriations. When actual expenditure is determined, the entry is reversed and the appropriation is reduced by the amount expended.

endogenous theory of business cycle. Any theory of the business cycle tracing the cause or causes of the cycle to economic movements or adjustments inherent in the very nature of the modern economy. Cf. *exogenous theory of business cycle.*

endogenous variable. A variable whose value in equilibrium of a system is determined by the operation of the system. Cf. *exogenous variable.*

endorsement. See *indorsement.*

endowment annuity insurance. A combination of *deferred annuity* and decreasing *term insurance* (covering the excess of the face amount of the insurance over the cash value).

endowment insurance. A combination of term insurance and investment. If the insured outlives the policy, the face value of it is paid to him when the insured period is over. If he dies during the period of insurance, the beneficiary receives the face value of the policy.

Engel's law. Based on a study of budgets of workingmen in Western Europe in the 1850's, the following empirical statement was derived: as the income of a family increases, it spends a smaller percentage on food. Other regularities observed are: (2) approximately the same percentage spent on clothing, (3) the same proportion for rent, heat, and light and (4) an increasing percentage on recreation, education, health, and miscellaneous items. Today an empirical study would yield somewhat different conclusions.

engross. To *corner* the market.

entail. The order of succession created by an owner of land so that those following him cannot sell or convey the land.

enterpriser. Any person or group of persons who assume the risks of a business enterprise. Also called entrepreneur. Managers of a business are classified as labor when they do not assume the risks of ownership.

entirety, estate by. Ownership by husband and wife in their two names. To this the right of survivorship applies. In most states this estate has been abolished and automatically creates a *joint tenancy.*

entre pot. French for "intermediate port." Same as *free port.*

entrepreneur. Originally a French word, meaning an *enterpriser.*

entropy. The amount of information that is available in a sequence of outcomes.

envelope curve. See *planning curve.*

E.O.M. End of month. In figuring discounts, E.O.M. means that computation is made from the end of the month (E.O.M.) rather than date of shipment or invoice. Cf. *R.O.G.*

EOQ. Abbreviation for "economic order quantity."

EPS. Abbreviation for "earnings per share."

equalization fund. Same as *exchange equalization fund.*

equalization (tax). In the U.S., most states or lower political units have equalization systems for property taxes. Because valuation assessment is carried out on a local basis but the tax is applied to several local units, it is necessary to have coordination, which is achieved through equalization which recognizes the differences between local units in assessing. Thus equalization is an effort to insure uniformity of tax burden within the taxing unit.

equation of exchange. In monetary theory, the statement that the quantity of money times its velocity equals (is identical with) the price level times the volume of transactions. Stated as $MV = PT$. Another variant is the *cash balance equation* in which V is $1/K$ with K the cash balance held.

equation of international demand. See *reciprocal demand.*

equilibrium. In economics, a condition which once achieved will continue indefinitely unless one of the variables (economic or noneconomic) is altered.

equilibrum, types of. See the following specific terms:

dynamic equilibrium
equilibrium of firm or industry (partial), long run
equilibrium of firm or industry (partial), short run
expectational equilibrium
general equilibrium, (under monopoly or monopolistic competition)
general equilibrium (under pure competition)
intermediate equilibrium
market equilibrium
momentary equilibrium
neutral equilibrium
normal equilibrium
partial equilibrium
stable equilibrium
static equilibrium
unstable equilibrium

equilibrium interest rate. The interest rate which keeps the price level constant. This rate coincides with the rate which keeps money incomes constant only in a stationary economy.

equilibrium level of income. In Keynesian theory, that level of equilibrium which will continue unless factors of the economy change.

equilibrium of firm or industry (partial), long run. Equilibrium of the firm or industry is achieved in the long run by adjustment of the number of firms until the *marginal revenue* equals *marginal cost* (see those terms) for the individual firms, and average total unit cost is equal to or less than price. In the special case of pure competition, this occurs where marginal cost of the firm equals average revenue, and minimum average total unit cost is equal to price. Cf. *dynamic equilibrium, equilibrium of firm or industry (partial) short run, expectational equilibrium, general equilibrium (under monopoly or monopolistic competition), general equilibrium (under pure competition), intermediate equilibrium, market equilibrium, momentary equilibrium, neutral equilibrium, normal equilibrium, partial equilibrium, stable equilibrium, static equilibrium,* and *unstable equilibrium.*

equilibrium of firm or industry (partial), short run. Equilibrium of the firm or industry is achieved in the short run at the point where for the individual firm *marginal revenue* equals *marginal cost* (see those terms), and average variable cost is equal to or less than price, but there is insufficient time for new firms to enter the industry. In the special case of pure competition, this occurs where marginal cost of the firm equals average revenue, and average variable cost is equal to or less than average revenue. Cf. *dynamic equilibrium, equilibrium of firm or industry (partial) long run, expectational equilibrium, general equilibrium, (under monopoly or monopolistic competition), general equilibrium (under pure competition), intermediate equilibrium, market equilibrium, momentary equilibrium, neutral equilibrium, normal equilibrium, partial equilibrium, stable equilibrium, static equilibrium,* and *unstable equilibrium.*

equimarginal principle. In dividing a fixed quantity of anything among a number of different uses, it will be apportioned to each use so that the gain from putting one unit into one use it just equal to the loss in the uses from which that unit is withdrawn. Cf. *marginal rate of substitution.*

equipment trust bond. See *equipment trust certificate.*

equipment trust certificate. A device widely used in the railroad, airline and trucking fields by which corporations can get new equipment. The equipment is held by a trustee who leases the equipment to the corporation. Thus the equipment does not become subject to claims against the corporation. The equipment must be plainly marked as to true ownership, however, to make this device effective. The trustee issues certificates similar to shares of stock to those who put up the money to finance the trustee's purchase of the equipment. The rent from the lease becomes the income distributed to the certificate holders. When rental payments total purchase price plus interest, the equipment is turned over to the lessee. Three forms of contract may be used: *chattel mortgage, conditional sale,* or *lease.*

equitable asset. An asset held by the executor of an estate but subject to debts only by a decree of an equity court for satisfaction of certain obligations. Cf. *legal asset.*

equitable conversion. In law, a rule that a court of equity will give effect to those things intended to be accomplished even though not all of the legal formalities have been performed. Thus if a contract to sell land has been entered but death intervenes before the deed is executed, equitable conversion will be applied so that the estate of the deceased vendor will be considered to have money and not land.

equitable lien. In law, a court of equity may impose a *lien* as a remedial device where possession of property has changed thus having terminated the legal lien.

equitable mortgage. An agreement to make certain property security for a debt will create a mortgage as soon as money is advanced even though the mortgage has not yet been executed. This mortgage is called *equitable* because it can be cut off by an actual mortgage to a good faith lender with no knowledge of the equitable mortgage.

equitable right. A right recognized in a court of equity. In older English and American days, two sets of courts were maintained, law courts and equity courts, and hence two sets of rights, legal and equitable, developed. This distinction in courts has now largely disappeared but the classification of rights continues. Cf. *legal rights.*

equity. (1) In business, it means the equity of ownership, i.e., the net worth of a firm or corporation (total assets less total debts). The "equity" belongs to the partners or stockholders. (2) In the law of English-speaking countries, there are two branches of civil "law," (a) the common law and (b) equity. Today the distinction persists, not formally but in the tradition of the law. Equity was devised to effect changes in the common law which had become frozen.

equity annuity. Same as *variable annuity.*

equity capital. The total funds invested in a business by the owners. Same as *net worth.*

equity of redemption. The interest of one who has mortgaged property for a loan. In so-called "title" states, the lender owns the mortgaged property and the borrower only has the right (equity) to get it back (redeem it) upon payment of the debt. In "lien" states, the mortgagor still retains title to the property and the mortgage is a lien

equity rate. In insurance, an adjusted rate for risks which deviate widely from the average risk (either higher or lower).

equity trading. See *trading on the equity.*

error. See *random error, sampling error, standard error, and systematic error.*

escalator clause. A clause in an agreement providing for adjustment of price based on some event or index. For example, a provision that the price due the seller will be increased in proportion to any increase in costs. Or a provision in a labor agreement that wage rates will fluctuate with the changes in the cost of living index.

escape clause. A provision in the current U.S. tariff act authorizing the tariff commission to request the President to set quotas and other terms upon proof that an increase in imports after a negotiated tariff reduction injures an American producer.

escape period. Most commonly applied in labor agreements involving *maintenance of membership clauses* to permit workers to withdraw from the union during the last month of one contract and before the beginning of the next contract.

escheat. The right of the state to take for itself any property left by a person who has made no will and who has no heirs to receive it. The term also applied in older days to the right of the king to take the property of one convicted of treason.

escrow. An arrangement under which two parties agree to clear a transaction through a third party (the escrower) who acts according to the terms specified. For example, the purchaser of land may deposit money with an escrower who will release the money to the seller of the land when the seller furnishes a deed.

establishment. In the census, a plant or place of business. Thus a number of establishments may be owned by one *firm.*

estate. In law, (1) the extent of an interest in property, e.g., an estate for 10 years is the ownership for 10 years; (2) the total of property left at death.

estate at sufferance. In law, the interest of a tenant holding over and continuing to occupy land after the lease under which he held possession has expired.

estate by entirety. See *entirety, estate by.*

estate tax. A tax on the right to transmit property to heirs. The federal death tax is an estate tax, i.e., the tax is assessed on the estate itself and the rate depends on the size of the estate and not on the number or kinds of heirs. It differs from the inheritance tax which is upon the one receiving the property, and makes distinctions as to relationship, heirs, and the size of inheritance by each heir.

estoppel. A general legal doctrine preventing a person from attempting to prove certain facts because he has acted in a manner which admits the contrary facts.

estovers. French for "necessaries." The right of a tenant to take wood for fuel, fences, and similar purposes, from the premises he has leased.

Euler theorem. The proposition that if production is a linear homogeneous function (such that an equal percentage increase in all the factors results in the same percentage increase in output), then if each factor is paid its marginal product, the total product will equal the total returns to each factor. Linear homogeneity would be true only of a constant cost industry, i.e., one with no economies (or diseconomies) of scale.

Eurodollar market. The market which deals in commitments payable in U.S. dollars held in Europe. The basis for the market is that such commitments can freely move between European countries without the restrictions imposed by such countries on the foreign investment of funds that involve their own currencies and without the restrictions imposed by the U.S. on export of dollars from the U.S.

European Common Market. See *EEC. European Economic Community.*

ever-normal granary. A device designed to stabilize the price of agricultural commodities through the purchase by the government of excess production for storage and the sale by the government from that storage in years of low production.

ex ante investment. Same as *planned investment.*

ex ante saving. Same as *planned savings.*

exceptions to classification. In transportation, a publication of classification ratings and rules different from the classification ratings and rules contained in a major classification.

excess bank reserves. The deposits which a member bank has with the Federal Reserve Bank plus vault cash over and above the amount required by law or by the Federal Reserve System.

excess capacity. The existence of idle ability to produce output in either a firm or an industry but excluding facilities unable to make a profit at prevailing prices for current output. Cf. *overcapacity.*

excess coverage. See *contribution clause.*

excess-demand inflation. A rise in the *price level* consequent upon an increase in *aggregate demand* more rapid than the increase in full-employment output.

excess insurance. Insurance covering only that part of a loss in excess of a stated amount with losses of the stated amount or less covered by other insurance or *self-insurance.*

excess present value. The difference between the purchase price of an asset and its *present value.*

excess profits tax. (1) The American excess profits tax of both World Wars was built on the same structure: the excess profits tax rate applied to all income over a certain "normal" amount. The "normal" income was computed at the option of the taxpayer as (a) the average of the incomes of a few preceding years or (b) a return of a given percent on the capital invested in the business. There were exceptions to these two bases. (2) Excess profits taxes may exist in peacetime. As a corollary of the tax on declared value of capital stock, a tax was levied for excessive earnings on that declared value. (3) There is also a separate tax levied on corporations for the unreasonable accumulation of surplus by a corporation to avoid taxes on corporate dividends, the so-called section 102 tax.

excess reinsurance. *Reinsurance* by a *reinsurer* (one insurance company insuring a risk of another insurance company) against loss by the *insurer* of an amount in excess of an agreed primary amount.

exchange. (1) One product or service given in return for another. Called barter if no money is involved. (2) A place where organized traders meet to buy and sell commodities or securities. Cf. *organized exchange.*

exchange clearing agreement. Same as *clearing agreement.*

exchange control. Governmental regulation of the purchase and sale of foreign exchange. Various programs may be employed: *blocked exchanges, clearing agreement, exchange equalization fund, multiple currency system, rationing of exchange.*

exchange distribution. In finance, the sale of a block of stock on a stock exchange by a holder (not the issuing corporation) during regular hours at a fixed price. Only the seller pays a commission. Cf. *secondary offering.*

Exchange Equalization Account. See *Exchange Stabilization Fund.*

exchange equalization fund. The purpose of the fund is to combine the advantages of fairly stable exchange rates in the short run with a degree of long-run flexibility. It is used when a country has left the gold standard. The fund is administered by the monetary authority of a country and consists of foreign exchange and gold which is used to manipulate the foreign exchange markets in an effort to provide stability.

exchange jobber. A banker who buys *foreign exchange* in large amounts for resale at a margin to smaller banks or individuals.

exchange rate. Used particularly with reference to the ratio at which the money of one country is exchanged for the money of another country.

Exchange Stabilization Fund. A department of the United States Treasury established in 1934 with the "profits" derived from the reduction in the gold content of the dollar for the purpose of stabilizing the foreign exchanges. A similar fund, the Exchange Equalization Account, was established by the British in 1932.

exchange value. The value of any good considered as the quantity of other things that will be given in exchange for it.

exchequer. In England, the branch of the government in charge of public revenues.

excise tax. A tax levied on the sale of certain commodities produced within a country, such as cigars, whiskey, automobiles, and amusements.

exclusion. In taxation, the recognition of an amount as not within the scope of tax computation. Thus in the federal *gift tax,* gifts of less than $3,000 to any one person in any one year are excluded. Cf. *exemption.*

exclusive agency listing. A contract between the owner of real estate and a broker such that the stated broker will receive a commission regardless of which broker makes the sale. Sale by the owner's efforts, however, will not entitle the broker to commission. Cf. *exclusive-right-to-sell listing.*

exclusive agent. An agent who has the sole rights to sell within a given geographical or other market area.

exclusive contract. A term that may embrace only *full requirements* or may extend to being a *tying contract.*

exclusive-right-to-sell listing. A contract between the owner of real estate and a broker such that the broker will receive a commission regardless of who sells the real estate, even the owner. Cf. *exclusive agency listing.*

exculpatory clause. A provision in an agreement which excuses one of the parties from liability for any negligence he may commit. Made illegal as to trustees of a bond indenture by the *Trust Indenture Act of 1939.*

ex dividend. Latin for "without dividend." Stock sold ex dividend is sold without the next dividend which has already been declared, that is, the seller of the stock will receive the next dividend when it is paid. Cf. *cum dividend.*

executed contract. A contract in which performance by both parties has been completed.

execution. In law, the writ of a court directing the sheriff to carry out the *judgment* of the court. In a criminal case, the sheriff delivers the person to prison. In a civil case, he seizes property or funds as directed.

executive committee. A group selected by the board of directors of a corporation, usually from among their own members, to act for the board (in so far as that is legally possible) between meetings of the board of directors. This device was developed because often part of the board of directors is active in the management of the company while another part of the board acts only in an advisory capacity. The active part of the board is usually named to the executive committee.

executor. The person named in a will to manage the estate of a deceased person according to the terms of the will and subject to the rules of law and the supervision of a judge. Cf. *administrator.*

executor's bond. A bond required of the executor named in a will to assure an estate against misconduct by the executor.

executor de son tort. Law French for "executor by his own wrongful act." One who improperly undertakes to deal with the property of a deceased person as if he were legally designated executory. He is held to the same standard of conduct as an executor.

executory contract. A contract in which something remains to be done to complete the original agreement. Cf. *executed contract.*

exemplary damages. Same as *punitive damages.*

exemption. In taxation, the recognition of an amount as within the scope of tax computation but not subjected to tax. Thus in the federal *gift tax* all amounts over the *exclusions* are subject to a cumulative exemption of (currently) $30,000. Cf. *exclusion.*

ex gratia payment. The payment of a claim, even though one is not legally obligated to pay, in order to avoid the expense of defending against the claim.

exhaust price. In the stock market, the price below which stock bought on *margin* will be sold unless more security is put up.

exogenous theory of business cycle. Any theory of the business cycle tracing the cause or causes of the cycle to disturbances external to the economic mechanism, such as crop changes, inventions, weather cycles, etc. Cf. *endogenous theory of business cycle.*

exogenous variable. A variable whose value is not determined by the operation of the system. Cf. *endogenous variable.*

exoneration. In law, the right of a *surety* to force the *principal* into the case immediately rather than proceeding against the principal later in a separate suit.

expansion. See *business cycle.*

ex parte. Literally, "from (one) side." In law, a proceeding which is unopposed but required to establish the legality of the court or commission judgment or order desired as a result of the proceeding.

expectational equilibrium. In economic theory, the situation in which people's expectations though they are changing, come to pass as anticipated. Cf. *dynamic equilibrium, equilibrium of firm or industry (partial) long run, equilibrium of firm or industry (partial) short run, general equilibrium, (under monopoly or monopolistic competition), general equilibrium, (under pure competition), intermediate equilibrium, market equilibrium, momentary equilibrium, neutral equilibrium, normal equilibrium, partial equilibrium, stable equilibrium, static equilibrium,* and *unstable equilibrium.*

expected income hypothesis. Sáme as *permanent income hypothesis.*

expected return. The *mean* value of a probability distribution of possible returns each weighted by its probability.

expected value. The *mean* value of a probability distribution, that is the average of the respective values each weighted by its probability.

expenditure. In accounting, the outlays of cash in a period, as distinguished from expense which includes: noncash items and expenditures made in a previous period but chargeable to the current period, and items attributable to the current period but not yet paid. Sometimes distinguished from *appropriation* which is an authorization to spend, and *disbursement* which is the cash payment. Then expenditure is the commitment of funds.

expenditure curve. Used in two senses: (1) same as *budget line.* (2) same as *income-consumption curve.*

expenditure equation. Same as *income equation.*

expense. (1) In accounting, the voluntary using up of a service or material through physical consumption or passage of time attended by the receipt of some anticipated benefit. (2) In economics, the cash outlays incurred in the production of a good or service. Cf. *cost, accrued income (or expense), deferred charge, prepaid expense.*

expense loading. In insurance, the amount added to pure risk premium to cover the expenses of the insurance company other than loss payments.

expense ratio. In insurance, the ratio of all expenses other than loss adjustments and federal income taxes to net premiums written (as distinguished from earned). Cf. *loss ratio.*

experience rating. In insurance, the variation of the premium rate to allow for the abnormal or subnormal risk experience of the insured, e.g., a 40% premium reduction on the ground that the insured has a past-risk record 40% better than normal. Used widely in workmen's compensation insurance. Cf. *manual rating, merit rating, retrospective rating, schedule rating.*

expired cost. A cost that should be expensed in the current period.

explained variance. Same as *associated variance.*

explicit cost. The cost determined by the price paid for a factor of production. Cf. *implicit cost.*

exploitation of labor. (1) In Marxian theory, giving labor anything less than the total of production after capital maintenance. (2) In Marshallian theory, paying labor less than its marginal product.

exponential smoothing. A form of *moving average* in which the items considered in the average are not weighted equally but are discounted in geometric proportion to their age, with older items carrying less weight. The weights are an exponential function of the ages of the data. Cf. *smoothing constant.*

export bounty. A subsidy paid by the government of the country from which goods are exported.

Export-Import Bank. Originally established in 1934, it was in 1945 made an independent agency of the United States government to aid in financing exports and imports. Most of the actual loans have been for the benefit of individual exporters in the U.S. and to foreign governments, banks, and firms for purchase of specific goods in the U.S.

export multiplier. See *foreign-trade multiplier.*

export quotas. Fixed amounts of goods which may be exported. Export quotas are determined by the government and may be used for the sake of national defense, to support price control schemes, etc.

export rate. In transportation, a rate applicable only to domestic shipment of goods en route to a foreign country.

exports. The goods (including services) sold to citizens of another country plus the services furnished to the citizens of the foreign country in shipping, financing, and otherwise facilitating the export. Cf. *invisible exports.*

ex post facto law. In law, a criminal statute attempting to increase punishment after the act to which it would apply has been performed. This can be done under English law but is unconstitutional in the United States. Retrospective civil legislation, however, is not unconstitutional, but it may not impair the obligation of contract.

ex post investment. Investment actually made. Cf. *ex ante investment.*

ex post saving. Ex post saving is realized saving. If hoards are considered as constant, ex post saving must equal ex post investment. Cf. *ex ante saving.*

express warranty. A statement or conduct by a seller to a buyer that a specific condition exists in the character of goods. Cf. *implied warranty.*

ex rights. Literally, without rights. Stock sold ex rights is sold without privileged subscription rights to a current new issue by a corporation. Cf. *cum rights.*

extended bond. A bond whose maturity date has been delayed with the consent of the bondholders.

extended coverage. In insurance, an indorsement on the policy covering risks in addition to those stated in the body of the policy. Sometimes the policy itself covers the added risks and is called an extended coverage policy.

extended term insurance. An option given to the holder of a life insurance policy entitling him to use the cash surrender value to remain insured in the original amount for a definite specified time without further payment of premiums. This is an advantage to a policyholder who cannot or does not wish to keep up his insurance premiums but wants to continue the insurance as long as possible.

extension bond. A bond secured by a mortgage on an addition or extension of a railroad.

extensive use of land. See *margin of cultivation, extensive.*

external bill. A bill of exchange drawn in one country but payable in another country. Cf. *foreign bill.*

external debt. The debt held by persons outside a country.

external economies and diseconomies. External economies are increases in efficiency within the producing unit, not paid for by the unit but resulting from action outside the unit. The unit may be a firm or an industry. E.g., the entry of a firm into an industry may lower the costs of all firms previously in the industry. This economy is external to the firm but internal to the industry. If a loss in efficiency were involved, the decrease would be termed a "diseconomy." Cf. *internal economies and diseconomies.*

external financing. Procurement of funds for a firm from sources outside the firm, e.g. by the sale of new bonds or stock. Cf. *internal financing.*

extractive industry. Any industry which uses up irreplaceable natural resources.

extra dividend. A dividend in addition to the regular dividend.

extrapolation. The process of estimating an unknown number or value *outside* the range of known numbers or values which are used as the basis for estimating. Projecting a curve beyond the limits of experience or data. Cf. *interpolation.*

Fabian socialism. That group of socialists who accept the principles of *socialism* but reject class struggle and violence in the belief that socialism will come about through evolution. The Fabian Society was organized in England in 1889.

FAC Federal Advisory Council. A group of twelve advisors representing the 12 Federal Reserve districts, which meets several times a year to confer with the Board of Governors of the Federal Reserve System.

face value. The value stated on the face of a security or insurance policy. This is the value at maturity or death.

factor. (1) In economics, same as *factor of production.* (2) In business, in England, an agent who represents another is called a factor. In the United States, the term refers particularly to the one financing and marketing textiles by assuming the responsibility for credit transactions, thus relieving the manufacturer of this function. (3) One who purchases accounts receivable from a manufacturer or merchandiser and thereby assumes the risk of their collection. Cf. *non-notification loan.*

factor analysis. See *discriminant analysis.*

factor cost. Payments to the *factors of production,* namely, materials, wages, rents, interest, and profits but not such items as *indirect business taxes* (such as *excise taxes* and *real property* taxes).

factor-cost line. Same as *iso-outlay curve.*

factoring. Sale of *accounts receivable* of a firm to a *factor* at a discounted price.

factor prices. A shortened form of *factor of production prices.*

factor reversal test. In statistics, a method of testing the mathematical validity of an index number. Separate indices are computed for price change and quantity change from one period to the next and these are multiplied by each other. If this equals the ratio of the base period's price times quantity to the next period's price times quantity, the test is met. Index numbers computed by the weighted *aggregative* and weighted *average of relatives* do not meet this test. The *ideal index* does. Cf. *time reversal test.*

factor's lien. The right of an agent selling merchandise to keep possession of the merchandise until his principal pays all money due him on the arrangement.

factors of production. The "ingredients" used by an enterprise in producing a commodity. The services derived from different resources, e.g., land, labor, etc.

factory system. Following the domestic system, the factory system is that stage in economic development where production is concentrated in a larger unit under one roof with the owner directing the work of others. Cf. *domestic system, handicraft system, household system.*

faculative reinsurance. In insurance, an agreement covering reinsurance and giving the reinsurer the right to reject any business if he acts promptly.

Fair Labor Standards Act. Federal law passed in 1938 applying to the production of all goods and services in interstate commerce providing for time and one-half pay for all work over 40 hours per week, establishing a minimum hourly wage (presently $1.60 per hour), and regulating other labor conditions including child labor.

fair list. A list of employers said to be fair to labor. Compiled by labor organizations and published in their papers and and magazines. Cf. *unfair list, blacklist.*

fair market value. In law, the price that would result between a willing buyer and a willing seller.

fair return. In utility or railroad rate making, fair return is the net income allowed to a utility as a profit. Computed as a percentage of the *rate base* (q.v.) which is a valuation of the property devoted to public use or of the amount of invested money. Cf. *fair value.*

fair return on fair value theory of rate making. See *Smyth v. Ames rule.*

fair trade laws. See *fair trade practices acts.*

fair trade practices acts. Forty-five states have passed such acts authorizing producers and others to set minimum resale prices binding retailers, except under unusual circumstances such as bona fide clearance sales. The principal application of such laws has been to branded goods. Cf. *unfair trade practice act, price floor laws.*

fair value. In utility and railroad rate making, the fair value of the property devoted to public use is the *rate base* on which the utility is entitled to a *fair return.* There is no exact definition of how "fair value" is measured—it is a judgment reached after considering one or more of the relevant factors including *original cost, investment cost, reproduction new cost,* and *prudent investment cost theories of rate-making.*

family income insurance. Life insurance designed to provide extra income during the period of maximum family dependency (during the period when children are growing up).

Fannie Mae. The colloquial term for *Federal National Mortgage Association.*

farm-price supports. The prices at which the U.S. Department of Agriculture will purchase (or lend on the security of) agricultural products. Such prices may be at *parity price* or above or below the parity price.

f.a.s. Free alongside ship. Means that the seller must deliver his goods alongside a ship with all charges to this point covered in the sales price. From then on the responsibility for loss and loading belongs to the buyer.

fascism. Applied to the system in Italy under Mussolini, 1921 to 1945. Also used in a wider sense to apply to all totalitarian systems, e.g., Germany under Hitler. Government under one man with the right to private property recognized in part but with political and economic rights severely restricted.

fashion goods. Goods whose primary appeal rests on frequently changing design or appearance. Cf. *convenience goods, impulse goods, point of purchase goods, shopping goods, specialty goods.*

favorable balance of trade theory. A theory of *mercantilism* that a favorable balance of trade was desirable. The balance is favorable when the money total of exports exceeds the money total of imports.

FCA Farm Credit Administration. The new name given to the administrative body handling farm credit since 1933. The FCA has a board of five commissioners. One is called the Governor. Each of the other four is the governing official of a set of twelve farm credit banks: the Federal Land Banks, the Intermediate Credit Corporations, the Production Credit Corporations, and the Banks for Cooperatives, respectively.

FCC Federal Communications Commission. The FCC was created by Congress in 1934 to provide for the regulation of interstate and foreign communication by wire, radio or TV centralizing these duties and responsibilities with a view to more effective communication service.

FCIC Federal Crop Insurance Corporation. The FCIC was created within the Department of Agriculture in 1938 to provide for the insurance of wheat and cotton crops. The program insures the potential crop up to fifty to seventy per cent of the past average yield against losses due to unavoidable causes. Premium rates are calculated for each farm according to the past history of the individual farm.

FDA Food and Drug Administration. Until 1940, an agency within the United States Department of Agriculture, since then a part of the Federal Security Agency. Administers the Food, Drug, and Cosmetics Act of 1938 and other federal laws affecting adulteration and false labeling.

FDIC Federal Deposit Insurance Corporation. Organized in 1933 to insure the repayment of bank deposits up to $5000 (since raised to $20,000) per account in any one insured bank. All members of the Federal Reserve System must belong and all nonmember banks which qualify may also belong. Insured members pay a premium semiannually based upon the annual average of deposits. A board of three, located at Washington, D.C., is in control.

featherbedding. Popular term applied to the establishment by unions of rules or practices designed to increase artificially the number in employment or their wages, e.g., requiring at least a minimum of 5 apprentices to each journeymen even though 3 would be sufficient to do the job.

federal funds. Colloquial term for deposits at a Federal Reserve Bank. Such funds are frequently lent overnight by a *member bank* with *excess bank reserves* to other member banks which are deficient in *required reserves.*

Federal Home Loan Banks. A system of 11 regional banks created in 1932 to provide credit for home financing carried on by its members which are principally savings and loan and building and loan associations.

Federal Home Loan Mortgage Corporation. An agency of the Federal Home Loan Banks packaging insured mortgages for buyers pursuant to commitment. Known colloquially as *Freddie Mac.* Cf. *Federal National Mortgage Association* (*Fannie Mae*) and *Government National Mortgage Association* (*Ginnie Mae*).

federal labor local union. An affiliated union of the *American Federation of Labor* consisting of workers in several trades in a given locality. Usually organized because the number in each trade is not sufficient for a separate union.

Federal Land Banks. A system of 12 farm loan banks created in 1916 and scattered over the United States, under the supervision of the Farm Credit Administration. Loans running from 5 to 40 years are made on farm land and buildings.

Federal National Mortgage Association. Chartered in 1938, reconstituted in 1954 as an independent federal agency and since converted to a privately owned corporation. Purchases and sells insured mortgages. Known colloquially as *Fannie Mae.* Cf. *Federal Home Loan Mortgage Corp.* (*Freddie Mac*) and *Government National Mortgage Association* (*Ginnie Mae*).

Federal Reserve Bank. See *Federal Reserve System.*

Federal Reserve Bank Note. A form of currency issued by the individual Federal Reserve Banks on the basis of dollar-for-dollar security of U.S. bonds issued for that purpose. In process of retirement since 1935.

Federal Reserve Note. A form of currency issued by the individual Federal Reserve Banks. These notes must be secured 25% by gold certificates. The balance of the security is commercial paper rediscounted by private banks and government bonds.

Federal Reserve Open Market Committee. Consists of the seven members of the Board of Governors of the Federal Reserve

System and of five representatives of the Federal Reserve Banks. The Committee has actual charge of the *open market operations* of all the Federal Reserve Banks.

Federal Reserve System. A system of twelve central banks created in 1913 and controlled by the Board of Governors of seven men in Washington. National banks must belong and state banks may. A member bank must invest 6% (of which only 3% or half has currently been called) of its own capital and surplus in the stock of its regional Federal Reserve Bank and must also keep a minimum reserve of 12% if a country bank, and 16.5% if a reserve city bank, of its demand deposits in the Reserve Bank or in vault cash and 4% of its time or savings deposits. The Board of Governors has the power to vary these percentages from a minimum of 7% for country banks and 10% for reserve city banks to a maximum of 14% and 22%, respectively. The twelve cities in which a Federal Reserve Bank is located are: (1) Boston, Mass., (2) New York, N.Y., (3) Philadelphia, Pa., (4) Cleveland, Ohio, (5) Richmond, Va., (6) Atlanta, Ga. (7) Chicago, Ill., (8) St. Louis, Mo., (9) Minneapolis, Minn., (10) Kansas City, Mo., (11) Dallas, Texas, (12) San Francisco, Cal. There are also 25 branch offices.

federal savings and loan associations. Under an act of 1933 several thousand of these associations have been formed and many building and loan associations with state charters have changed to federal charters. Each must belong to the Federal Home Loan Bank of its district. Their accounts are insured up to $10,000 each by the Federal Savings and Loan Insurance Corporation. See *Savings and Loan Insurance Corporation, Federal.*

Federal Savings and Loan Insurance Corporation. See *Savings and Loan Insurance Corporation, Federal.*

fee. (1) The payment to government for a service which confers a special benefit, or for a special cost imposed upon the government in performing a service for the common benefit. (2) The charges of professional people, e.g., physicians, attorneys, accountants, etc. (3) The full title or ownership of real estate.

feedback. The further refinement of a plan or computation by introducing into a revision of the plan or computation results from the original plan or computation, or introducing changes in the conditions assumed in the original plan or computation.

feedback system. See explanation under *cybernetics.*

fee simple. The full title or ownership of real estate with no limitation as to time.

felicific calculus. The argument that in economic analysis, the satisfaction or utility received by one person from one unit of a good is comparable to that received by another person.

felony. A crime which is usually defined by statute, often in terms of the maximum period of imprisonment that could be imposed. This dividing line in some states is a maximum sentence of one year. Crimes with a maximum over one year are then classed as felonies. A felony requires proof of criminal intent (mens rea), although this can be inferred from conduct. Cf. *misdemeanor.*

feoffment. In law, the conveyance by gift of the *fee simple* in land.

fee simple. The full and unconditional ownership of land.

fee tail. See *entail.*

fellow servant rule. A common law principle that where a fellow employee is negligent, an injured workman cannot recover from his employer. The principle has been negatived by *workmen's compensation laws.*

feudalism. The form of political organization which developed in Europe after the dissolution of the Roman Empire. Political organization was dependent on the personal relations of the lord of manor and his subjects. There was no strong central government, no absolute ownership of land, but complete stratification of society.

FHA Federal Housing Administration. Created in 1934 under the National Housing Act to encourage home building and home ownership by insuring loans made by private lending institutions.

fiat money. Paper money called "fiat" because its use as money depends upon the credit of the government issuing it and not upon any right to convert paper into metallic currency.

fiat standard. See fiat money. Cf. *monetary standard, types of.*

fidelity bond. An agreement by an insurer guaranteeing proper performance of his duties by a person in a position of trust and upon default in performance the insurer will pay losses to the insured up to the face of the bond.

fidelity insurance. See *fidelity bond.*

final equation. In *econometrics,* the algebraic elimination from each *reduced form equation* of the lagged values of all endogenous variables other than the one explained by the equation. Thus a final equation is essentially a *difference equation* in one endogenous variable expressing the current value of that variable as a function of a number of its lagged values and of parameters, exogenous variables and disturbances. Cf. *adjustment equation, behavioral equation, reduced form equation, restraint equation, and structural equation.*

fiduciary. One holding a position of trust or confidence as far as the law is concerned. Trustees, executors, administrators, corporate directors, etc. are fiduciaries although the standards applicable to each are not the same. The mere fact that somebody is trusted by somebody else, however, does not establish a fiduciary relation. The relation must be one fitting a recognized legal category.

fiduciary bond. A *surety bond* required of trustees and other fiduciaries in a court proceeding insuring against damages from failure to perform their duties.

fiduciary loan. An unsecured loan.

fiduciary money. Paper money which is convertible into gold or silver, but which is not fully backed by gold or silver, so that simultaneous conversion of all such money would be impossible. Hence "faith" or confidence is required. Distinguish *fiat money.*

fiduciary standard of money. See *fiduciary money.*

field warehouse. A warehouse established on the premises of a merchandiser or producer by a professional warehouseman through a lease of the premises in order to avoid unnecessary handling of goods.

field warehousing loan. A loan made on inventories held in field warehouses established on the premises of the borrower.

fieri facias. Latin for "You may cause it to be done." A writ of execution commanding an officer of the law to sell the property of a party to a law suit in order to satisfy a judgment.

fi. fa. Abbreviation for *fieri facias.*

FIFO. First in, first out method of inventory. See that term.

final equation. In *econometrics*, the algebraic elimination from each *reduced from equation* of the lagged values of all *endogenous variables* other than the one explained by the equation. Thus a final equation is essentially a *difference equation* in one *endogenous variable* expressing the current value of that variable as a function of a number of its lagged values and of parameters, exogenous variables and disturbances. Cf. *adjustment equation, behavioral equation, definitional equation, reduced form equation, restraint equation*, and *structural equation.*

final good. In national income accounting, a good produced and purchased or merely purchased by the ultimate consumer during the accounting period. Such goods enter the national product total. Goods purchased for resale (with or without further processing) are intermediate and do not enter the national product total.

finance bill. A bill of exchange drawn by a bank in one country on a bank in another country on securities held by the latter.

finance company. Any company (other than a bank) engaged in lending money usually against the security of goods.

financial break-even point. Assuming a plant organized for a given output, if units of output are put on one axis and total dollars on the other axis, the financial break-even point is the intersection of the total cash revenue curve and the total cash outlay curve, excluding interest and dividends.

financial budget. The plan for securing the deficit of cash from future operations or employing the excess of cash from future operations. Starting with the *cash budget,* the financial budget plans the borrowing or investing required by the cash budget balances.

financial indifference point. With debt at a given rate of interest, and the income tax rate constant, there is a level of earnings before interest and taxes at which the resulting earnings per common share will be the same regardless of the percentage of debt and equity. There is one such point for each combination of interest rate and income tax rate.

financial intermediaries. Financial institutions such as commercial banks, insurance companies, and mutual trust funds that act as an intermediary between lenders (and savers) and borrowers. In national income accounting the fact that services and costs are offset (such as no interest on a checking account but "free service" allowed) requires inputing values to such situations.

financial lease. Such a lease as provides for rental payments that cover the full repayment of original cost of the asset plus interest (with zero terminal value) and is noncancellable. Cf. *operating lease.*

financial leverage. See *leverage factor* (1).

financial paper. Accommodation paper, that is, a short-term loan not supported by a specific commercial transaction or transfer of goods. Cf. *commercial paper, commodity paper.*

financial plan. The financial plan of a corporation is the pattern of stocks and bonds issued at the time the corporation is

FINANCIAL BREAK-EVEN POINT

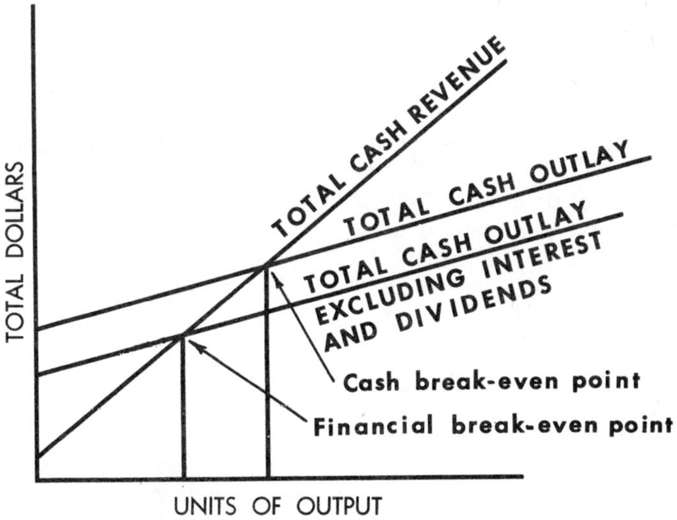

Figure 19.

organized, or after failure when it is reorganized.

financial responsibility law. In insurance, a *statute* requiring an automobile driver to present evidence of his ability to pay damages. It may be required as a condition for obtaining a license, or it may be required only after an accident as a condition for retaining a license pending the final determination of responsibility and payment of any judgment.

financial risk. In investments, used in contradistinction to *interest rate risk* and *purchasing power risk* to refer to the risk of default in performing the obligations of a security.

financial statement. Any report summarizing the financial condition or financial results of an organization on any date or for any period. The two principal types of financial statement are: (1) *balance sheet* and (2) *profit-and-loss statement*.

financial structure. All of the financial resources of a firm, short term and long term, debt and equity. Distinguish *capital structure* which includes only long-term resources.

fine or fineness. The degree of purity when speaking of gold or silver coin. United States coin was formerly nine-tenths fine or pure and one-tenth alloy.

finished goods turnover. Cost of goods sold during a period divided by the average finished goods inventory at cost of that period.

fink. A slang term for a worker engaged in *strike-breaking* or in reporting to the employer on union activities.

fire insurance. See *standard fire policy*.

firm. (1) A business entity under one ownership; it may have more than one establishment (plant or place of business). (2) In economics, that business engaged in producing one product or group of closely related products.

first in, first out method of inventory. Under the first in, first out rule (FIFO), items of inventory issued are priced out at the purchase price of the oldest batch in stock, then the purchase price of the next oldest batch, and so on. Inventory value is thus computed by assuming that goods on hand are those most recently purchased and are valued at the successively latest purchase prices. See *inventory valuation methods* for other types.

first order goods. Same as *consumption goods*.

first, second, or third mortgage. The words first, second, or third applied to a mortgage indicate the priority of the interest of the mortgagee in the property given as security for a debt. Mortgages are ranked in the time order in which they are made unless earlier mortgagees consent otherwise.

fiscal. (1) Pertaining to financial affairs. (2) More recently used in a special sense as opposed, for example, to "monetary." Then it refers to the "fisc," that is, the financial aspect of the government.

fiscal agent. One who takes over the care of certain financial affairs of a person, firm, or a government.

fiscal drag. The effect on *disposable personal income* caused by the more than proportionate increase in personal income taxes when personal income increases under a static schedule of *progressive* income tax rates. In the absence of a redistribution of personal incomes, individuals having an increase in personal income are taxed at higher rates on the increase in income. The same effect follows whether the increase is in *real income* or only *money income* (inflation).

fiscal monopoly. Monopolization by a government of the manufacture and sale of certain commodities in general use for the purpose of getting revenue for the treasury. Tobacco has been a prime favorite, being so used in Austria, France, Italy, Japan, Portugal, Rumania, Spain, and Sweden. Also matches, camphor, and salt are frequently used for this purpose.

fiscal period. Any period of time established for accounting purposes, usually a month, quarter-year or year. The particular characteristic is that the period can be geared to a date which does not coincide with the calendar, e.g., a fiscal year from March 14 to March 14, a fiscal month from May 21 to June 21.

fiscal policy. A term developed in the 1930's and referring to comprehensive governmental planning of budgets, so as to consider not only the individual merits of particular items of the budget but also the over-all effect of the budget on the economy and particularly the cyclical problem. The term fiscal policy is used particularly in contrast to *monetary policy,* with the former term emphasizing that activities directed at modifying the business cycle and reducing unemployment must be more comprehensive than the controls over the quantities of money and bank credit, which are emphasized as the prime tools of monetary policy. Cf. *monetary policy, compensatory finance,* and *functional finance.*

fiscal year. The particular twelve-month period used as a year for accounting purposes by a business or government. The twelve months need not begin with January.

Fisher equation. In monetary theory, the Fisher equation is $PT = MV$, where P is the general price level, T is the total volume of transactions, V is the transactions velocity of money and M is the quantity of money. Cf. *cash balance equation, income equation, income velocity of money.*

Fisher identity. Same as *Fisher equation.*

Fisher's index. Same as *ideal index.*

fishy-back. A marine service parallel to *piggyback* in which motor-truck trailers are handled on carferries.

five-twenty. A U.S. government bond redeemable after five years at the option of the U.S. and payable after twenty years. Cf. *ten-forty.*

fixed asset. Any property used in carrying on the operation of a business, which will not be consumed through use or converted into cash during the current fiscal period.

fixed asset turnover. See *plant turnover.*

fixed budget. A *budget* or estimate of receipts and expenditures which is not altered once it is established and does not recognize the effects of changes in the volume of sales or production or in product mix. Cf. *variable budget.*

fixed capital. (1) In economics, the capital invested in goods which can be used over and over again before wearing out, as buildings, machinery, and equipment. (2) In finance, the permanent amount of invested money in a business.

fixed charge coverage. The ratio of earnings before interest and taxes to fixed charges (total interest on all debt and any debt amortization commitments).

fixed charges. The expenses which have to be borne whether any business is done or not. The chief items are the company's interest on bonds, some taxes levied by the government, insurance payments, and depreciation due to obsolescence.

fixed cost. The cost of a business which goes on regardless of the amount of production. For example, depreciation of a building or insurance.

fixed credit line. Same as *irrevocable credit.*

fixed debt. Same as *funded debt.*

fixed exchange rate. In foreign exchange, an agreement between two or more countries that their governments will exchange each other's currency at a set rate of exchange. Cf. *floating exchange rate.*

fixed income. An income the amount of which has been fixed in advance by law, contract, or circumstances.

fixed interval reorder system. Reordering for inventory at fixed time intervals with the quantity of the reorder varying. Cf. *fixed order system.*

fixed investment trust. An investment trust which limits itself to purchasing from a fixed list of securities agreed upon at the commencement of its business. Ordinarily, the ratio in which new money will be invested in this fixed list is also fixed.

fixed obligation. An obligation which is fixed at the time the agreement is made and continues to run during the life of the agreement, e.g., interest on bonds except income or adjustment bonds.

fixed order system. Reordering for inventory in a fixed quantity but with variation in the time interval between orders. Cf. *fixed interval reorder system.*

fixed or long term liability. A liability which will not be paid in the normal operation of a business at an early date. All liabilities to be paid more than one year hence are usually called fixed.

fixed penalty bond. A *surety bond* in which the maximum the *surety* will have to pay for failure of the *principal* to perform is limited to the *face value* of the policy. Cf. *open covenant bond.*

fixed trust. A trust whose terms leave no room for the exercise of judgment by the trustee. Cf. *discretionary trust.*

fixture. In law, personal property which has been affixed to real estate but may be removed. The rule as to whether the property may be removed varies with the type of property and the relationship between the parties involved, which are used to establish an implied intention that may be altered by express agreement.

fixture rates. In public utilities, a specified sum for each fixture regardless of use.

flat. (1) In insurance, a flat policy is one without a coinsurance clause. (2) In insurance, cancelling flat is the termination of a renewal policy within 60 days after the anniversary date without charge to the insured or the agent. (3) In finance, stock is sold flat, that is, the price is not adjusted for any accrued dividends that may exist. (4) In finance, stock is loaned flat when the demand for borrowing it is great relative to the supply and lenders of the stock refuse to pay any interest on money advanced against the stock.

flat bond. A bond whose price includes accrued interest in the quoted price. Bonds in default and *income bonds* are usually quoted this way.

flat cancellation. In *insurance,* the cancellation of a policy as of its effective date without premium charge.

flat rate. In public utilities, a flat rate requires each customer to pay a fixed sum per period without regard to use. Also termed rental rate.

fleet policy. An automobile liability insurance policy covering a number of vehicles owned by the same insured.

flexible budget. A *budget* which provides estimates for varying levels of sales and hence estimates of cash requirements, profits, and financing needs for these several levels. Also called *variable budget.*

flexible exchange. Same as *floating exchange standard.*

flexible markup pricing. A pricing method which gears prices to changing economic conditions, such as the different stages of the business cycle. Cf. *cost-plus pricing.*

flexible tariff. A tariff permitting administrative officials to use discretion in altering tariff rates to deal with emergency conditions disturbing competitive conditions between countries, particularly where the conditions give rise to *dumping.*

flight of capital. A movement of capital from one country to another caused by fear on the part of the owners that something may happen to imperil its value or safety, such as inflation, confiscation, or war.

float. (1) In banking practice, checks and other items in process of collection. (2) In manufacturing, the amount of goods in process of production, usually measured in terms of number of units in process divided by number of finished units produced per average day, and expressed as, e.g., "six days float." (3) In finance, the unsold part of a security issue.

floater policy. In insurance, a policy covering property for all risks without regard to its location at the time of loss.

floating capital. That part of capital in *current assets* such as inventory and receivables.

floating debt. Any debt not yet funded, that is, not formally evidenced by a bond issue. Cf. *funding a debt.*

floating exchange. That monetary system under which the exchange rates between the currencies of several countries are permitted to move freely in response to demand and supply conditions for the currencies. Cf. *monetary standard, types of.*

floating exchange rate. In foreign exchange, the determination of the rate of exchange of one country's currency for that of another by market forces rather than at a *fixed exchange rate* agreed upon by the countries.

floor broker. The member of a stock exchange who transacts his firm's business on the floor of the exchange.

floor planning. Any method such as a *trust receipt* by which the borrower keeps possession of goods which are pledged as security for a loan.

floor stock. (1) That stock of inexpensive items maintained on the floor of a factory which can be used by workers without requisitions. (2) In merchandising, the amount of inventory maintained either solely for display or for immediate sale as opposed to drawing items from a warehouse or storage.

floor-trader. In finance, a member of a stock exchange who deals for his own account. Cf. *commission broker.*

flotation cost. The expenses of selling securities such as underwriting *spread*, legal and accounting fees and printing and engraving charges.

flow chart. A diagrammatic tool to show the movement (flow) of goods, money, or other items.

flow of funds statement. In *macroeconomics*, an accounting statement for a period showing source and application of funds for various sectors of the economy (such as households, business, and government) of various types of funds such as financial and savings.

fly-power. On the stock exchange, a written assignment on a separate sheet, but similar to the form used on the reverse of stock certificates and to be attached to such a certificate. When signed and attached, this assignment transfers the ownership of the certificate as if the endorsement were on the certificate.

f.o.b. Free on board. Used in price quotations to indicate that the sale price covers all charges, including delivery of goods free on board truck, car, or vessel at a designated point, either the origin or the destination of a shipment. Cf. *c.i.f.,* (cost, insurance, freight).

f.o.b. pricing. A system of prices in which the buyer pays the freight from the seller's premises. Cf. *delivered price, basing point system, mill base system,* and *zone pricing.*

forced choice ratings. Also called preference check list. In personnel management, a chart for rating personnel designed in such a way that the rater is offered specific descriptive phrases so arranged that their selection permits scoring but does not disclose their scoring effect. Intended to reduce the tendency to give average ratings.

forced distribution rating. In personnel management, a rating system requiring the rater to place, for example, 10% of the people in the lowest category, 20% in the next, 40% in the next, etc. This "normalizes" the distribution of ratings and avoids excessive use of an average rating.

forced loan. A loan that cannot be collected at maturity and is extended without much possibility of the lender's doing otherwise.

forced sale. A sale required to be made in a period of time shorter than that normally used. Usually brought about by an unsatisfied creditor.

forced savings. (1) In a general sense, the savings over which the individual has no control even though he has rights of ownership to them, such as corporate surpluses. (2) In monetary theory, individuals whose incomes in terms of money remain constant as (or do not rise so fast as) the price level rises are said to have been forced to save, that is, their consumption in real terms is reduced and what they cannot consume is saved from the point of view of economy.

forecasting. The estimation of future values of an economic variable or variables from known values of the same or another variable or variables on the assumption that a past known relationship of lag by the first variable continues to exist.

foreclosure. (1) The legal procedure which provides for the sale of mortgaged property when the mortgagor fails to pay the debt. The proceeds of the sale are then applied to the mortgage debt. Any excess of proceeds over the debt is refunded to the debtor; any deficiency is charged against the debtor in a *deficiency judgment* if that is asked for. (2) Strict foreclosure involves forfeiture of the mortgaged property upon default.

foreign. In law, belonging to another jurisdiction such as another state of the United States, not necessarily another country.

foreign bill. (1) In law, a draft drawn in one state but payable in another state. A bill payable in the same state in which it is drawn is a domestic bill. A bill payable outside the country is an external bill. (2) In economics, foreign bills are bills payable outside the country.

foreign car. In transportation, a car on the rails of a carrier other than its owner.

foreign corporation. (1) In law, a corporation is foreign in all states except the state in which it is chartered. (2) In business, a corporation chartered in a foreign country, more properly called an alien corporation.

foreign exchange. (1) Money or promises to pay money of one country in another country. (2) More broadly, the process by which balances resulting from transactions between countries are settled.

foreign exchange rate. The rate at which the money of one country can be exchanged for the money of another country; the price of a foreign currency in terms of the domestic currency.

foreign trade. Usually means trade between persons who are residents of different countries. May also be between the governments of countries.

foreign trade multiplier. Analogous to the *investment multiplier* is the foreign trade multiplier: the increase in money expenditure for the production of goods for export divided into the increase in the national income of the exporting country. The latter will eventually be considerably greater than the increase in exports of goods and imports of gold. This rests on the assumption of underemployment of productive resources in the exporting or importing country, or both.

foreign-trade zone. Same as *free port*.

foreman. A supervisor who has the power effectively to recommend hiring and firing of workers. Declared by Taft-Hartley Act amending the National Labor Relations Act as ineligible for union membership.

formula investing, types of. See the following specific terms:

constant dollar plan	*dollar averaging*
constant ratio plan	*variable ratio plan*

forward exchange. Also called foreign exchange futures. The purchase (or sale) at the present time of foreign exchange in order to meet a payment due at a future date in a foreign currency without being exposed to fluctuations from the present exchange rate.

forwarding. In an account extending over several pages, carrying the balance from one page to the top of the next page of an account as the first entry on the new page.

forwarding agent. (1) A service by trucking companies which pick up rail shipments for delivery to points not served by rails. (2) More generally, assembling less than carload freight and consolidating it into carload lots for shipment.

forward shifting tax. A tax which is included in the selling price by the taxpayer and thus shifted "forward" to the buyer.

founders' stock. Stock given promoters and management personnel at the time of incorporation for services rendered.

fourth section order. In transportation, an order of the Interstate Commerce Commission permitting carriers to charge higher rates for a shorter than for a longer haul over the same route, to avoid violation of Section Four of the Interstate Commerce Act. Cf. *long and short haul clause.*

FPC Federal Power Commission. An independent body of five commissioners appointed by the President with the consent of the Senate. The Commission operates under many federal statutes: Federal Power Act, TVA Act, Bonneville Act, Fort Peck Act, Flood Control Act, Natural Gas Act, and others. Its purpose is to regulate the development and use of power in interstate commerce, its rates, conservation, etc.

fractional money. Coins of smaller value such as the half-dollar, quarter, dime, and nickel in the United States; the shilling, penny, and half-penny in England.

franchise. (1) A right granted by a government to a corporation, firm, or individual to carry on a certain kind of business in a certain place. Public utilities, such as railroads and trolley companies, operate under franchises. (2) By analogy, a similar grant by a manufacturer to a distributor with respect to products.

franchise clause. In insurance, a clause providing that no part of a loss under a stated amount will be paid, but that all of the loss will be paid if the loss exceeds the stated amount. Distinguish *deductible coverage.*

franking. The privilege of free use of the mails granted to congressmen and agencies of the U.S. government.

F ratio. See *F value.*

fraud. Securing consent to a contract by misrepresentation made with knowledge or by tricks.

fraudulent conveyance. A transfer of property for the purpose of defeating or delaying creditors in their pursuit of payment. Such a transfer is void so far as the creditors are concerned.

Freddie Mac. Colloquial term for *Federal Home Loan Mortgage Corporation.*

free alongside ship. See *f.a.s.*

free coinage. The right to bring the standard metal (gold or silver) to the mint to be made into coins for a minting charge. Cf. *gratuitous coinage.*

free cycle. A business cycle whose limits are determined by endogenous variables and not by physical factors such as full employment of the factors of production. Cf. *constrained cycle.*

free enterprise. Same as *capitalism, laissez faire.*

free entry. The absence of restrictions preventing new firms from entering an industry or old firms from leaving it. A legitimate restriction is defined as protection of the public against its own ignorance or the fraud of those who wish to sell to it, and is not considered to bar free entry.

Freefloating Exchange. See *floating exchange.*

free gold. The amount of gold in the treasury in excess of gold needed to meet gold certificates and other indebtedness due in gold.

free goods. Those goods that nature furnishes freely and in such abundance that all demand for them is satisfied without work.

freehold estate. An estate in fee or for one's life is a freehold estate; a lease for years regardless how long its duration is not.

free list. In foreign trade, a list of goods not liable to payment of customs duties.

free port. An area, usually part of a port, set outside the customs area of the country, where foreign goods may be unloaded, stored, repacked, processed, and reloaded for shipment without entering customs.

free reserves. The unused lending power of *member banks* of the *Federal Reserve System.* Hence, *excess free reserves* less borrowing from the *Federal Reserve Banks* by the *member banks.*

free rider. One who subscribes for a block of new bonds when the offering is announced and then sells them at a profit before the date when full payment for the bonds is due. Similarly for stocks. The free rider is exposed to the risk that the price may fall and not advance before he sells. Now made illegal by *SEC* and the *New York Stock Exchange.*

free trade. The policy of having no controls over imports or exports thus letting the law of *comparative cost* operate freely.

free trade zone. See *free port.*

freight classification. The grouping of thousands of commodities into various classes for purposes of applying class rates.

freight equalization. Charging the buyer the freight charge he would pay from the nearest source of supply rather than the actual freight. Cf. *basing point system.*

freight density. The number of tons of freight carried one mile divided by the number of miles of road.

freight forwarder. A private agency which consolidates the small freight shipments of a number of shippers and takes advantage of carload rates. In return, the shipper gets faster service.

freight rate. See the following specific terms:

blanket rate
class rate
combination rate
combination through rate
commodity rate
group rate
joint rate
joint combination rate
joint through rate
released rate
zone freight rate

frequency curve. A curve on a graph with frequency count on the y axis and the magnitude on the x axis, connecting the plotted points of a frequency distribution.

frequency distribution. The classification of data to show the number of items having the same value. For example, 10 A's, 5 B's, 6 C's, etc.

frequency polygon. The area under a *frequency curve.*

frictional unemployment. Unemployment due to temporary want of balance between supply and demand for specialized labor, e.g., a sudden decrease in demand for a good may cause unemployment until the specialized labor force in that industry can shift to other jobs.

friendly fire. In fire insurance, a clause excluding liability for damage resulting from a fire which does not leave its proper place such as damage from a fire which never leaves a stove.

fringe benefit. In collective bargaining, fringe benefits include such employer-paid benefits to workers as *call-in-pay,* vaca-

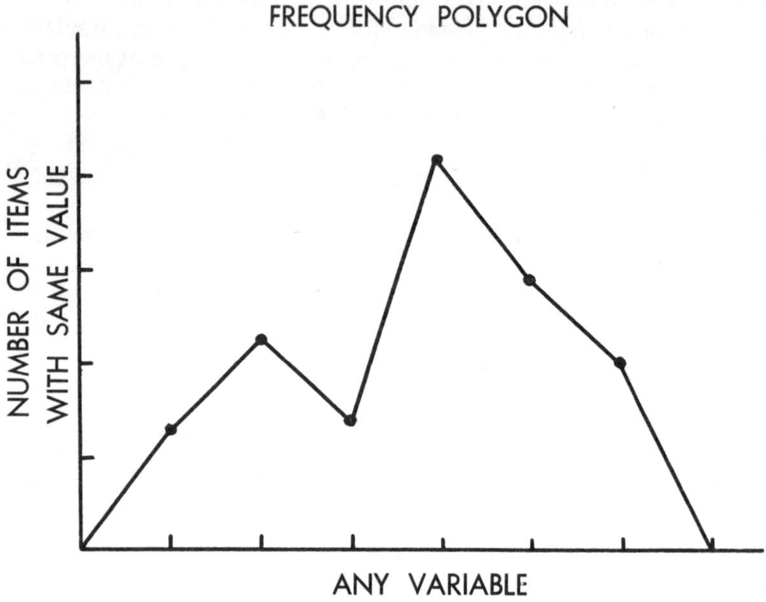

Figure 20.

tions, hospitalization and medical programs, life insurance, profit-sharing plans, welfare funds, etc.

fringe issues. Minor questions in a labor agreement. For example, shift premiums, etc.

front end load plan. Same as *contractual plan.*

frozen assets. Those assets of a business which are not readily salable, or which cannot be sold immediately without serious loss.

FSA Federal Security Agency. The agency established to handle the social security program including the administration of the Social Security Act itself, the Federal Unemployment Insurance Act, and similar functions.

FSLIC Federal Savings and Loan Insurance Corporation. See *Savings and Loan Insurance Corporation, Federal.*

FSRC Federal Surplus Relief Corporation. Established in October, 1933, to acquire surplus agricultural products.

FTC Federal Trade Commission. Consists of five members appointed by the President with the approval of the Senate, with its office in Washington, D.C. Its function is to prevent unfair trade practices and certain restraints of trade. Cf. *unfair methods of competition.*

full contribution mortgage clause. In fire insurance of mortgaged property, a clause providing that if there is more than one mortgage held on the same property, the insurer will first pay the first mortgage in full, then the second, etc. Cf. *noncontribution clause.*

full cost pricing. Also called average cost pricing. Pricing each good so that the price covers all direct costs, the allocable portion of overhead, and a profit. Cf. *marginal cost pricing.*

full coverage. In insurance, a provision that all the loss is covered and not merely that in excess of a minimum figure. Cf. *deductible coverage, divided coverage, franchise clause.*

full crew rule. A union practice requiring the employment of a minimum number of union men for a stated job.

full employment. In economic theory, the condition where all factors of production (not just labor) within an economy are being used in production so that factor prices are in equilibrium, and specifically as to labor, that all laborers who are willing to work at the going rate are employed (with some allowance for *frictional unemployment*). Thus full employment is reached where there are an equal number of job openings and laborers looking for that type of work.

full faith and credit bond. Same as *general obligation bond.*

full function wholesaler. A middleman who performs many services. Thus he takes title to the goods he deals in, stores an inventory, grants credit, undertakes promotion and performs other marketing functions.

full-line forcing. The practice of requiring a buyer, as a condition of the sale to him of one or more popular or highly desired items in a vendor's line of merchandise, to purchase less popular or less desired items in the line. Cf. *tying contract.*

full lot. Same as *round lot.*

full-paid stock. Same as *paid-up stock.*

full requirements contract. An agreement by a buyer to buy all of a product he needs in a given period from the named seller, but it may or may not involve a commitment to purchase anything.

full stock. A stock whose par is $100 per share. Cf. *half stock.*

fully diluted earnings. In accounting, the adjustment of current earnings per share to show the result if all options and conversion privileges of bonds and preferred stock were exercised.

functional costing. Classification of costs for allocation to various operations such as storing, delivery, billing, etc.

functional discount. Same as *trade discount.*

functional finance. The analysis of financial matters for purposes other than the usual problems of balancing budgets. E.g., for the effects upon *national income*.

functional middleman or agent. A middleman who negotiates purchases or sales but does not take title to the goods in which he deals, and who commonly receives remuneration in the form of a commission or fee. Cf. *merchant middleman*.

fund. (1) In general, a sum of money, bonds or similar assets set aside for a particular person or use. (2) In governmental accounting, a sum of money or other resources set aside for the purpose of carrying on specific activities according to statutes or regulations. Each fund is treated as though it were a separate business entity. Distinguish *appropriation*.

fund, types of. See the following specific terms:

bond fund
general fund
imprest fund
revolving fund
sinking fund
special assessment fund
trust and agency fund
utility fund
working capital fund

funded debt. The indebtedness of a business or government which has been formally evidenced as in a bond issue. Usually the line is drawn at debt due more than one year hence.

funded pension plan. A pension plan providing for accumulation of the funds needed for pensions so that upon the individual's retirement the full fund will be on hand. This may be achieved by the purchase of annuity contracts or by the deposit of funds with a trustee. Cf. *group annuity* and *qualified pension plan*.

funded reserve. A *reserve* invested in earmarked interest-bearing securities.

funding. (1) The process of converting accounts payable or other short-term debt into fixed obligations with a maturity date and ordinarily represented by formal documents such as bonds.

fungible goods. Goods which are standardized, one unit like the other. Fungible goods owned by one person can be mixed with similar goods owned by another person without affecting legal rights. Cf. *accession*.

futures. Contracts whose fulfillment by actual delivery of goods is not required until a specified time in the future. Most of the dealings on commodity exchanges, especially in wheat, corn, cotton, and coffee, are in futures, that is, in contracts calling for "future delivery." The system requires that products be standardized. Cf. *spot trading*.

F value. The distribution of the *variance* of *random samples* from a *normal* population is neither symmetrical nor normal but skewed to the right or j-shaped when the *degree of freedom* are 3 or more and reverse j-shaped for degrees of freedom of 1 and 2. The shape of the distribution curve depends on the variance and on the degrees of freedom. In application, the ratio (*F*) of the variances of two independent samples follows the *F* distribution. By comparing this ratio with a table of critical values of *F* for given degrees of freedom and levels of probability, it can be estimated whether the two samples come from the same universe. In *correlation analysis,* the *F* value is the sum of the squares due to the regression divided by the sum of the squares due to the deviation about the regression when each such square has been divided by the degrees of freedom.

gain from trade. The total increase in output of two or more countries gained by specialization of each country in producing the goods where it has the *comparative advantage.* From this gross gain are deducted the added costs of trading such as transportation.

gambler's ruin. Same as *probability of ruin.*

game theory. As applied to economics and business, the analysis of strategies by analogy to games such as poker.

Gantt chart. A device developed by H. L. Gantt, an American engineer, to present production data in graphic form, e.g., planned vs. actual production, or individual employee performance against a standard.

Gantt premium plan. An incentive wage plan under which the employee receives a minimum wage for all work up to the standard output and thereafter a piece rate on additional output determined as the standard piece rate plus a 20 to 50% premium on such rate. Cf. *Bedaux, Emerson, Halsey, Merrick, Rowan* and *Taylor plans.*

GAO General Accounting Office. An agency established by Congress in 1921 to supervise and coordinate the accounting for government expenditures.

gap sheet. In personnel management, a summary statement of what an individual has achieved in various skills at the executive level and what skills remain to be developed by him. Used in promotion questions.

garnishee. A person who holds money or property belonging to another which has been attached for debt. In a garnishment proceeding, the garnishee is always a third party to an action by a creditor against a debtor.

garnishment. Subjection to court order at the demand of a creditor (first party) of a debt owed by a third party to the debtor (second party) who is being sued by his creditor.

GATT General Agreement on Tariffs and Trade. At a Geneva conference in 1947, twenty-three countries entered a multilateral agreement designed to increase international trade by the reduction or elimination of duties and quotas.

Gaussian curve. A type of normal curve developed by Gauss for the probable distribution of large numbers and generally referred to as "the" *normal curve.*

general agent. An agent who can act as fully as his principal.

general average. In *marine insurance,* a provision that the loss to any cargo from navigation risks will be borne proportionately to value by all the cargo. Cf. *particular average.*

general depository. A member bank of the Federal Reserve System authorized to handle deposits of the U.S. Treasury.

general equilibrium (under monopoly or monopolistic competition). The situation where there is no reason for firms to enter or leave any industry, to expand or to contract. Thus there can be general equilibrium under monopoly but not in the strict sense under monopolistic competition, because attempts at product differentiation could be made at any time, although the situation can become relatively stable. Cf. *dynamic equilibrium, equilibrium of firm or industry (partial) long run, expectational equilibrium, general equilibrium, (under pure competition), intermediate equilibrium, market equilibrium, momentary equilibrium, neutral equilibrium, normal equilibrium, partial equilibrium, stable equilibrium, static equilibrium,* and *unstable equilibrium.*

general equilibrium (under pure competition). Various definitions exist, e.g., (1) the situation where all expectations will be fulfilled, (2) the situation where the only disturbing factor would be innovation, absence of which is postulated, (3) a static state where all prices are at their long run equilibrium, individuals are spending their incomes to yield maximum satisfaction, and the demand and supply for factors of production are equated, and (4) other definitions. Cf. *dynamic equilibrium, equilibrium of firm or industry (partial) long run, equilibrium of firm or industry (partial) short run, exceptional equilibrium, general equilibrium (under monopoly or monopolistic competition), intermediate equilibrium, market equilibrium, momentary equilibrium, neutral equilibrium,* *normal equilibrium, partial equilibrium, stable equilibrium, static equilibrium,* and *unstable equilibrium.*

general equilibrium theory. A theoretical framework of the entire economy recognizing the interrelation of price and output for both commodities produced and the factors of production. This is done by a system of equations each showing the dependency or relationship of a change in one item to the others. There are three sets of equations: (1) relating quantities of commodities demanded to their prices and the prices of factors (including an equation for money as such), (2) relating the prices of all commodities to their costs of production, and (3) relating the supplies of factors available to the total used for production of commodities. Solution of the equations gives a determinate value to each variable.

general fund. In governmental accounting, the fund used to account for revenues and expenditures not allocated to specific purposes by law or contractual agreement.

general indorsement. Same as *blank indorsement.*

general ledger. A ledger which contains all those accounts appearing in the trial balance.

general legacy. A gift by will to be paid out of the general assets of an estate and not from a particular source. Cf. *demonstrative legacy, lapsed legacy, residuary legacy,* and *specific legacy.*

general management trust. An investment trust that is not limited to a fixed list of securities from which to select its purchases but has discretion in the purchase of securities. Cf. *fixed investment trust.*

general merchandise store. A *retail store* handling many lines of goods. Includes both *department stores* and *variety stores.*

general mortgage bond. A bond secured by a general mortgage on the borrower's property, but it may be outranked as to individual assets by other bonds secured by prior mortgages.

general obligation bond. In municipal finance, a bond secured by a pledge of the issuing governmental unit's full faith, credit, and taxing power.

general operating expenses. In transportation, those expenses that do not vary greatly with the amount of business done, e.g., road-bed maintenance. Considered as different from fixed charges which continue whether any business is done or not, e.g., interest on debt. Cf. *particular operating expense.*

general price level. See *price level, general.*

general property tax. A tax on wealth and property rights regardless of their nature, but exceptions of types of property are frequently made. An important tax in the United States for local and state revenue.

general sales tax. A tax levied on all articles as they are sold at retail, but exceptions of certain commodities such as food are frequently made. Over half of the 50 states have such a tax. Cf. *turnover tax.*

general strike. The cessation of work in all industries everywhere in a country. Usually regarded as a revolution against public authority.

general tax bond. Same as *general obligation bond.*

general verdict. In law, a verdict which finds simply for one of the parties. Cf. *special verdict.*

geometric mean. This value is obtained by adding the logarithms of all the values of the items in a series, then dividing this total by the number of items and taking the antilog of this quotient. Or the values may be multiplied successively by each other and the *n*th root extracted of this product where *n* is the number of items. Cf. *arithmetic, harmonic* and *quadratic mean.*

geometric progression. A succession of terms which increases or decreases by multiplication of the preceding term by a constant factor, e.g., 2, 4, 8, 16, 32, or 32, 16, 8, 4, 2 but cannot go below zero. Cf. *arithmetic progression.*

Gibrat's distribution. A statement by a French economist in 1931 explaining the size distribution of firms. Specifically, the statement is that the distribution of percentage changes in size of the firms in a given size class is the same for all size classes above a minimum size class. Cf. *log-normal distribution, normal distribution, Pareto distribution, Poisson distribution, t distribution, Yule distribution.*

Gibrat's law of proportionate effect. Same as *Gibrat's distribution.*

Giffin effect. The situation noted by Sir R. Giffin that a rise in the price of all goods will, in the case of the poor whose incomes do not increase, cause an increase in the quantity of staple items of food consumed despite the increase in their price in order to make the income cover the needs.

gift causa mortis. A gift made in anticipation of death. The gift is contingent upon death following the sickness during which it is made, else it is revocable.

gift certificate. A retail merchandising device used by the certificate purchaser to give the recipient a free choice of goods to the dollar amount of the certificate.

gift inter vivos. A gift made between living parties, requiring a donative intention and some outward manifestation of that intention.

gift tax. A tax on the transfer of property by gift. Under federal law the tax is levied against the donor, under state laws against the donee. The tax is primarily a supplement to inheritance taxation to prevent easy evasion of death taxes.

Gini coefficient. A measure of the degree of inequality in the distribution of two variables arranged cumulatively in a *Lorenz curve,* e.g., percentage of population and percentage of income. The coefficient is the ratio of (a) the area between the Lorenz curve and the line of perfectly equal distribution (45° line) to (b) the area under the line of perfectly equal distribution. This ratio measures the departure of the Lorenz curve from complete equality, expressed as a ratio to complete inequality (which would be represented by the full right-angle triangle under the diagonal). Cf. *Pareto's measure of inequality.*

Ginnie Mae. Colloquial term for *Government National Mortgage Association.*

give-out order. In securities and commodities, an order to a *broker* given out by him to a specialist for execution.

GNP. Abbreviation for *gross national product.*

going public. A colloquial term describing the first offering of the stock of a company for purchase by the general public.

going value or going concern value. (1) The "value" which an enterprise has as a unit as opposed to the total "values" of each of its parts taken separately. (2) In the same sense as good will, the capitalization of above average earning power of a firm by dividing the annual earnings of a firm by the average earning rate of the industry in which the firm is. (3) In public utilities, (a) the actual cash outlays for intangibles such as promotional expenditures which under conservative accounting practice do not appear as a balance sheet asset, plus (b) any operating losses or sub-par earnings in the early days of the business before normal volume is established. Computed for inclusion in the *rate base.*

gold bonds. Bonds whose principal and interest are specifically payable in gold coin of a certain weight and fineness. This provision in American bonds was nullified by Congress in 1933.

gold bullion standard. That monetary system under which paper money is the sole legal tender, and the national stock of gold is not coined but used as a reserve and for payments to foreign countries. Cf. *monetary standard, types of.*

gold certificate. A note secured 100% by gold. Before 1934 these certificates circulated as money, but since 1934 they are held only by the Federal Reserve System which buys them from the Treasury.

gold clause. The provision in contracts calling for payment in a stipulated quantity of gold or a stipulated number of dollars at the option of the party to be paid. Not binding in the United States since 1933. Cf. *gold bonds.*

gold currency system. A monetary system where currency and gold can be freely converted one into the other at established rates.

gold exchange standard. A monetary system that came into prominence after World War I. Instead of convertibility between gold and currency (the gold standard), countries on the gold exchange standard are willing to buy or sell the currency of some gold standard country at a fixed price. Cf. *monetary standard, types of.*

gold exporting point. The rate of exchange at which the importer of goods can at the same cost buy gold and export it in payment of his imports. Before 1931 the gold exporting point between the U.S. and England was about $4.88 or two cents (the cost of shipping $4.86 worth of gold) above the par of gold exchange ($4.86).

gold importing point. The rate of exchange at which the exporter can at the same cost arrange to have gold sent to him in payment of his goods. Before 1931, the gold importing point between the U.S. and England was about $4.84 or two cents (the cost of shipping $4.86 worth of gold) below the par of gold exchange ($4.86).

gold settlement fund. The fund of gold certificates deposited by the 12 Federal Reserve Banks with the Interdistrict Fund of the Federal Reserve System and used for clearance of debits and credits of each Reserve Bank against the other 11 banks in order to save transportation of money between the banks.

gold standard. That monetary system under which money is convertible into gold at a specified rate and vice versa and free shipment of gold internationally is permitted. Cf. *monetary* *standard, types of.*

Gompertz curve. An exponential curve; a series in which the increments of the logarithms for each successive item are declining by a constant percentage. Many series of data in insurance conform to this curve. Likewise new industries and new products are thought to follow this curve.

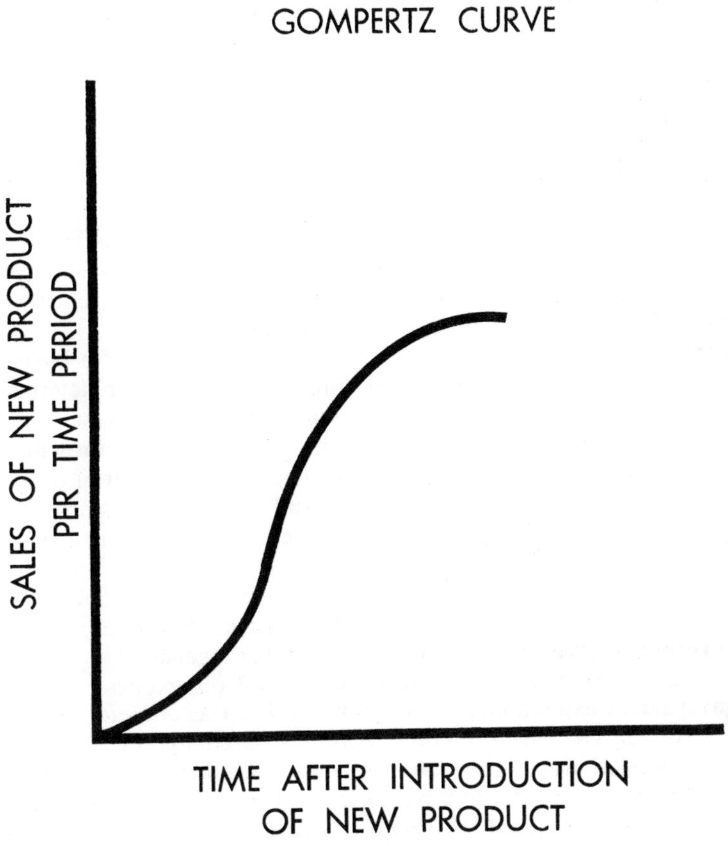

Figure 21.

good. (1) Any material thing that is capable of satisfying a human want as distinguished from a service. (2) In economics, no distinction is made between a physical good and a service—both are goods.

goods, types of. See the following specific terms:

capital goods
complementary goods
consumption or consumer goods
convenience goods
durable goods
economic goods
fashion goods
first order goods
free goods
fungible goods
hard goods
higher order goods
impulse goods
inferior goods
intermediate goods
joint cost goods
joint demand goods
lower order goods
point of purchase goods
prestige goods
producers' goods
semi-durable goods
shopping goods
soft goods
specialty goods
standard goods
substitutional goods

good and marketable title. A complete and unbroken record showing the transfer of all rights in property by each prior owner to the next successor and so on to the present owner.

goods in process. Same as *work in process.*

good will. A value in excess of the tangible assets of a business, brought about by superior future earning power determined by the capitalization at an assumed rate of interest of those earnings which are in excess of the "normal" return in that industry for a similar business. The actual amount of the good will is negotiated by the buyer and seller of a business.

goon. A slang term for a person hired to terrorize management or workers.

government bond. A colloquial term designating bonds of the United States government and not including *municipal bonds.*

government depository. A bank or other agency designated by a government to receive its taxes and other dues.

government expenditures multiplier. In *macroeconomics*, the ratio of the change in *national income* to a change in government expenditures. The value of this multiplier depends on the particular model and *parameters* of the economy assumed.

Government National Mortgage Association. A federal agency packaging insured mortgages for buyers pursuant to commitments. Known colloquially as *Ginnie Mae.* Cf. *Federal National Mortgage Association* (*Fannie Mae*) and *Federal Home Loan Mortgage Corporation* (*Freddie Mac*).

government sector. See *sector accounts.*

GPO Government Printing Office. The GPO was created by Congress in 1860. Its purpose is to execute orders for printing and binding placed by Congress and the departments, independent establishments, and agencies of the federal government.

grace period. (1) The period (usually 30 days) after the due date of a premium during which the insurance company will accept payment without penalty. (2) Occasionally used in a more general sense to describe any period beyond due date granted to a debtor by a creditor.

grade. A unit of measurement covering a fixed number of degrees of each of a list of selected characteristics, and occupying a fixed position in a scale.

graded premium life insurance. A life insurance policy providing that the premiums will increase each year for a period and then level. It is intended for people who expect to increase their earnings through the graded period.

graded tax. A form of real property tax with rates higher on unimproved land than on improvements of land so as to encourage improvement. Cf. *graduated tax.*

grade labeling. The practice of indicating the quality of a product (e.g., canned fruits or vegetables) on the label of the package by means of a letter (as A, B, C, grades) or numeral. The grade is determined by measuring various characteristics of the commodity against unvarying standards, and weighting these measurements according to some standard plan in order to establish the final (or composite) grade. Cf. *descriptive labeling.*

grade standard. The center or middle point from which the scope of a grade is measured.

grading. Classifying commodities according to agreed-upon standards of quality, size, etc. Commonly done in grains, etc.

graduated tax. A tax such that the rate increases as the amount of property or income of the taxpayer increases.

graduation. The term applied to the process of "smoothing" raw data, that is, adjusting actual data to establish a table which follows a mathematical formula. Curve fitting is one of the methods of graduation.

grain pit. One of the circular platforms on the floor of an exchange, e.g., the Chicago Board of Trade, where brokers meet to buy and sell a specific grain, e.g., wheat or corn.

grandfather clause. (1) In general, a provision in new regulations exempting existing business from the new requirements. (2) In the Public Utility Holding Company Act, the prohibition of more than three tiers of utility corporations, i.e., the limit is one *holding company* with stock of another *holding company*. Cf. *death sentence*.

granger movement. A movement in the farming states of the upper Mississippi valley in the late 19th century against monopolistic control of railroads and warehouses, calling for legislative control of such services and later spreading to other types of businesses, particularly public utilities.

granter. See *grantor*.

grantor. The person who makes a grant or transfer of property. The person receiving the grant is the grantee.

grants-in-aid. The usual method is for the federal government to offer to put up the bulk of the costs of a venture if the state or other recipient will put up part of the cost and administer the program according to federal rules. To a lesser extent the states now act similarly with respect to small units of government.

graph. A system of coordinates for plotting data. Cf. *chart*.

gratuitous coinage. A system under which there is no charge for making coins. Cf. *free coinage*.

graveyard shift. The usual term for the eight-hour shift beginning at midnight. Cf. *swing shift*.

gray market. A generic term describing transactions made for immediate delivery at a premium over usual prices because of a suddent or unexpected shortage of a commodity. Distinguish from such transactions made in violation of a law, in which case the term used is *black market*.

greenbacks. Paper money first issued during the Civil War on the general credit of the Federal government and not convertible into a precious metal. Because they had green ink on one side they came to be called "greenbacks." This does not serve to identify them any longer since other forms of paper money are also printed in green.

Gresham's law. Bad money drives out good. When two kinds of money circulate in a country, the money which the mint overvalues (through the *mint ratio*) tends to drive the undervalued money out of circulation. The undervalued money is hoarded, melted down, or exported, and thus disappears from circulation to the extent that the overvalued (or cheaper) is put into circulation.

grievance procedure. In a labor agreement, the grievance procedure includes the various steps specified by the contract to be taken in an effort to settle disputes between the employer and the union or its members about matters which the contract recognizes as subject to the procedure.

gross. One dozen dozen. Hence 144 units.

gross debt. The total debt of an obligor which is legally outstanding. Cf. *net debt.*

gross income (individual). In income taxation, the gains from the disposition of assets, profits, personal compensation, rents, interest, and dividends before allowances or deductions. Cf. *net income (individual).*

gross income margin. The ratio of (1) the difference between *net sales* and *cost of goods sold to* (2) net sales.

gross interest. The net interest plus charges added to cover risk and administrative costs. Gross interest is the interest payment made by the borrower.

gross lease. A lease under which the lessor agrees to pay rent and all the charges that an owner would usually pay, such as taxes and insurance.

gross margin. In accounting, net sales less net cost of sales, otherwise described as gross profit on sales. Gross margin is the typical term used in merchandising; *gross profit* is the typical term in manufacturing. Cf. *maintained mark-up.*

gross national debt. The total outstanding debt of the central or national government regardless of any duplications or overlapping.

gross national product. The money value of the total output of goods and services within a country in a given period of time, usually a year, before allowance for depreciation and consumption of capital goods. Cf. *net national product, national income.*

gross net premiums. In insurance, gross premiums less returned premiums but before any premiums paid by the *insurer* for *reinsurance.*

gross plant turnover. *Net sales* divided by gross plant, i.e., undepreciated plant.

gross profit. In accounting, the total allocable receipts of a period's operations less the cost of the goods sold, before allowance for operating expenses and income taxes.

gross profit margin. Same as *gross profit ratio.*

gross profit on sales. Same as *gross margin.*

gross profit ratio. The ratio to sales of the difference between sales and the *cost of merchandise sold.*

gross profits test. In auditing, a method of verifying the book valuation of a closing inventory. Having determined the gross profit (sales less cost of sales) of a previous period, the auditor takes the sales of the current period and applies the gross profit percentage of the previous period to obtain a theoretical cost of sales. Then taking the opening inventory, adding purchases during the current period, and deducting this theoretical cost of sales should yield a figure approximating the closing inventory shown on the books. This method is also used in settling fire losses where no inventory records exist or survive.

gross receipts tax. A tax based on total receipts (sales) rather than on profits. E.g., a sales tax with no exemptions.

gross regression coefficient. See *regression coefficient.*

gross sales. The total of all sales before deducting returned sales. Cf. *net sales.*

gross spread. In finance, the difference between the price paid by an investment banker for an issue and the price paid by the buying public.

gross tonnage (vessel). With reference to vessels and not cargo, gross tonnage is the cubic feet of closed-in space of the vessel divided by 100, on the assumption that 100 cubic feet is equal to one ton. Cf. *deadweight tonnage (vessel), net tonnage (vessel), registered tonnage (vessel).*

gross up. Colloquial term in taxation of U.S. international businesses under which U.S. corporations must "gross up" any income from foreign subsidiaries, that is, include pre-foreign tax income in U.S. income tax returns in order to claim credit against U.S. income taxes for foreign income taxes paid.

gross working capital. Same as *current assets.*

ground rent. The rent or periodic charge payable for the use of land as distinct from the rent payable for use of buildings. More specifically, a system of selling land by long-term leases with the original owner retaining the title to the land after the expiration of the lease.

group annuity. A pension plan providing annuities upon retirement for individual employees under a master contract. The usual type provides for the purchase each year of a paid-up *deferred annuity* for each employee. Cf. *funded pension plan* and *qualified pension plan.*

group banking. Same as *chain banking.*

group bonus. *Piecework* wages paid not on the basis of individual production but on the basis of the production of an entire group of employees who share proportionately.

group creditor insurance. Insurance issued to a creditor (such as a bank) covering the lives of many debtors for the purpose of minimizing the problem of collection from the estate of a deceased debtor.

group insurance. Insurance of a group of individuals (usually employees or others having a common characteristic). Ordinarily the insurance is in smaller amounts and at lower rates because of lower overhead costs to the insurer.

group rate. Same as *blanket rate.*

growth. See *economic growth.*

growth curve. See *Gompertz curve* and *logarithmic curve.*

growth stock. The stock of a corporation with prospects for future expansion at a rate above the average of other companies.

GTC order. Good until cancelled order. On the stock market, a customer's order to his broker to buy or sell a security at a set price, the order to remain in effect until executed or cancelled.

guarantee. The undertaking to answer for the debt or obligation of another if he does not perform. Not to be confused with a suretyship in which the principal and the surety are each directly liable to perform. Indemnity is a broader word than guarantee but essentially the same. This deviates from the popular use of "guarantee" in which a person assures his own performance.

guaranteed annual wage. A system under which employees are assured of regular income for twelve months of the year. Under the *Fair Labor Standards Act* employers using this system can have employees work 2,000 hours per year without overtime and up to 12 hours per day or 56 hours per week without overtime.

guaranteed bonds. Usually arise when one corporation leases some property of another one and guarantees the principal or interest, or both, of the bonds of the corporation whose property is leased.

guaranteed mortgage. A mortgage whose principal and/or interest payment is guaranteed by a guarantor. Today most guarantees are by the Federal Housing Administration or the Veterans Administration, but some guarantees are by a mortgage guarantee corporation.

guaranteed mortgage certificate. A participation certificate representing a share or part of a large guaranteed mortgage being resold in smaller units.

guaranteed stock. Stock whose dividends are guaranteed by a corporation other than the corporation which issued the stock.

guaranty bond. A combined *fidelity bond* and *surety bond.*

guaranty insurance. The English term for *fidelity insurance.*

guaranty of title. Protection provided by some insurance companies to pay for the loss due to invalidity of real estate titles. By means of such a policy bought for a moderate fee, a person who buys a piece of real estate or lends money on a mortgage can obtain a guarantee against loss through any defect in the title. The insurance is of an indemnity nature and therefore not transferable. Cf. *Torrens system.*

guaranty stock. Stock representing ownership in a type of *savings and loan association* permitted in some states, notably California and Ohio. In this situation the usual stock of savers has priority over the guaranty stock. In turn, the guaranty stock receives all residual earnings after the dividend on the usual savers' stock has been paid.

guaranty stock savings and loan associations. In some states, notably California and Ohio, the laws permit *savings and loan associations* to be organized on a nonmutual basis so that the holders of the "guaranty stock" are junior in priority to the savings accounts and receive the residual earnings. In such associations savings accounts may be liabilities and not constitute ownership.

guardian or guardian ad litem. A guardian is a person designated by the court to administer the affairs of a person declared to be legally incompetent. A guardian ad litem is a person designated by the court to handle the affairs of the incompetent in a particular legal proceeding. The guardianship of the person and of the person's property may be placed in separate people.

guild economy. Refers particularly to the economic organization which prevailed in the time of the Middle Ages. The economy was organized by groups, each representing the association of all (employers and employees) working in a particular trade or craft.

guild socialism. A system of socialism advocated in England after World War I, involving the organization of the economy into modern "guilds" (industries) with minimum government interference.

Haavelmo principle. In *econometrics,* the statistical method used must be derived from a model that specifies the relations among the jointly dependent variables.

habeas corpus. A legal action hailing someone (usually a government official) into court on the ground that he is holding or attempting to hold a person illegally. A complaint is made by the person held or one of his friends stating the facts and the court issues an order (writ of habeas corpus) commanding the person charged to produce the body of the person held at a stated time and place for decision by the court of the legality of continuing to hold the person.

habendum clause. The clause in a real estate document which specifies the extent of the interest in the land conveyed such as for life or in *fee.*

half stock. A stock whose par is $50 per share. Cf. *full stock.*

Halsey premium plan. An incentive wage plan under which the employee receives a minimum wage for all work up to the standard output and thereafter compensation for additional output at 30 to 50% of the time wage rate for time saved. Cf. *Bedaux, Emerson, Gantt, Merrick, Rowan* and *Taylor plans.*

handicraft system. That stage in the economic development of industry when skilled artisans carried on industries, fashioning their products by hand without the aid of complicated machinery. Cf. *household system, domestic system, factory system.*

hand-to-mouth buying. The practice of buying in the smallest possible quantities and only as immediately necessary, thus holding inventories at a minimum level.

hard goods. Durable consumers' goods. Cf. *soft goods.*

hard money. (1) Metallic money as opposed to paper money, the latter being called soft money. (2) Sometimes, money with stability in purchasing power or international exchange.

harmonic mean. This value is obtained by adding the reciprocals of all the values of the items in a series, then dividing this total by the number of items and taking the reciprocal of this quotient. Cf. *arithmetic, geometric* and *quadratic mean.*

harmonic series. A series such that the reciprocal of each term forms an arithmetic series. For example, ½, ⅓, ¼, etc.

Harrod-Domar model. The Domar equation is:

$$r = \frac{\Delta I}{I} = \alpha\sigma$$

where r is the natural (full employment) rate of growth, α is the fraction of income saved, I is investment and σ is the potential increase of output per unit of new investment. The Harrod equation is:

$$G_w = \left(\frac{\Delta Y}{Y}\right)_w = \frac{s}{c}$$

where G_w is the warranted rate of growth, Y is income, c is the number of units of new investment needed to produce an extra unit of output and s is the fraction of income saved. The subscript w indicates that the equation defines the conditions for the rate of growth which keeps savings and investment equal.

Hawkinson-Simon conditions. In *input-output analysis,* the proposition that a negative requirement for a resource may result (no solution would exist in the positive X and positive Y quadrant) unless the slopes of the production equations bear the proper relationship to each other.

Hawley-Smoot Tariff Act. The U.S. tariff law of 1930, raising tariff rates on more than 1,000 commodities but permitting variation of rates within a 50% limit by the President on the advice of the U.S. Tariff Commission.

head. The difference between the height of water behind a dam and that below the dam.

headright. The grant of 50 acres of land "per head" by certain southern colonies to 17th century immigrants.

head tax. A tax of a flat amount per person.

hearsay. In law, testimony of one person as to the statement of another, not to prove what the other said but to prove the truth of the fact asserted by the other.

heavy market. In securities and commodities, a market in which prices are falling.

hedge clause. (1) Before 1933, brokers, banks, promoters, and underwriters who were selling issues of stocks or bonds, many of which belonged to the "cats and dogs" class, would escape prosecution for damages or fraud by merely putting in tiny print at the foot of the abbreviated promotional circular or at some other inconspicuous place the following statement, known as the "hedge clause": "The statements in this circular have been obtained from sources which we regard as reliable, and while we do not guarantee them, we believe them to be accurate." Such a hedge is no longer a legal protection.' (2) Currently, a clause permitting underwriters to terminate the underwriting contract under stated conditions.

hedging. Any method of minimizing the risks of possible changes in prices. Grain producers and storers of grain may hedge their holdings of the commodity by selling for future delivery such quantities of cash or spot grain as they may buy or hold. Since the movement, up or down, of cash (spot) prices is usually in the same direction and about in the same degree as the movement of the present prices of contracts for future delivery, any loss (or gain) resulting from carrying the actual merchandise is usually approximately offset by a corresponding gain (or loss) when the futures contract is liquidated.

hedonism. The principle that individuals are motivated by a desire to maximize benefits, e.g., through less work, greater quantity of physical goods, etc.

heir. (1) Any person who succeeds to or acquires the estate of a deceased person by right of blood and by operation of law in the absence of a will. (2) Generally speaking the term "heir" is applied to all who receive property from a deceased person's estate.

Hepburn Act. The 1906 act of Congress permitting the Interstate Commerce Commission to announce rate changes and make them effective within 30 days until suspended by a court. The act also expanded the jurisdiction of the Commission to cover pipelines and sleeping cars.

hereditaments. Things capable of being inherited.

heuristic. Proceeding to the discovery of the solution of a problem not by step by step, final, and strict proof but by the use of a series of plausible, proposed solutions whose testing determines in which direction to proceed for the next proposed solution likely to approximate the final solution more closely than the proposed solution just tested.

hidden asset. An asset carried on the books at substantially less than its fair market value. The hidden asset thus is the difference between the book value and the market value.

hidden inflation. A deterioration in the quality of goods deliberately done to hide a price increase.

hidden reserve. By undervaluing assets or overvaluing liabilities, a hidden reserve is created, i.e., the surplus amount thus created is not apparent from an examination of a financial statement.

hidden tax. An indirect tax which is incorporated in the price of goods and services.

higgling. "Dickering" back and forth by buyer and seller in an effort to arrive at a mutually satisfactory price or contract.

higher order goods. Same as *intermediate goods.*

high finance. A colloquial term for large scale, complicated, or speculative financing.

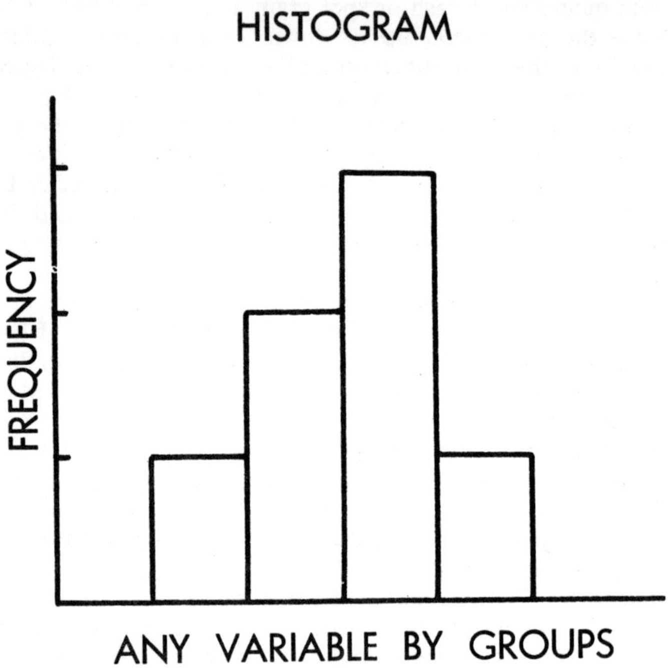

Figure 22.

histogram. A graph composed of a series of rectangles with the areas of the rectangles proportional to class frequency, grouping all items by ranges. Cf. *charts.*

historical school of economics. The group of economists, primarily Germans of the 19th century, who reacted to the theoretical approach of *classical economics* and emphasized the study of economic history as the method of verifying economic principles.

hoarding. An effort by individuals to accumulate idle goods or money. Hoarding can be done by individuals but when everyone tries to hoard *money* the result is a decline in the velocity of circulation or in the amount of money in circulation.

HOLC Home Owners Loan Corporation. A federal corporation organized in 1933 for the purpose of making loans to owners of small homes who were either delinquent in their payments and in danger of losing their homes or on the verge of becoming delinquent.

hold-back pay. That part of wages withheld by the employer (1) because of the time gap needed to compute pay and prepare payroll, or (2) because of various advances on the account of the employee by the employer (e.g., cash advances or tools) against which the hold-back pay gives protection in the event of sudden quitting by the employee.

holder in due course. In law, with reference to negotiable instruments, a holder in due course is one who has received an instrument that is (1) complete and regular on its face, (2) received before maturity without notice of dishonor of the instrument, (3) received in good faith and for value, and (4) received without notice of any infirmity in the instrument or defect in the title of the person negotiating it.

hold harmless. A clause agreeing to assume the liabilities or losses involved.

holding company. A corporation which controls the voting power of other individual corporations for the purpose of united action. A holding company may also be an operating company, as the American Telephone and Telegraph Company which operates long distance lines and controls local telephone companies.

holding the line. This term describes efforts used to maintain any given economic position, e.g., efforts to prevent further price increases or to prevent increase in unemployment.

holographic will. In law, a *will* in the handwriting of the decedent. Some states relax formalities for such wills.

home car. In transportation, a railroad car on the rails of its owner.

home economics. The organized knowledge which treats of foods, clothing, shelter, and household management in their physical, economic, and social aspects as related to the life and welfare of the individual, the family, and the community.

homeowner's insurance. A form of *comprehensive* insurance including in one policy fire and extended coverage, liability, theft, and other coverages.

homestead. The term is applied in several ways: (1) the homestead laws of the 19th century permitting settlers to acquire free land from the public domain, (2) the exemption provisions in the law of bankruptcy preventing the seizure of a minimum amount of land and house, (3) the provisions in inheritance laws securing to a widow the right to live in the family homestead after her husband's death.

homework system. A system of industrial organization designed to permit employees to perform some manufacturing operations at home rather than in a factory.

homogeneous function. A function such that if all independent variables are multiplied by a factor, t, the dependent variables are multiplied by t^n, n being the degree of the equation. An illustration of its application to economics would be the situation in production where if all inputs of the factors of production are changed by a given proportion, the output is changed in the same proportion. This situation is *constant returns to scale* (q.v.), and is a linear (first degree) homogeneous function.

homogeneous variance. Same as *homoscedasticity.*

homoscedasticity. In sampling, the condition in which the error of a distribution with respect to one variable (say Y) is the same at all levels of the values of X.

honoring. Meeting a claim or obligation when it is due.

Hope case rule. See *Symth v. Ames rule.*

Hopkinson rate. In public utilities, a rate made up of two parts. The demand charge is a specific charge for fixed capacity costs. The energy charge is based on the variable output costs.

horizontal combination. A combination which unites under one ownership a number of firms engaged in the same or in overlapping processes or stages of production and marketing. Distinguish *circular combination* and *vertical combination.*

horizontal union. Same as *craft union.*

horizontal trust. Same as *horizontal combination.*

hot cargo. A colloquial term in labor relations referring to the right of union labor to refuse to handle products shipped to their employers from another firm which the union considers offensive to organized labor. Distinguish from *secondary boycott* which is a strike against one's employer to force him to cease relations with another employer to whom the union objects.

hotel lien. Same as *innkeeper's lien.*

"hot money." Used in three senses: (1) money of investors who jump from one investment to another on the slightest change in current rate of return, (2) money in international movement to avoid depreciation of a country's currency, (3) in general parlance, any "tainted" money.

house brand. The branding by a wholesaler with his own name, of goods he has purchased from a producer unlabeled. Also called dealer's brand and private brand.

household system. Predominant during early agricultural stages of society. Characterized by isolated households which are economically self-sufficing. Cf. *handicraft system, domestic system, factory system.*

hurdle rate. In *capital budgeting*, the minimum *rate of return* acceptable to a firm on an investment. Also called *cutoff rate.*

Hurwicz criterion. Same as *optimism criterion.*

hyperinflation. The situation in which monetary demand increases too rapidly, particularly after the economy is fully employed. People seek to spend quickly before prices rise further and prevent the equilibrating effect of a redistribution of real incomes which follows on less drastic inflation.

hypothecate. To pledge something as security for a debt. Technically, there is no pledging since possession is not transferred but only the right to order sale upon default.

hysteresis. In economics, a term referring to the nonreversibility of an economic function, e.g., if in expansion, the cost curve goes down, then after the expansion an effort to contract to the original position will not proceed along the same cost curve. This is due to the fact that not all economies (or diseconomies) inherent in the expansion are lost in the contraction.

ICC Interstate Commerce Commission. Originally established in 1887. Now consists of 11 men in Washington, D.C., appointed by the President with the consent of the Senate, with the duty of supervision and regulation of interstate railroads, trucks, buses, oil pipelines, inland water transportation, and other miscellaneous powers.

iconic model. A *model* which differs from reality only in scale such as a model dam. Cf. *analogue model, econometric model,* and *mathematical model.*

ideal index. A method of computing index numbers, devised by Fisher, in which two indices err but compensate each other. The formula is

$$\frac{p_1q_0}{p_0q_0} \times \frac{p_1q_1}{p_0q_1}$$

where p_0 is the price in the base period
q_0 is the quantity in the base period

p_1 is the price in the other period
q_1 is the quantity in the other period

Cf. *Laspeyres price index.*

identification. In *econometrics,* the problem of estimating the coefficients of the variables in a system of equations. Cf. *just identified model, overidentified model,* and *underidentified model.*

identification. In *econometrics*, the variables involved in one economic relationship may also be involved in other economic relationships. The identification problem is to separate that past movement of the variables which is related to the economic relationship being studied from that associated with other economic relationships. Cf. *just identified model, overidentified model*, and *underidentified model.*

illness frequency rate. The number of illnesses suffered by employees per 1,000,000 man-hours of work on an annual basis. The proportion is

$$\frac{\text{I.F.R.}}{\text{1,000,000 man-hours}} = \frac{\text{disabling illnesses/year}}{\text{man-hours/year}}$$

illness severity rate. The number of days lost from disabling illnesses or death per 1,000 man-hours of work with 6,000 days charged for death. The proportion is

$$\frac{\text{I.S.R.}}{\text{1,000 man-hours}} = \frac{\text{days lost by illness/year}}{\text{man-hours/year}}$$

ILO International Labor Organization. An association established in 1920 as an autonomous part of the League of Nations and including the U.S., to further the interests and standards of labor. Affiliated with the United Nations since 1947

IMF International Monetary Fund. Established by the Bretton Woods (1944) conference and designed to meet the requirements of international monetary cooperation, this fund has as its purposes (1) international monetary cooperation, (2) balanced growth of trade, (3) avoidance of competitive exchange depreciation, (4) a multilateral system of payments for transactions. Cf. *International Bank of Reconstruction and Development.*

immediate annuity. An annuity policy on which there is no deferment period and the annuitant begins to receive payments immediately upon purchase.

impaired capital. A negative surplus account. Hence the amount represented by the capital stock of the corporation has been reduced below what it was at the time the stock was issued.

impair investment. The purchase of securities after initial issue, as distinguished from the initial purchase of securities which results in expenditures on capital goods.

imperfect market. A market in which the price (or *terms of trade*) falls as the quantity exchanged increases. Cf. *perfect market* and *pluperfect market.*

imperfect oligopoly. The situation in which a few sellers dominating the market for a product offer slightly differentiated products and hence are not concerned about arousing reactions by their competitors. Cf. *complete oligopoly* and *partial oligopoly.*

imperfect competition. Used in two senses: (1) as the equivalent of *monopolistic competition,* (2) the market situation in which there is imperfect knowledge of the market by buyers or sellers and/or lack of an unlimited supply of the ingredients of production at existing prices. Cf. *perfect competition.*

imperialism. In economics, the penetration of less advanced countries by more advanced countries either (1) to develop outlets for the investment of excessive savings of the advanced country, or (2) to develop markets for the excess production of the advanced country, or both.

implicit cost. Same as *opportunity cost.*

implicit rent. The amount of the income from a business which the owner attributes to the land he owns as an estimate of the rental he would have had to pay if he leased it from an owner.

implied contract. A contract in which the parties speak by their actions rather than by their oral or written words. The most common example is the furnishing by one party of goods or services under circumstances that leave no doubt it is mutually intended that they be paid for.

implied powers doctrine. As opposed to express powers which are specifically enumerated in the U.S. Constitution, the doctrine of implied powers was developed early in the 19th century on the principle that if the end is clearly within the express powers then the means, if suitable to that end, are permitted as implied powers.

implied warranty. Conditions concerning a sale of goods whose existence a buyer is entitled to assume when nothing is said to the contrary by the seller. Under the Uniform Sales Act, the general implied warranties by a seller are: (1) the right to pass title, (2) quiet possession by the buyer, (3) freedom of the goods from encumbrance, and (4) quality of the goods only in sales by sample, description, or for a particular purpose. Cf. *express warranty.*

import multiplier. See *foreign trade multiplier.*

import quotas. The fixed amounts of goods which may be imported. Import quotas are imposed by governments to conserve foreign exchange or to reduce or restrict the use of certain commodities to force a foreign country to terms, etc.

import rate. In transportation, a rate applicable only to domestic shipment of goods brought in from a foreign country.

imports. Commodities or services bought from foreign countries. Cf. *invisible imports.*

impost. A tax, particularly used to describe import duties.

imprest fund. In accounting, a fund created for purposes of internal control. Withdrawals from the fund are by authorized documents which are used as the basis for periodic payments to restore the fund to its original balance. At the time of such payments, the accumulated disbursements from the fund are entered in the proper accounts from the disbursement memoranda.

improper accumulation. A tax term describing the retention of earnings in a corporation for the purposes of delaying personal income taxes that would be payable by stockholders if dividends were declared. A penalty tax is levied to discourage this practice.

impulse goods. Goods purchased without advance planning and because the buyer was induced to purchase at first sight. Cf. *convenience goods, fashion goods, shopping goods, specialty goods.*

imputed cost. In economics, where no cash payment is involved but an opportunity to use a factor is foregone, the price commanded by the opportunity is called an imputed cost of the use in the alternative selected.

imputed cost. Same as *opportunity cost.*

inactive stock. A stock infrequently traded.

inadmitted asset. In insurance, those assets of the *insurer* which are not recognized by the regulating state as qualifying in the determination of various financial standards which the insurer must by law maintain.

incentive pay. Includes any system of wages which is designed to pay the worker according to his productivity. For example, a piecework system or a bonus system based on output. Cf. *piecework.*

incentive taxation. The use of taxation not only for purposes of public revenue but to encourage economic development along any given line. Cf. *regulatory taxation.*

incentive wage. Same as *incentive pay.*

inchmaree. A clause in *ocean marine insurance* policies covering risks other than perils of the sea.

inchoate. In law, a right that has not matured. Thus a widow's *dower* right is inchoate as long as her husband lives.

incidence (of taxation). See *tax incidence.*

inclosures. See *enclosures.*

income. (1) In accounting, the gross earnings of a given period including noncash items and excluding cash payments received in the current period but attributable to preceding or succeeding periods, minus the expenses similarly reckoned as regards cash and noncash items. (2) In economics, income individually speaking is the payment received by a factor of production. Collectively it is the total of these payments. In the case of the entrepreneur, it is the excess of the value of his finished product over his prime cost, with prime cost defined as the factor payments made by the entrepreneur plus the user costs of the assets he employs, with user cost defined as the difference between the value of an asset when it is used and when it is not used, allowing for maintenance of the asset.

income, types and classifications of. See the following specific terms:

accrued income
deferred income
discretionary income
disposable personal income
earned income
fixed income
gross (individual) income
life income
money income
national income
net (business) income
net (individual) income
nonoperating income
operating income
other income
personal income
real income
real national income
transfer income

income basis. The ratio of the dollars of interest or dividend to the price paid for the security rather than to the face or par value. Cf. *maturity basis* and *yield to maturity.*

income bonds. Bonds that receive interest only when it is earned during any one year. Ordinarily other fixed charges are paid first, then the income bonds, and then dividends on stocks.

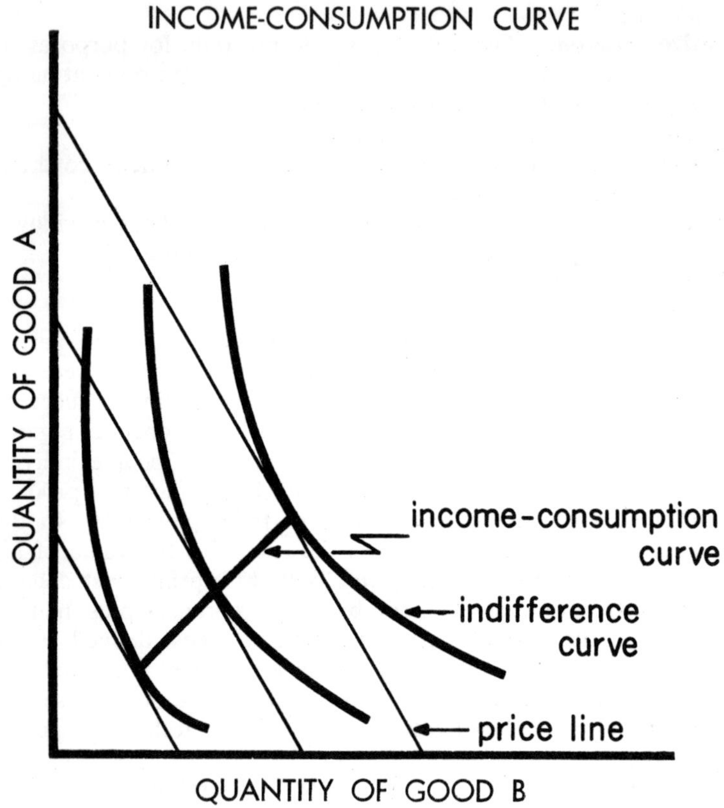

Figure 23.

income-consumption curve. Sometimes called the "standard of life" curve. Using a map of *indifference curves* for an individual with commodity *A* on the *y* axis and commodity *B* on the *x* axis, each indifference curve shows all the combinations of the two commodities yielding equal satisfaction to the individual. A straight line between a point on the *x* axis and a point on the *y* axis is a price line the slope of which shows the rate of exchange between *A* and *B* in the market. Lines parallel to this straight line then reflect other income levels of the individual (prices of the two goods remaining constant). The points of tangency of the price lines and the indifference curves trace out the income-consumption curve.

income effect. The effect of a change in the price of a commodity upon the demand for that commodity by changing the purchasing power of the income available for expenditure. Cf. *substitution effect.*

income elasticity. See *elasticity of demand, income.*

income equation. (1) The national income and its disposition between consumption and investment. Thus Y_1 (national income) = C_0 (consumption) plus I_0 (investment) where the subscript "$_0$" indicates an earlier period and the subscript "$_1$" the next later period. (2) In monetary theory the income approach can be applied to either the Fisher equation or the cash balance (Cambridge) equation. See those terms. The cash balance income equation is $Py = M/(Ty\ Ky)$ where

Py = average price level of Ty below

M = quantity of money

Ty = goods and services constituting the real annual income. (It excludes money expenditures which are not expenditures of real income).

$K = 1/Vy$ where Vy = number of times a unit of money is spent on the real constituents of the national income. Cf *income velocity of money.*

income in kind. Goods or services received by an individual directly as income rather than through money payments. Cf. *real income.*

income leakages. Removals from the stream of *consumption* plus *investment.* Hence taxes and savings in excess of intended investment. But these income leakages may be partially, wholly, or more than offset by compensating expenditures such as government expenditures and intended investment. Imports are also classified as leakages, with exports as compensating expenditures.

income multiplier. See *multiplier.*

income—offer line. (Applied to labor.) Using a map of *indifference curves* for a worker, with work income on the *y* axis and leisure on the *x* axis, a straight line connecting one point on the *x* axis and one point on the *y* axis shows all the combinations of leisure and income that the worker can have (the wage rate remaining constant). This is called a budget line the slope of which shows a particular wage rate. On the same map, indifference curves (convex with respect to the origin) show all the combinations of leisure and income giving equal satisfaction to the worker. Lines parallel to the budget line will be tangent to these indifference curves. The points of tangency trace out the income-offer line. If the budget lines are anchored to one point on the work axis (creating a fan), the income offer line reflects willingness to work at different wage rates. See figure 44, page 343.

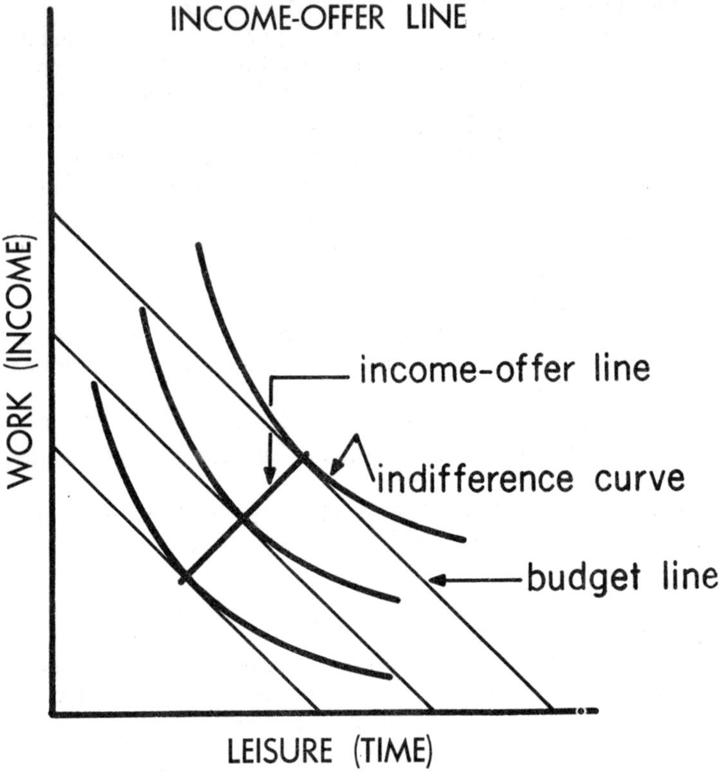

Figure 24.

income payments to individuals. Same as *personal income.*

income-purchase line. Using a map of *indifference curves* for a buyer of commodity *A* with income on the *y* axis and quantity of *A* on the *x* axis, a straight line connecting one point on the *x* axis and one point on the *y* axis shows all the combinations of *A* and income that the buyer can have (the price of *A* remaining constant). This is called a budget line, the slope of which shows the price or particular rate of exchange of money and that good. On the same map, indifference curves (convex with respect to the origin) show all the combinations of *A* and income giving equal satisfaction to the buyer. Lines

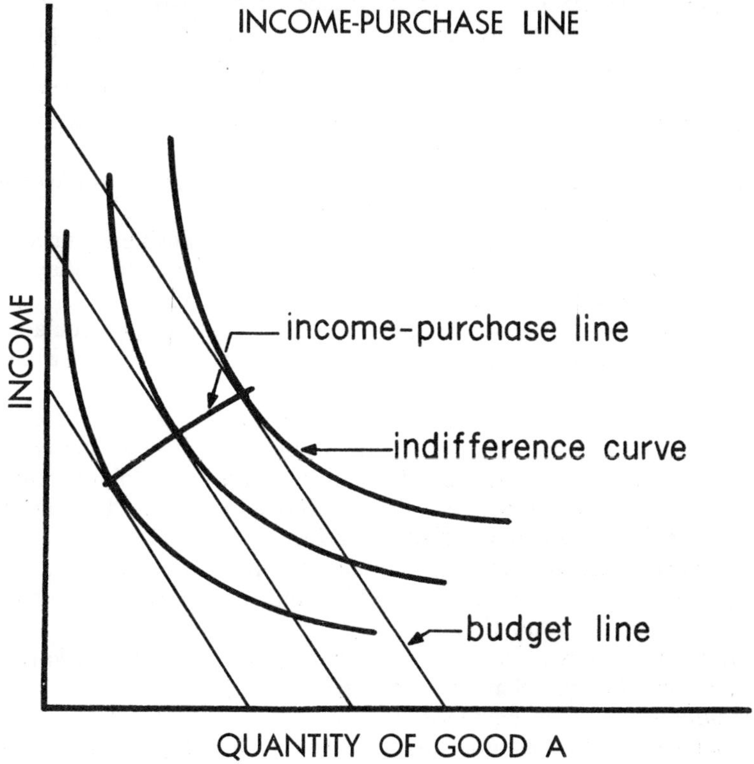

Figure 25.

parallel to the budget line will be tangent to these indifference curves. The points of tangency trace out the income-purchase line.

income statement. Same as *profit-and-loss statement.*

income statement account. Same as *nominal account.*

income tax. A tax imposed by the federal government and most of the states on the income of an individual, a firm, or a corporation. It is a direct tax and is levied on the ability-to-pay principle.

income velocity of money. The ratio of income generating expenditures in a time period to the quantity of money. Income generating expenditures include both expenditures on consumers' goods and expenditure on new investment goods. Distinguish *transactions velocity of money.*

incontestable clause. A life insurance clause providing that the insurance company cannot "contest" the validity of the policy after the insured survives for a period of time (usually one or two years) except for nonpayment of premium. In case of misstatement of age the policy usually provides for a recomputation of premiums based on the correct age.

inconvertible money. Paper money which cannot be redeemed for a standard amount of precious metal.

"Inc." or Incorporated. Some states require business corporations to have "Inc." after their name to indicate that they are concerns with limited liability of stockholders.

incorporation. The process or procedure by which an association or group of individuals becomes a legal entity called a corporation.

increasing cost. The situation in which *average total unit costs* of a business increase as the volume of business increases. True over large ranges of output for farming, mining, fishing, and lumbering, the so-called extractive industries. Distinguish *constant cost* and *decreasing cost.*

increasing cost industry. An industry whose *average total unit cost* increases as production volume increases over a given range of production.

increasing returns. See *diminishing marginal productivity, law of.*

incremental cost. Same as *marginal cost.*

incumbrance. See *encumbrance.*

indemnity. (1) An undertaking to answer for the damage resulting from non-performance or misconduct by a party. An indemnity right arises only after the party indemnified has suffered a loss. Distinguish *suretyship.* (2) Same as *straddle.*

indemnity bond. A general term covering bonds which provide for reimbursement for loss resulting from infidelity or failure to perform duties.

indent. An importer's purchase order to an exporter or middleman to be filled at the best prices possible or stated prices for the specifications, and usually within certain time limits. Originated in Far East trade.

indent house. A firm specializing in importing goods pursuant to specific orders from domestic buyers. The advantage of the firm lies in its contacts and experience particularly in procuring the lowest possible price.

indenture. (1) Any written agreement. The term derives from the former practice of tearing the edges of two copies of a document so that later matching of the torn edges will establish the identity of the copies. (2) The contract between an *apprentice* and his master. (3) Historically, the indentured servant contract of Colonial times which provided for a term of personal service by a servant to his master.

indenture deed. See *deed poll.*

indentured servant. One who pays indebtedness by personal services for a stated number of years. E.g., in Colonial days immigrants might be indentured for the price of their passage from Europe to the United States.

independent contractor. The independent contractor is distinguished from an agent in that he uses his own judgment as to how to accomplish the result, is free from the control of others, and accountable only for the end result specified in a contract. Cf. *agent.*

independent equations. A system of equations such that none of them can be obtained by combining any two or more of the other equations in the system.

independent union. A union not affiliated with a federation of unions.

independent variable. A variable not dependent on another variable for its value. For example, in a time series of wheat output per year and rainfall per year, wheat output is the dependent variable and rainfall the independent variable. Cf. *dependent variable.*

index number. A mathematical device or number which is used to express the price level, volume of trade, etc., of a given period, in comparison with that of a base period the value for which is given as 100. Useful in comparing relative changes in various phenomena from month to month or year to year. Cf. *aggregative index number, average of relatives index number, ideal index number, link relative index number.*

index of correlation. The square root of the *index of determination.* The symbol is i.

index of determination. The ratio of the *associated variance* to the total *variance* when a curvilinear *regression line* is fitted to two variables. When the fitted line is curvilinear, the symbol is i^2, whereas when the line fitted is straight, the symbol is r^2 and the term is *coefficient of determination.*

index of disparity. A scale for comparing the size of the leading firms of different industries with each other. If all the firms in an industry are of the same size, the index is zero, but if one is much larger, then the index figure approaches 15. Cf. *concentration ratio.*

index of multiple correlation. The square root of the *index of multiple determination.* The symbol is I.

index of multiple determination. The ratio of the *associated variance* to the total *variance* when a curvilinear *regression line* is fitted to more than two variables. When the regression line is curvilinear, the symbol is I^2 rather than R^2 and the term is index of multiple correlation rather than coefficient of multiple determination, since the latter applies to a straight-line regression.

index of profitability. The ratio of the *present value* of an asset to its purchase price.

indictment. The finding of a grand jury in a criminal case that there is reasonable ground to believe an accused person may be guilty. It also serves to inform the defendant of what he is accused.

INDIFFERENCE CURVE

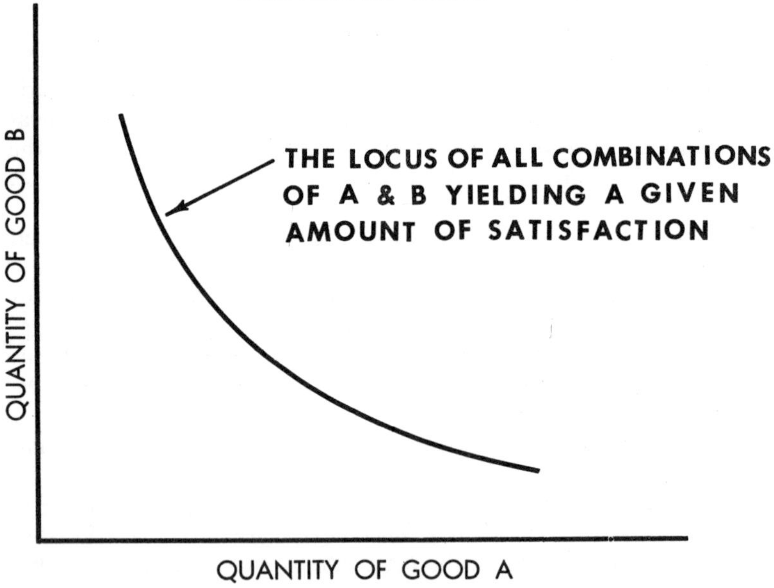

Figure 26.

indifference curve. (Consumer and others.) Using a graph with quantity of commodity A on one axis and quantity of commodity B on the other axis, the indifference curve is the locus of all points indicating those combinations of the two commodities which will yield equal satisfaction to a given individual. This is a consumer indifference curve. Such a curve must be convex to the origin because of diminishing marginal utility of each good as its quantity increases. Analogous use of this device can be made in other ways, e.g., in production by putting factors in place of commodities, the indifference curve then traces equal outputs obtained by different combinations of the factors of production. This then is called an *isoquant*.

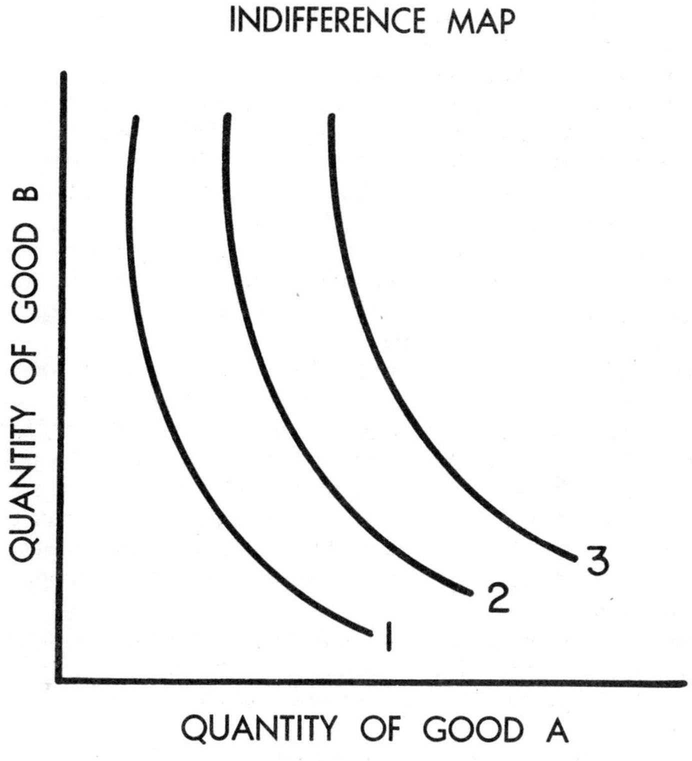

Figure 27.

indifference map. A series of *indifference curves* for one individual with regard to his consumption preferences as to two commodities with each curve showing the various combinations of the two goods which are considered equal in satisfaction by the individual, but each separate curve indicating a higher level of satisfaction as the curves remove from the origin. Also used with regard to an entrepreneur and the factors of production in which case the indifference curve is called an *isoquant* curve, and for other problems.

indirect business taxes. In national income accounting, indirect business taxes are such taxes as *excise* and *real property* but not *income taxes. National income* is determined after the deduction of indirect business taxes (as well as depreciation) from *gross national product.* This is done because otherwise a change in an indirect business tax would cause a change in the factor income total without a corresponding change in employment or factor prices.

indirect cost. Same as *fixed cost.*

indirect labor. In accounting, the amount of wages paid to employees which cannot be charged directly to specific finished products because the wages do not vary proportionately with the units of that product made, but must be allocated in some logical manner to all jobs. Cf. *direct labor.*

indirect tax. A tax which one person is directed by law to collect with the clear expectation that the person paying the tax to the government will in turn exact it from another. Eg. *customs duties* or *sales taxes.*

individual bargaining. Negotiation of an agreement by one individual with another. In labor, the process in which each worker settles his own wages, hours, etc., with the employer.

individualism. (1) Usually equivalent to "laissez faire." A policy or theory that the economic welfare of society is best served by permitting individuals or groups of them to conduct their businesses with the least possible amount of public or government interference. (2) In a broader sense, any system opposed to *collectivism.*

individual proprietorship. An individual conducting a business as an individual. He is subject to all the risks, e.g., in insolvency his nonbusiness assets can be reached to satisfy business liabilities.

indorsed bond. Same as *assumed bond*, that is, bonds of an original debtor which have been assumed by a second debtor who indorses them.

indorsee. One to whom an instrument is transferred by indorsement.

indorsement. (1) Transferring title (ownership) or guaranteeing payment by writing one's name on the back of a *negotiable instrument* where one is not the maker, drawer or acceptor. In general, the indorser warrants that he had good title, that the instrument is genuine, that all prior parties were competent and capable to contract, and that he has no knowledge of a fact rendering the paper invalid. An unqualified indorser guarantees to those coming after him that payment will be made. (2) In insurance, any change in the terms of the original policy, e.g., change of the name of the insured. (3) In general, the signing of any financial document.

indorsement, types of. See the following specific terms.

accommodation indorsement
blank indorsement
conditional indorsement
general indorsement
qualified indorsement
restrictive indorsement
special indorsement

indorsement in full. Same as *special indorsement.*

indorser. One who has put his name on a negotiable paper in order to transfer title (ownership) from himself to another or to guarantee payment.

induced consumption. An increase in consumer spending resulting from an increase in investment.

induced investment. New investment caused by an increase in consumption expenditure. Some increases in consumption may merely activate idle facilities. Cf. *autonomous investment, acceleration principle.*

industrial bank. Originally a bank organized particularly to receive small deposits of workers and to make small loans. Today the industrial bank has largely become a commercial bank.

industrial carrier. A carrier owned by one or more of the industries served by it. It may be either a *common, contract,* or *private carrier.*

industrial life insurance. Life insurance designed for the wage-earning or industrial population, usually sold in smaller face amounts and on a weekly premium basis. This form of insurance is higher in cost than regular life insurance because of the higher overhead cost and no medical selection.

industrial relations. In careful usage, all the relationships that grow out of the fact of employment. Distinguish *personnel management* and *labor relations.*

industrial revolution. The great economic changes which began with the mechanical inventions, factory system, and industrial capitalism in England in the 18th century. In the U.S. the industrial revolution occurred somewhat later, in the middle of the 19th century.

industrial union. A union that takes into its membership all the workers that work for a given employer or in a given industry. Examples are the United Mine Workers of America, the United Automobile Workers (CIO), etc.

industry. A group of *firms* closely related in competition because of great substitutability of their products and distinguished from other firms by a "gap" in the range of substitute products.

industry effect. The role played by the number of firms in determining the *elasticity of demand and supply* of a product. The elasticity of the total supply curve for an industry depends not only on the effect that a rise in price will have on the output of each firm but also on the effect the rise in price will have on the number of firms offering outputs. By analogy, a similar effect on the demand curve as price changes increase or decrease the number of customers wanting the product. Thus an individual's demand may be highly inelastic but total demand for the product be elastic because the price change causes a large change in the numbers of customers.

industry-wide bargaining. The negotiation of a collective-bargaining agreement between a union or group of unions and substantially all the employers in a given industry within one country.

inelastic demand or supply (price). Demand (or supply) is said to be inelastic when quantity demanded (or supplied) does not change so much proportionately as price when price changes. Cf. *elasticity of demand and supply.*

infant industry. Generally used with reference to tariffs and subsidies to describe an industry which has not had opportunity to arrive at what would be its mature level under existing conditions.

infant (or minor). In the U.S., a person who is under 21 years old and hence not of legal age and unable to enter a contract binding on him (except for necessities) unless expressly authorized by statute.

inferior good. A good whose consumption decreases as income increases and increases as income decreases, e.g., bread in the average family's budget. Also called a "poor man's good."

infeoffment. The act or instrument of *feoffment.*

infinitely elastic demand (or supply). Same as *perfectly elastic demand (*or *supply).*

infinitely inelastic demand (or supply). Same as *perfectly inelastic demand (or supply).*

inflation. A period when purchasing power of the monetary unit is falling. Sometimes defined as a period of generally rising prices and wages. However, in an economy where prices are falling but costs are falling faster (profits are increasing) there is inflation sometimes described as relative inflation.

inflation, types of. See the following specific terms.

bottleneck inflation	*hyperinflation*
cost-push inflation	*open inflation*
creeping inflation	*reflation*
demand-pull inflation	*repressed inflation*
excess-demand inflation	*suppressed inflation*

inflationary gap. The amount by which actual consumption and investment expenditures of both private and governmental sources exceed the expenditures theoretically calculated as necessary to absorb all goods and services produced at current prices.

information. A sworn statement either by an officer or a citizen that a named person committed a crime and what the crime is. In most states this is an alternative to *indictment* as a method of starting a criminal action.

information returns. Forms required to be furnished to the government by the employer or other party making payment of wages, salaries, dividends, or interest, showing the name of the one paid, the amount, and the kind of payment. Used by the government to verify tax statements made by the party receiving the payment.

infringement. In *patent, trade-mark,* and *copyright* law, the invasion of the exclusive right in the owner of a patent, trademark, or copyright to produce or reproduce that which is within the scope of the right. Such an owner may license others or refuse to do so during the term of the right.

ingrossing. In law, copying a document into final form from a rough draft.

inheritance tax. A tax collected from heirs on the right to receive an inheritance. The amount of the tax depends on the amount left by the deceased person to the heir and his family relation to the deceased. Cf. *estate tax.*

initial reserve. That reserve upon an insurance policy consisting of the *terminal reserve* of the prior policy year plus the net premium for the next year. Cf. *mean reserve.*

injunction. A court order restraining someone from doing something under penalty of contempt of court which can mean a fine or imprisonment or both. Most commonly used to restrain strikers from doing irreparable damage to the employer's property, until restricted by *Norris-La Guardia Act*. Distinguish two types of injunction: *permanent* and *temporary*. Cf. *pendente lite*.

inland bill. *A bill of exchange* drawn and payable in the same state.

inland marine insurance. See *marine insurance*.

in lieu tax. A substitute for property taxes in the case of public utilities. Usually a tax based on gross earnings.

in loco parentis. Latin for "in place of the parent." A guardian for a child or a master to a servant.

innkeeper's lien. The right of an innkeeper to keep possession of baggage and property of a guest for unpaid charges.

innovation theory of the cycle. This explanation of the business cycle emphasizes the role of innovations (all forms of cost reduction or new products) in stimulating investment and hence incomes. As the innovation becomes widely adopted, this effect on incomes disappears due to the fact that the profit margin narrows and further new investment declines. Since innovations are not developed uniformly through time but come in groups, incomes rise and fall.

in personam. A legal proceeding against a person in which the judgment will personally bind the losing party. Distinguish *in rem*.

input-output analysis. Upon the assumption of fixed technological coefficients (e.g., that it takes a given amount of material and a given amount of man-hours to produce a unit of a given good), the empirical analysis of production by *general equilibrium* techniques (using simultaneous equations and matrix algebra). The effort is to determine what can be produced and the quantity of each intermediate product to be used up in the production process, given the quantities of available resources and the state of technology.

in rem. A legal proceeding against a piece of property or a status (a relationship) as opposed to a proceeding against a person which is called in personam.

insider. In security regulation, anyone who has knowledge of facts not available to the general public. Specifically includes directors, officers, and holders of more than 10 per cent of a corporation's stock who must report all transactions to the *SEC*.

insolvency. The term is used in two senses: (1) the inability of a person to meet his obligations as they mature (this is the "equity" sense), (2) the excess of liabilities (in the case of a corporation, excluding capital stock) over assets (this is the "bankruptcy" sense).

insolvency guarantee funds. There are three major insolvency guarantee funds: (1) FDIC guaranteeing to $20,000 per account, depositors in insured banks; (2) *FSLIC* guaranteeing to $20,000 per account in insured savings and loan associates; and (3) federal insurance guaranteeing to $60,000 per account, individual accounts with brokers. In addition, as to brokerage accounts, the New York Stock Exchange has unlimited protection covering accounts with its member firms.

installment account. A credit granted upon purchase of services or goods with the provision that payment is to be made in a number of more or less equal partial payments, usually one each month until the entire purchase price (plus financing charges) is paid. The period of payment is usually shorter than the expected life of the item purchased.

installment bond. A bond that is to be repaid to the bondholder in installments over a period of time.

installment buying. Buying articles or services by making a down payment (usually) and agreeing thereafter to pay stated sums at stated intervals until the account is settled. Title to (ownership of) the goods may or may not remain with the seller until payments are completed. Cf. *conditional sale*.

installment equipment financing. Buying equipment for a down payment with an agreement to pay installments thereafter until the account is settled.

installment refund life annuity. An *annuity* policy that provides for the payment of periodic income for the life of the annuitant but guarantees that in the event of the premature death of the annuitant, the periodic payments will continue to his estate until total payments made equal the purchase price of the annuity. Cf. *cash refund annuity*.

institutional economics. An approach to the study of economics which emphasizes the dominant role played by institutional phenomena (such as the corporation or the labor union) in determining economic development, rather than profit decisions by individuals.

instrument. In law, any written document.

instrumental variable. In *econometrics*, a variable used to separate the relationship between an *independent variable* and the *disturbance term* when analyzing a *dependent variable* as a function of one or more independent variables plus a disturbance term. If an independent variable is related to the disturbance term, the estimate of the coefficient of the independent variable by a technique such as regression analysis will be biased unless the relationship of the independent variable to the disturbance term is removed. Cf. *endogenous variable, exogenous variable, jointly dependent variable, predetermined variable, shift variable.*

insurable interest. An interest in property such that a loss will be suffered by the person insured if the person or property covered dies, is lost, destroyed, or damaged. In the absence of such an interest, an insurance contract is void.

insurance. A method of pooling or shifting probable losses among a group generally. The essential conditions are (1) the presence of a large enough number of separate but combinable risks; (2) an event whose average occurrence can be reduced to mathematical formulae with a relatively small margin of error. This makes it possible to predict probable losses and to calculate the annual cost.

insurance, types of. See the following specific terms:

accident insurance
accounts receivable insurance
all-risk insurance
annuity insurance
assessment insurance
business insurance
business interruption insurance
casualty insurance
coinsurance
collision insurance
comprehensive insurance
concurrent insurance
constructive total loss insurance
convertible collision insurance
convertible life insurance
cooperative insurance
credit insurance
credit life insurance
deposit insurance
disability premium waiver insurance
employer's liability insurance
endowment insurance
endowment annuity insurance
excess insurance
experience rating insurance
extended term insurance
family income insurance
fidelity insurance
graded premium life insurance
group insurance
group creditor insurance
guaranty insurance
homeowner's insurance
industrial insurance
inland marine insurance
legal reserve insurance
level premium insurance
liability insurance
life insurance
limited-pay life insurance

major medical insurance
malpractice insurance
manual rating insurance
marine insurance
merit rating insurance
mutual insurance
ordinary life insurance
paid-up insurance
participating insurance
product liability insurance
profit insurance
protection and indemnity insurance
public liability insurance
reciprocal insurance
reinsurance
renewable term life insurance
replacement insurance
retirement income insurance
schedule rating insurance
self-insurance
social insurance
single premium life insurance insurance
standard fire policy
step-rate premium insurance
stock company insurance
straight life insurance
term insurance
title insurance
underinsurance
unemployment insurance
use and occupancy insurance
whole life insurance
workmen's compensation insurance

insurance age change. In life insurance, the one-year period starting one-halfyear before and ending one-half year after the birthday is used to determine age for premium purposes but in *annuities,* the last birthday is used.

insurance policy. The written contract between the insurance company and the party insured containing all the terms and conditions of the agreement. See the specific types of policy under the term *policy.*

"insurance poor." Carrying so much insurance, such as life, health, accident, automobile, property, theft, tornado, etc., that there is nothing left to live comfortably on without much scraping and pinching.

insurance premium. The amount payable in advance by the insured to the insurer once only, annually, semi-annually, quarterly, monthly, or weekly.

insurance rating. In insurance, risks are rated for purposes of determination of premiums. Such rating may include exposures over which the insured has no control as well as exposures which can be affected by the insured.

insurance rating, types of. See the following specific terms:

experience rating
manual rating
merit rating
retrospective rating
schedule rating

insured. One who is protected against loss by an insurance company through the purchase of insurance.

insured pension plan. A type of group *annuity* sold by life insurance companies with the purpose of relieving the employer of the management of the pension fund which is carried out by the life insurance company.

insurer. The insurance company which takes the risks and guarantees to make good any losses covered by the insurance policy.

in tail. A limitation on land made by the grantor of a deed so that only the blood descendants of the new owner can inherit. If there are no blood descendants at any time, the land reverts to the grantor.

intangible asset. (1) In law and taxation, any nonmaterial property rights such as securities, notes and claims. (2) In accounting and finance, in a narrower sense which includes only good will, patents, copyrights, trademarks, secret processes, and like items; whereas securities and notes and claims are considered tangible.

intangible personal property. Rights to personal property as distinguished from the property itself. E.g., stocks, bonds, notes, and contracts.

integer programming. The addition of a constraint that the answers to a problem of *linear programming* must be in integers (whole numbers) and not a fraction or an integer plus a fraction.

integration of industry. Organizing the different processes in the production of economic goods under a single management. Cf. *vertical, horizontal, and circular combinations.*

intended investment. The investment contemplated by businessmen in inventories on the basis of estimated future sales volume. Cf. *realized investment* and *unintended investment.*

intensive use of land. See *margin of cultivation, intensive.*

inter alia. Latin for "among other things."

inter alios. Latin for "among other persons." In law, refers to people who are strangers to the case at hand.

interchangeable bond. A bond with the right to be exchanged, at the option of the holder, for another bond.

intercompany dividends. Dividends from one corporation fully taxable under the income tax law to another fully taxable corporation are excluded as to 85 per cent of such dividends from taxable income

intercorrelation. The situation in which there is correlation between *independent variables* being examined as well as between the independent variables and the *dependent variable.*

interdiction. In law, the prohibition of commercial traffic between the country so proclaiming and specified countries or ports.

interest (net). Payment for the use of funds. Variously explained as (1) the reward for sacrificing consumption of present income (*abstinence theory*), (2) the price adjusting different people's views of *liquidity preference,* (3) the price overcoming the preference for the present over the future (*time preference theory*), (4) the measure of the productivity of various investments (*marginal efficiency of capital*), and (5) the price adjusting the supply and demand for loanable funds (*loanable funds theory*).

interest, types of. See the following specific terms:

accrued interest
Boston interest
compound interest
gross interest
New York interest
nominal interest
ordinary interest
simple interest

interest bond. A bond issued in payment of interest on other bonds because of a shortage of cash to pay the interest.

interest coverage. Same as *times interest earned.*

interest rate risk. In investments, used in contradistinction to *financial risk* and *purchasing power risk* to refer to the risk that the interest rate may change thus affecting the market value of a security even though its obligations continue to be met.

interest rate, types of. See the following specific terms:

equilibrium interest rate
legal rate of interest
money interest rate
nominal interest rate
real interest rate

interest, theories of. Cf. *abstinence theory of interest, agio theory of interest, liquidity preference theory of interest, loanable funds theory of interest, marginal productivity theory of interest, time preference theory of interest.*

interim bond. A temporary certificate which will be replaced by a permanent bond at a later date.

interim certificate (stock or bond). A temporary certificate issued to the purchaser of a security until the properly engraved certificate is issued in its place.

interlocking directorates. A number of separately organized and functioning corporations managed by the same or nearly the same group of directors. This brings about a community of interest between these companies. Competition can be limited or eliminated; prices can be fixed or held relatively stable; similar labor policies, pro-union or anti-union, can be pursued; or if the corporations are noncompetitive they can help one another in a friendly and profitable manner. Some effort at government regulation has been made by the *Clayton Act.*

interlocking stock ownership. Either the direct ownership of the stock of one company by another or the ownership of stock by a stockholder common to two or more corporations.

interlocutory decree. A decree of a court of equity which does not finally dispose of a matter but settles intervening questions.

intermediate equilibrium. See *equilibrium of firm or industry, (partial) short run.*

intermediate financing. Sometimes defined in terms of length of time to maturity, such as more than one year but less than 5 or 10 years. However, intermediate financing is not merely a matter of time to maturity but rather of the type of arrangement, namely a *private placement,* which allows easy refinancing arrangements.

intermediate goods. Intermediate goods are between the raw materials and consumer's goods. Intermediate goods are classified into "higher order" and "lower order" goods depending on the degree to which they are removed from the consumer. Goods of the "first order" are consumption goods. Cf. *final goods.*

internal audit. An *audit* conducted by an employee of the business being audited and not by an independent auditor.

internal check. A method of effecting safeguards against errors and fraud by (1) procedures to prevent errors and discover errors when made, and (2) interrelation of the work of various members of an organization to prevent the concealment of fraud unless two or more persons are in collusion.

internal economies and diseconomies. Internal economies are increases in efficiency within the producing unit through better organization or differences in the scale of operations. Care must be taken to distinguish the unit used, e.g., economies that are external to the firm may be internal to the industry. Economies that are increases in efficiency but outside the unit referred to are called external. An example of an internal economy to a firm: doubling the volume of production to lower the unit cost of a high-priced plant manager. An example of an economy external to the firm but internal to the industry: industry-wide advertising to which a number of firms contribute. Diseconomies are decreases in efficiency similarly classified. Cf. *external economies and diseconomies.*

internal financing. Securing the funds needed by a firm from retained earnings and depreciation rather than going outside the firm to borrow or sell stock. Cf. *external financing.*

internal growth. The expansion of a firm from increased sales of its products rather than by acquiring new firms through *merger.*

internal national debt. That part of the national debt owed to persons within the country owing the debt.

internal rate of return method. Same as *yield method.*

internal revenue. In the U.S., all federal tax revenues except customs duties.

International Bank for Reconstruction and Development. Established by the Bretton Woods (1944) conference and designed for capital adjustments between countries in order to (1) restore countries devastated by World War II, and (2) develop backward areas through loans and guarantees of loans. Popularly called World Bank. Cf. *International Monetary Fund.*

international union. A labor union with affiliates in other countries. In this sense AFL and CIO are international only with regard to Canadian affiliates.

international unit. A statistical unit used to compare living standards in different countries. The unit is based on the average purchasing power of the dollar in the United States for 1925–34.

interpleader. In law, the procedural step by which a party (such as an insurance company) admits liability but questions which one of two parties is entitled to performance and thus brings in the third party for a complete determination. Cf. *intervention.*

interpolation. The process of establishing a theoretical value for a point between two points of known value. The process assumes a constant relationship for the distance between the two points for the factors involved. Cf. *extrapolation.*

interquartile range. The difference between the third *quartile* point and the first quartile point.

interrogatories. In law, questions in writing presented to one who is to testify in a case so that he may answer. Cf. *discovery.*

inter se or inter sese. Latin, meaning "among themselves."

interstate commerce. See *commerce clause.*

intervention. In law, the introduction into a judicial proceeding between two parties (plaintiff and defendant) of a third party called the "intervener." The third party seeks to enter the proceeding on his own initiative, generally. Some proceedings (ex parte) have only one party and then the intervener would be the second party. Cf. *interpleader.*

inter vivos trust. A trust created by a living person as opposed to a trust created by a will. Cf. *testamentary trust.*

intestate. One dying without disposing of his property by a valid will.

intestate succession. Where a decedent leaves no valid will, the inheritance of his property is determined by the statute on intestate succession of the state of his domicile.

in transit privileges. Rights of the shipper to interrupt shipment for manufacturing or treating. For example, steel bought in Pittsburgh might be heat treated in Chicago and reshipped to Minneapolis at the through rate from Pittsburgh to Minneapolis.

in transitu. From the Latin, meaning in the course of transportation.

intrastate traffic. Traffic which originates in one state and terminates in the same state.

intrinsic value. The value which an analyst judges to be supported by the facts when the price in the current market temporarily deviates from a normal market price.

inventory. (1) A written schedule of all items owned by a person or firm, showing the value of each item as well as the total. (2) More narrowly, the schedule of raw materials, goods in process, and finished goods of a business as separate from the fixed assets of a business.

inventory count. The type and number of items in an inventory. This may be done by *physical* (count) *inventory* or computed by a system called *perpetual inventory*.

inventory cycle. (1) A business cycle term for a cycle measured by fluctuations in inventories. (2) Same as *inventory turnover* when applied to an individual business.

inventory theory of business cycle. The argument that the business cycle originates in efforts of business to increase or decrease inventories in response to expectations as to future sales.

inventory turnover. Cost of goods sold during a period divided by average inventory at cost of that period.

inventory valuation methods. See the following specific terms:

base stock method of inventory
cost method (average) of inventory
cost or market whichever is lower method of inventory
first in, first out method of inventory
last in, first out method of inventory
retail method of inventory
standard cost method of inventory

invested capital. In finance, same as *capital structure,* namely, the total of long term debt plus net worth.

invested capital turnover. *Net sales* divided by invested capital.

investment. (1) The purchase of stocks, bonds, and property, which, upon analysis, promise safety of principal and a satisfactory return. These factors distinguish investment from speculation. (2) In economic theory, investment means the acquisition of means of production (including goods for selling) with money capital.

Investment Advisers Act. Passed by Congress in 1940, and administered by the SEC (Securities and Exchange Commission), the principal provisions require registration of advisers and reporting of their activities and fees, and forbid compensation based on capital gains or appreciation as well as acting as principal or broker in dealings with clients. The act does not apply when (1) all clients are within one state and no advice is given about listed securities, or (2) when the only clients are investment or insurance companies or (3) when the number of clients is less than fifteen and there is no holding out to the public as an adviser.

investment banking. Underwriting and selling primarily new issues of stocks and bonds to investors.

investment bill. A bill of exchange purchased at a discount with the intention of holding to maturity as an investment.

investment broker. One who negotiates only cash transactions and not those *on margin.*

investment certificate. A loan contract carrying a rate of interest and maturity date. Typically issued by a *savings and loan association* and is not stock but a debt.

investment company. A corporation or trust organized for the purpose of dealing in securities. Shares in the company are sold to the public. The supporting argument is that this device "spreads the risk" and cost of handling by pooling the investments of many people. Cf. *closed-end investment company, fixed investment company, management investment company, mutual* or *open-end investment company.*

investment Company Act. Passed by Congress in 1940, this law regulates investment companies, i.e., companies whose business is making investments and who sell shares to the public.

investment cost theory of rate making. In utility and railroad rate making, investment cost is the cost of acquisition by the *present* owner of property devoted to public use. On this base the rate of return is computed. Cf. *cost of capital, fair return on fair value, original cost, prudent investment* and *reproduction cost theories of rate making.*

investment credit. Credit represented by corporation bonds and notes and thus long term credit. Such promises may be secured or unsecured. Also used as an estimated amount in the formation or establishment of firms.

investment function. The relation between investment expenditure and income.

investment letter. A letter given by a buyer of stock to the seller stating that the purchase is for investment with no intent to reoffer the stock. Then registration of the stock with the *SEC* may not be required.

investment multiplier. In *macroeconomics*, the ratio of the change in *national income* following on a change in investment to the change in investment. The value of the multiplier depends on the particular model and parameters of the economy assumed.

investment portfolio. A list of securities owned by a person.

investment tax credit. Federal legislation designed to stimulate purchase of capital goods by allowing a percentage of the purchase price as a credit against taxes due and not merely as a deduction from taxable income. The percentage is in addition to *depreciation.*

investment trust. Same as *investment company.*

investment turnover. The ratio of sales to the total of bonds and *net worth.* Also called *capital turnover.*

investors method. Same as *yield method* (in capital budgeting).

invisible exports. Services, financial or personal, rendered by citizens of one country to foreigners. These may consist of insurance, freight and passenger charges, interest on domestic bonds, dividends of domestic corporations, etc. So called because the "visible" or commodity exports pass through customs and are recorded in statistics of foreign trade, whereas the "invisibles" were formerly not so recorded.

invisible hand. A term used by Adam Smith to describe the proposition that the economy is guided by the self-interest of individuals and that such a process leads to increased general welfare of society.

invisible imports. Services, financial or personal, rendered by foreigners to the natives of a given country. These may consist of freight and passenger charges, insurance and banking services, etc.

invisible items of foreign trade. Freight, insurance charges, tourist expenditures, and similar items. Distinguish *visible items of foreign trade.*

invitation to bid. An advertisement issued by one who desires a number of different persons to bid on the job. The invitation usually contains the specifications for the job or materials on which bids are desired. Used in connection with either open or sealed bids.

invoice. A business form showing the items shipped and charges therefor sent by the seller at the time of shipment to the buyer.

involuntary bankruptcy. Bankruptcy proceedings begun by the petition of a creditor who seeks to wind up the affairs of a debtor.

IOU "I owe you." (1) In law, a form of an admission of debt. It is not a promise to pay, is not negotiable, and does not carry interest. (2) In colloquial use, any unsecured promise to pay.

ipso facto. Latin for "by the fact itself," or "by the mere fact." Cf. *ipso jure.*

ipso jure. Latin for "by operation of law," or "by mere law." Cf. *ipso facto.*

Irish dividend. A facetious term used when an assessment is levied against the stockholders of a corporation. E.g., this was formerly possible when bank stock carried *double liability.*

iron law of wages. The theory was attributed to David Ricardo by LaSalle. The "law" is a generalization that wages tend to be merely sufficient to maintain the laboring class at the minimum standard of living.

IRR. Abbreviation for *"internal rate of return."*

irrecusable. In law, a category of obligations imposed upon a person regardless of his consent or actions.

irredeemable bond. Same as *annuity bond,* that is, without maturity date.

irredeemable money. Same as *inconvertible money.*

irrevocable credit. A credit which cannot, before the date it expires, be cancelled, revoked, or withdrawn without the consent of a person in whose favor the credit is given. Used mostly in foreign travel and trade, but also used in domestic business. Also called fixed credit line.

irrevocable letter of credit. A *letter of credit* which cannot be cancelled until after a stated date without the consent of the person in whose favor it is drawn.

IRS. Internal Revenue Service. The division of the Treasury Department of the federal government which collects all internal taxes, including excise and income taxes. Formerly called *BIR*, Bureau of Internal Revenue.

iso-cost contour or curve. Same as *iso-outlay curve.*

iso-outlay curve. Using quantity of factor of production *A* on one axis and quantity of factor of production *B* on the other axis, the iso-outlay curve is the straight line connecting any point on one axis with a point on the other axis, representing all combinations of the two factors which can be purchased for the same amount of money. Cf. *iso-product curve, scale line.*

iso-product curve. A production *indifference curve.* If quantity of one factor of production is plotted on one axis and quantity of another factor of production on the other axis, the isoquant is a curve tracing the various combinations of the two factors which will yield the same quantity of product, and is convex to the origin. Cf. *iso-outlay curve, scale line.*

isoquant. (1) Same as *iso-product curve.* (2) Sometimes used in a broader sense to describe any curve representing equal quantities and not just equal quantities of output.

isorevenue curve. Plotting units of good A on the x axis and units of good B on the y axis, a straight line connecting any

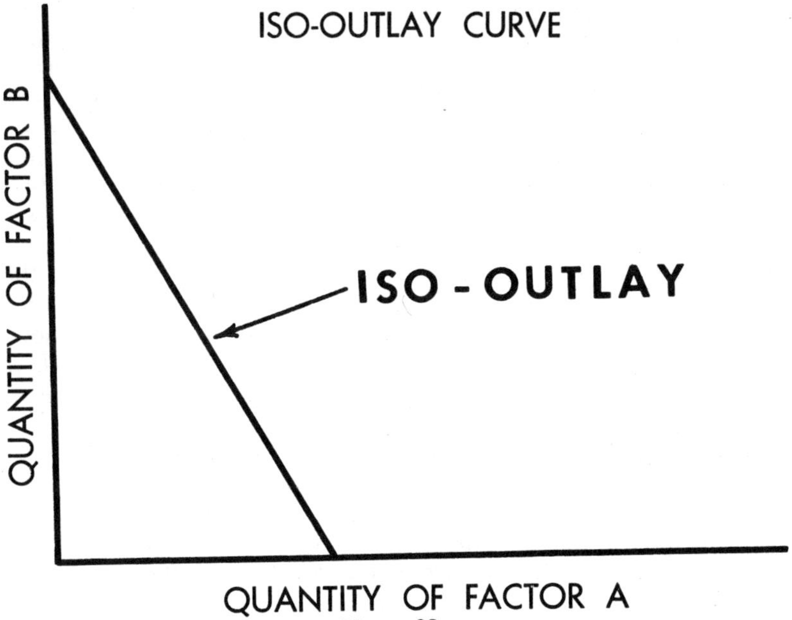

Figure 28.

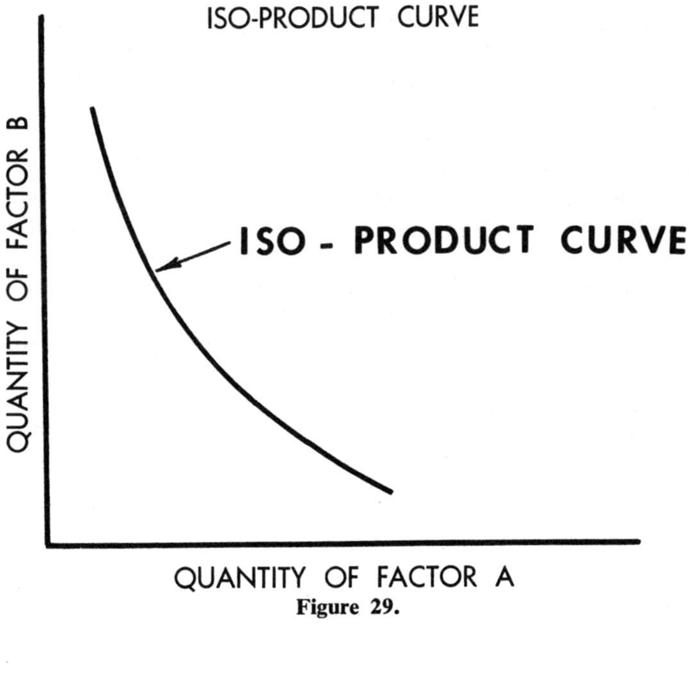

Figure 29.

point on one axis with that *one* point on the other axis which will result in the same total dollar sales (for only the second good). Then all points on this curve represent various combinations of quantities of the two goods whose sale will yield the same total dollars so long as the unit price of each good does not change. Such a *price line* is also called an *isorevenue curve*. See diagram under *price line*. (Figure 43, page 342)

iso-utility curve. Same as *indifference curve (consumer)*.

issue. (1) Used as a noun, the entire stocks or bonds sold by a corporation at a particular time. (2) In law, either (a) the children who are conceived by parents or ancestors, or (b) a

ITO International Trade Organization. As a result of the Geneva conference of 1947 and the Havana conference of 1947–8, a charter for a proposed organization directed to handling international trade and economic matters was developed.

IWW Industrial Workers of the World. Formed in 1905 as a radical rival of the AFL, and advocating sabotage and the *general strike* as means to their goal of a workers' society without a wage system. Lost its significance after World War I because of factionalism and governmental suppression.

jeopardy assessment. The power of the government to make an immediate assessment and seizure upon claim of income taxes where there is danger of either the taxpayer leaving the country or of assets disappearing.

job analysis. The process of discovering and interpreting the component elements of a job.

jobber. (1) Same as *wholesaler*. (2) More narrowly, a middleman dealing in relatively small ("job") lots, who buys from a manufacturer, importer, or wholesaler and sells to a retailer. Cf. *exchange jobber, rack jobber,* and *wagon jobber*.

job classification. A system of defining the skills and duties of a given occupation or level of achievement within a given occupation. Used for wage classification and general personnel purposes.

job description. See *job specification*.

job evaluation. See *job rating*.

job lot. Miscellaneous goods offered for sale as a unit. Cf. *broken lot*.

job method of cost accounting. A system of allocating costs among various products by maintaining a ticket for each "job" and cumulating thereon the various charges incurred at each step in production.

job order. An order or ticket directing the work to be done on a particular lot of materials.

job rating (or evaluation). The process of evaluating one job in relation to other jobs by means of a system of weighting for the various elements of the jobs compared.

job shop. One who produces to customer order rather than for the producer's inventory. Also usually involves orders of small numbers of units of the same kind and likewise a complexity in routings from one production center to another rather than a single (or few) production line flow(s).

job specification (or description). The process of determining the qualifications for the effective performance of a job.

joinder. In law, the term applies to combining or adding *causes of action* (claims) or (2) parties or persons, as well as (3) establishing the disputed issue.

joinder of issue. In law, the point in the *pleadings* by the parties to a law suit when the disputed facts have been identified.

joint and several. When signers of an obligation use this phrase, they are all bound jointly as well as each of them individually for the full amount of the debt. Joint and several liability can exist in other legal relations besides contracts, e.g., in the field of tort law.

joint and several bond. A bond whose principal and interest is guaranteed by two or more debtors.

joint and survivor annuity. An annuity payable during the longer life of either of two persons.

joint combination rate. In transportation, a *joint rate* which is obtained by combining two or more rates published in one tariff. Cf. *joint through rate.*

joint correlation. The situation in which there is a difference in the relationship between two variables (in a three-variable case) depending on what the level of the third variable is.

joint cost. The situation in which two or more products result from one process of production in such a way that no logically satisfactory method of apportioning the costs between the products can be devised.

joint-cost goods. Goods which appear jointly as the result of the same production costs. For example, beef, hides, horns, etc., are the result of the same expenses incurred in the slaughtering of cattle.

joint-demand goods. Same as *complementary goods.*

joint liability. In law, the liability of two or more persons arising from their association with regard to a contract, tort, or other legal relationship. Whether each is liable for the whole or only his part of the liability depends on the law of each state, but at common law, each is liable for the whole. Cf. *joint and several.*

jointly dependent variable. In *econometrics*, jointly dependent variables consist of the non-lagged *endogenous variables.* Cf. *endogenous variable, exogenous variable, instrumental variable, predetermined variable, shift variable.*

joint-product method of cost accounting. A system of allocating costs between two or more products produced simultaneously by distributing costs on some index basis (e.g., selling price, space occupancy, direct labor, etc.). Distinguish *process method of cost accounting.*

joint rate. In transportation, a rate applicable from a point on one carrier's route to a point on another's line, made by agreement between the two or more carriers involved and published as a single rate.

joint return. In U.S. income taxation, a return reporting the income of both the husband and the wife. This return renders each fully liable for the total tax due.

joint stock company. An organization whose capital has been divided into transferable shares among its members who, however, have the personal liability of partners for the debts of the concern. In use in England but not generally in the United States.

joint tariff. See *joint rate.*

joint tenancy. The ownership by two or more people of property in common with the right of survivorship, i.e., when one dies, his interest passes to his cotenants rather than his heirs. Cf. *tenancy in common.*

joint through rate. In transportation, a *joint rate* which is published as a unit to apply from a point on one transportation line to a point on another. Cf. *joint combination rate.*

jointure. An agreement before marriage providing lands for a wife upon the death of the husband for the life of the wife. Such an agreement, if accepted by the wife, cuts off *dower.*

joint venture. An association of individuals to carry out a limited business transaction. For example, several men associate together to share a ship's charter for a specific voyage. Unlimited liability exists but the scope of the business is much more limited than in a partnership. Cf. *underwriting syndicate.*

journal. In accounting, the first record of a transaction is made in a book called the journal from which the entry will be transferred to the ledger accounts. Entering a transaction in the journal is called journalizing. Cf. *transfer journal.*

journeyman. A carry-over from medieval days. The term is applied to the level of skill in a trade or craft between the lowest level (apprentice) and the highest level (master).

journeyman guild. An organization of the workers above the level of apprentices in an occupation during the Middle Ages. The forerunner of the modern union.

judgment. The final decision or order of a court closing a lawsuit. The judgment, however, may be subject to appeal to a higher court.

judgment bond. A bond given by one appealing from the decision of a lower court that the judgment of the lower court will be paid if the appeal is denied.

judgment creditor. A creditor whose claim has, by court action, been reduced to a judgment against the debtor.

judgment debtor. A debtor against whom a court has issued a judgment in favor of one called the judgment creditor.

judgment lien. The priority acquired by a *judgment creditor* (as of the date the judgment is docketed) against real estate of the *judgment debtor.* The lien continues for a statutory period during which the creditor may foreclose.

judgment note. Same as *cognovit note.*

judgment roll. The record of the proceedings in a lawsuit. Usually this includes the pleadings, the verdict, and the *judgment* as well as any orders made before judgment.

judicial sale. A sale conducted under the authority and supervision of a court, such as in *foreclosure* of a *mortgage.*

Juglar cycle. See *business cycle.*

junior bonds. Bonds of one issue which are subordinate in priority as regards principal or interest to another bond issue.

junior lien. A lien that is outranked by another lien.

jurat. That part of a document containing the certification by an officer empowered to take oaths that the document was sworn to before him.

jurisdiction. Jurisdiction is the power of the court or government agency over the parties and subject matter. Thus (1) a court or agency cannot render a judgment affecting a person or subject matter unless certain formalities designed to give notice to the parties have been complied with, and (2) a court or agency can act only to the extent that the constitution or legislature grants it power over a given area of human relations.

jurisdictional strike. A disagreement between two or more unions as to which shall perform a given kind of work or which shall be the representative of a given group of employees, with one of the unions striking to force the employer to yield to it. Outlawed by the Taft-Hartley Act.

jury, grand. Literally, the "large" jury. Often composed of 24 individuals who act in criminal cases on whether an *indictment* will be issued. If an indictment is returned, the defendant will be tried before a petit jury.

jury, petit. Literally, the "little" jury. Usually composed of 6 to 12 individuals who pass a verdict in a lawsuit. In criminal cases, the *grand jury* will previously have passed an indictment or a criminal complaint will have been sworn.

jus gentium. Latin for "the law of nations." In Roman law, the concept extended beyond international law as it is understood today and embraced all relations between the citizens of one state and the citizens of another.

just determined system. A system of *consistent* and *independent equations* such that the number of equations is equal to the number of variables and hence only one set of values of the variables will satisfy the system. Cf. *overdetermined system* and *underdetermined system.*

jus tertii. Latin for "the right of a third party." In law, the term refers to the position of the defendant denying that the plaintiff is entitled to the property and claiming that the right is in a third party.

just identified model. See *just determined system.*

Kaldor criterion. In *welfare economics,* a change in the economy is an improvement if those who gain evaluate their gains at a higher figure than the value which the losers set upon their losses. Cf. *Bergson criterion, Paretian optimality,* and *Scitovsky double criterion.*

kameralism. Alternate spelling for *cameralism.*

k.d. "knocked down." (1) In transportation, a good shipped in unassembled parts instead of set up (S.U.). (2) At an auction sale it means that the auctioneer brought his hammer down and sold the goods for the price reached at that moment.

keelage. Money paid for the use of port or harbor facilities.

Kefauver-Celler Act. An amendment enacted by Congress in 1950 to plug a loophole in the *Clayton Antitrust Act* of 1914 (which forbids the acquisition of the stock of another company in the same area of business when the effect is to lessen competition.) The Kefauver-Celler Anti-merger Act forbids the acquisition of the assets of another company in this situation.

Keynesian cross. With consumption on the vertical axis of a quadrant and with income in the horizontal axis, the intersection of the curve tracing (1) the path of consumption as income increases (the *consumption function*) with (2) a straight line from the origin at 45 degrees (to either axis) is called the Keynesian cross.

Keynesian economics. The school of economic thought following J. M. Keynes (1883–1946). The school holds changes in *national income* bring the economy to equilibrium rather than changes in price as argued by the *classical school.*

Keynes effect. The proposition that wage-rate reductions lower the income level and interest rates, but may not increase investment. Cf. *Pigou effect.*

keystone pricing. Nominal pricing in which the marked price is intended as higher than the selling price to make the buyer feel he is getting a bargain.

kickback. A payment by a worker of part of his wages either to a company representative or a union representative in order to evade some requirement or agreement. Now illegal under the Federal Antikickback Law except that payment of union dues is not considered a "kickback."

kinked demand. A firm's demand curve which becomes discontinuous at the market price. This is associated with the phenomenon of an industry in which there are few firms but no price leader. Here if a firm raises a price the others will not follow but if it cuts a price the others will follow.

Kinne rule. In insurance, where a blanket policy covers two items also insured by two specific policies, one on each item, the blanket insurance is apportioned in proportion to the losses experienced on each item until the insured is indemnified or the insurance exhausted and the usual contribution applies between the blanket policy and each specific policy. Cf. *Cromie, Page,* and *Reading rules* for this general situation.

Kitchin cycle. See *business cycle.*

kiting. (1) A banking term applied to the process of issuing checks for a larger amount than the balance in the account, taking advantage of the time interval needed for collection of checks and the fact that accounts may be credited by a bank

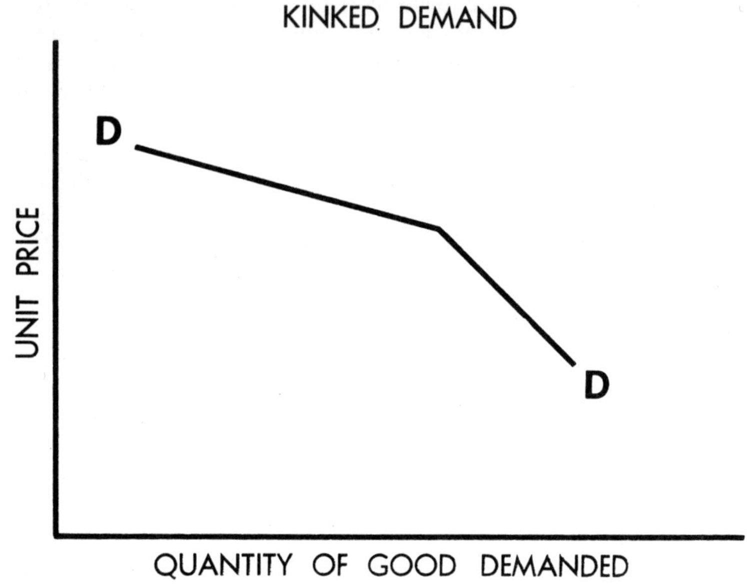

Figure 30.

as soon as the checks are deposited by the holder of the check but are charged with a check only when the check is presented for payment. (2) A banking term applied to the alteration of a check to raise the amount originally shown or authorized.

Knights of Labor. A centralized organization of American labor organized in 1869 and dominant between 1876 and 1890. Devoted primarily to humanitarian and educational objectives rather than collective bargaining.

Kondratieff cycle. See *business cycle*.

Koopmans principle. In *econometrics*, the hypothetical model specifying that the relations among the variables should be such as to allow for identification of the *parameters*.

K ratio. The reciprocal of *velocity of circulation*. Cf. *cash balance equation*.

kurtosis. In statistics, a measure of the degree to which a curve of frequency distribution is peaked or flat-topped by comparison with the peakedness of the *normal curve*. Cf. *leptokurtic*, *mesokurtic*, and *platykurtic*.

labor exchange bank. A scheme appearing in the 19th century with the aim of facilitating exchange of commodities in proportion to their labor content.

labor force. (1) In economics, the total number of workers willing to work at prevailing wage rates. Thus both the employed and unemployed (but willing to work) are included. (2) In the census definition, all persons over 14 years old not in institutions who are gainfully employed or temporarily out of work (more than 15 hours per week without pay for a family farm or business).

labor-hour method of depreciation. Taking the initial cost of a capital asset, deducting the expected salvage value at the time it is discarded, and spreading the difference on the basis of labor hours of use in an accounting period as a per cent of the total labor hours of use expected to constitute the life of the asset.

Labor Management Relations Act of 1947. See *Taft-Hartley Act.*

Labor Management Reporting and Disclosure Act of 1959. See *Landrum-Griffin Act.*

labor piracy. Taking workers from other employers by higher wages or better working conditions.

labor relations. In careful usage, the in-employment relations among employers and organized groups of employees, particularly the employer-union relationships. Distinguish *personnel management* and *industrial relations.*

labor theory of value. The theory that the value of commodities is or should be in proportion to the amount of labor spent in their production.

labor turnover. The number of people hired per unit of time in order to maintain a working force at a given figure is spoken of as the labor turnover. The most frequently used formula to measure labor turnover is: $T = R/F$ where T = turnover rate, R = replacements per unit of time and F = average working force.

labor union. See *union.*

laches. In law, a doctrine in *equity* which regardless of the *statute of limitations* bars a person from recovering in a suit where he has delayed too long in asserting his claims.

LAFTA. Latin American Free Trade Association. An association of Argentina, Bolivia, Brazil, Chile, Columbia, Ecuador, Mexico, Paraguay, Peru, Uruguay, and Venezuela to remove internal trade barriers but not to adopt a common tariff for imports from outside the association. Cf.

lag. The length of time by which a change in one variable follows a change in another. Cf. *lead.*

laissez faire, laissez passer. French for "let things go ahead, let them occur." No governmental interference in the economy. The term was developed in the 18th century particularly by those opposed to *mercantilism.*

"lambs." Ignorant or inexperienced speculators in stocks. The term is of Wall Street origin.

land bank. (1) In Colonial America, landowners grouped together and issued currency secured by mortgages on their land. (2) Sometimes used to describe banks organized under the Federal Farm Loan Act of 1916.

land contract. A written agreement for the sale of land. The purpose of using the agreement instead of a *deed* and *mortgage* is to protect the seller's interest in the unpaid balance of the purchase price. Mortgage foreclosure requires more time than land contract *foreclosure* and a margin of safety is needed to protect the seller against loss due to the possibility of a falling market during the period of foreclosure.

Landrum-Griffin Act. A federal law passed in 1959, providing for disclosure of certain financial transactions and administrative practices of labor organizations and employers and set-Also called Labor Management Reporting and Disclosure Act of 1959. Also bars employers from entering labor agreements requiring them not to buy from firms with which the union has a dispute. Cf. *secondary boycott* and *hot cargo.*

land grant. Same as *land patent.*

land-grant railroads. In the earlier days of railroad building (1850 to 1900), Congress encouraged the railroads to build, particularly in the West, by grants of land for each mile of railroad constructed. As part of the same scheme, those railroads were required to handle government freight at reduced rates until this was repealed in 1946.

land patent. The legal document used by the federal government in conveying the title of land to a citizen or individual.

land trust certificate. While any land can be placed in trust and beneficial ownership divided into shares represented by certificates, the typical use involves land subject to a long-term lease. Thus the ownership of the *remainder* interest (after the lease expires) is represented by the land trust certificates and the certificate holders participate in the lease income.

Lanham Act. An act of Congress in 1947 revising the law on trademarks.

Laplace criterion. In a situation of uncertainty where the probabilities of various eventualities (states of nature) are unknown, it should be assumed each eventuality is equally probable. Cf. *maximin, optimistic criterion,* and *regret criterion.*

lapping. In accounting, a method of concealing shortages by a series of entries postponing from one accounting period to the next the receipt of cash or some other asset.

lapse. (1) In insurance, the termination of an insurance policy by nonpayment of the premium due. (2) In law, the death of a person named in a will (a legatee) before the death of the *testator* cancels the legacy in the absence of a *statute* specifying a different resolution.

lapsed legacy. A *legacy* which falls into the residue of the estate because the legatee predeceased the *testator.* This rule is altered by statutes. Cf. *demonstrative legacy, general legacy, residuary legacy,* and *specific legacy.*

lapse ratio. In insurance, the ratio of the number of insurance policies lapsed without value or surrendered for cash during a year to the number in force at the beginning of the year.

larceny. The wrongful taking of property from another's possession without the use of force. Distinguish *embezzlement.*

Laspeyres price index. An index number computed as the value of current purchases of products (current quantity) at base-year prices divided by the actual base-year expenditure (base-year price times base-year quantity) multiplied by 100. Hence

$$\frac{p_0q_1}{p_0q_0} \text{ X } 100$$

where p_0 is the price in the base year, q_0 is the quantity in the base year, and q_1 is the quantity in the current year. Cf. *ideal index.*

last in, first out method of inventory. Under the last in, first out rule (LIFO), items of inventory used are priced out at the latest purchase prices of the stock. Inventory value is thus computed by assuming that goods on hand are those most remotely purchased and are valued at the successively most remote purchase prices.

last survivor annuity. Same as *survivorship annuity.*

Latin square. As applied to economic data, a controlled experiment in which the variable to be tested is randomly rotated by rows and columns so that the effect of other variables can be eliminated by studying row and column differences.

lawful money. (1) Money which is defined as lawful by a statute for a specific purpose. Different statutes may have different definitions, e.g., gold certificates are lawful money for reserve purposes for the Federal Reserve Banks. (2) Colloquially any money which has legal tender rights.

law merchant, or lex mercatoria, or lex mercatorum. (1) The law developed in Europe by the special courts for merchants which were more informal and speedier than the common law. Later absorbed by the common law. (2) In a general sense denotes the usages or customs which regulate matters of commerce. It includes the law of shipping, of marine insurance, of negotiable instruments, and of sales.

law of the case. The legal rule that once a matter has been finally determined in a case (as in an interlocutory appeal), this matter can no longer be reexamined even if admittedly incorrectly decided.

layaway plan. An installment purchase plan under which merchandise is set aside until payments are completed.

layoff. Temporary termination of employment by the employer.

lay-up refund. In insurance, the return of part of the premium because a ship is in port and not exposed to the perils of the sea.

lay-up warranty. In insurance, the statement of a policy holder as to the period a ship will be in port and not exposed to the perils of the sea.

l.c.l. Less-than-carload lots. Based on the fact that freight handled in carload lots for a shipper costs the carrier less than freight handled in small lots, two different rates are established for carload or less-than-carload freight.

lead. The length of time by which a change in one variable precedes a change in another. Cf. *lag.*

lead-lag technique. A forecasting technique, based on the proposition that there is a stable relationship between one economic series (the indicator) and another series which is being forecast on the basis of the movements of the first economic series.

lead time. In purchasing, the time which must be allowed between the day goods are ordered and the day delivery can be expected.

leakage. In monetary theory, the removal of funds from the income stream for repayment of debts previously contracted, or for addition to hoards.

learning curve. This curve traces over time the degree of skill developed from experience.

lease, or leasehold. A contract for the possession of lands, tenements, machinery, patents, copyrights, etc., for a limited time in return for a periodic payment of a certain sum of money or other valuable things. See *tenancy* (for different types of lease). Cf. *financial lease, net lease, operating lease.*

leaseback. See *sale and lease back.*

leased department. Often in a department store, a department operated by a specialist organization that leases the space for the department under a contract which covers all their relations. Millinery and shoes or meats are the most commonly leased departments.

leasehold mortgage. A mortgage secured by the lease of property.

leasehold mortgage bond. A bond secured by a building constructed on leased real estate. This bond is subject to the compliance by the lessee (who issues the bond) with the terms of the lease and upon default in the terms of the lease, the lessor of the leased real estate has priority over the holders of the leasehold bonds.

least outlay (or cost) combination. If quantities of one factor of production are plotted on one axis and quantities of another factor on the other axis, a set of parallel straight lines *(iso-outlay curves)* will trace all combinations of the two factors which can be purchased for the same amount of money. Another set of curves convex to the origin (*iso-product curves*) will trace all combinations of the two factors which yield the same quantity of product. The least cost combination will be the point of tangency of the iso-outlay curve and the iso-product curve, this point being the cheapest combination of the factors for that given quantity of output. The series of least cost combinations traces the least cost combination curve or *scale line.*

least squares method. In statistics, a method to fit a chosen type of curve (not necessarily a straight line) to a given set of data such that the sum of the squares of the distances (taken either horizontally or vertically) from each point of the data to the fitted curve is a minimum.

The fit of a straight line to two variables (X and Y) is achieved by solving simultaneously the following equations to get the a and b coefficients to put in the general formula for a straight line ($Y = a + bX$):

$$b = \frac{\Sigma(XY) - nM_xM_y}{\Sigma(X)^2 - n\ (M_x)^2}$$

$$a = M_y - bM_x$$

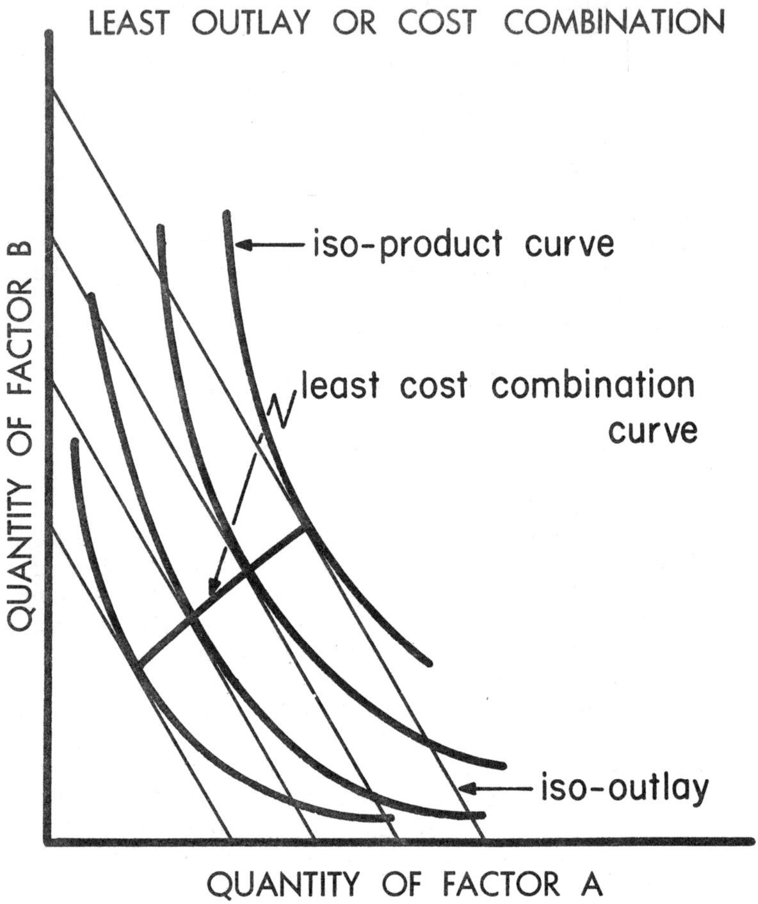

Figure 31.

where Σ means "the sum of," X and Y are the values of the two variables, n is the number of items, M_x is the arithmetic mean of the X values and M_y is the arithmetic mean of the Y values. The value of b is obtained first so it can be used in the second equation to get the value of a.

Alternatively, a and b can be determined by solving the normal equations simultaneously

$$\Sigma Y = na + b\Sigma(X)$$
$$\Sigma XY = a\Sigma(X) + b\Sigma(X)^2$$

The preceding computations will fit the line minimizing the sum of the squares of the vertical deviations (the *Y* deviation). To fit a line minimizing the sum of the squares of the horizontal deviations (the *X* deviations), replace *Y* with *X* and *X* with *Y* at all points in the preceding. Cf. *semiaverage line fitting.*

ledger. A bound book, loose-leaf book, or file of accounts. The accounts are usually arrayed in five groups: assets, liabilities, net worth, income, and expense. The information for each account is transferred to it from a journal. This process is called posting. Cf. *general ledger, subsidiary ledger.*

legacy. Strictly, a gift of personal property by will. Also called a bequest. A gift of real property (land) by will is a *devise.*

legacy, types of. See the following specific terms:

demonstrative legacy
general legacy
lapsed legacy
residuary legacy
specific legacy

legal asset. An asset held by the executor of an estate and subject to all debts under common law. Cf. *equitable asset.*

legal investments. Also called "legals" or "legal list." The investments to which savings banks, trust funds, insurance reserves, and the like are restricted by law. Usually consist of United States government obligations, certain municipal bonds, high grade railroad and public utility bonds, real estate first mortgages, etc.

legal list. See *legal investments.*

legal monopoly. A monopoly created by law, e.g., a patent or copyright.

legal rate of interest. The rate of interest which the law implies in the absence of agreement by the parties on the question of interest. It is not to be confused with the usurious rate of interest which is the maximum rate of interest which the law allows and is in excess of the legal rate.

legal reserve (legal bank reserve). The deposits which a member bank has with the Federal Reserve Bank plus the vault cash of the member bank are legal reserves. Such reserves are classified into (1) *required reserves* and (2) *excess reserves.*

legal reserve (in insurance). Same as *mean reserve.*

legal reserve insurance. Insurance for which there is a reserve or fund which with future premiums, if any, based on assumed rates of interest and mortality, will pay estimated future claims.

legal reserve life insurance. *Life insurance* conforming to the state laws which specify what minimum assets must be maintained against each policy at each point in time in order for the insurer to be recognized as solvent. The aggregate of these amounts for all a company's policies are its "legal reserves."

legal right. A right recognized in a court of law. In older English and American days, two sets of courts were maintained, law courts and equity courts, and hence two sets of rights, legal and equitable, developed. This distinction in courts has now largely disappeared but the classification of rights continues. Cf. *equitable right.*

legal tender. Any kind of money which by law must be accepted when offered in payment of a debt expressed in the country's money unit.

legatee. One to whom a *legacy* is given.

leisure class. A term devised by Veblen to describe the economic group which, largely because of wealth or income, concerns itself primarily with the spending of money and the enjoyment of leisure.

lending rate in capital budgeting. The rate which an investor can get in the market for his funds. This rate is usually (but not always) below the rate the investor pays for borrowing funds from the market. Cf. *borrowing rate in capital budgeting.*

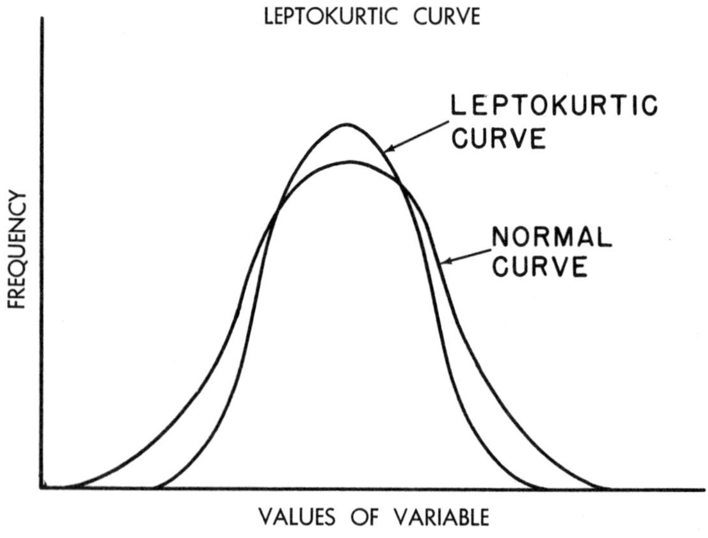

Figure 32.

leptokurtic curve. A frequency distribution curve which is more peaked than the *normal curve.* Cf. *mesokurtic* and *platykurtic.*

Lerner effect. The increase in consumption following on an increase in the supply of liquid assets relative to *disposable personal income.*

Lerner index of market power. The ratio of the difference between price and *marginal cost* to price. Hence (P — MC)/P.

lessee. The person taking possession of property for a period of time pursuant to a contract.

lessor. The person giving up the possession of property for a period of time pursuant to a contract.

less than carload rate. See *l.c.l.*

letter of administration. The written authority of a probate court issued to the administrator who will act for the estate of one dying without a will or who succeeds an *executor* who dies before he has finished the administration of an estate.

letter of attorney. Same as *power of attorney.*

letter of credit. A letter authorizing the extension of credit or the advance of money to the bearer who is usually named in the letter, the credit or advance to be charged to the person issuing the letter.

letter of credit, types of. See the following specific terms:

circular letter of credit
confirmed letter of credit
irrevocable letter of credit
open letter of credit
revocable letter of credit
revolving letter of credit
straight letter of credit
traveler's letter of credit
unconfirmed letter of credit

letter of indemnity. A contract by which one party agrees to reimburse another party for loss resulting upon a stated contingency. In effect, an insurance contract.

letter of license. A letter by a creditor permitting a debtor to proceed as stated to avoid bankruptcy.

letter of lien. A document signed by the buyer admitting that he holds the goods in trust for the seller until payment has been made for the goods. Used particularly in foreign trade.

letter of marque and reprisal. Permission granted by a government to private shipowners to attack enemy ships and seize and retain property carried by such ships.

letters patent. Same as *land patent.*

letters testamentary. The written authority from a probate court issued to the executor of a will to act for the estate. Cf. *letter of administration.*

letter stock. Stock not registered under the Securities Act of 1933 where the buyer gives the seller a letter stating the buyer intends to hold for investment purposes and does not contemplate reoffering the stock to others.

level charge plan. In *investment companies,* a plan under which the *sales charge* is deducted at the same rate as periodic (installment) purchases of shares are made. Cf. *contractual plan.*

level of service. The percentage of orders (in volume) filled from inventory as opposed to satisfied by production after receipt of the order.

level-payment mortgage. Same as *direct-reduction mortgage.*

level premium insurance. A fixed rate of premium on a life insurance policy determined by the age of the insured person at the time he takes out the policy and remaining the same thereafter.

leverage coefficient. The ratio of the total increase in national income to an increase in initial expenditures. Cf. *multiplier* (several types), *acceleration principle.*

leverage factor. (1) In finance, the extent to which a corporation can effect, by the use of bonds and preferred stocks, proportionate changes in return to common stock greater than the changes in operating income. If the bulk of the corporation's capital is represented by bonds and preferred stock, the corporation has a high leverage factor. The process of using the leverage factor is called trading on the equity. (2) The increase in the rate of profit which follows an increase in the volume of sales or production when fixed costs are spread over more units.

leveraging earnings. Changing the return on *equity* by issuing debt or preferred stock.

lex fori. Latin for "the law of the forum." The law of the place of the trial as opposed to the law of the place of the tort, contract, or other activity. The law of the forum governs matters of procedure; the law of the place governs matters of substance. Cf. *lex loci.*

lex loci. Latin for "the law of the place." In contracts, the law of the place where the contract was made. Cf. *lex fori.*

lex mercatoria. Same as *law merchant.*

liabilities. The claims of creditors. The assets of an individual or business are subject to payment of these claims.

liability, types of. See the following specific terms:

contingent liability
current liability
fixed or long term liability
single liability
unlimited liability

liability insurance. There are four principal types: *automobile liability*, *product liability*, *public liability*, and *workman's compensation*. Each of these insures a liability (or obligation to pay) imposed by law on the insured person.

liability reserve. An amount set up to show a liability such as income taxes but in the form of a reserve to show that the amount is estimated.

libel. (1) A written or printed untruth which damages a party about whom the statement is untrue. Cf. *slander*. (2) In *admiralty* law, the complaint is called a libel, the plaintiff is the libellant and the defendant the libellee.

liberty bond. A bond issued by the United States government to finance its activities in the first World War.

license. (1) A personal, nontransferable, formal permission from the government to perform certain acts or to carry on a certain business. (2) A permit granted by a private person, e.g., a license under a patent.

license tax. A tax upon individuals or corporations for the right of engaging in some business enterprise.

lien. A right by way of security against real estate or personal property for the satisfaction of a debt. May be created by specific act of the individual (e.g., a *mortgage*), or by operation of law (e.g., *mechanic's lien* for work done or a *vendor's lien* for the unpaid purchase price). A lien is lost when possession is surrendered, but a court of equity may impose an *equitable lien* where possession has been lost.

lien, types of. See the following specific terms:

agent's lien
attorney's lien
bailee's lien
carrier's lien
equitable lien
hotel lien
innkeeper's lien
judgment lien
mechanic's lien
seller's lien
vendor's lien

life annuity. An *annuity* policy that provides for the payment of income to the annuitant during his lifetime but with no payments after death even though death occurs prematurely. Also called *life income* annuity.

life annuity certain. An *annuity* policy that provides for the payment of income for the life of the annuitant but guarantees a minimum number of payments so that if the annuitant dies within the guaranteed period, the balance of the payments is made to his estate. Cf. *cash refund annuity*.

life cycle income hypothesis. That people plan consumption and saving over a life-time to achieve no net saving over their life time, that is, saving in years of higher income to spend in years of lower income. Identified with Modigliani-Brumberg-Ando. Cf. *absolute income hypothesis, past income hypothesis, permanent income hypothesis, relative income hypothesis.*

life estate. The right to possession of land for a period of time measured by the life either of the party having the right to possession or of another person. More than one life span may be used to measure the period, e.g., for the period of the longer living of *A* or *B*.

life expectancy. The number of years of life remaining at any attained age for the average of persons of that attained age. Such a number of years is determined from one of the mortality tables. Cf. *American experience table of mortality* and *Commissioners' Standard Ordinary Mortality Table.*

life income annuity. (1) Most commonly, an annuity or a life insurance policy guaranteeing the holder an income for life after reaching a certain age. (2) Also any arrangement providing income for life.

life insurance. A contract providing for payment of a stated amount upon the death of an individual called the insured in return for the payment of premiums. A protection against the risk of premature death and loss of income to the family by means of spreading the risk over a great many others who are also participants in the plan. The unit of time is the year. The usual unit of insurance is $1,000.

life or nonrefund annuity. An annuity such that the annuitant (party receiving the annuity) is assured of a fixed income for life. If he dies before the annuity is exhausted, the company takes the unexpended balance. If he lives beyond the life of the fund, the company stands the loss.

life table. In insurance, a table showing the mortality and survivorship characteristics of a given population. Thus the experience of fifteen American insurance companies in the period before 1895 forms the basis for the *American experience table of mortality.*

life tenant. The one owning a *life estate.*

LIFO. See *last in, first out method of inventory.*

lighterage. A charge made for the conveyance of goods by water, either in a lighter or a barge.

limit. In trading, the definite price stated by a customer to a broker restricting the execution of an order to buy for not more than or to sell for not less than the stated price.

limited (Ltd.). "Limited" means shareholders in the concern have only limited liability for corporation debts, namely, to the extent of their investment. In some states and countries required to be placed after the title of a corporation. In general, Ltd. and Inc. are the English and American terms representing the same concept.

limited coinage. The situation in which only a certain amount of a given metal is coined, as under the Bland-Allison Act of 1878, or the Sherman Silver Act of 1890. Cf. *limping standard.*

limited company. English term for a *corporation* or company in which the liability of stockholders is limited to their investment. Cf. *joint stock company.*

limited function wholesaler. A middleman who takes title to the goods he deals in but performs only one or two of the functions of wholesaler. The principal categories are (see each item): cash-carry wholesalers, drop shippers, rack jobbers, truck wholesalers.

limited gold standard. Same as *gold bullion standard.*

limited legal tender. Moneys which formerly were legal tender in payment of debts up to a specified amount, e.g., pennies were legal tender up to 25 cents. This was changed by law June 5, 1933.

limited liability. Restriction of the liability of an investor to the amount invested. In a limited partnership the limited partners, and in a business corporation all the stockholders, have such limited liability. Formerly, in the case of a bank, liability of stockholders extended to double the par value of stock owned. Cf. *double liability.*

limited-line store. A nondepartmentalized retail store with the bulk of its sales in a given broad line of merchandise.

limited partnership. A partnership which has one or more partners whose loss is limited to the investment in the business. The name of a limited partner cannot be used in the firm name unless identified as limited. The limited partner cannot engage in business for the partnership. The limited partnership must also have one or more general partners who have unlimited personal liability for the debts of the partnership. Under the Uniform Limited Partnership Act, the agreement of partnership must be publicly recorded.

limited-pay life insurance. Life insurance in which the insured pays a limited number of years but is insured for life. The annual payments may be from one on up, commonly for five, ten, twenty, and twenty-five years.

limited tax bond. In municipal finance, a bond secured by the pledge of a tax that is limited as to rate or amount, e.g., a state constitutional limit as to rate or amount of tax that a municipality can levy.

limit of liability. In insurance, the maximum amount which an insurer is bound by the policy to pay in the case of proved losses covered by the terms of the policy.

limit order. An order to buy or sell on a stock exchange subject to some limitation as to price. Cf. *market order, day order, open order.*

limping standard. A monetary system involving two metals with a restriction on coinage of one metal thus distinguishing it from true bimetallism. Cf. *monetary standard, types of.*

linear model. A system relating quantifiable factors either as variables or constants with the relationships of the variables expressed in the form of linear equations. Cf. *nonlinear model.*

linear programming. A system of determining maximum output and minimum cost, giving particular recognition to the fact that at any given point in time methods of production, supplies of factors, or other elements are fixed and the paths of expansion are linear. The system employs constraints (limitations that must be met by the answer) and an *objective function* (that which will be maximized or minimized) which are then manipulated by matrix algebra.

linear regression. See *regression analysis.*

line-balancing stock. Same as *decoupling inventory.*

line haul. In transportation, the distance from point of origin to point of destination over truck or rail routes, excluding pickup and delivery.

line of credit. A commitment by a bank or other financial institution to a borrower to lend on future request on presently agreed terms, up to the amount of the "line." The lending may be secured or not and usually is contingent upon maintenance by the borrower of the same financial condition.

line of discount. Essentially the same as *line of credit.*

line position. A place in the "line" organization, which includes all those from the president to common labor, whose duty it is to operate or get out production. Distinguish *staff position.*

link financing. An arrangement by a bank borrower for an insurance company to purchase a *certificate of deposit* to be posted with the bank as the *compensatory balance* for the loan of the bank to the borrower.

link relative index number. An index number computed from a series of data stating each datum not as a percentage of the original base but as a percentage of the preceding datum.

liquid asset. Same as *quick asset.*

liquidated. In law, a claim that is in the form of a determinate money amount.

liquidated damages. See the explanation under *damages for breach of contract.*

liquidation. (1) The winding up of affairs, selling assets for cash. (2) More narrowly, the termination of liabilities or selling of assets even though there is no winding up.

liquidity. The measure of liquidity is the extent to which a person has cash or can procure cash through sale of property.

liquidity function. An equation in which the quantity of money desired for liquid holding (dependent variable) is taken as a function of one or more independent variables. Thus $M_L = f(X, Y)$ where M_L is the quantity of money desired for liquid purposes.

liquidity preference. The schedule of the amount of resources valued in terms of money or of wage-units which an individual wishes to retain in the form of money in different sets of circumstances.

liquidity preference theory of interest. An explanation of the rate of interest as the price adjusting (a) the *liquidity preferences* of individuals, which determine demand for money and (b) banking policy, which determines the supply of money. Cf. *abstinence theory of interest, agio theory of interest, marginal productivity theory of interest, time preference theory of interest.*

liquidity ratios. The principal liquidity ratios are: *acid test, cash-to-daily-purchases, current ratio,* and *quick ratio.* These ratios measure the ability of a firm to meet its debts as they come due.

liquidity risk. Same as *market risk.*

liquidity trap. The point at which the demand for money (liquidity) is infinitely elastic with respect to the interest rate and further increases in the supply of money yield no fall in the interest rate. Such a situation arises when the yield on earning assets is so low that the risk of holding such assets is (or is thought to be) so high that investors prefer to hold any increases in the money supply in liquid form.

lis pendens. Latin for "a case is pending." Particularly in connection with real estate, a notice placed in the public record of property that questions have been raised bearing on the title to the property so that any buyer will take the risk of what the ultimate decision of the case may be.

listed security. A security which has met the requirements of a stock exchange for listing. Such requirements include submitting of financial reports, consent to certain supervision, etc.

listing. (1) In real estate, the contract of an owner authorizing a broker to sell the owner's real estate. (2) In securities, the contract between a firm and a stock exchange covering the trading of that firm's securities on the stock exchange.

listing, types of. See the following specific terms:

exclusive agency listing
exclusive right to sell listing
multiple listing
open listing

list price. The price shown in the sales list of the seller. Used as the basis from which discounts may be computed for various classes of buyers.

lite pendente. Latin for "a suit being pending." In law, a court may issue orders for the duration of the lawsuit, i.e., until the matter is finally resolved.

little steel. Colloquial term for the smaller steel-producing companies.

littoral rights. The shore line rights of a body of water between the high water and low water marks of a sea or lake. Cf. *riparian rights.*

livery company. At the end of the Middle Ages the rich guild masters who could own costly liveries formed livery companies (as opposed to the yeomanry of the smaller masters) to dominate a particular craft.

livery of seisin. In law, the delivery of possession of *real estate.* In the United States, this occurs with the delivery of the *deed* to the property to the new owner.

living trust. Same as *inter vivos trust.*

Lloyd's. An association in London whose members deal in various kinds of insurance, and in particular keep a Register of all British and many foreign-owned ships. A Lloyd's policy binds only those members of the association who underwrite the particular risk on which the insurance is issued. Similar insurance groups in the United States are also called Lloyd's groups.

load factor. In public utilities, the ratio of the average output to the peak output for a given period of time. Used as the basis for price differentiation between different classes of customers. The higher the load factor, the lower the rate charged the customer. Cf. *capacity factor, diversity factor, utilization factor.*

loading charge. Especially in insurance, the addition of a uniform charge covering overhead costs to the bare premium required by actuarial tables to cover mortality and interest factors. In the case of open-end investment companies, the charge made at the time of purchase to cover overhead such as commissions.

loan. (1) A sum of money lent by the lender to the borrower. (2) Other property whose use but not ownership is transferred by the owner to the user.

loans, types of. See the following specific terms:

broker's loan
call loan
collateral loan
consumption loan
day loan
deposit loan
fiduciary loan
field warehousing loan
forced loan
morning loan
nonnotification loan
participation loan
production loan
secured loan
term loan
tied loan
warehousing loan
workout loan

loanable funds theory of interest. An explanation of interest as the price adjusting the demand for and supply of loanable funds available at any particular time, with demand determined mainly by investment opportunities and supply by savings and credit creation. Cf. *abstinence theory of interest, agio theory of interest, liquidity preference theory of interest, marginal productivity theory of interest, time preference theory of interest.*

loan crowd. The term applied to those brokers on the stock exchange who loan stock to other brokers who are engaged in *selling short.*

loaned flat. Usually, when stock is sold short (see *selling short*), and a person borrows stock to effect delivery and deposits cash with the lender of the stock equal to the market value of the borrowed stock, interest is allowed on this deposit, but if the stock is scarce, no interest is allowed on the deposit, that is, the stock is loaned flat.

loan shark. One who takes advantage of a person's needs to lend him money at exorbitant rates of interest, usually requiring the pledge of property many times the value of the loan.

loan value. In life insurance, the maximum amount that the insurer must lend the insured on his request. Usually this amount is identical with the cash surrender value of the policy.

local brand. A brand sponsored by a distributor or manufacturer in a limited area. Cf. *manufacturer's brand.*

local option. Used to refer to the state constitutional or legislative grant to local communities of the right to regulate certain activities such as liquor licensing and taxicab licenses.

local rate. In transportation, a rate applicable to shipments between stations located on the same transportation line. Cf. *joint rate.*

lock-box financing. The operation of a system of lock boxes in post offices in many cities with instruction to customers of a firm to mail payments to the nearest city in order to speed the collection of funds. A bank in each city collects the contents of each box at frequent intervals.

locked in. In the stock market, a term describing an investor who owns securities on which he has a profit but which he is unwilling to sell because of the *capital gains tax.*

lockout. Action by an employer closing his plant to enforce his demands against workmen or to avoid workmen's demands.

lock-up. A note or obligation that has been renewed.

loco parentis. See *in loco parentis.*

locus sigilii. Latin for "the place of the seal." In law, a sealed contract may have different consequences from one not sealed. Thus in some states, the statute of limitations applicable to a sealed contract is double that for an unsealed contract. A person is free to adopt any mark as his seal. Hence, the frequently used "L.S." on printed forms.

logarithm. An exponent indicating a power to which a base must be raised to equal a number. Common logarithms are based on 10. Natural logarithms are based on e (2.7182818).

logarithmic curve. A curve whose values on one axis increase arithmetically while the values on the other axis increase logarithmically. Many patterns of growth conform to this curve. The general formula of the curve is $\log y = \log a + x \log b$ where x is the arithmetic axis and y is the logarithmic axis and a is the intercept on the y axis when x is zero and b is the *slope* of the curve.

logistic curve. A modified exponential curve; a series in which progression is by small absolute amounts in the early stages, then by large absolute amounts, and finally again by smaller absolute amounts until an upper limit or saturation is ap-

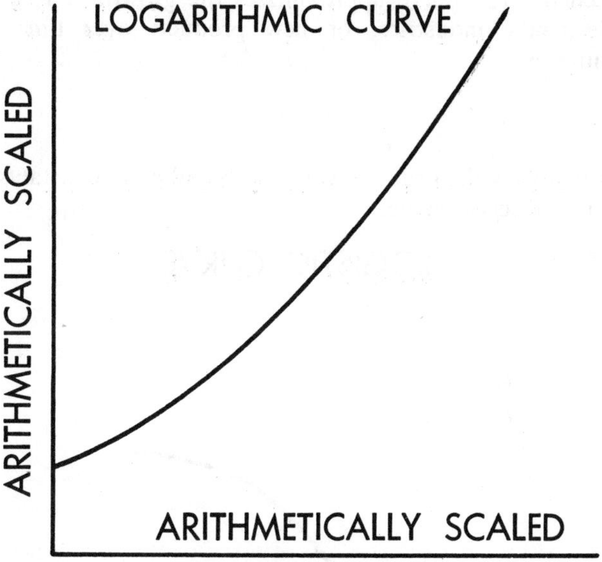

Figure 33.

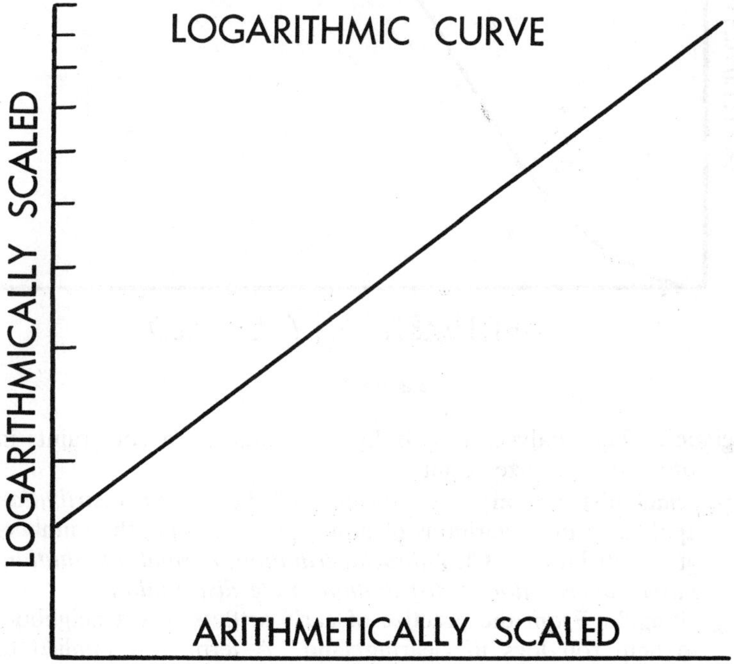

Figure 34.

proached. The curve approximates the growth of new companies, new industries, or new products over time. The formula is

$$\frac{1}{y_c} = a + bc^x$$

in which y_c is the ordinate value; a, b and c are constants; and x is the abscissa value.

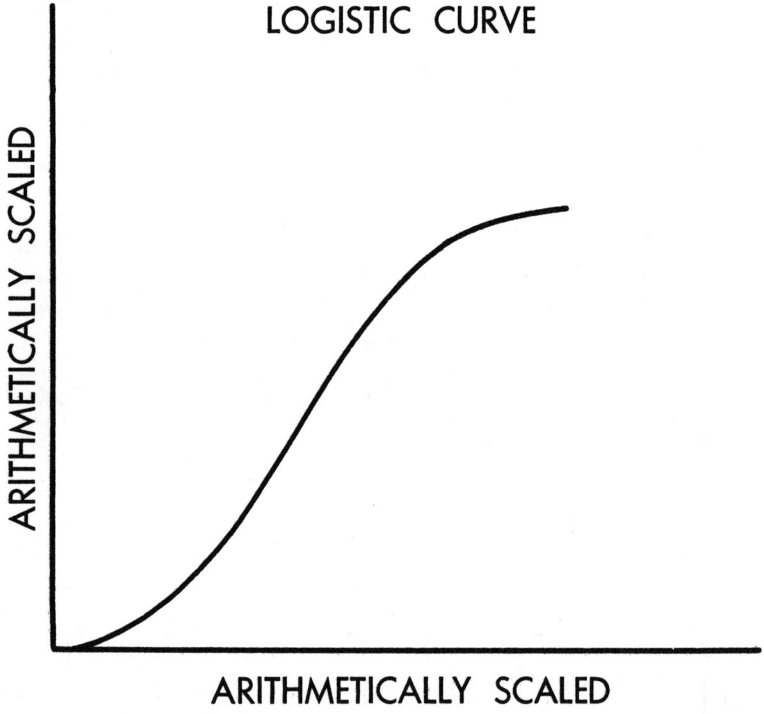

Figure 35.

logistics. The analysis, usually by mathematics, of constraints in order to optimize results.

log-normal distribution. The formula of the *normal distribution* applied to the logarithms of numbers rather than the numbers of a distribution. Cf. *Gibrat distribution, normal distribution, Pareto distribution, t distribution, Yule distribution.*

"logrolling." From the practice of early settlers to get neighbors to help roll logs in clearing land. A term now applied to legislators and their practice of trading votes on legislation. For example, a legislator who had no direct interest in the tariff on fish might agree to vote in favor of a high tariff if another legislator who was vitally interested in the fish tariff would go along on a measure in which the first legislator was vitally interested. Now the term is used generally to describe this principle in business transactions.

Lombard Street. The street in London where most financial institutions are located. The British equivalent of the American term, Wall Street.

long. See *buying long.*

long and short haul clause. The provision in the Interstate Commerce Act, as amended, which prohibits carriers from charging higher rates for a short haul than for a longer haul which includes the short haul.

longevity pay. A pay differential allowed to employees on the basis of length of service.

long rate. In insurance, the premium rate for a policy extending more than one year. This rate is lower than the annual rate.

long run. A general term in economic theory. (1) The period of time in which *all* costs (including the "fixed costs") of a particular firm are to be considered variable. For example, time long enough to add to plant whereas the time period required to add an extra shift is the short run. (2) The same concept applied to the period of time needed so that all the factors of an economy are variable.

long run cost. In the long run there are no *fixed costs* and hence both the *average cost curve* and *marginal cost curve* (see Figure 2, page 27) will be flatter than in the short run. In the long run all resources used in production are variable.

long run equilibrium. See *equilibrium of firm or industry, (partial) long run.*

long ton. 2,240 pounds. Cf. *short ton.*

long wave. See *business cycle.*

Lorenz curve. With percentages from 0 to 100 on each axis, the curve shows the cumulative percentage relationships between two variables, one on each axis. The curve is used to measure the degree of departure from a uniform distribution in which 1% of one variable would be matched by 1% in the other variable. A completely uniform distribution would appear as a straight line of 45°. The more hollow the curve, the more unequal the distribution. This curve is commonly used to show the effect of a tax on the distribution of income.

The *Gini coefficient* is used to measure the inequality of a Lorenz distribution. One of the famous uses of the Lorenz curve is the *Pareto distribution.* See Figure 36.

loss-and-expense ratio. In insurance, the sum of the *loss ratio* plus the *expense ratio.*

lost carry-back and loss carry-forward. See *carry back* (or *carry forward*).

loss constant. In workmen's compensation insurance, a flat sum included in the premium for a risk that is too small for the use of experience ratings.

loss conversion factor. In workmen's compensation insurance, the amount added to actual losses paid to cover expenses in handling claims. This figure is then used in *retrospective rating.*

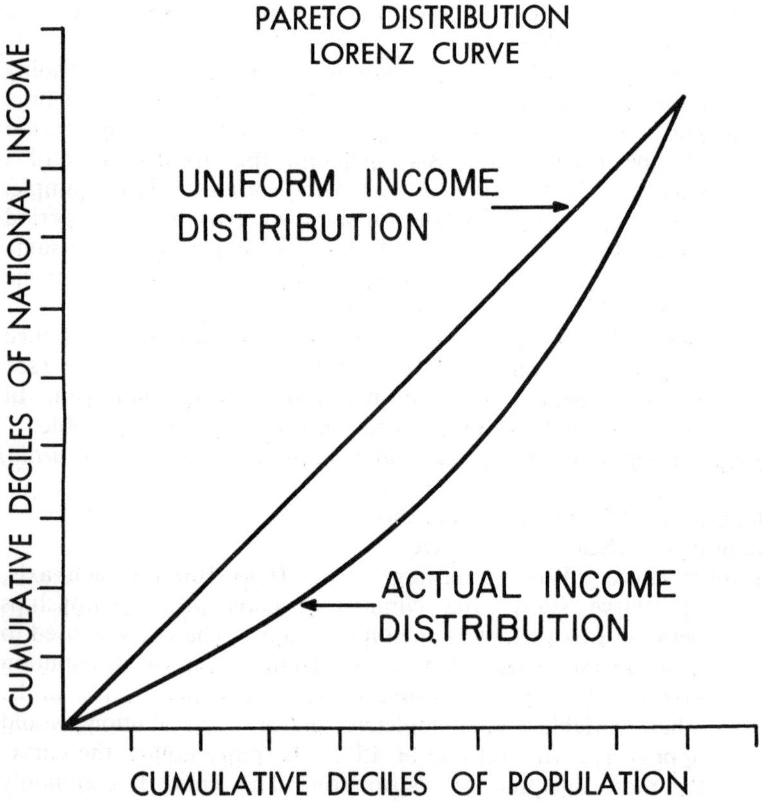

Figure 36.

loss leader price. A "loss leader" is a popular, fast selling product offered for sale at a price which may be less than cost in order to attract customers, with the expectation that sales of other merchandise, bearing normal or higher than normal markup, will increase enough to more than compensate for the "loss" on the popular item.

loss payable clause. In insurance, a clause providing for the payment of any loss to someone other than the *insured.*

loss ratio. In insurance, the ratio of losses paid to premiums earned, i.e., the losses of a period against the premiums allocable to that period.

loss reserve. In insurance, a fund for payment of losses that have been incurred but are not yet due.

lot size. See *optimum lot size.*

lot-size stock. In inventory analysis, the amount of inventory needed to minimize inventory costs. See *optimum lot-size.* Docs not include *safety stock* (to reduce normal outages due to demand variation and replenishment time) and *anticipation stock* (to meet specific and anticipated variations such as seasonal variation.) Cf. *cycle stock.*

lower order goods. Cf. *intermediate goods.*

l.s. See *locus sigilii.*

Ltd. See *limited.*

l.t.l. Less than truckload. See explanation under *l.c.l.*

lucrum cessans. Latin for "profit lost." In breach of contract, one element of damages is lost profit. Cf. *damnum emergens.*

lump of labor theory of wages. A generalization that at any given time, the amount of labor demanded by producers is fixed and does not change with the rate of pay demanded by the workers, but that increased productivity by workers would shorten the number of hours of work available. Cf. *bargaining theory of wages, marginal productivity theory of wages, residual theory of wages, subsistence theory of wages, wages fund theory of wages.*

luxuries. Articles of consumption which some persons argue are not needed for health or welfare but which are purchased by some consumers. Economists often prefer to avoid the ethical implications of the word by measuring the degree of luxury in terms of *price elasticity* of demand and *income elasticity* of demand for a commodity, holding that low elasticity indicates in fact that the item is not a luxury at all but a necessity, e.g., cigarettes or beer.

macroeconomics. Modern economic analysis is divided into macroeconomics and microeconomics. Macroeconomics is the study of *aggregates* of firms, households, prices, wages, and incomes, as opposed to *single* or *individual* firms or households. Cf. *microeconomics.*

maintained mark-up. See *mark-up, maintained.*

maintenance of membership. A clause in a labor contract providing that once an employee joins a union he must remain a union member for the term of the current contract, usually under penalty of losing his job. Ordinarily an *escape period* is provided between contracts.

major medical insurance. Insurance designed to cover medical expenditures above a deductible amount but not in excess of the *face value* of the policy.

mala fide. Latin for "in bad faith."

mala in se. Latin for "wrong in itself," i.e., morally wrong. In criminal law, intent must be shown (by conduct or otherwise) to do such an act. Cf. *mala prohibita.*

mala prohibita. Latin for "wrong by reason of law." In criminal law, no intent need be proved to establish guilt of mala prohibita. Mere violation is sufficient. Cf. *mala in se.*

malicious prosecution. The tort of bringing a lawsuit in bad faith without reasonable grounds to believe the action will be successful.

Maloney Act. Passed by Congress in 1938 as an amendment to the *Securities Exchange Act* and providing for registration with the SEC of all brokers dealing in the over-the-counter market except those dealing exclusively intrastate or in exempt securities. Regulation occurs cooperatively with the National Association of Securities Dealers.

malpractice insurance. Insurance protecting professional people from claims resulting from negligent performance of professional services.

Malthusian law of population. As stated by Malthus, population tends to increase faster than the food supply.

managed currency. A currency whose quantity is increased or decreased according to changes in the general price level or other objectives. The management is by the government of a country or its central bank. The management may be designed to influence the internal price level of a country or the ratio of that price level to the price levels of other countries, or both, or to pursue other objectives.

managed money. Same as *managed currency.*

management fee. The annual charge (as distinct from the *sales charge*) of the manager of an *investment company* fund. Usually based on the value of the assets and for the income handled.

management ratio. The ratio of the number of management personnel to 1000 employees. Further broken down into the ratio of top-management and middle-management personnel per 1000 employees.

management science. The broad field employing information systems and the techniques of *operations research* and *decision theory* to arrive at business decisions scientifically. *Data processing* and scientific programming on computing machines have been important tools for development of this area.

management trust. Same as *general management trust*.

Manchester school. A 19th century group of English economists who applied the doctrines of the *classical school* to achieve reforms such as repeal of the corn laws.

mandamus. Latin for "we command." A court order requiring an official to do something which he is under a duty to do. Corporate officers are generally held to be officials for purposes of this type of action.

manifest. A shipping document recording the value, count, point of origin, and destination of each item of cargo. The term has been extended beyond marine transportation to warehousing, land transportation, etc.

manipulation. In the stock market, the illegal practice of buying or selling to create the impression of an active market or to affect the price to induce others to buy or sell. Cf. *bear raiding*.

manit. An abbreviation for "man-minutes." Used in connection with an incentive wage plan in which the worker is paid a premium for man-minutes of work achieved over the standard output per worker.

Mann-Elkins Act. An act of Congress in 1910 revising laws governing interstate commerce by including communication systems (now under FCC jurisdiction) and by broadening the powers of the Interstate Commerce Commission.

manorial system. The medieval land ownership system under which the feudal lord of the manor owned large tracts of land which were farmed by serfs, who in return furnished services to the lord.

manual rating. In insurance, the determination of the premium rate from a manual classifying the types of risk on a general basis (e.g., by industries) without reference to the particular conditions of an individual case. Cf. *experience rating, merit rating, retrospective rating, schedule rating.*

manufacturer's agent. An agent middleman who sells only in a specific market area where he may also represent noncompeting lines. He is bound by the price policy of the manufacturer. He may operate a warehouse for the manufacturer but seldom handles credits and collections. He differs from a broker in that his relationship to the manufacturer is continuous.

manufacturer's brand. A brand sponsored by one or more manufacturers without limitation as to area. Cf. *local brand.*

manufacturer's representative. Same as *manufacturer's agent.*

manufacturing overhead. All the costs of the manufacturing department except raw materials, purchased parts, and *direct labor.*

margin. In commercial transactions, the difference between the purchase price paid by a middleman or retailer and his selling price. Also called *gross margin.*

margin (or "on margin"). In trading, the purchase of a stock or commodity with payment in part in cash (called the margin) and in part by a loan. Usually the loan is made by the broker effecting the purchase.

marginal analysis. The analysis of economic data in terms of the addition to the value of one variable (e.g., to output, revenues, or costs) resulting from the addition of one unit to another variable (e.g., to input, prices, or output).

marginal buyer. The buyer whose willingness to buy is just great enough to cause him to pay a given price.

marginal cost. At any given point of production, the addition to total costs of the last unit produced. With dollars of cost on the y axis and quantity of output on the x axis, the marginal cost curve will be U-shaped. (See Figure 2, page 27.)

marginal costing. Same as *direct costing.*

marginal cost pricing. Pricing each good so that the price covers all direct costs, plus the variable part of overhead. Cf. *average cost pricing, full cost pricing.*

marginal efficiency of capital. For the firm, the declining returns from capital investment as the use of capital increases. For the economy, the supply price of capital rises as its use increases.

marginal farmers. Farmers who work land which produces only enough to cover the cost of production at given prices. If prices fall, marginal land becomes idle or is operated at a loss.

marginal laborer. The laborer who produces goods whose value just equals the amount of his wages.

marginal land. See *margin of cultivation, extensive.*

marginal output curve. At any given volume of production, the addition to total physical output by the last physical unit of variable input (such as labor) added, while one or more *factors of production* (such as plant size) are held fixed. With units of marginal output on the *y* axis and units of the variable input factor on the *x* axis, the marginal output curve will be shaped like an inverted u because of first the less efficient, then efficient, and finally less efficient use of the fixed factor.

marginal pair. The *marginal seller* and the *marginal buyer.* Sometimes the term "marginal pairs" is used to refer to the marginal seller and marginal buyer plus the first seller whose price is above the market price and the first buyer whose price is just below the market price.

marginal physical product. At any given point in production, the addition to the total physical product by the last unit of input. Cf. *marginal revenue product.*

marginal productivity of capital. Same as *marginal efficiency of capital.*

marginal productivity theory of interest. An interest theory explaining the interest rate as tending under competitive conditions to equal the marginal addition to output by the last unit of capital when the amount of available capital is assumed fixed.

marginal productivity theory of wages. A wage theory holding that wages of all workers under competitive conditions tend to equal the marginal addition to the product attributable to the marginal laborer. Cf. *bargaining theory of wages, lump of labor theory of wages, residual theory of wages, subsistence theory of wages, wage fund theory of wages.*

marginal propensity to consume. The ratio between a) the increase in consumption which follows on a small increase in income and b) the increase in income.

marginal propensity to invest. The ratio between a) the increase in new capital formed which follows on a small increase in income and b) that small increase in income.

marginal propensity to save. The ratio between a) the increase in income not spent on consumption which follows on a small increase in income and b) that small increase in income.

marginal rate of substitution (diminishing). A refinement of the basic idea of the principle of *diminishing marginal utility.*

Assuming a consumer with a given quantity of each of two goods, *x* and *y*, and varying the quantities of each so that the consumer retains the same total satisfaction, the principle states that the more *x* is substituted for *y*, the more of *y* will have to be received for further decreases of *x*. The rate of this substitution must diminish when the goods are substitutional and not complementary. Marginal rate of substitution is also applicable to questions of substituting one factor of production for another and similar problems.

marginal revenue. At any given volume of sales, the addition (positive or negative) to total revenue by the last unit of product sold at the point under consideration. With dollars of revenue on the *y* axis and quantity of output on the *x* axis, the marginal revenue curve will be a horizontal straight line at the level of price in the case of *pure competition* and a curve descending to the right and under the average revenue curve in the case of *monopolistic competition*. (See Figure 5, page 29.)

marginal revenue product. At any given point in a schedule relating revenue and input, the addition to total revenue by the last unit of input. When there is *pure competition,* the marginal revenue product is equal to the *marginal physical product* multiplied by the price of the product. In *monopolistic competition,* the marginal revenue product is less than the marginal physical product because the demand curve is sloping downward to the right, and the loss of revenue from previous units due to the lower price of expanded output must be deducted from the revenue added by the marginal unit. Cf. *marginal physical product*.

marginal seller. (1) Under pure competition in the long run, the seller whose costs of production (including wages of management and "normal" return on capital) just equal the market price for the good he is selling. Proper adjustments would have to be made for "expectations" as to future price in order to make this a workable concept. (2) In the short run, the seller whose marginal costs just equal market price. (3) In momentary transactions, the seller whose *reservation price* is equal to market price.

marginal utility. At any given point of consumption, the addition (positive or negative) to total utility by the last unit of a good. The older group of the marginal utility school assumed that utility can be measured; the new group argues that it is only possible to establish preferences but not to measure their differences.

marginal utility school. A 19th century group of economists headed by W. S. Jevons in England, Leon Walras in France, and Karl Menger in Austria, who related prices and product preferences through marginal utility: the added amount of satisfaction from an additional unit of a good. Sometimes confused with *Austrian school.*

marginal value product. Same as *marginal revenue product.*

margin call. A demand by a broker to put up money or securities upon purchase of a stock or if the stock is already owned on margin, to increase the money or securities where the price of the stock has fallen since purchase. The last process is remargining.

margin of cultivation, extensive. The situation in which unit doses of labor and capital applied to less and less productive land finally reach land of such poor quality that the product just pays for the labor and capital.

margin of cultivation, intensive. The situation in which the last dose of labor and capital applied to land on which previous doses have been applied yields a product that is just large enough to pay for itself.

margin of profit. (1) Net profit from operations divided by net sales. This is a rate. (2) The amount of profit remaining after costs have been deducted from income. This is an amount.

margin of safety. In investment banking, the difference between the total face value of a bond issue and the actual value of property put up as security for the issue.

marine insurance. (1) Ocean marine insurance. Insurance on property that is transported on the high seas, including the vessels and their contents. Probably the oldest form of insurance known, dating back to ancient history. (2) Inland marine insurance. Insurance covering any of four major risks: (1) transportation of goods other than on the ocean, (2) fixed transportation and communication property, (3) personal property at large (floating), and (4) liability as a bailee.

marital deduction. The provision of the federal *estate tax* that property left to a surviving spouse is not includable within the estate of the deceased spouse for estate tax purposes up to one-half of the estate of the deceased spouse. A parallel provision of the federal *gift tax* classifies one-half of any gift by a spouse as being given by the other spouse. In both the federal estate tax and the federal gift tax, the marital deduction is allowed before any exemption or exclusion is applied.

maritime law. Same as *admiralty.*

mark-down. A reduction in the price below that at which the goods have been offered. When expressed as a percentage, the *new* selling price is used as the base (e.g., a price reduction from $1. to 50c is a 100% mark-down).

mark-down cancellation. Additions that do not raise the selling price above that at which the goods were offered for sale prior to a mark-down.

market. (1) With reference to a commodity, the area in which buyers and sellers of the commodity are in communication with one another, and an area in which exchange takes place. (2) A particular group of buyers, e.g., the juvenile market. (3) Buyers and sellers of a given commodity, e.g., the wheat market. (4) A *trading area,* e.g., the New England market, the Atlanta market. (5) In Marshallian economics, an area within which, ideally, prices at any given time are the same for all buyers and sellers. (6) Colloquially for *market value.*

market, types of. See the following specific terms:

bear market
black market
broad market
brokers' market
bull market
buyers' market
capital market
cash or spot market
futures market
gray market
imperfect market
money market
narrow market
open market
over-the-counter market
perfect market
pluperfect market
primary market
secondary market
sellers' market
soft market
speculative market
thin market

marketability. In investments, ready salability at a price not materially lower than that at which it can be bought.

marketable title. See *good and marketable title.*

market area. That territory within which the purchase or sale of a commodity affects the price generally prevailing for that commodity.

market demand. The quantity of goods and services demanded at prices currently prevailing in the market place.

market equilibrium. Same as *momentary equilibrium.*

market functions. Those positions as to assets, liabilities, and other variables to which an economic unit can move by the process of exchange with other economic units. Cf. *production function.*

marketing. Those business activities involved in the flow of goods and services from production to consumption, including buying, selling, advertising, standardizing and grading, transporting, storing, financing, and the market information function.

marketing cooperative. An association of producers to market their products jointly, e.g., California Fruit Growers Exchange.

market order. An order to buy or sell on a stock or commodity exchange at the current price when the order reaches the floor of the exchange. Cf. *day order, limit order, open order.*

market-out clause. A clause in some *underwriting* agreements permitting the underwriter to withdraw if the market becomes unfavorable.

market price. The price at which a good is exchanged in the market from day to day, or the current ruling price in the market.

market ratio. The power of one good to command another in exchange for itself in a free market. Often used with reference to the relative value of gold and silver.

market risk. In finance, the risk of being unable to sell securities or assets at a price near the last price.

markets, Say's law of. See *Say's law of markets.*

market sealing. The situation in which goods sold in a low-price market cannot be resold in a higher-priced market.

market segmentation. Separating the market into categories for the purpose of imposing different terms (such as prices) on each part of the market.

market transformation. The exchange of one good by an economic unit for another good in the market place. Cf. *production transformation.*

market value. The price at which stocks, bonds, notes, or goods sell in a given market at a given time. If no current transactions are taking place, an average of *bid* and *ask* is used.

Markov chain. A sequence of transitions in a system such that when the variable is in state i at the beginning of a period, the probability that it will be in state j at the beginning of the next period is such that (1) the probability of j following i, that is, p_{ij}, depends only on the states i and j and (2) for each i, $\Sigma p_{ij} = 1$.

mark-up. The amount added to cost in order to determine selling price. Mark-up percentages are usually calculated with selling price as the base (e.g., an addition of $1. to a cost of $1. is a 50% mark-up). Sometimes mark-up is expressed as a percent of cost but this must be specifically indicated because it is not the prevalent practice.

mark-up, maintained. The difference between net sales and gross cost of merchandise sold. While "gross margin" takes account of cash discounts and workroom costs, maintained mark-up does not. Maintained mark-up is expressed as a per cent of net sales.

marline rate. A shortened form of market line rate: the ratio of cost per agate line of advertising to the dollar volume of sales reached by a publication.

marriage settlement. Settling before marriage certain property rights on one or both members of the matrimonial contract.

marshaling of assets. A rule for the distribution by a court of equity of a debtor's property among his creditors, requiring that each creditor so exhaust his rights as to permit all others to be paid if possible. Thus in a case of partnership, the firm creditors must first exhaust the firm assets, and personal creditors the personal assets of the partners before either group "crosses over" to reach the other remaining assets.

Marshallian cross. With price on the vertical axis of a quadrant and quantity demanded on the horizontal axis, the intersection of the *demand curve* and the *supply curve* is called the Marshallian cross.

Marshallian K ratio. Same as *K ratio*.

Marshallian school. The school of economic thought following Alfred Marshall (1837–1924). Also called *neoclassicism* to distinguish it from *classical economics*. In general, the school is analytical rather than historical, and devotes primary emphasis to the pricing process and *partial equilibrium* analysis.

Marxian rate of exploitation. Defined as S/V where S is surplus (all income not paid to labor) and V is variable capital (akin to *current assets*).

Marxian rate of profit. Defined as S/(V + C) where S is surplus (all income not paid to labor), V is variable capital (akin to *current assets*) and C is constant capital (akin to *fixed assets*).

Marxian wage rate. Defined as V/(S + V) where S is surplus (all income not paid to labor) and V is variable capital (akin to *current assets.*) This rate is in labor hours per labor hour.

Marxian school. The school of economic thought following Karl

Marx (1818–1883) with the central thesis that only labor gives value, and since workers do not get all the proceeds of the productive process, they are exploited. Exploitation ultimately would culminate in violent revolution and the establishment of collectivism.

Massachusetts trust. A form of business organization under which the control and management of a business as well as the legal title to the property of the business are in the hands of a trustee or group of trustees, while the ownership and equitable title to the property of the business are in beneficiaries whose ownership is evidenced by trust certificates. Named after Massachusetts where the device originated because the laws of that state forbade ownership of real estate by a corporation. This trust has limited liability, like a corporation.

mass picketing. Picketing by large numbers for dramatic effect or forcibly to prevent entry of non-strikers or customers.

mass production. The production of goods in large quantities to take advantage of increased efficiency of machinery and the division of labor as well as standardization of the product and economies of scale.

master. One who has achieved the highest level of skill in a trade or craft and employs others as *journeymen* or *apprentices.*

master in chancery. See *chancery.*

master policy. In insurance, the policy covering a group of persons or risks, as in group health insurance, and containing all the contract provisions. The individual members of the group are furnished with certificates referring to the master policy and giving a summary of the provisions of the master policy.

master's deed. A *deed* signed by a *master in chancery* pursuant to the judgment or order of a court.

matched and lost. On the stock market, when the *bids* at a fixed price equal or exceed the stock offered, the flip of a coin decides which bid is successful. Likewise for two *asks.*

matched order. An order to buy and sell the same stock, the purpose being artificially to raise or lower the price of the given security. See *wash sale.*

material. In accounting, an item of sufficient size to merit separate disclosure or computation.

mathematical economics. The application of mathematical analysis (use of equations, symbols, etc.) to economics particularly in the handling of relationships between a number of variable factors.

mathematical model. A set of relations among a number of economic variables theoretically constructed and tested against reality for consistency and reasonableness but using only partial information from the real world for this purpose. Cf. *econometric model.*

mathematics of finance. The term applied to various applications of the concept of interest, such as compounding and discounting, present value, annuities, etc.

matter in pais. "In pais" is French for "in the country," but the phrase means "a matter of fact" as opposed to a matter of law.

matrix. The arrangement of data in tabular form for analysis. For example, the outcomes of possible actions may be classified by column tabs and various possible strategies may be classified by row tabs. The table or matrix may then be systematically checked for an optimum solution, or the constants and the coefficients of the variables of a system or set of equations may likewise be put in tabular form for analysis by mathematical methods such as determinants.

mats. Short term for "matrices" which include all printing devices serving as dies from which the printing plate is made.

mature economy. The national situation in which the rate of population growth and new investment are declining heavily and the proportion of national income spent in consumption is increasing.

maturity basis. The ratio of the dollars of interest payable on a bond to the maturity value, thus ignoring any premium or discount at the time of acquisition. Cf. *yield to maturity* and *income basis.*

maturity date. The date on which an obligation is due.

maturity value. The amount which must be paid on the date an obligation is due.

maximin. In a situation of uncertainty, the principle of selecting that strategy yielding the maximum of possible minimum payoffs from alternative strategies. This employs the criterion of pessimism. Cf. *Laplace criterion, optimism criterion,* and *regret criterion.*

maximum and minimum tariff. A tariff providing maximum and minimum rates used for the purpose of negotiating with foreign countries as to the exact tariff to apply.

maximum efficiency. Cf. *least cost combination.*

McClintock tables. Same as *American experience mortality table.*

McGuire Act. A 1952 amendment of the *Miller-Tydings Act* extending the legality of *resale price maintenance agreements* (in states which authorize such agreements in intrastate commerce) not only where written agreements so providing have been entered into by purchasers but binding nonsigners as well.

mean. A measure of central tendency of data. There are four primary types of mean:

arithmetic mean	*quadratic mean*
geometric mean	*harmonic mean*

When nothing is specified, it is implied that the word "mean" refers to the arithmetic mean.

mean deviation. Same as *average deviation.*

mean reserve. In insurance, the average of the *initial reserve* and the *terminal reserve*. This is the legal reserve, i.e., the policy value which the insurer is required by law to maintain.

measured day rate. A wage system under which the employee's rate of pay is periodically adjusted according to his efficiency in working.

measurement goods. In transportation, goods whose freight charge is determined by cubic feet rather than weight.

mechanic's lien. In order to protect laborers and men who supply materials, the statutes of most states give them a lien for unpaid balances directly against the property supplied or worked on. The common law did not grant such a lien, although certain liens were automatic at common law, e.g., the lien of an innkeeper on baggage for his services.

median. The value which separates an arrangement of items in the order of their magnitude so that an equal number of items are smaller and an equal number are larger than the median.

mediation. The process by which a third party (the mediator) endeavors to bring two parties to a dispute into agreement. If the individual has power to impose his decision, it is arbitration; if he can only suggest a solution, it is conciliation.

medium of exchange. A device by which indirect exchanges may be made, thus avoiding the inconvenience of direct exchange and barter. Money serves as this device.

member bank. A state or national bank which belongs to the Federal Reserve System.

membership corporation. A corporation which does not issue stock but which members join by paying a membership fee.

memorandum check. A check drawn by a borrower in favor of his creditor to be used to reduce a loan if the loan is not paid at the due date. Hence this check is *postdated.*

memorandum clause. In marine insurance, a policy clause releasing the insurer from liability for losses from stated causes.

mens rea. Literally "a criminal intent." No one can be convicted of a felony without proof of a criminal intent, but such intent may be inferred from conduct. In the case of a misdemeanor, one can be convicted without any proof of a criminal intent.

mercantile agency. One who supplies prospective creditors with information about businesses seeking credit.

mercantilism. A political and economic theory that precious metals are the most important form of wealth and that an excess of exports over imports is the way of increasing the supply of these metals held by a country. Achievement of this end would require public control of exports, imports, prices, wages, etc.

merchandise broker. An *agent middleman* who acts for buyers and sellers and negotiates for specific lots of goods but takes no title or possession of them.

merchandise car. In transportation, a car containing less than carload lots.

merchandise turnover. Same as *inventory turnover.*

merchant guild. An organization of merchants during the Middle Ages.

merchant middleman (or wholesaler). A middleman who takes title to the goods he deals in and thus bears all the risks of ownership. Cf. *agent middleman.*

merchant's rule. A rule for partial payments of delinquent interest-bearing debts under which repayments are considered to earn interest until final settlement and not considered as applied to past-due interest. Cf. *United States rule.*

merger. (1) In a broad sense, the combination of two or more corporations by any of several devices. (2) The acquisition by one corporation of the stock of another corporation. The acquiring corporation then retires the other corporation's stock and dissolves it. Cf. *consolidation, holding company.*

merit rating. (1) In labor relations, the system of reappraising the job qualifications of employees periodically for purposes of wage adjustments and promotions. (2) In insurance, the generic term covering *experience rating* and *schedule rating,* both of which give effect in determining premium rate to factors over which the insured has controls. Cf. *experience* *rating, manual rating, retrospective rating, schedule rating.*

Merrick multiple piece rate plan. An incentive wage plan deriving from the *Taylor differential piece rate* plan and providing for progressively increasing piece rates for additional ranges of output. Cf. *Bedaux, Emerson, Gantt, Halsey, Rowan* and *Taylor plans.*

mesne profits. The profits taken by the wrongful possession of land. Such profits can be recovered in the same lawsuit seeking to eject one who is wrongfully in possession.

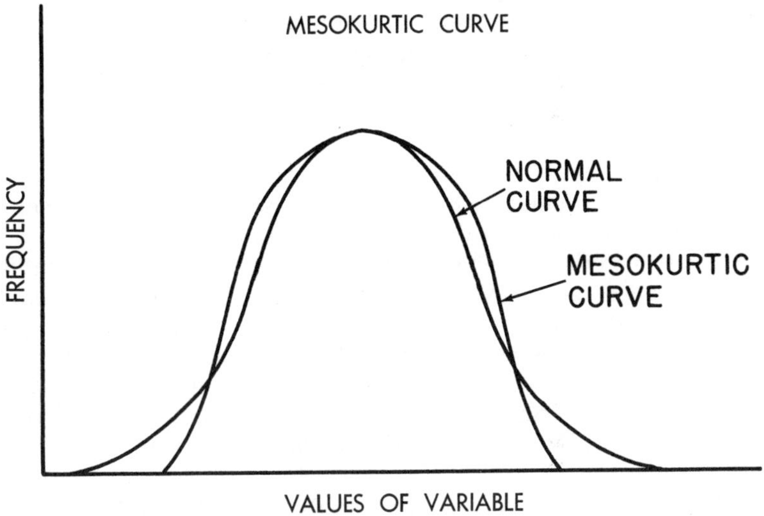

Figure 37.

mesokurtic curve. A frequency distribution curve which follows the *normal curve* as regards peakedness or flat-toppedness. Cf. *leptokurtic* and *platykurtic.*

metayer system. The European term equivalent to American *sharecropping.*

meter rate (straight line). In public utilities, a constant charge per unit of service as reported by a meter.

metes and bounds. A system of describing land in conveyances employing measurements (metes) and boundaries (bounds) which is used in states not employing United States surveys. Most of the older states in the East use metes and bounds.

microeconomics. Modern economic analysis is divided into microeconomics and macroeconomics. Microeconomics is the study of individual firms, households, prices, wages, and incomes as opposed to aggregates of such data. Cf. *macroeconomics*.

middlemen. The jobbers, merchants, brokers, agents, retailers, etc., who handle goods between the point of production and their final sale.

migratory worker. A worker moving periodically from one region to another to find work, often moving according to the harvest schedule of the different crops.

mill base pricing. A pricing system in which prices are quoted for delivery at the point of production with the buyer to pay freight from that point. Cf. *basing-point system*.

Miller-Tydings Act. An amendment enacted in 1937 to the *Sherman Antitrust Act* providing that *resale price maintenance agreements* are not violations of the antitrust law.

milling in transit. A privilege applicable to the freight rates of some commodities permitting the shipment of goods from an originating point with processing at some intermediate point and reshipment to destination with the *through rate* for the raw material (original shipped good) applicable for the entire distance rather than the raw material rate to the point of processing and another (higher) rate applicable from the point of processing to destination.

mineral rights. The rights of the owner of real estate extending below the surface of his land. Such rights may be sold separately from the land (surface) rights by the owner. Cf. *air rights*.

minimax. The principle of selection of strategies under the *regret criterion:* that the decision-maker should select that alternative with the least of the maximum regrets possible.

minimum inventory buying. See *buying to minimum inventory*.

minimum resale price. See *resale price maintenance agreement*.

minimum wage. The lowest wage, established by law or contract, which can be paid by the employer.

min-max system. In inventory control, one type of *fixed interval reorder system*. Upon periodic review of stocks, a replenishment order issues when stock on hand plus an order falls to or below a specific minimum. The replenishment order then brings the stock up to a specific maximum.

minor. In law, same as *infant*.

mintage. The charge made by a government for converting bullion into coins.

mint par of exchange. Same as *par of exchange*.

mint price of gold. The price for gold which the government will pay upon delivery to the mint. This is now $35. per fine troy ounce in the United States.

mint ratio. The relation between the price of gold and silver as set by the mint under a system of *bimetallism.* The ratio is fixed and does not fluctuate with the market situation.

minute book. A book containing a summary of the events of a meeting of an organization. Ordinarily kept by the secretary of the organization.

MIP Monthly Investment Plan. The plan devised by the N.Y. Stock Exchange under which investors can buy one or more securities through their broker by uniform dollar payments per month. Cf. *dollar averaging.*

misdemeanor. A crime which is usually defined by statute, often in terms of the upper limit of imprisonment that could be imposed. This dividing line in some states is a maximum sentence of one year. Crimes with an upper sentence less than this maximum are classed as misdemeanors. No criminal intent need be proven, just the violating conduct. Cf. *felony.*

misfeasance. In law, the inadequate performance of a duty. Cf. *nonfeasance.*

misjoinder. In law, the improper union of causes of action or of parties in a lawsuit.

misprison. In criminal law, the term to signify every misdemeanor not specifically identified by name.

mixed account. The balance in these accounts contains both a *real* and a *nominal* element. For example, expense or income accounts requiring adjustment for deferred expenses or income; or the sales account, the real element being cost of goods sold or decrease in merchandise, and the nominal element being profit or loss on sales.

mixed carload rate. In transportation, a rate applicable to a carload of different commodities in a single consignment.

mixed cost. A cost with both fixed and variable elements.

mixed currency. A currency consisting of (1) precious metals and notes, or, (2) various kinds of precious metals.

mixed economy. An economy having some of the characteristics of free enterprise and some of socialism, with the socialist aspect appearing through government intervention.

mixed policy. In marine insurance, a combination of a time policy with a voyage policy, e.g., all voyages during one year.

mixed strategy. The combination of two strategies and of the probabilities of each of the strategies.

mixed tariff. Same as *compound tariff.*

mode. Mode, or modal item, in a series is that item whose value occurs most frequently. There may be one, more than one, or no mode in a given series. If items are arranged in groups or ranges, the modal class is the group with the largest number of items.

model. In economics, the consideration of quantifiable factors which may be either variables or constants and the construction of relations among them that may be expressed in the form of equations. Cf. *analogue model, iconic model, econometric model* and *mathematical model.*

model, types of. See the following specific terms:

analogue model
closed model
dynamic model
econometric model
iconic model
linear model
mathematical model
nonlinear model
open model
stable model
static model
steady state model
transient state model
unstable model

modified union shop. A labor agreement providing that existing employees may continue as union or nonunion members but new employees must join the union.

Modigliani-Miller hypothesis. In finance, the proposition that, in the absence of income taxes, there is no optimal ratio of debt to equity in a firm. The increase of cost of one as the ratio is changed is offset by a decrease in the cost of the other.

moment. The moment around any point is the sum of the deviations of all items from that point, divided by the number of items. This is the first moment. The second is the sum of the squares of these deviations similarly divided; the third moment is the sum of the cubes of these deviations; the fourth moment is the sum of these deviations to the fourth power, etc. The first moment is symbolized by the Greek letter μ_1, the second by μ_2, etc. If the moment is around the arithmetic mean, it is symbolized by the Greek letter γ_1 for the first moment, etc.

momentary equilibrium. Momentary or market equilibrium in economic theory refers to the immediate price in the market at which exchange of goods currently takes place and the goods are cleared from the market. If a distinction is made between speculative (futures) contracts and contracts covering exchange of goods actually in existence, two equilibriums can be distinguished under this heading. Cf. *dynamic equilibrium,*

equilibrium of firm or industry (partial) long run, equilibrium of firm or industry (partial) short run, expectational equilibrium, general equilibrium (under monopoly or monopolistic competition), general equilibrium (under pure competition), intermediate equilibrium, market equilibrium, neutral equilibrium, normal equilibrium, partial equilibrium, stable equilibrium, static equilibrium, and *unstable equilibrium.*

monetary policy. A term used in juxtaposition to *fiscal policy* to describe the activities directed at effective changes in the quantities of money and bank credit on the premise that control of these quantities is the prime way of maintaining a stable price level and modifying the *business cycle.* Cf. *fiscal policy.*

monetary standard. The basis upon which a money is issued, that is the principle that determines the quantity of money.

monetary standard, types of. See the following specific terms:

bimetallism standard
commodity standard
crawling peg standard
dollar-gold standard
dollar-only standard
fiat standard
flexible exchange standard
floating exchange standard
gold bullion standard
gold exchange standard
gold standard
limping standard
paper standard
silver standard

monetary theory of the cycle. Although there are many forms of the theory, emphasis is placed on the shift by people from money to goods (or vice versa) or upon fractional reserve banking or upon both as the main reasons for the business cycle.

monetary underconsumption theory. That type which emphasizes some aspect of money, such as its liquidity, as the origin of underconsumption. Cf. *real underconsumption theory.*

monetary unit. The unit of money of a country. In the U.S., the dollar is the monetary unit; in Great Britain, the pound sterling. The monetary unit may or may not be defined in terms of a commodity into which it is convertible.

monetization of the debt. See *debt monetization.*

money. Any generally accepted medium of exchange and unit of account. The characteristics of good money are: general desirability, great value in small bulk, portability, durability, uniform quality, easy recognizability, and stability of value.

money, type of. See the following specific terms:

bank money
cheap money
check book money
convertible (paper) money
credit money
dear money
earnest money
fiat money
fiduciary money
fractional money
hard money
inconvertible money
irredeemable money
lawful money
managed money
representative money
soft money
standard money
tight money
token money
wildcat money

money broker. One who deals in *foreign exchange* but often on his own account and then he is a *dealer.*

money desk. The department at a bank buying and selling short-term funds.

money functions. There are four generally accepted functions of money: as (1) a unit of account, (2) a medium of exchange, (3) a store of value, and (4) a standard of deferred payment.

money illusion. The erroneous belief that one's position has been improved by the receipt of more units of money at a time when the price level is rising in proportion (therefore the value of a unit of money is falling).

money income. Income measured in money units.

money market. The institutions and practices through which short-term funds are channeled to borrowers and entrepreneurs. Cf. *capital market.*

money order. A document purchased by a party who desires to transmit money. The document is purchased from a post office, bank, or express company which "orders" the payment of money by its branch or affiliate at the location to which it is to be sent by the person named on the order as the payor.

money rate of interest. Same as *nominal rate of interest.*

money rate risk. Same as *interest rate risk.*

money wages. Wages expressed in terms of money without regard to changes in the purchasing power of money; also called nominal wages. Cf. *real wages.*

monometallism. A monetary system in which only one metal is used as standard money, i.e., only one metal may be coined in unlimited amounts or melted down. Cf. *bimetallism, symmetallism.*

monopolistic competition. (1) General meaning: the market situation in which there are only a few producers or a few dominate the market. (2) In economic theory, competition among sellers who are individually able to influence the market often because of slight differences among the products they produce. Cf. *product differentiation.* (See Figure 5, page 29.)

monopoly. In a general sense, the market situation in which one person or a group has such a control of the supply of a commodity as to be able to regulate its price.

monopoly, types of. See the following specific terms:

buyers' monopoly
fiscal monopoly
legal monopoly
public monopoly
sellers' monopoly

monopsony. The market situation in which there is only one buyer for a particular commodity.

Monte Carlo technique. A technique which assigns one number to each item or event using the numbers in regular numerical order. Then a table of random numbers is matched against this numerical array to establish the sequence of values that would develop by chance. Comparing the actual data with the chance data reveals the degree of regularity in the actual data.

Monte Carlo technique. Any procedure using random sampling techniques to obtain a probabilistic approximation to the solution of a mathematical problem. The estimate is a statistical parameter, the sampling is from a population and the mathematical expressions are built up of one or more probability functions.

month order. See *day order.*

Monthly Investment Plan. See *MIP.*

moot case. A question whose decision would be (1) premature or (2) useless because it has already been agreed upon or otherwise resolved.

moral hazard. In insurance, the risk which an insurer takes that either the insured or the beneficiary will bring about a loss in order to recover under the policy.

moral suasion. Used particularly with reference to efforts by the *Federal Reserve System* to influence future conduct of businesses in production and investment and of consumers. Under this concept, reliance is placed by the Federal Reserve for influence on the conduct of producers and consumers not upon formal regulation but upon mere statement of the policy the Federal Reserve intends to pursue particularly regarding credit expansion or contraction.

moratorium. The declaration of a period during which a debtor is given the legal right to delay the meeting of an obligation that has fallen due.

more favorable terms clause. A clause in a labor agreement under which the union agrees not to enter other contracts more favorable to the employer with competing producers.

morning loan. An unsecured loan of an unspecified amount to a stockbroker to carry on his business during the day.

Morris plan bank. Same as *industrial bank.*

mortality ratio. In *life insurance,* the ratio of actual mortality experienced by an insurer to the mortality expected from a mortality table such as the *Commissioners' Standard Ordinary Mortality Table.*

mortality table. See *life table.*

mortgage. A conveyance of property as security for the payment of a debt. The mortgage may specify that the property is now upon nonpayment of the debt the property is to be conveyed automatically.

mortgage, types of. See the following specific terms:

amortized mortgage
blanket mortgage
chattel mortgage
closed-end mortgage
consolidated mortgage
direct-reduction mortgage
equitable mortgage
first, etc., mortgage
leasehold mortgage
level-payment mortgage
open-end mortgage
overlying mortgage
purchase-money mortgage
refunding mortgage (bonds)
straight mortgage
underlying mortgage

mortgage banker. One engaged in dealing in mortgages either as principal or agent.

mortgage bonds. Bonds for which real estate or personal property is pledged as security that the bond will be paid as per its terms. May be first, second, refunding, etc.

mortgage certificate. A certificate covering a partial interest in a large mortgage issued by the depository who holds the entire mortgage for the benefit of all the certificate holders.

mortgage clause. In insurance, the clause providing protection for the mortgagee's interest and dealing with the allocation of the insurer's liability if the property is also insured by the mortgagor.

mortgage company. A private enterprise engaged principally in originating mortgages which are then sold to investors.

mortgagee. The one receiving the *mortgage,* i.e., the one who is loaning money and receiving the mortgaged property as security. Cf. *mortgagor.*

mortgage loss clause. An insurance policy clause protecting the mortgagee from loss through acts by the mortgagor which otherwise would invalidate the policy. Also called New York, standard, or union loss clause.

mortgagor. The one issuing the *mortgage,* i.e., the one who is putting up his property as security for a loan. Cf. *mortgagee.*

mortality table. See *American experience table of mortality.*

mortmain. In law, the policy stemming from English statutes forbidding the holding of land by religious corporations and restricting other corporations to holding land at the discretion of the king. These restrictions do not exist in the United States today.

most-favored-nation clause. A clause in commercial treaties between two countries specifying that if subsequently either party to the agreement grants a favor (usually a tariff reduction) to a third country, the other party to the treaty will be granted the same favor. The clause is conditional if the favor is granted to the other party to the treaty only on condition that the same reciprocal advantage obtained from the third country is granted to the other party to the treaty; it is unconditional if the favor is granted without regard to a reciprocal advantage.

motion study. See *time and motion study.*

movable exchange. Instruments quoted in the currency of the country in which payment is to be made rather than in which the instrument is drawn.

moving average. An average computed from part of a series of items, progressively adding unused items as items already used are eliminated. E.g., a three-year moving average of the following: 1930, 5; 1931, 6; 1932, 7; 1933, 8; would be $5 + 6 + 7/3 = 6$, centered at 1931; $6 + 7 + 8/3 = 7$, centered at 1932.

multicollinearity. The situation in which two or more *independent variables* are related to each other as well as each related to a *dependent variable.* See *bunch map.*

multilateralism. An international economic policy having as its object the freeing of international trade from the restrictions involved in *bilateralism* in an effort to permit countries to specialize in production and exchange in accordance with the principal of *comparative advantage.*

multinational. Used to describe a company that has operations centers in many countries as opposed to an international company which imports or exports goods but has its operations center in only one country.

multiple budget. A *budget* extending two or more periods of time into the future and extended as each time period elapses.

multiple-commodity reserve dollar. See *commodity reserve theory*.

multiple correlation. The correlation between one dependent variable and two or more independent variables, weighted by the net regression coefficients between the dependent and each of the independent variables. The symbol used for the coefficient of multiple correlation is R. See *correlation* for an illustration of simple, multiple, and partial correlation. If the independent variables are regarded as random variables, then the appropriate term is multiple correlation. If the independent variables are fixed in advance then the term is multiple regression.

multiple currency system. Governmental control of the use of a country's currency in foreign trade, so that the currency's value in any transaction depends upon the type of commodity purchased abroad for which exchange is sought.

multiple-line underwriter. In insurance, an underwriter *(insurer)* handling a number of different types of risks.

multiple listing. A contract between the owner of real estate and a broker giving the broker an *exclusive-right-to-sell listing,* with the understanding that the broker will permit other brokers to sell for a percentage of the commission.

multiple prices. A price system of a producer in which the same basic product is sold in many different models, each at a different price, in order to take advantage of those customers who buy for prestige reasons. Cf. *class price*.

multiple regression. See *multiple correlation*.

multiple tariff. A tariff specifying different duties for the same item imported from different countries.

multiplicative predicting equation. A predicting equation in which the dependent variable is a function of a constant and several independent variables with a multiplication sign between the terms, Thus $Y = aX^bZ^c$. Cf. *additive predicting equation.*

multiplier. In *macroeconomics*, the ratio (called the multiplier) of the change in *national income* following on a change in investment (or governmental expenditures or excess of exports over imports). The value of the multiplier depends on the particular model and *parameters* of the economy assumed.

multiplier, types of. See the following specific terms:

balanced budget multiplier
employment multiplier
export multiplier
foreign trade multiplier
government-expenditures multiplier
investment multiplier

multivariate analysis. The analysis of values of more than two variables, e.g., determination of the *coefficient of multiple correlation.* Cf. *univariate analysis* and *bivariate analysis.*

municipal bond. The bond of a state or of a *municipal corporation.* Interest on such bonds is exempt from U.S. income taxes.

municipal corporation. A political subdivision of the state, constituted for local government, which exercises a portion of the power of the state under legislative grant from the state. Like a corporation in that the governmental unit is considered a legal entity, but unlike a corporation in the absence of stockholders.

muniment. The documents which the owner of land has by which he defends his ownership or title.

mutatis mutandis. Latin for "changing those things which must be changed." In economic analysis which proceeds by assuming constant all things except the variables being studied, a change in a variable may necessarily involve a change in other conditions which are not within the particular consequences being studied. *Caeteris paribus* (other things being unchanged) is sometimes less exactly used to include what is meant by mutatis mutandis.

mutual benefit association. In insurance, a fraternal or social organization operating on an assessment basis. Assessments are made to meet claims that have occurred rather than the collection of premiums in advance of claims. Each member is liable for his share of unpaid assessments.

mutual company. A corporation without capital stock, in which profits are distributed among the members in proportion to the quantity of business each did with the company, as in a mutual insurance company.

mutual fund. An *open-end investment trust* which gives its management discretion in the choice of investments. Cf. *fixed investment trust.*

mutual insurance. In a mutual insurance company there are no stockholders and there is no stock. The "owners" of the insurance company are the policyholders. The company may be of the assessment type or it may be nonassessable and use fixed premiums which set the maximum liability of a policyholder. Cf. *stock insurance company.*

mutual investment trust. Same as *mutual fund.*

mutualism. The argument developed by Proudhon (1809-1865) that services exchanged for each other would be mutually equal if rent, interest, and profits were eliminated.

mutual mistake. Same as *bilateral mistake.*

mutual savings bank. A bank in which the depositors are the owners and share the earnings.

naked contract. Same as *nudum pactum.*

NAM National Association of Manufacturers. Organized in 1895, the National Association of Manufacturers is an association of manufacturers in all fields to promote their common interests.

name bond. A bond covering the fidelity or performance of a named person regardless of the position he holds. Cf. *position bond.*

narrow market. The market situation in which the volume of trading is small. Also called *thin market.*

NASD National Association of Securities Dealers, Inc. A non-profit organization established for cooperative regulation of the over-the-counter market for securities in conjunction with the Securities and Exchange Commission. Membership is maintained through the discounts and price concessions which dealers allow to members.

Nash criterion. In game theory, the proposition that if the situation is evaluated at zero for each of two players, and if the players' payoffs are evaluated by the players as X and X_1, then a fair division is one which maximizes the product of the utilities, XX_1.

national bank. A bank whose charter is granted by the federal government, hence is under its control and must be a member of the Federal Reserve System and of the Federal Deposit Insurance Corporation.

national bank notes. Notes, formerly issued by national banks and now in the process of redemption, secured 100% by federal government bonds and 5% lawful money, both kept at the Treasury in Washington, D.C.

national brand. Loosely used to designate a *manufacturer's brand* which has wide circulation.

national debt. The debt of the central or national government as opposed to the debt of state or local governments within that country. Cf. *public debt.*

national fraternal congress table of mortality. A *mortality table* prepared in 1898 for the use of fraternal organizations engaged in insurance underwriting. Cf. American experience mortality table.

national income. The aggregate earnings of all factors in current production. Also equal to *net national product* minus *indirect business taxes* and *business transfer payments.* Cf. *personal income.*

national income accounts budget. In *macroeconomics*, a government budget that includes payments into and out of trust funds and records taxes when incurred rather than when received. Cf. *administrative budget.*

nationalization. The acquisition and operation by the government of a previously privately-owned and operated business.

national product. See *gross national product, net national product.*

natural interest rate. The interest rate at which the demand for loanable funds just equals the supply of savings. The interest rate which keeps the flow of money incomes constant rather than the interest rate which keeps the price level constant.

natural law. A body of moral principles dictated by reason or conscience.

natural premium. In life insurance, a premium that increases with the risk each year and is paid on a one year renewable term basis.

natural rate of growth. That rate of growth of *national income* which will maintain full employment. See explanation under *Harrod-Domar model.* Cf. *actual rate of growth* and *warranted rate of growth.*

navicert. A wartime document issued by a belligerent nation authorizing the ship of a neutral to sail to a designated destination through blockaded waters.

near money. Assets quickly convertible into money, e.g., savings deposits and government bonds.

ne exeat. Latin for "that he should not leave." In law, a writ enjoining a person from leaving the jurisdiction of the court.

negative income tax. A system of payments (transfers) to individuals in inverse proportion to incomes below some break-even level. Cf. *negative wage tax.*

negative investment. Same as *disinvestment.*

negative pledge clause. A clause in a mortgage providing that the borrower will not pledge any of his assets or will pledge his assets only if the notes or bonds outstanding have certain protection.

negative wage tax. A system of payments (transfers) to individuals to subsidize the prices at which they sell their labor services. The subsidy varies inversely with the wage rate received in the market place. Cf. *negative income tax.*

negligence. In law, injury resulting from the failure to act as a reasonable man would under the circumstances with respect to a person to whom a duty in law is owned.

negotiable. (1) In a popular sense it means transferable by delivery. (2) In law, however, a document is negotiable when it meets certain legal formalities (for example, it must be in order or in bearer form). Then, as a consequence, one taking such a document is relieved of certain claims which could otherwise be made against him, provided the document has been received in good faith, for value, before maturity, and without knowledge of any defect in it. The other requirements of form to make a document negotiable are: 1) in writing and signed by the maker or drawer, 2) payable on demand or at a fixed or determinable time, 3) unconditional promise or order to pay a definite amount of money and 4) if a bill of exchange, the drawer must be named or identified.

negotiable check. A check payable "to order" or "to bearer." A negotiable check in order form can be made nonnegotiable by a *restrictive indorsement.*

negotiated purchase. The process of preparation of a security issue by the issuing company by negotiation with the underwriting investment banking firms. Cf. *competitive bidding.*

neoclassical economics. Cf. *Marshallian school.*

net amount at risk. In insurance, the difference between the face amount of a policy and the reserve held against the policy.

net asset value. In *investment companies,* the market value of all the assets less the liabilities and divided by the number of shares outstanding. Usually computed at least daily.

net borrowed reserves. The excess of total borrowings from Federal Reserve banks by member banks of the *Federal Reserve System* over the total *excess bank reserves* of such member banks with the total excess bank reserves being the actual total reserves of such member banks in excess of the *required bank reserves* of such banks.

net cost. In insurance, the total premiums paid on a policy less the dividends received and the *cash surrender* value as of the date the net cost is determined.

net current assets. Same as *net working capital.*

net debt. The total debt (gross debt) of an obligor less sinking fund accumulations or other provisions for debt retirement. Cf. *gross debt.*

net income (business). Same as *net profit.*

net income (individual). Gross income less the expenses incurred in getting such income. For the individual's income tax report it means the income from all sources less certain permissible deductions. Cf. *gross income (individual).*

net lease. A lease under which the tenant pays taxes, insurance, and repairs.

net national debt. The total national debt less that part held by the government in various trust funds.

net national product. The money value of the total output of goods and services within a country in a given period of time, usually a year, after allowance for depreciation and consumption of capital goods. Cf. *gross national product.*

net operating assets. The assets, net of depreciation and bad debts, employed in the ordinary course of business. Hence, excludes investments in stocks and bonds owned by a manufacturing company, for example.

net operating income. Income before interest and income taxes but after depreciation produced by *operating assets.*

net operating margin. *Net operating income* divided by sales for the period.

net option. Same as *option.*

net position. In trading, the difference between the contracts long and the contracts short held by a trader. Cf. *buying long, selling short.*

net premium. In insurace, the amount received by the *insurer.* This is variously defined as the billed premiums (1) less the agent's commission, or (2) less the returned premiums, or (3) less the returned premiums and *reinsurance* premiums.

net present value. The difference between future cash inflows of an investment discounted to the present at an assumed rate and all cash outflows similarly discounted.

net price. The price after discounts and other allowances.

net product. Same as *produit net.*

net profit. Deducting the cost of goods sold from sales gives the gross profit. Deducting the operating expenses (overhead) from gross profit gives the operating profit. Deducting income taxes from operating profit gives the net profit.

net profit margin. The ratio of *net profit* to *net sales.*

net rate. In insurance, either (1) the premium paid less dividends received, or (2) the premium paid less the expense loading.

net regression coefficient. In *multiple correlation,* the coefficient of each *independent variable* in the regression equation is the net regression coefficient. The term "net" indicates that the relation of the dependent variable to that particular independent variable is free of the associated influences of the other independent variable or variables upon the dependent variable. The term partial regression coefficient is used by some for the net regression coefficient.

net reproduction rate. The ratio of the number of females (daughters) who will become mothers to the number of females (mothers) who reproduced them. If this ratio is one, population is stationary, if it is less than one, population is declining and if more than one, population is increasing.

net sales. The total of all sales after deducting returned sales. Cf. *gross sales.*

net tonnage (vessel). With reference to vessels, net tonnage is *gross tonnage* less space for crew, machinery, and fuel. Cf. *deadweight tonnage (vessel), gross tonnage (vessel), registered tonnage (vessel).*

network analysis. The analysis of a complex of many separate activities going on simultaneously. An example is *PERT*.

net working capital. See *working capital* (net).

net worth. The total assets of a person or business less the total liabilities (amounts due to creditors) is the net worth. In the case of a corporation, net worth includes both capital stock and surplus; in the case of a partnership or single proprietorship, it is the original investment plus accumulated and reinvested profits.

net yield. The income of a bond less annual amortization if bought at a premium, but plus annual accumulation if bought at a discount. In the case of stock, dividends divided by purchase price.

Neumann. See under *von Neumann.*

neutral equilibrium. In economics, a condition which once achieved will continue indefinitely unless one of the variables (economic or noneconomic) is altered and then the system will come to rest with new and different adjustment. Cf. *dynamic equilibrium, equilibrium of firm or industry (partial) long run, equilibrium of firm or industry (partial) short run, expectational equilibrium, general equilibrium (under monopoly or monopolistic competition), general equilibrium (under pure* *competition), intermediate equilibrium, market equilibrium, normal equilibrium, partial equilibrium, stable equilibrium, static equilibrium,* and *unstable equilibrium.*

neutral money. A system under which the dollar would be convertible into commodities at a fixed price with the object of stabilizing the price level.

New Deal. A general term given to the economic, social, and political program and philosophy of Franklin Delano Roosevelt as carried out by legislation, administration, and court decisions after 1932.

New York interest. Interest computed by the exact days in a month rather than by use of a 30 day month, etc. Cf. *Boston interest.*

New York loss clause. Same as *mortgage loss clause.*

New York plan. An *equipment trust* arrangement using a conditional sale as the legal device. Cf. *Philadelphia plan.*

New York Stock Exchange. An unincorporated association of 1,375 members founded in 1792 and handling the purchase and sale of corporate stocks for themselves and others. The largest security market in the U.S.

New York stock right. See *stock right.*

next of kin. Technically those related by blood as opposed to those related by marriage.

NIL Negotiable instruments law. In an effort to establish uniformity and therefore increase certainty and speed of transactions involving negotiable instruments, all 50 states have enacted the uniform negotiable instruments law. This law is now embodied in the Uniform Commercial Code which is in effect in many states.

NIRA National Industrial Recovery Act. An act passed by Congress in 1933 giving President Roosevelt great power to regulate trade, industry, labor, and prices through appointed agencies. Declared unconstitutional in 1935 on two counts: (1) Congress cannot delegate its legislative powers, (2) Congress cannot regulate intrastate commerce.

nisi prius. Latin for "unless before." In law, a term to identify those courts which try civil cases with the aid of a jury.

NLRA National Labor Relations Act (Wagner Act). Federal law enacted in 1935 regulating interstate commerce with these primary provisions: (1) assurance of recognition of unions through certification, (2) selection of employee representatives through elections, (3) specification of unfair labor practices of which the management of a business could be guilty.

NLRB National Labor Relations Board. The board of 5 members administering the Wagner Act and the Taft-Hartley Act. The board conducts elections to determine bargaining agents, determines bargaining units and adjudicates unfair labor practice charges. The board seeks enforcement of its orders through the court system.

no-action letter. An opinion issued by the attorney for a governmental agency that if facts stated in a request for a ruling are later presented, the attorney will advise the governmental agency not to act, that is, that the facts do not warrant a prosecution.

noibn. "Not otherwise indexed by name." Used in transportation to refer to that freight classification which applies if no other specific class exists.

nolle prosequi. In law, the dropping of a case at the request of the prosecuting attorney. This does not foreclose the possibility of another case being brought for the same matter, unless under the double jeopardy rule the case had already reached a point where the defendant might have been found guilty.

no-load fund. A fund of an *investment company* which makes no *sales charge* but may charge a *management fee.*

nolo contendere. A plea by an accused in a criminal case that he does not wish to contest the matter and thus impliedly consents to a finding of conviction.

nominal account. An account established to analyze the changes in the surplus account. These include expense and income accounts which are closed into surplus at the end of each fiscal period. Cf. *real account.*

nominal cost. Cost measured in monetary units at the time it was incurred, that is, ignoring changes in the purchasing power of money.

nominal damages. In law, damages awarded when the *plaintiff* proves his case but the damages are negligible. Cf. *exemplary damages.*

nominal interest rate. The rate of interest stated in a security as opposed to the actual interest yield which is based upon the price at which the interest-bearing property is purchased and the length of time to maturity of the obligation.

nominal price. The estimated price of a commodity infrequently sold.

nominal yield. The rate of return specified in a security. This is calculated on the face or par value.

nomograph. A graph of three or more scaled lines such that an equation of two or more independent variables may be solved by laying a straight edge on two or more known points and reading the value at the intersection of the straight edge with the line scaled with the unknown.

nonadmitted asset. In insurance, an asset that cannot be used in making reports of financial condition to regulatory bodies.

nonassessable insurance. Insurance in which the liability of the insured (policyholder) is limited to the premium he pays and no assessments can be made against him.

nonassessable policy. See *nonassessable insurance.*

nonassessable stock. Stock on which the owner is not obliged to make payments in the event of insolvency provided he has already paid the purchase price.

nonassignable. A contract whose rights cannot be transferred to another person. Contracts are assignable unless both parties have agreed they are not assignable or unless the law prevents assignment in the particular case.

noncancellable policy. In insurance, a policy that cannot be terminated during its term without the consent of both the *insurer* and the *insured.* Most policies are cancellable by the insured or the insurer after a minimum notice period except that life insurance is usually not cancellable by the company in the absence of fraud or misrepresentation by the insured.

noncompeting groups. The theory that workers within a given category compete sharply with each other, but that workers in one category do not compete with workers in another category. The classification often used for his purpose is: entrepreneurs, "white collar," skilled labor, and unskilled labor groups.

non compos mentis. Latin for "a person lacking sufficient understanding" to comprehend what he is doing.

nonconcurrent insurance. Insurance under two or more policies which differ in some respect other than who the insurer is, the amount of the insurance, and the policy dates.

noncontribution clause. In fire insurance on mortgaged property, the most widely used form of clause to protect the interest of a mortgagee. Under this clause, only the interests of the owner of the property and the holder of the first mortgage will be protected by the policy. Cf. *full contribution clause.*

noncumulative preferred stock. A stock which has no right to unpaid and undeclared dividends of past years, but only a prior claim to any dividends declared during the current year.

noncupative will. An oral will declared in the last illness of the *testator* before witnesses and then reduced to writing within a given time. The recognition of such wills is subject to statutes that vary from state to state.

nondiscretionary trust. Same as *fixed investment trust.*

nondiversifiable risk. The systematic tendency of a stock (or investment) to move in price (or rate of return) with the market as a whole. Cf. *diversifiable risk.*

nonfeasance. In law, the failure to perform a duty. Cf. *misfeasance.*

nonforfeiture options or values. In life insurance, the rights of an insured upon default in premium payment. These rights are (1) to receive the *cash surrender value,* (2) to apply this value either to secure *paid-up insurance* of a lower face amount or to continue the policy's face amount for as long as this value will allow.

noninsurable risk. A risk, the occurrence of which is not measurable by actuarial science and hence is noninsurable. Examples are: changes in demand for a product, inventions, social changes, etc. In modern economics, a synonym for "uncertainty."

nonlinear correlation. Any correlation based on regression lines which are not straight lines, such as parabolas or hyperbolas.

nonlinear model. A system relating quantifiable factors either as variables or constants with the relationships of the variables expressed in the form of nonlinear equations. Cf. *linear model.*

nonnegotiable. Frequently misunderstood to mean not transferable. Correctly, nonnegotiable means wanting in one of the requirements of a *negotiable instrument,* and as a consequence not entitled to the benefits of negotiability such as freedom from many defenses which could otherwise be raised by the maker, e.g., fraudulent inducement. A nonnegotiable document is transferable by assignment. To prevent transfer, the label nontransferable should be used.

nonnotification loan. A loan made by a bank or commercial finance company on the security of accounts receivable. The original debtor is not notified that the account has been pledged; the loan is made with recourse, that is, if an account receivable is not paid, the borrower still remains liable for the amount loaned against the receivable.

non obstante verdicto. Latin for, notwithstanding the verdict. After a jury has rendered a verdict, the judge may give judgment to the contrary if there is no evidence from which a jury could have arrived at its decision, or for other reasons specified by statutes.

nonoperating assets. See *operating assets.*

nonoperating income. The income which a business concern receives from investments it holds either from earnings on the investment or from *capital gains.*

nonparticipating policy. In insurance, a policy for which the insured is charged a premium approximating the anticipated cost but with no provision for refunding of part of the premium in the form of a dividend.

nonprice competition. Competition through quality of product, added services, advertising, packaging, etc.

nonprofit corporation. A corporation organized for charitable, educational, humanitarian, or other such limited purposes. May be a stock or nonstock corporation and has exemption from income taxes but is obligated for other taxes to the extent the corporation has income-yielding property or operations.

nonproportional output, law of. Same as *diminishing marginal productivity, law of.*

nonrecourse loan. A loan under the U.S. agricultural program to farmers on the security of surplus crops which are delivered to the government and held off the market. The loan must be liquidated as provided by the government's program but the government has no recourse against the farmer for a deficiency if the security fails to bring the amount of the loan.

nonreversibility of function. See *hysteresis.*

nonstock corporation. One type of *nonprofit corporation* in which the members hold no stock. Among these are religious, charitable, mutual insurance, and municipal corporations.

nonstochastic model. A model using no random variables. Cf. *stochastic model.*

nonsuit. In law, a judgment against a plaintiff who has failed to prove his case, or defaulted. Up to the point where the plaintiff has finished with his evidence, he can usually withdraw without being barred from starting again.

nonvalued policy. An insurance policy for a specific total amount of coverage but with the value of a particular item to be determined at the time of loss. Cf. *valued policy.*

nonvoting stock. Stock which does not give the holder the right to vote at corporate meetings.

nonwaiver clause. In insurance, the clause providing that investigation of the value of a claim by the *insurer* does not admit that liability is assumed.

no par stock. Stock without par value but which represents a proportionate share of the ownership of a corporation based on the number of shares. One issue of stock in a corporation may have par value and another issue in the same corporation may have no par value. New York was the first state to pass a no-par-value law in 1912.

normal distribution. The curve expressing the relationship between the frequency (measured on the y axis) and the deviations (positive or negative) from the mean (measured on the x axis) of a series of measurements. Many kinds of variables have magnitudes distributed according to the pattern of the normal curve. Over 99% of a normal distribution will lie within a range of three *standard deviations* either side of the *arithmetic mean,* 95% within a range of two standard deviations either side, and 68% within a range of one standard deviation either side. The formula is

$$y = \frac{n}{\sigma\sqrt{2\Pi}} e^{-x^2/2\sigma^2}$$

where y = the frequency of any X value
x = the deviation from the mean of each item in the distribution
n = the total frequency
σ = the standard deviation
e = the Naperian constant, 2.71828
Π = the circular constant, 3.14159

Cf. *Gibrat's distribution, log-normal distribution, Pareto's measure of inequality of a distribution, Poisson distribution, t distribution, Yule distribution.*

normal probability curve. Same as *normal distribution.*

normal equilibrium. See *equilibrium of firm or industry, partial.*

normal price. That price which will in the long run make the rate of production and rate of consumption equal.

normal profit. The least sum that must be paid a capitalist to induce him to allow the use of his capital in a process.

normal stock. Same as *base stock.*

normative economics. Economics which extends beyond analysis and description to include policy statements and judgments about the advisability of actions. Cf. *positive economics.*

Norris-La Guardia Act. Act of Congress in 1932 (also called the

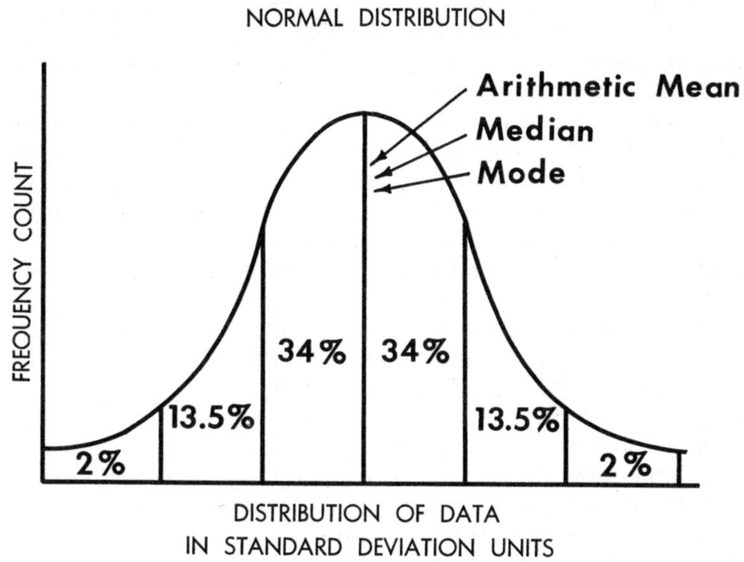

Figure 38.

anti-injunction act) severely limiting the power of a federal court to grant an injunction in a labor dispute and outlawing the *"yellow dog"* contract. Modified by the *Taft-Hartley Act* of 1947.

notary public. An official usually appointed by the governor of a state to administer oaths, certify documents, protest negotiable documents upon default, and perform similar duties.

notch problem. The situation arising when tax rates increase progressively and a single rate is applied to the entire taxable amount. Thus if the rate increases at $2,000, the tax on $2,001 will be so much larger than the tax on $1,999, that it would be better to forego the $2. This notch problem is avoided by the bracket system applying different rates to different ranges rather than to the total.

note. An abbreviation of the term "promissory note." A written promise to pay a designated person or bearer a certain sum at a definite time. Interest may be promised or not. Cf. *circular note, cognovit note, judgment note.*

Notes of 1890, Treasury. Issued to pay for the monthly purchase of 4½ million ounces of silver authorized by Congress, and redeemable in silver or gold. The law was repealed in 1893 and the notes have been almost completely displaced by silver certificates, as provided by the Gold Standard Act of 1900.

notice of dishonor. The notice given by the holder of a negotiable instrument upon which there has been default by the maker to all indorsers whom the holder seeks to hold liable for payment.

noting a bill. The notation on a bill of exchange by a notary public after presentation of the bill protesting its nonpayment. The notation consists of the date, notary's initials, reason for nonpayment and the notary's charges.

novation. An agreement replacing an old party to a contract by a new party. This requires the consent of all the original parties and of the new party, and involves the transfer of both rights *and* duties. Not to be confused with an *assignment* which involves only the transfer of rights.

np No protest. A check, draft or note marked this way is not to be protested if not paid, that is, the legal requirement of formal presentation with demand for payment need not be fulfilled and no protest fee can be changed by any bank or agent entrusted with its collection.

NPV. Abbreviation for *"net present value."*

NRA National Recovery Administration. Used to designate the machinery which made the *NIRA* effective.

nsf Not sufficient funds. The term stamped on a check by the bank on which it is drawn when the drawer of the check does not have sufficient funds to his credit to pay the check.

nudum pactum. Literally, "a naked promise." A promise not legally binding because not supported by a consideration.

nuisance tax. A small tax placed on articles of common use, often involving annoying detail in its collection.

numeraire. In dealing with multiple exchange and to avoid the special problems raised by the peculiar characteristics of money (such as liquidity), the particular commodity chosen as a standard of value is called the numeraire.

numerical rating system. In life insurance, a method of determining the premiums for substandard risks. A normal risk is rated 100 and individual advantages or disadvantages are assigned values with disadvantages assigned higher values than the normal for that factor and advantages assigned smaller values than the normal of another factor to arrive at the *net* deviation of a substandard risk.

nunc pro tunc. Latin for "now as well as then." In law, the phrase indicating the decision of a court is effective retroactively.

nuncupative will. An oral will declared in the last illness of the *testator* before witnesses and then reduced to writing within a given time. The recognition of such wills is subject to statutes that vary from state to state.

OASI Old Age and Survivors' Insurance. See *Social Security Act.*

obiter dictum. Latin for "what is said in passing." A statement or opinion by a court not necessary to the decision of a case and therefore not so binding in authority as a proposition necessarily involved in a decision.

objective function. An equation which states what is to be maximized or minimized. A common objective function states the profit to be derived. Thus if X product can be sold for $1 and Y product for $2, the objective function would be Profit $= 1X + 2Y$.

obligation. (1) In business, any enforceable debt, such as a bond, note, contract, charge account, etc. (2) In law, a duty owed by one person to another.

obligee. The person entitled to receive discharge of an obligation. Cf. *obligor.*

obligor. The person who owes discharge of an obligation to another, the *obligee.*

obsolescence. The decrease in value of an existing article due to invention, change in demand, or similar factors, but not wear and tear. Cf. *depreciation.*

occupancy ratio. The percentage of available housing units fit for occupancy that are occupied. Cf. *vacancy ratio.*

ocean marine insurance. See *marine insurance.*

odd-lot broker. Strictly speaking, same as *odd-lot dealer.*

odd-lot dealers. Members of a stock exchange who handle transactions in less than the usual trading unit. The ordinary unit on the stock exchange is 100 shares, although a few inactive stocks have smaller units.

OEM original equipment manufacturer. A term used to distinguish sales made to or by the manufacturer of an entire unit, such as a refrigerator, by contrast with other sales such as repair parts.

off-board security. Same as *unlisted security.*

off-board trading. Buying and selling a security listed on an exchange without routing the transaction over the exchange. Cf. *third market.*

offer. The terms of a contract proposed by one party (the offeror) to another party (the offeree).

offer curve. Same as *price-consumption curve.*

offeree. One to whom an offer has been made.

offering price. Same as *ask.*

offeror. One who makes an offer.

official classification. See *classification territory.*

official exchange rate. The ratio that is applied by the monetary authority of one country in exchanging its money for that of another country.

off-peak service. In public utilities, the off-peak service is service during those hours when the normal demand for service is low. Cf. *peak load.*

offsets to saving. The sum of investment plus the government deficit offsets saving.

ogive. A curve of frequency distribution (with frequency on the y axis and the measured magnitude on the x axis) which is cumulative so that at any given point on the curve all items of that value or less are included (or that value or more, if the ogive is to run in the other direction).

oligopoly. More than two but only a few *sellers* of a particular commodity. Cf. *complete oligopoly, imperfect oligopoly,* and *partial oligopoly.*

oligopsony. More than two but only a few *buyers* of a particular commodity.

omnibus clause. In automobile *liability insurance,* the clause providing that the insurance protection also extends to those persons (other than the owner-insured) who are using the car with the consent of the insured and within the conditions of the policy.

omnibus risk. In insurance, the coverage of an assortment of risks such as may be involved in the case of the tenants of a building who are engaged in different businesses.

one hundred per cent reserve money. A plan to require commercial banks to hold *legal reserves* equal to their *deposits.* Thus no loans could be made by commercial banks except to the extent of the bank's *net worth.* The purpose is to prevent changes in the volume of bank credit.

one-name paper. A negotiable instrument which has not yet been indorsed. When it is indorsed, it becomes two-name paper.

on-line, real-time. Compiling information as it occurs (on line) by a computer so that managers can exercise immediate control (real time).

on margin. See *margin.*

open account. Same as *open book account.*

open bid. An offer to perform a contract together with the price for the materials or work but with the right to reduce the price to meet the price quoted by others for the same job. Cf. *sealed bid.*

open book account. An entry on the books of the seller charging the buyer with the price of the goods.

open certificate. In insurance, a policy whose rates and policy provisions may be changed.

open corporation. A corporation whose stock is widely held. Examples are the American Telephone and Telegraph Co., General Motors, U.S. Steel, and others. Cf. *close corporation.*

open covenant bond. In insurance, a *surety bond* in which the surety agrees to pay any amount of damages assessed against the *principal* for failure to perform the function insured. Cf. *fixed penalty bond.*

open credit. A credit established by a bank (or business house) permitting a borrower (or customer) to make withdrawals (or buy goods) up to a stated amount without depositing security (or making payments for the goods).

open door policy. The policy of admitting citizens of foreign countries to a country to trade on equal terms with the country's own citizens.

open economy. An economic system which is free to interact with other economic systems. Cf. *closed economy.*

open-end contract. A contract which permits the buyer to order additional units upon the same terms without additional consent by the seller.

open-end investment trust. An investment company that sells and rebuys its own stock at book value plus a handling charge. Cf. *closed-end investment trust.*

open-end mortgage. A mortgage which allows the borrowing of additional sums, usually providing that at least the stated ratio of assets to the debt must be maintained.

open-end mortgage bond. A bond secured by a mortgage which authorizes the issuance of additional bonds against the same mortgage.

open indent. An importer's purchase order to an exporter, which may be filled with goods from any manufacturer or firm provided the goods meet specifications. Cf. *closed indent.*

open inflation. The situation where there is no control of prices and there is an increase in money demand for goods relative to the supply of goods. Shortages are adjusted then by a rise in prices.

opening entry. (1) The entry made to begin a set of books; the entry debiting all existing assets and crediting liabilities, reserves, and capital accounts. (2) The first entry in an account.

opening price. The price at which the first sale on an organized market is made on a particular day.

open interest. In trading, the amount of a commodity required to satisfy unliquidated futures contracts at any given time.

open letter of credit. A *letter of credit* without special conditions.

open line. A *line of credit* which may be cancelled by the creditor as opposed to a *standby line* which is noncancellable.

open listing. A contract between the owner of real estate and an agent such that anyone selling the real estate will receive the commission.

open market operations. The purchase or sale of government bonds and bills of exchange by the Federal Reserve System for several possible objectives: (1) to support the market price of government bonds, (2) to affect member bank reserves and thus their lending policy. In the second case, purchasing by the Federal Reserve makes possible the expansion of credit through the increase of reserves and vice versa for selling.

open market paper. Bills of exchange or notes drawn by one with high credit standing, made payable to himself and indorsed in blank. These are sold to financial institutions other than banks.

open market rate. The interest or discount rate for *commercial paper* in the open market.

open model. In *econometrics,* a model that involves changes in the values of the *exogenous variables* but does not involve a feedback of earlier values of the *endogenous variables* for the determination of future values of the endogenous variables. Cf. *closed model.*

open mortgage. (1) A mortgage of property against which the mortgagor can increase his indebtedness, thus reducing the percentage of security. Cf. *closed-end mortgage*. (2) A mortgage whose note has passed maturity with an unpaid balance due.

open order. In finance, an order to buy or sell on a stock exchange at (or above, or below) a stated price whenever the order can be filled. Subject to cancellation if the order has not been fulfilled at the time it is cancelled. Cf. *day order, limit order, market order.*

open policy. In insurance, a policy covering a risk for a specified time or a stated value, but permitting interchange of the goods insured. Most frequently used in transportation.

open price association. A trade association which gathers and distributes information about prices and quantities sold. Cf. *trade association.*

open price filing. A system of filing shipment reports, monthly production records, and price lists of producers with a trade association. Can be used for purposes of collusion to evade the antitrust laws.

open rate. Same as *open market rate.*

open shop. A business firm in which union and nonunion men may work and in which the employer can choose his employees as he sees fit. Distinguish *open union.* Cf. *agency shop, closed shop, preferential shop, union shop.*

open stock. In merchandising, the term for goods kept on hand particularly to fill in sets, as in silverware, with individual pieces.

open to buy. In merchandising, the term indicates that a retailer has a given sum he considers available to commit to buying.

open trade. In securities and commodities, the term to describe partially completed deals, e.g., an uncovered *short sale.*

open union. A union that makes no effort to exclude workers from membership through high initiation fees and dues, severe examinations, approval votes, or other devices. Distinguish *open shop.* Cf. *closed union.*

operating asset turnover. The ratio of sales to average tangible *operating assets.*

operating assets. Those assets which contribute to the regular income from the operations of a business. Thus stocks and bonds owned, unused real estate, loans to officers, etc., are excluded from operating assets.

operating costs. *Cost of goods sold* plus operating expenses.

operating curve. A *short run cost* curve.

operating expenses. (1) Commercial overhead; those expenses other than direct labor, materials, and manufacturing expense and other than financing expenses and income taxes. (2) In transportation, the expenses of operating the service. Broken down into *general operating expenses* and *particular operating expenses.*

operating lease. Such a lease as provides for rental payments covering less than the full cost of an asset plus interest assuming zero value at the end of the lease. May or may not provide for the lessor to bear costs of maintenance. Cf. *financial lease.*

operating leverage. See *leverage factor, (2).*

operating margin. Net *operating income* divided by sales for the period.

operating profit. Deducting the *cost of goods* sold from sales gives the *gross profit.* Deducting the *operating expenses* (overhead) from gross profit gives the operating profit.

operating ratio. Total of expenses of operation divided by total of operating revenues. Usually this includes only the ratio of (1) cost of goods sold plus selling, administrative, and general expenses to (2) net sales.

operating statement. Often used as the equivalent of the *profit and loss statement.* Technically, the operating statement reports only the results of the operations of a business and thus excludes income from other sources such as investments held or expenses such as financing costs.

operations research. A generic term embracing all activities concerned with quantification and analysis of business data by scientific methods to guide decision making. Decision theory applied to business problems. It embraces such techniques as *queuing theory, search theory, linear programming,* and *Monte Carlo technique.*

opportunity cost. In economics, the dollar amount that would be derived from the employment of a *factor of production* in the best alternative use.

optimism criterion. In a situation of uncertainty where the probabilities of various eventualities (states of nature) are unknown, the basis of decision should be (1) to determine a coefficient of optimism, namely, that probability for the maximum and minimum payoffs which is acceptable and then (2) to select the highest expected payoff using the weights of this coefficient to establish expected payoff values. Cf. *Laplace criterion, maximin,* and *regret criterion.*

optimum level of inventory. See *optimum size lot.*

optimum population. In any given state of the arts and accumulation of capital, there is a certain number of people whose labor will produce the largest possible per capita product from a given territory. A population of this effective size is sometimes called an "optimum population."

optimum size lot. That size of purchase which equalizes the cost of carrying inventory against the cost of processing additional orders so as to minimize the cost of feeding a production line. The equation is $x = \sqrt{2tu/c}$ where x = minimum-cost quantity size, t = reorder cost, u = annual usuage in units, c = annual cost of inventorying one unit for one year.

option. A contract (and hence must have all the requirements of a contract if it is to be valid) giving a party rights with respect to property, usually the right to buy or sell. Cf. *call, put, futures.*

options (in life insurance). (1) Settlement options upon the death of the *insured* which permit the *beneficiary* to select (unless the insured restricted selection) (a) lump-sum payment, (b) leaving the proceeds to earn interest, (c) paying out over a set number of years, (d) combinations of the preceding. (2) *Dividend options,* (3) *nonforfeiture options.*

optional bond. A bond that may be redeemed at the option of the issuer.

optional date. The date at which a municipality or corporation has the right to redeem its obligations under certain conditions.

optional dividend. A dividend payable in cash or stock whichever is preferred by the stockholder.

order (stock market), types of. See the following specific terms:

cross order
day order
give-out order
G(ood) T(il) C(ancelled) Order
limit order
market order
matched order
month order
open order
split order
stop-loss order
stop order
week order

order bill of exchange. See *order paper.*

order bill of lading. A negotiable *bill of lading* stating that goods are to be delivered to the person named on the bill or to his order upon his indorsement. Cf. *straight bill of lading.*

order buying. The purchasing policy of a producer who buys materials only after he has an order, and thus minimizes his inventory. Cf. *buying to minimum inventory, quota buying.*

"order paper." In dealing with negotiable instruments, an instrument is called "order paper" when it is in such form as to require indorsement by the payee or indorsee. "Order paper" can be converted to "bearer paper" by a *blank indorsement.* Cf. *"bearer paper."*

order point. The inventory level which triggers reordering. In simple form, *safety stock* plus average usage during lead time for an order.

order to show cause. In law, an order by a court to bring a question on for a hearing. The order states that the party served with the order is directed to show cause on the date set why the action desired by the party bringing the order should not be taken.

ordinal utility theory. The proposition that economic analysis must proceed from a ranking of pleasurable alternatives since there is no unit for measurement of pleasure. Cf. *cardinal utility theory* and *von Neumann-Morgenstern utility index.*

ordinary asset. Whatever is regularly bought and sold in the taxpayer's business. Gains on the sale of such assets are ordinary income although for taxpayers not regularly dealing in such assets the gain would be classed as a *capital gain.*

ordinary discount. The difference between the value at maturity and the present value which at an assumed rate of interest will accumulate to the value of maturity.

ordinary interest. Same as *simple interest.*

ordinary life insurance. Formerly used in the same sense as *whole life insurance;* more recently used to distinguish the usual singly issued, larger amount policy from *group insurance* and *industrial life insurance.*

ordinary stock. Same as *common stock.*

ordinary voting. The stockholder under this principle is entitled to one vote for each voting share and directors are elected one at a time. Cf. *common law voting, cumulative voting.*

ore tenus. In law, a *pleading* made orally.

organized exchange. The place where goods or property rights are bought and sold according to recognized rules. Examples are stock and bond exchanges, grain, butter, sugar, and other exchanges.

original cost theory of rate making. In public utility and railroad rate making, original cost is the cost of the property at the time it was first devoted to public service less accrued depreciation. On this base, the rate of return is allowed. Cf. *cost of capital, fair return on fair value, investment cost, prudent investment cost,* and *reproduction new cost theories of rate making.*

other income or expense. Same as *non-operating income (or expense).*

other insurance clause. In insurance, the clause providing the distribution of losses between two or more policies covering the same property. Cf. *Cromie, Kinne, Page* and *Reading rules.*

Ottawa agreements. Agreements entered into at Ottawa, Canada, in 1932, between the self-governing members of the British Commonwealth, establishing preferential tariffs ("imperial preference") among the members.

outlay contour or curve. (1) Same as *iso-outlay curve.* (2) Same as second meaning of *price line.*

outlay or capital outlay. In governmental accounting, expenditures that result in the acquisition of *fixed assets.*

out-of-pocket costs. An inexact term used to describe those *variable costs* that are paid in cash (i.e., immediately). In transportation, the term has acquired greater precision and is applied to a specific group of costs, such as the wages of a train crew and the fuel for a specific trip.

output costs. In public utilities, the costs that vary with the output of service consumed by a particular customer. Cf. *customer costs, demand costs.*

output rate. In public utilities, the part of the rate charge based on *output costs.*

outside broker. One who is not a member of an exchange but who works through a member.

outstanding bonds. Bonds which have been issued to the public and are in the public's hands.

outstanding stock. Issued stock in the hands of owners.

overabsorbed overhead. The excess of the amount of overhead cost applied by an accounting standard over the actual overhead incurred.

overallotment. In underwriting, the sale of more stock than is actually available so that the underwriter must enter the market to buy some shares to meet all his selling commitments. Such purchases stabilize the price of the stock offered.

over and short. Any document, account, or report showing the difference between an actual count of items and the stated quantity of items on the document or account.

overapplied overhead. Same as *overabsorbed overhead.*

over-bought. (1) In securities or commodities, a description that a price is too high. (2) More generally, any businessman who has excessive inventories.

overcapacity. The existence of more firms in an industry with the ability to produce a greater output than can be sold at prices sufficient to yield a profit on the funds invested in the industry. Cf. *excess capacity.*

overcapitalization. In finance, generally means the issuance of (1) securities with a stated value in excess of the market value of the net worth of an enterprise, or (2) securities bearing a rate of return above that which the income of the enterprise can maintain. Cf. *watered stock.*

overcertification. The certification of a check by a bank for an amount in excess of the depositor's balance, used primarily to enable brokers to buy stock to be deposited as security for the loan.

overdetermined system. In *econometrics,* a system of equations (even though *consistent* and *independent*) such that the number of equations is greater than the number of variables and different solutions are obtained, depending on which variable is eliminated first. Cf. *just determined system* and *underdetermined system.*

overdraft. A draft drawn in excess of the amount owed by the party upon whom the draft is drawn. Hence the term is particularly applied to checks in excess of the amount of a person's deposit in a bank.

overextended. A high ratio of liabilities to current assets.

overhead (costs). (1) All costs except direct labor and material charges, but sometimes excluding *manufacturing overhead.* (2) More narrowly, financial and other fixed costs are also excluded. Cf. *direct costs.*

overidentified model. See *overdetermined system.*

overinsurance. Insurance in excess of the possible amount of loss.

overinvestment theory of the cycle. This theory argues that the business cycle is caused by an excess of investment. There are two variants: (1) that more projects (investments) are undertaken than the savings can complete; or (2) that more savings and investments occur than are needed, and when the resulting investments are finished the output cannot be sold at profitable prices. In the latter sense, the same as the *underconsumption theory of the cycle.*

overissue. The issuance of more securities than are authorized by the articles of incorporation or by the action of the board of directors.

overlapping debt. In municipal finance, that portion of the debt of governmental units for which the residents of a particular community are responsible. For example, the residents of a city which is part of a large sewer district (which itself is a municipal entity) and part of a county (an even larger unit), would be liable for the city's proportionate share of the debt of the sewer district and the county.

overlapping insurance. Insurance by two or more *insurers* or policies covering the same property or risk. When the same property is involved, see *Cromie, Kinne, Page* and *Reading* rules. When the same liability of the *insured* is covered, the rules vary.

overlying bonds. Bonds subject to the prior claim of other bonds. Cf. *underlying bonds.*

overlying mortgage. A mortgage subject to the claim of another mortgage, e.g., when speaking of the first mortgage, the second mortgage is overlying.

overproduction. (1) Production of a greater amount of all goods than can be sold at or above cost, resulting in excessively low prices and disorganization of markets. (2) Production of a specific good or goods in excess of what can be sold at any price.

override. An extra compensation payable to one on salary or in addition to regular commission. Sometimes paid to the manager of salesmen on commission on the basis of the earnings of the salesmen under his supervision.

oversaving. (1) More saving than can profitably be used in maintaining the current (and future) scale of consumption of an economy. (2) More liquid or money saving than entrepreneurs are currently willing to invest.

oversaving theory of the business cycle. Same as *underconsumption theory of the business cycle.*

oversold. (1) In securities or commodities, the situation in which the amount of *selling short* is excessive in relation to the available items. (2) More generally, any business man who has committed himself for more than he can do.

oversubscription. An issue of securities for which there are more buyers than stock available.

over-the-counter market. Generally applied to security transactions which take place outside of an organized stock exchange whether the securities are listed on an organized exchange or not.

over-the-counter securities. Those securities *not listed* on an organized exchange.

overtime. All time worked in excess of a stipulated number of hours per day or per week as defined by law or agreement.

Usually paid for at a higher rate than the normal working time which is called "straight time." Under the federal *Fair Labor Standards Act,* all time over 40 hours per week in interstate commerce must be paid a premium of 50% over the regular pay. By agreement, work on Saturdays, Sundays, or holidays is sometimes classified automatically as overtime. Distinguish *shift premium.*

package car. In transportation, a car for less-than-carload lots destined for distant points and moving on fast trains.

package pay. Used particularly with reference to executive compensation where other components of pay loom large in comparison with salary: stock options, increased pensions, profit-sharing and bonus arrangements, and similar devices.

packing list. A business form showing the contents of a shipment, item by item, to permit checking by customs officials and by the customer.

Page rule. In insurance, where a *blanket* policy covers property also insured by a specific policy and there is a loss on this item only, the two policies contribute in proportion to their face amounts for this loss under the Page rule. Cf. *Cromie, Kinne* and *Reading* rules for this general situation.

paid-in capital. The amount paid in for that part of the stock of a corporation which has been sold.

paid-in surplus. Surplus which is contributed by the stockholders and does not arise from profits. Frequently in opening a bank, surplus is paid-in at the time of organization. The sale of stock by a corporation at prices above the par value results in paid-in surplus equal to the excess of sale price over par value.

paid-up additions. In life insurance, units of single premium insurance bought by application of the dividends on a *policy* under the insured's option as to disposition of dividends. Cf. *dividend options.*

paid-up insurance. Insurance for which the policy holder has completed the payments, but the policy has not yet matured. Or where the insured has ceased paying premiums, but instead of dropping the policy or taking extended term insurance he has elected to buy with the cash value a paid-up contract, payable at his death but in an amount less than the original face amount.

paid-up (or full-paid) stock. Any share for which subscribers have paid the full amount of par value into the corporation's treasury.

paid-up value. Used in connection with life insurance to designate the amount of insurance which will be allowed the insured on the policy with no further payment due should he discontinue premium payments on the existing policy. Distinguish *cash surrender value.*

paired combination rating. In personnel management, a rating system in which paired names of all those to be rated appear on cards so that each person to be rated appears on a card with every other person to be rated. Each rater marks the preferred person on each card. The totals are then related to standard scores.

pais. See *matter in pais.*

Palmer rule. The "Rule of 1832" or "Palmer rule" (after Palmer, governor of the Bank of England at that time) sought to make fluctuations in English currency conform to what would occur under purely metallic currency by keeping bank-owned paper at a constant level.

panic. When people are madly selling securities or other commodities at the best price they will fetch or staging a "run" on a bank to withdraw deposits. Cf. *business cycle.*

paper money. See *paper standard.*

paper profits. Profits that would exist at a given moment if a person closed transactions of sale or purchase. E.g., a house was purchased for $5,000. The present price if it were to be sold would be $8,000. There is a "paper profit" of $3,000.

paper rate. In transportation, a published rate under which no traffic moves.

paper standard. The meaning of this term varies. Any monetary standard which does not qualify as the gold, silver, or commodity standard can be called a paper standard. Hence the essence of the paper standard lies in the fact that the money involved is not convertible into gold, silver, or another commodity. Cf. *monetary standard, types of.*

par. See *par value.*

parallel standards. A monetary system in which two or more metals are coined but in which the monetary authority has no established ratio for metal content of either in the monetary unit of the country.

parameter. In *econometrics,* a constant or the coefficient of a variable in a model or system of equations.

pardon. See *reprieve.*

Paretian optimality. A condition in which no further improvement of one individual's total utility can be achieved without taking utility away from someone else. Cf. *Bergson criterion, Kaldor criterion,* and *Scitovsky double criterion.*

Pareto distribution. Using the personal distribution of the national income in the nineteenth century for many countries, Pareto found that if X signifies a given income level, and N the number of persons with incomes exceeding X, and if a curve is drawn with the logarithms of X as ordinates and the logarithms of N as abscissae, the curve is a straight line inclined to the axis of X at 56 degrees with a variation of 3 or 4 degrees. Since tangent 56 degrees = 1.5, then the number of incomes greater than mX for any value m is $\frac{1}{m^{1.5}} N$. Cf. *Gibrat distribution, log-normal distribution, normal distribution, Poisson distribution, t distribution, and Yule distribution.* (See Figure 36, page 264.)

Pareto's law. A generalization regarding the distribution of incomes by size in a population. The generalization is that a frequency distribution of incomes at different times and places will show a high degree of stability. A *frequency distribution* of income sizes would be highly *skewed* towards the low size income.

Pareto's measure of inequality of a distribution. Following directly from *Pareto's distribution,* this is

$$\frac{\text{logarithm of amount } X}{\text{logarithm of number of incomes in excess of } X}$$

where X is a given income level and a straight line has been fitted as stated in *Pareto distribution.* Cf. *Gini coefficient.*

pari materia. Latin for "the same subject." All language (in statutes, contracts, etc.) treating of the same subject is to be considered to get at the meaning so that one consistant meaning is applied throughout (if that is possible).

pari passu. Latin for "by the same step." In law, used particularly in situations calling for equal treatment of those with equal rights.

parity price. In the United States, that price of an agricultural commodity which gives the commodity a purchasing power, with respect to articles which farmers buy, equivilant to that which it had in a base period (usually August, 1909, to July, 1914, a period of relatively high prosperity for farmers as a class.) Parity prices are published monthly for about 31 basic commodities, semi-annually for about 150 others, by the Department of Agriculture.

parity ratio. Same as *parity price.*

Parkinson's law. Work expands to use available time. All slack in a system will be exhausted. Thus any amount in a budget is sure to get spent.

parliamentary law. The body of rules governing the internal procedure of a legislative group. In the United States, the rules of Congress have been codified as *Robert's rules of order.* These rules apply to the meetings of stockholders and directors of a corporation.

par-list bank. All member banks of the Federal Reserve System must clear their checks at par. Many nonmembers take a collection charge out of each check and hence do not clear at par. Some nonmembers clear at par. These constitute the par list.

par of exchange. The rate of exchange determined by the ratio between the metallic content of the standard monetary units of two countries. Before 1931 English par of exchange was $4.866 in American money for the English pound; today it is $2.80.

parol contract. An oral or verbal agreement.

parol evidence. Evidence offered in a court of a verbal statement.

par or face value. The value printed on the face of the stock or bond certificate. This value may be any amount, small or large. In the United States the most common par value of stock has been one hundred dollars per share, while in England it is one pound. The par value of a bond is generally $100, $500, or $1,000. Cf. *no par stock.*

partial correlation. The net relationship of a dependent variable to one or more independent variables after the effect of one or more other independent variables has been held constant statistically. Cf. *correlation* for an illustration of simple, multiple and partial correlation.

partial equilibrium. An *equilibrium* reached from a consideration of only a few endogenous variables and holding other economic variables constant. Cf. *equilibrium of firm or industry (partial) long run* and *equilibrium of firm or industry (partial) short run.*

partial limitation clause. In insurance, a clause providing that claims less than a stated amount will not be paid, but the entire claim will be paid if the amount exceeds the stated figure. Cf. *deductible coverage.*

partial oligopoly. The situation in which a few sellers dominate the selling side of the market for a product but do not act in a manner to maximize the joint profits of the group due primarily to uncertainty about the responses of the other large sellers to any action by one of them. Cf. *complete oligopoly* and *imperfect oligopoly.*

partial regression coefficient. Same as *net regression coefficient* but not to be confused with *coefficient of partial determination,* which is the square root of the ratio of *associated variance* to total *variance* with the effect of the other independent variables held statistically constant.

participating bond. A bond which shares in earnings but in any event receives a minimum stated amount as interest.

participating insurance. (1) Insurance written by a mutual insurance company is called participating because any "profits" (overcharges) are refunded to the policy holders. Stock insurance companies usually write nonparticipating policies. (2) Insurance in which the insured is required to bear part of the loss.

participating policy. In insurance, a policy for which the insured is charged a premium greater than the anticipated cost with the excess to be refunded in the form of dividends.

participating preferred stock. Preferred stock that entitles the owner after receiving the regular preferred dividend to share the profits declared as dividends with the holders of common stock, either immediately or after a stipulated amount has been paid to the holders of common stock.

participation certificate. A document stating the share of ownership of the holder in a security of large denomination.

participation loan. A loan extended by several banks or other lenders working together.

particular average. In *marine insurance,* any loss resulting from accident other than normal perils of the sea (such as water leakage) is not apportioned among the shippers but borne by the particular owner of the damaged goods. Cf. *general average.*

particular balance of trade. See *balance of trade.*

particular operating expenses. Those expenses that vary directly with the amount of business done. E.g., in running a particular train, the coal and wages of the crew. Cf. *general operating expenses.*

partition. In law, the division of property among co-owners, Where division in kind is impractical, the whole is sold and the proceeds divided.

partnership. An association of two or more persons who own a business jointly for profit. The chief characteristics of a partnership are: (1) unlimited liability of its members (except for a limited partnership), (2) nontransferability of ownership unless the other partners consent, (3) instability of existence (death and other events can terminate the partnership). Cf. *limited partnership.*

part-paid stock. Stock for which the holder has made only partial payment to the corporation and on which he still owes a balance.

party wall. A wall on the boundary line of two parcels of real estate with the owners of the two parcels having common rights in the wall.

par value. In the case of bonds and stock, the face value appearing on the certificate is the par value. Those stocks not containing such a statement have no-par value. Cf. *stated value.*

pass book. A booklet which commercial banks, savings banks, savings and loan associations, and others give to their depositors and into which are entered the deposits and withdrawals of money made by the depositors. Legally, a pass book has only the value of a memorandum.

passenger density. The total number of miles travelled by all passengers divided by the total number of miles of the system.

passenger mile cost. Total passenger travel costs divided by total passenger miles travelled.

passenger miles. The total number of miles travelled by all passengers. Cf. *car mile.*

passing a dividend. Not paying a dividend at the usual time.

passive bond. A bond that carries no interest.

passive trade balance. Same as *unfavorable balance of trade.*

passive trust. Same as *dry trust.*

past income hypothesis. The argument that current consumption is largely a function of the prior income of individuals. Identified with Dusenberry. Cf. *absolute income hypothesis, life-cycle income hypothesis, permanent income hypothesis,* and *relative income hypothesis.*

patent. (1) The exclusive right to "any new and useful art, machine, manufacture, or composition of matter, or any new and useful improvement thereof . . . (or) asexually reproduced distinct and new variety of plant, other than a tuberpropogated plant . . . (or) any new, original, and ornamental design for an article of manufacture not patented or described in any printed publication in this or any foreign country . . . more than one year prior to . . . application." In short, a legal monopoly to an invention or discovery limited as above. The term of patent in the U.S. is 17 years, except that design patents run for 14, 7 or 3½ years at the option of the patentee. (2) The conveyance of land title by the government is also called a "patent."

patent infringement. Unauthorized use, sale, or manufacture of a patented article. Various remedies are available to the holder of the patent.

patent pooling. Any arrangement by which a number of producers agree to the interchange of patent licenses between the members of the pool.

paternalism. The term applied to a policy of a business or government in dealing with employees or citizens as a father (pater) would. Thus a unilateral basis of decisions.

pawnbrokers. Money lenders who extend loans upon the security of jewelry and other valuable personal property.

pay, types of. See the following specific terms:

call-in pay
dismissal pay
longevity pay
severance pay
vacation pay

payback period. In *capital budgeting*, the cost of an investment divided by the annual cash inflow from the investment gives the number of years to recover the cost of the investment. An alternate form computes the payback period using profit earned rather than cash return.

payback reciprocal. Approximation of the rate of return when the project life is at least twice the payback period and cash inflows are uniform.

payee. The party named in an instrument as the one to whom (or to whose order) payment is to be made.

pay load. That part of the total load yielding revenue.

payment bill. A *bill of exchange* presented for payment instead of acceptance.

payment supra protest. Payment after *protest*. An indorser liable on a dishonored negotiable instrument which has been protested receives a right to reimbursement from the drawer for paying the instrument.

payoff matrix. A matrix (table) with "states of nature" (situations that may develop) classified by rows (or columns) against available strategies (alternatives) classified by columns (or rows) for the purpose of analysis in view of the probabilities attaching to each of the states of nature. Cf. *decision theory*.

payoff period. In *capital budgeting,* the period of time required to recover the funds committed to an investment giving consideration to the fact that funds have a rate of discount and hence receipts are to be discounted back to the time of investment.

payor benefit rider. An attachment for a life insurance policy issued on the life of a child and waiving premiums if the parent dies or becomes disabled. Hence similar to the *disability premium* waiver which covers premium payments in the event of disability of the *insured.*

payout period. In *capital budgeting* the ratio of the original investment to the average annual cash earnings (after income taxes) plus depreciation. The result is in units of years.

pay-out ratio. The ratio of dividends paid to earnings in a given period.

payroll tax. A tax based on the payroll of a business. Social security taxes are of this kind, being a per cent of the wages paid.

P/E. Abbreviation for *"price-earnings ratio."*

peak. See *business cycle.*

peak demand capacity. See *peak load.*

peak load. In public utilities, refers to the period and size of the maximum demand for service during a given unit of time. E.g., the hour during a week when the greatest consumption of electricity or gas occurs. Cf. *off-peak service.*

peddler car. In transportation, a car for less than carload lots from one shipper over a specified route with deliveries to various consignees along the route.

Peel's Act. See *currency school principle.*

"pegging" exchange rates. The attempt by government to stabilize exchange rates through sales or purchases of foreign exchange.

"pegging" prices. Prices are spoken of as "pegged" when they are artificially held at a given level, usually through governmental action.

penalty bond. A bond providing for the payment of a stated sum if a future event happens (or does not happen) such as failure to appear in court.

penalty rate. The rate charged a member bank by the Federal Reserve Bank for a deficiency in the legal reserves required to be held against the deposits of that member bank.

pendente lite. See *lite pendente*.

penny stock. A low-priced and often speculative stock selling for less than $1 a share.

pension. An amount paid to a worker who has retired because of age or disability. The pension may be under *social security* or under a private retirement plan of the employer. Cf. *qualified pension, profit sharing and stock bonus plans*.

pension pool. A plan under which employers group together to create a common pension fund so that employees changing places of employment have no difficulty in transferring accrued pension rights.

peonage. Compulsory servitude based on the indebtedness of a laborer to his creditor, usually his employer.

peppercorn rent. A nominal rental maintained to give formal recognition to the status of landlord and tenant.

per capita. (1) Latin for "by the heads." Used as a basis for comparison, e.g., per capita national debt is the national debt divided by the number of individuals in the nation. (2) In law, used in contradistinction to *per stirpes* as regards the property of a person dying without a will. Under the per capita rule, distribution would be made equally to the surviving relatives of the same degree of relationship. Cf. *per stirpes*.

percentage completion accounting. Where the period of production exceeds the annual accounting period, one method of accounting is to accrue the profit or loss in each year by estimating the percentage of completion of the contract and the profit or loss accrued to date. The alternate method is *completed contract accounting*.

percentage distribution. A *frequency distribution* in which the percentage of items falling within each category is shown rather than the actual number of the items in each category.

percentage lease. A lease of business property providing that the rental will be a percentage of the sales or profits or of some similar measure of the activity of the lessee. The rent thus becomes a variable cost.

percentile. Any one-hundredth part of an array of values. Each such part contains the same number of values.

per contra item. In accounting, the opposite or offsetting account usually involving a guarantee or contingent liability. Thus where a bank has indicated acceptance on a bill of exchange which has not yet been paid, the asset is the customer's liability to pay the bank the amount of the bill of exchange and the liability is the bank's obligation to pay the holder in the same amount.

per curiam. Latin for "by the court." Applied to a court opinion which is not credited to one individual judge but rather the expression of a group of judges.

preemptory challenge. The right of a party to a lawsuit to object to a juror without giving any reason. The right is limited to a stated number of times for each side.

perfect competition. Used in two senses: (1) same as *pure competition,* (2) the market situation in which there is perfect knowledge of the market by buyers and sellers and an unlimited supply of the ingredients of production at existing prices. Cf. *imperfect competition.*

perfectly elastic demand (or supply). Perfect elasticity of demand (or supply) is the situation in which a small price change results in an unlimited increase in the quantity bought (or offered for sale). (See Figure 17, page 147.)

perfectly inelastic demand (or supply). Perfect inelasticity of demand (or supply) is the situation in which a small price change results in no change in the quantity bought (or offered for sale.). See Figure 39, page 324.

perfect market. A market in which the price does not change no matter how great the quantities of goods exchanged. Cf. *imperfect market* and *pluperfect market.*

performance bond. A bond protecting the insured against loss due to the inability of a contractor to perform. Also called a *contract bond.*

performance stock. Shares of stock in a corporation offered to a key employee at zero cost on the basis of achievement of specific objectives. Contrasted with *stock options* which specify some payment for stock and are directed at general objectives such as increased earnings per share.

peril point. The point beyond which reductions in tariff would substantially injure domestic industry. In American legislation, the U.S. Tariff Commission was directed to determine this point for each commodity, and any discretionary lowering of the tariff below this point by the President required a formal statement of reasons.

period analysis. In monetary theory, the effort to analyze the

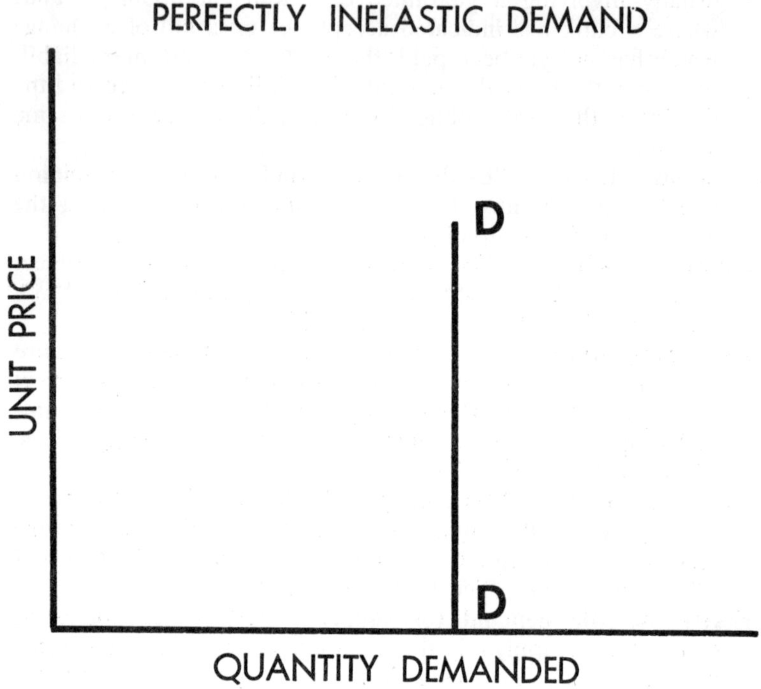

Figure 39.

cumulative effects as regards income, price level, employment, etc., of changes in investment, expenditures, hoarding, etc., over time by breaking time into periods with changes taking place discontinuously between periods and not continuously within a period.

periodic inventory method. Accounting for inventory by a physical count at various points in time. Cf. *perpetual inventory.*

period of production. The period of waiting involved in time-consuming processes of production. The concept depends on the particular author and type of problem he is dealing with. Sometimes the "average" period of production is defined as total capital divided by total income. Cf. *roundabout production.*

perjury. A false statement as to a material fact either orally in court or in writing under oath. Sometimes such statements are further classified into perjury and the lesser crimes of false swearing and misrepresentation.

permanent income hypothesis. The argument that current consumption is largely a function of a "life-time average" income including especially expected. One form of hypothesis (Friedman) employs three propositions. (1) Observed income has a transitory and a permanent component. The permanent component is the product of two factors: the wealth of the consumer (discounted present value of future expected income) and the rate at which these expected receipts are discounted. (2) Permanent consumption is a function of permanent income but independent of the level of that income. (3) Transitory and permanent income are uncorrelated, as are transitory and permanent consumption as well as transitory consumption and transitory income. The other form of the hypothesis (Modigliani) is that the consumer determines the amount available for consumption over his life. This is the sum of his net worth at the beginning of the period plus the present value of nonproperty income less the present value of planned bequests. The amount allocated to consumption is a given proportion of this total. Actual consumption differs from allocated consumption by the amount of transitory expenditures. Cf. *absolute income hypothesis, life-cycle income hypothesis, past income hypothesis, relative income hypothesis.*

permanent injunction. A court order restraining someone from doing something under penalty of contempt of court which can mean a fine or imprisonment or both. If this order is on the final decision of a court it is permanent.

permit card. A card issued by a union consenting to the employment of a non-union worker for a temporary period where there is a *closed shop* agreement.

per my et per tout. Law, French for "by the half and by the whole." This is the mode of description for property held in *joint tenancy.* For possession and survivorship, each joint tenant holds the whole; but for purposes of conveying away, each owns half.

perpetual bond. Same as *annuity bond,* that is, without maturity date. Cf. *consol, rentes.*

perpetual insurance. A seldom-used type of fire insurance policy that has no expiration date but is still subject to cancellation by either the *insured* or the *insurer.* Periodic premiums are payable.

perpetual inventory. The determination of what is on hand by starting at one point in time with a physical count and thereafter adding acquisitions and deducting disbursements so that the amount on hand can always be determined easily. Cf. *periodic inventory method, physical inventory.*

perpetuity. (1) In general a scheme designed to continue an ownership through time indefinitely. By statute law in most states such provisions are forbidden if they extend beyond the period of existing lives and twenty-one years. (2) Government bonds in some foreign countries are issued on a perpetuity or annuity basis, that is, they have no definite maturity date.

perquisite. (1) In law, property acquired through one's own effort and not inherited, (2) Any compensation over and above the regular wage.

personal bond. A document signed by a person as formal recognition of a specific obligation on his part either to pay money or to perform an act (such as turning in a lost stock certificate if he finds it after a duplicate has been issued to him.)

personal check. A *check* drawn by an individual.

personal consumption expenditures. That part of *disposable personal income (personal income* less personal income taxes) spent on *consumer goods,* including *consumer semidurable goods* and *consumer durable goods* as well as nondurable *consumer goods.*

personal credit. The power of an individual to secure money, goods, or services in the present for his promise to pay in the future.

personal effects floater. Same as *personal property floater.*

personal finance companies. A business which makes small loans for personal needs. Most of this business is done on the security of chattel mortgages, although wage assignments are sometimes taken. Now called *consumer loan companies.*

personal holding company. A holding company which under income tax law derives at least 60% of its gross income from royalties, dividends, interest, annuities, and sale of securities, and in which over 50% of the outstanding stock is owned by not more than five persons.

personal income (formerly, income payments to individuals). The aggregate income of individuals from all sources. Equal to national income minus undistributed corporate profits, inventory valuation adjustments, and direct corporate taxes plus government interest payments and transfer payments. Cf. *national income.*

personal property. All property other than interests in real estate (land). Short-term interests in land, such as leases, are called chattels real.

personal property floater. In insurance, a policy that protects against losses of *personal property* away from the home of the *insured.* Personal property at the home is covered by a *contents policy.*

personal representative. In law, the term applied to the person carrying out the disposition of the estate of a decedent. He is called an *executor* in case he is named in a will and an *administrator* where there is no will or when he is acting in place of an executor who has not taken his office or not completed his work as executor.

personal savings. That part of *personal income* not spent on *personal consumption expenditures* and not paid in personal income taxes. Thus *personal savings* is *disposable personal income* (*personal income* less personal income taxes) less *personal consumption expenditures.*

personal sector. See *sector accounts.*

personal surety. An individual acting as a surety contrasted with a corporation, usually an insurance company, so acting.

personalty. Same as *personal property.*

personnel management. In careful usage, the employer's activities in dealing with employees as *individuals.* Distinguish *labor relations* and *industrial relations.*

personnel ratio. The ratio of the number of specialized manpower staff members per 100 employees. The average is 0.8 for employers in this country.

per stirpes. Latin for "through the branches." A rule for descent of property where a person dies without a will. The property is to be completely and equally divided between those of the nearest equal degree of relationship, but where one of those of this degree has predeceased and left descendants, the descendants of nearest equal degree to this predeceased person will share equally in what would have been the predeceased's share had he survived. This is called the right of representation. Used in contradistinction to the *per capita* rule under which all relatives of the same degree of relationship to the deceased would share equally.

PERT Program Evaluation and Review Technique. A probabilistic diagram of a complex activity to analyze the intertemporal relationships of various segments of that activity to identify critical areas.

pessimism criterion. Same as *maximin.*

pet bank. A term applied to banks in which government deposits were made after the expiration of the second United States Bank in 1836.

Peter principle. The customary promotion practices of organizations result in promotion of individuals to one level above their competence. The level of incompetence is not known until after the promotion.

petty cash. A cash fund for small disbursements. Usually handled as an *imprest fund.*

phantom freight. A freight charge collected for a distance not travelled by goods. This arises usually in connection with the *basing point system* of pricing.

Philadelphia plan. An *equipment trust* arrangement using a lease as the legal device. Cf. *New York plan.*

Philadelphia stock right. See *stock right.*

Phillips curve. The strong inverse relation between the rate of money wage increase (plotted on one axis) and the unemployment rate (plotted on the other axis). The curve for the United States suggests that with 5 to 6 per cent unemployment, the price level will remain stable; but if unemployment were reduced to 3 per cent, an annual rise in prices of 4 to 5 per cent would be expected. This relation was first advanced by Phillips in 1958 for England.

physical inventory. The physical counting at intervals of all items to show exactly what is on hand. Cf. *perpetual inventory.*

physical value. A term loosely used to describe *replacement cost.*

physiocrat school. The school of economic thought holding that only land is value-creating in its product, which was called the *produit net,* but also holding that economics should analyze transactions in terms of flows of income to get at the fundamental changes in relationships. This was done by a chart called tableau economique attributed to many French economists of the seventeenth and eighteenth centuries.

picketing. In a labor dispute, the process of having some workers, or hired nonworkers, appear before a place of business carrying signs and banners urging workers not to work and customers not to patronize the establishment. Sometimes pickets are also placed before the homes of owners and managers of the business having the labor dispute. Picketing is legal if it is peaceful and constitutes only advertising. It is illegal when it involves violence or physical prevention of entrance to a plant.

pickup and delivery. The railroad service of calling for less than carload freight at the door of the sender and delivering at the door of the receiver. Now offered by other transportation agencies.

pictogram. Use of a picture or drawing to represent a statistical unit. For example, the figure of a man as 10,000 men and then by items showing the symbol repeatedly to show the number of groups of 10,000. There are four rules: (1) the symbol should be self-explanatory, (2) larger quantities should be shown by *more* symbols, not *larger* symbols, (3) *symbols* should be used for *comparative* statements only, (4) symbols should compare *approximate* quantities.

piecework. A system of wages based on the principle that the wage should vary with the amount of work done, the amount of work being measured by the number of pieces produced and the wage being determined at a fixed rate for each piece. Many variations of this principle exist. It is opposed in principle to the hourly rate system under which the employee is paid a fixed rate per hour worked, regardless of the volume produced. The two systems can be dovetailed; for example, a guaranteed hourly rate with a bonus arrangement for all work produced in excess of a standard amount. Cf. *group bonus.*

piggyback service. The loading of motor-truck trailers on railroad flat cars (t.o.f.c., trailer on flat car) for the *line haul* with the pickup and delivery done by the motor-truck trailer. Cf. *fishyback.*

pignorative contract. In European law, the pledging of property as security. Thus the counterpart of the English and American *mortgage.*

Pigou effect. The proposition that a fall in the price level will cause an increase in consumption, due to lower prices, sufficient to prevent a fall in employment. More generally, consumption (C) is viewed as varying directly with the quantity of money (M) and inversely with the price level (P). $C = f(M/P)$. Named for English economist A. C. Pigou.

piscary. The right to fish in another's waters.

pit. The ring or place on an exchange for trading.

Pittsburgh plus. For many years a favorite device of the steel industry. Steel prices were quoted at the Pittsburgh price plus the cost of transportation from Pittsburgh to the point of delivery, no matter where the shipment originated. Cf. *basing point system.*

plaintiff. In law, the party commencing a judicial proceeding. Cf. *defendant.*

plaintiff in error. In law, the party appealing to a higher court on a *writ of error.* Such a party might have been the *plaintiff* or *defendant* in the lower court, depending on who won in the lower court.

planned economy. An economy in which the use of resources is planned and controlled by government. The extent of government interference with the operation of the profit motive as the allocator of resources varies with the different advocates of such a system. Cf. *controlled economy.*

planned investment. In *Keynesian economics,* the amount of investment that people anticipate making.

planned saving. In *Keynesian economics* the amount of saving that people anticipate doing.

planning curve. When a new firm is considering entering an industry (or an existing firm is considering expansion or contraction) it is not committed to a plant of a particular size. A series of cost curves can be developed for the various possible plant sizes. These curves will overlap and create a new curve called a planning curve which consists of the near-minimum points of the series of cost curves. Cf. *operating curve.*

PLANNING CURVE

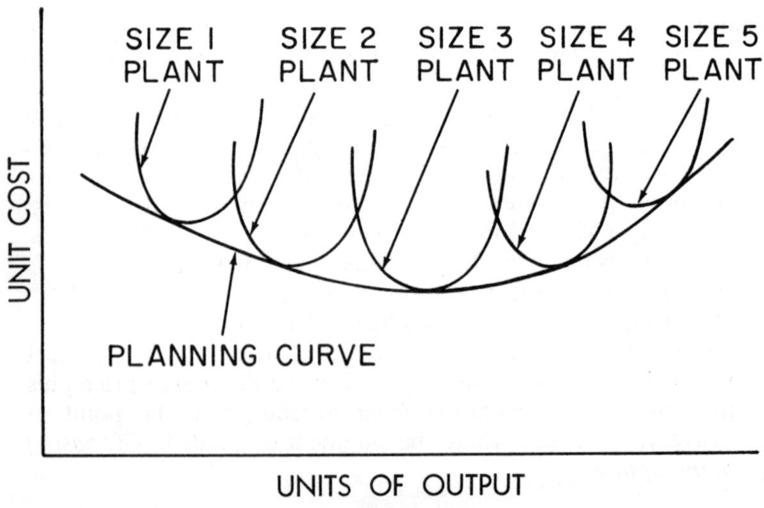

Figure 40.

plant factor. Same as *capacity factor*.

plant turnover. Net sales of a period divided by fixed assets before depreciation.

plat. A map or chart of a given area of real estate, usually prepared by a surveyor showing the size and location of various parcels of real estate as well as streets, alleys, easements of utilities, etc. Such a plat is often recorded in the *register of deeds* and referred to in conveyances of such parcels for accuracy and convenience.

platykurtic curve. A *frequency distribution* curve which is "flat-topped" by comparison with the *normal curve*. Cf. *leptokurtic* and *mesokurtic*.

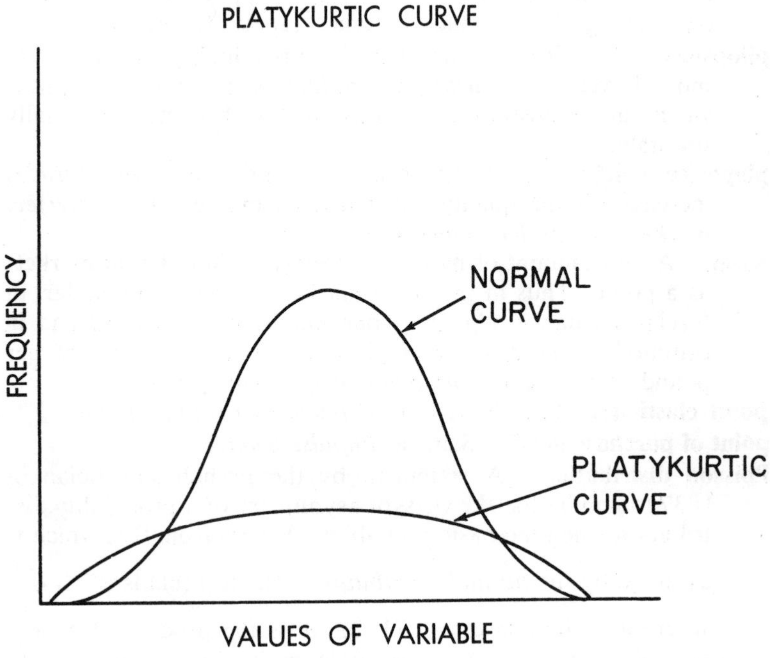

Figure 41.

pleadings. In law, the written complaint of the plaintiff or the answer of the defendant or subsequent written statements (such as reply, replication, or rejoinder) dealing with the last preceding written statement by either party.

pledge. A pledge is a *bailment* of personal property by the owner to another as security for a debt. The essential difference from a mortgage is that the pledge is valid only as long as the creditor has possession of the property. Wrong doings by either party with the property create much more complicated legal questions than is true in the case of mortgaged real property because of the absence of a recording system, although there are some provisions for recording mortgages of personal property.

Plimsoll lines. Markings on the side of a ship to indicate maximum draft of a loaded vessel. Different lines are used for different seasons and different waters.

pliopoly. The situation in which there is a high probability that more sellers of a product are likely to appear when an industry making that product becomes especially profitable.

pliopsony. The situation in which there is a high probability that more buyers of a *factor of production* are likely to appear when an industry using this factor becomes especially profitable.

pluperfect market. A market in which the price (or *terms of trade*) increases as the quantity exchanged increases. Cf. *imperfect market* and *perfect market.*

point. A unit amount of money is referred to in different markets as a point. Thus in the stock market a point is one dollar, in foreign exchange a point is one hundredth of a cent, and in commodity markets a point is one hundredth of a cent per pound. Cf. *gold import point, gold export point.*

point elasticity. See *elasticity of demand and supply, point.*

point of purchase good. Same as *impulse good.*

Poisson distribution. A statement by the French statistician in 1837 to handle the skewness or asymmetry of a probability distribution when the basic probability departs from 0.5, which is assumed by the *normal distribution.* The formula is $e^{-m} \cdot \frac{m^c}{c!}$ where e is the constant 2.71828, m is the product of N, the size of sample, times p the basic probability (which would be 1/6 in the case of six-sided dice), and c is the number of times the event occurs in a sample. Cf. *Gibrat's distribution, log-normal distribution, normal distribution, Pareto distribution, t distribution, Yule distribution.*

police power. The power, reserved to the states by the U.S. Constitution, to regulate activities in the interest of the safety, morals, health, and welfare of the people.

policy. In insurance, the contract between the insurer and the insured setting forth the premium, what risks are included and what risks not covered, the procedures to establish a claim, and all other terms and conditions applicable.

policy, types of. See the following specific terms:

adjustable policy
assessable policy
blanket policy
block policy
combination policy
coupon policy
endowment policy
extended coverage policy
fleet policy
floater policy
nonparticipating policy
open policy
participating policy
reporting policy
retention policy
schedule policy
standard fire policy
valued policy

See also types of insurance, under *insurance*.

policy loan. In insurance, a loan made by the insurer to the policyholder against the security of the *cash surrender value* of the policy.

policy reserve. See *reserve value*.

policy year. The twelve months beginning with the date of a policy.

political economy. (1) A synonym for *economics*. (2) Sometimes used as distinct from pure economics to stress the importance of political conditions and social institutions. Originally the term signified the application of "household management" to the body politic.

polling a jury. In law, asking each member of a jury what his finding is. This is directed at uncovering any individual who may want to change his vote between leaving the jury room and the reading of the verdict in the court room.

poll tax. A flat tax which some states and local governments levy on persons regardless of wealth or income. Some states levy on all persons over 21, some only on male voters over 21.

polyopsony. The market situation in which the number of buyers is so few that their actions materially affect the market price, yet large enough that each buyer cannot with confidence judge the effect of his actions on the conduct of other buyers in the market.

polypoly. The market situation in which the number of sellers is so few that their actions materially affect the market price, yet large enough that each seller cannot with confidence judge the effect of his actions on the conduct of the other sellers in the market.

polypsony. The situation in which a buyer believes his purchasing policy will not produce any reactions on the part of other buyers.

polypsony, pure. The situation in which the buyer assumes that he will be able to purchase at a given price any quantity that he may care to purchase.

pool. (1) An agreement between competitors to maintain prices by dividing traffic, territory, or earnings among themselves upon some basis of size or strength to restrict competition. (2) In insurance, a grouping of insurers to spread the risk of a large policy.

pool car. A service provided by railroads which permits combining a number of small shipments in a single carload at a lower cost than the less-than-carload rate. Ultimately the shipments will be carried separately to their destination from an intermediate point where the pool car stops. The *trap car* is a special type of pool car.

pooling of interests. That method of accounting for a *merger* in which the asset and liability accounts of each company are combined with any difference between the merger terms and the book values of net worth accounted for in the *capital surplus* account of the combined companies. The *earned surplus* of the acquired company is added to the earned surplus of the acquiring company. Cf. *purchase method of accounting.*

poor debtor's oath. In some states, an impoverished debtor may summon a creditor before a judge, and by taking a "poor debtor's oath," be absolved from paying that particular debt. A poor man's method of bankruptcy.

population. (1) The number of people living within a given area, such as a city, county, state, or nation, or the world. (2) In statistics, not limited to people but applied to any collection of items from which a sample is taken.

portal-to-portal act. A federal law of 1947 modifying the liability of employers which might exist for *portal-to-portal pay* under the *Fair Labor Standards Act, the Walsh-Healy Act,* or the *Bacon-Davis Act.*

portal-to-portal pay. Payment to workers for time spent in traveling from the entrance to an employer's premises to their working area.

port differential. The difference in freight charges on the same item from a point of origin to two or more competing ports.

portfolio. In investments, the collective term for all the securities held by one person or institution.

portfolio effect. The offsetting of the risk of one project with the risk of another whose returns fluctuate in the opposite direction from the first project. Thus the combined risk (variation in return) of the portfolio is smaller than of the individual items in the portfolio.

position bond. A *bond* covering the fidelity or performance of the duties of a particular job regardless of what person may hold the job. Cf. *name bond.*

positive economics. Economics as limited to analysis and description with no attempt at judgment or policy statements. Cf. *normative economics.*

possession. Merely the right to use, and this can be transferred without the transfer of ownership.

possibility curve. Same as *transformation curve.*

post. (1) A horseshoe-shaped enclosure on the main floor of a stock exchange around which trading in certain stocks takes place. (2) In accounting, the transfer of an entry from a *journal* to a *ledger.*

post-audit. Verification of the record of transactions which have already occurred. Cf. *pre-audit.*

postdating. Dating an instrument with a date later than that on which it was signed.

posting. In accounting, the transfer of entries from the *journal* to the *ledger* accounts.

pound sterling, English. The English monetary unit formerly worth $4.86 in American money and consisting of 113.001 grains pure gold, or 4.866 times the weight of the dollar (23.22 grains) before its devaluation in 1934. .The ratio now is 2.8. The symbol is £.

power of attorney. A written instrument authorizing someone else to act as your agent (your "attorney"). The power may be general (without limit) or special (restricted in some way, for example, a power of attorney to collect accounts only). The power of attorney must conform to formalities if it is to be used for purposes which require formalities. For example, a power of attorney to convey real estate must be witnessed and notarized because if the party himself were acting there would be this requirement.

pre-audit. An examination of the propriety of proposed transactions or as yet unrecorded transactions. Cf. *post-audit.*

precatory trust. A trust established by words of desire rather than the usual form of declaration.

precautionary demand for money. The amount of liquid resources which people desire to hold for emergencies and unexpected adversities. C. *speculative demand for money* and *transactions demand for money*.

precision. The degree of reproducibility of calculations or measurements produced by a process. The smaller the *standard deviation*, the higher the precision. Cf. *accuracy*.

predetermined variable. In *econometrics*, predetermined variables consist of *exogenous variables* and any lagged *endogenous variables* when analyzing a *dependent variable* as a function of one or more *independent variables* and a *disturbance term*. Cf. *endogenous variable, exogenous variable, instrumental variable, jointly dependent variable, shift variable*.

predicting equation. See *additive predicting equation, multiplicative predicting equation*.

preemption. (1) In foreign trade, the right of a government to seize goods and sell them at the value declared by the importer if suspicion exists that the value declared is too low. (2) As to public lands, the securing of the prior right to such lands by the party first taking possession and recording a claim together with a nominal payment. This statutory right was repealed in 1891 and the *Homestead Law* substituted.

preemptive right. The right of a stockholder in a corporation to participate proportionately in an increase of the capital stock. In short, the stockholder has a right to maintain his percentage interest in a corporation by requiring the corporation to offer to him the opportunity of buying his proportion of shares in a new issue before others can buy. The right is not recognized in the law of some states and in some can be eliminated by the stockholders.

preference bond. An infrequent term for *income bond*.

preference check list. Same as *forced choice rating*.

preference stock. An uncommon word for *preferred stock*.

preferential duty. Same as *differential duty*.

preferential shop. A business firm which gives preference in hiring to qualified union members over nonunion members. Cf. *agency shop, closed shop, open shop, union shop*.

preferential tariff. A tariff which grants lower rates of duty on goods imported from certain "preferred" countries than on the same goods from other countries. Cf. *most favored nation clause, Ottawa Agreements*.

preferential union shop. A business firm in which union men are hired first and if the union cannot supply sufficient men, nonunion men may be hired but must join the union after a stated period. Cf. *closed shop, open shop, union shop*.

preferred creditor. A creditor whose claim by law enjoys a priority in bankruptcy, e.g., a mortgage, a wage claim, or a tax claim.

preferred stock. Stock with a claim to earnings and/or assets of a corporation prior to that of some other class of stock.

preferred stock ratio. The stated or par value of preferred stock divided by the total value of bonds, preferred stock, common stock, reserves, and surplus.

preferring creditors. A solvent debtor may prefer his creditors that is, pay them as he sees fit. An insolvent debtor who has within four months before bankruptcy paid creditors who did not *at the time of payment* give full consideration is presumed to have preferred them, and the payment may be recalled unless it can be shown that the payment did not defraud the other creditors. Even payments prior to four months may be proven to be fraudulent preferences, but the burden of so proving is on the party claiming fraud.

prejudice. (1) In transportation, the detriment to one shipper from the refusal of the carrier to allow the same treatment accorded another shipper under similar circumstances. (2) In law, the termination of the right to sue on a particular basis. "Dismissed with prejudice" terminates the matter on the basis advanced.

preliminary examination. In criminal law, the hearing granted the accused to ascertain whether there is sufficient evidence to warrant holding the person for a trial.

preliminary injunction. Same as *temporary injunction.*

premium. It has five meanings depending upon the connection in which it is used: (1) the amount paid for insurance; (2) the amount paid as a bounty; (3) an amount paid for a loan either in lieu of or in addition to interest; (4) the difference between the established, normal, or nominal price of an article and the price at which it can be obtained; (5) the excess of a cash commodity price over a futures price or of one futures contract price over another.

premium discount plan. In insurance, concessions in premium rate for policies of larger face amount in recognition of the lower overhead costs associated with such a policy.

premium loan. In life insurance, a *policy loan* to the owner of the policy (secured by the *cash surrender value* of the policy) for the purpose of paying *premiums* of the policy.

premium pay. Same as *incentive pay.*

premium rate. (1) In insurance, the price for a unit of insurance.

(2) In finance, some stocks receive a premium fee when borrowed for trading, as in *selling short.*

premium stock. A stock which receives a premium fee when it is borrowed for trading, as in short selling.

premium wage system. Any system of wages which involves the payment of more than proportionate pay for increased output. Cf. *Bedaux, Emerson, Gantt, Merrick, Rowan* and *Taylor plans.*

prepaid expense. In accounting, an expense paid before the accounting period to which it is attributable (such as a long term insurance policy whose full premium has been paid but which has not yet expired). Hence the unused part of this expense is shown as an asset. Cf. *deferred charge.*

prepaying. Paying before the date on which payment is due.

prescription. In law, the right of ownership which results from long and continuous possession. Hence, the right that is the end product of *adverse possession* for the required legal period.

presentment. Presentment is the requirement in the law of negotiable instruments that in order to bind indorsers on their liability, the instrument must be presented to the maker or other party primarily liable for payment as specified on the document. Failure promptly to do so discharges the liability of the indorsers for the default of the drawer or acceptor.

present value. The sum of future payments due discounted back to the present date at an assumed rate of interest.

present value method (in capital budgeting). The determination of the net excess (or deficiency) of the cash flows (periodic cash) received from an investment over (or under) the cash flows laid out for an investment when applying a given rate to discounting (and accruing) both of these cash flows. Cf. *accounting method, yield method.*

pressure index. An index reflecting the amplitude of deviations of a given economic series (or average of such series) from a reference point on the hypothesis that the amplitude built up in one direction (positive or negative) will be followed by a deviation of equal amplitude in the opposite direction from the reference point. Cf. *diffusion index.*

prestige good. A good whose consumption is sought primarily because the price for that good is high, e.g., diamonds for display.

presumption. In law, either an assumed fact or an inference assumed from a fact. There are two fundamental types of presumption: (1) irrefutable, that is, no evidence will be received to the contrary as a matter of policy; (2) refutable, that is, the fact or inference will prevail until the opposite side introduces some evidence to make it a disputed matter.

presumptive tax. A tax based on some circumstance of living such as a hearth tax, a window tax, or a carriage tax on the presumption that such a tax indicates ability to pay and economic or social status.

price. The amount of money which expresses the exchange value of a single unit of a good, as five cents for a pound of sugar.

price, types of. See the following specific terms:

accounting price
administered price
ask (price)
base price
bid (price)
call price
ceiling price
class price
closing price
conversion price
delivered price
exhaust price
list price
market price
minimum resale price
multiple price
normal price
nominal price
offering price
opening price
parity price
redemption price
rendu price
reservation price
shadow price
spot price
stop price
street price
support price
to arrive price
transfer price
upset price
zone price

price-consumption curve. Using an *indifference map* for an individual and plotting quantities of commodity *A* on one axis and quantities of commodity *B* on the other axis, an indifference curve traces all the combinations of the two goods which yield equal satisfaction to the individual. A series of such curves then traces different levels of satisfaction. Superimposing on this same map a fan of straight lines from any one point on either axis, each such straight line represents a different price ratio in the market place. That line which traces the points of tangency of each indifference curve with one of these straight lines is the price-consumption curve. Cf. *income-consumption curve*.

PRICE-CONSUMPTION CURVE

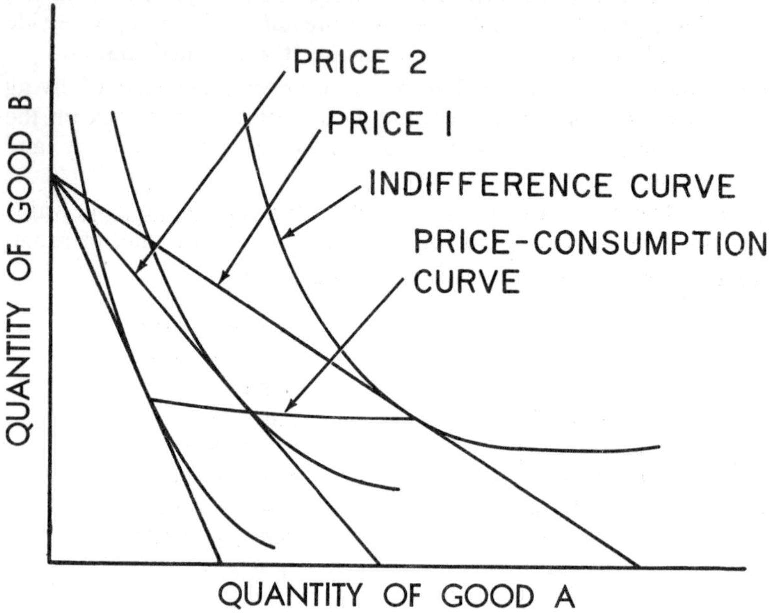

Figure 42.

price control. Governmental regulation of prices through setting a maximum price for sales of a commodity or service; may be selective or universal. Distinguish from private price regulation *(resale price maintenance).*

price discrimination. Essentially an effort to avoid treating different buyers (or sellers) in the same way as regards price. Such discrimination may be practiced in many ways, for example, selling the same product in two different countries at two different prices after allowing for tariff and freight differentials. Certain price discrimination on sales within the U.S. is forbidden by the *Robinson-Patman Act.*

price discrimination, first degree. The situation in which each buyer is forced to pay the maximum sum he is willing to pay for each item purchased.

price discrimination, second degree. The situation in which each buyer is forced to pay a different price but not the maximum sum he is willing to pay for each item purchased.

price discrimination, third degree. The situation in which buyers are classified into groups according to the elasticity of their demands for the product, and different prices charged each group.

price-earnings ratio. The market price of a security divided by the earnings per share.

price elasticity. See *elasticity of demand and supply, price.*

price fixing or stabilization. 1) The regulation by law of the price of one or more commodities. The commodities chosen for regulation usually have relatively *inelastic demand* so that slight changes in quantity brought to market or demanded would cause disproportionate changes in price in the absence of price fixing. 2) Similar efforts to control price by collusion of individuals or companies are illegal. But some controls on price by individuals are legal, e.g., *resale price maintenance.*

price floor laws. Statutes establishing minimum prices below which vendors may not legally sell. Cf. *fair trade practice acts, unfair trade practice acts.*

price index. A device to show the relative change in the price of a good over time or the relative change in an average of the prices of a number of selected goods over time. Setting a base period and taking the price in that year as 100, prices in succeeding years may each be divided by the base year price and multiplied by 100 and this will give the price index for each successive year. Cf. *price level, general* and the various types of index numbers shown under *index number.*

price leadership. In some industries which produce highly similar products it is customary for all producers to be guided by one (the "leader") in changing prices up or down. This practice is known as price leadership.

price level, general. The average of all prices is called the general price level. This average is a price index. Comparison of this average for one year with the same average for another year shows the change in the general price level.

price line. (1) In marketing, a single retail price fixed for goods that would otherwise be marked at different prices within some rather limited range, e.g., $39.50 for all goods that would otherwise be priced from $37 to $42. (2) In economic theory, using an *indifference map* with commodity *A* on the *x* axis and commodity *B* on the *y* axis, a straight line connecting

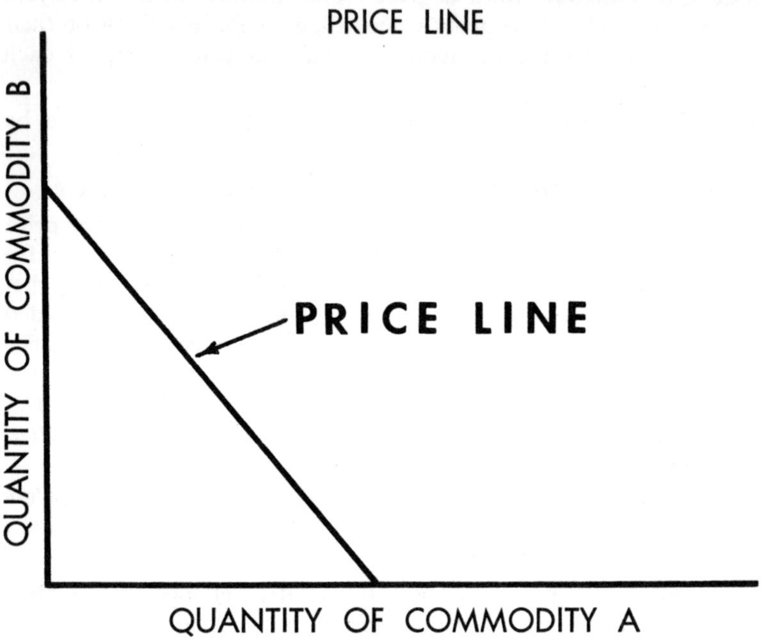

Figure 43.

any point on the x axis with any point on the y axis is a price line. This is called a price line because the individual can move along this line without any change in total expenditure by simply exchanging one good for the other at the ratio indicated by the line's slope, provided the line is drawn to reflect market price, i.e., the ratio in the market between the two goods. Commodity *A* and commodity *B* may be consumer goods or factors of production, and in both cases the straight line is a price line.

price lining. The practice of offering a class of merchandise (such as shoes) in a limited number of price categories reflecting differences in workmanship, materials, design, or other characteristics.

price maintenance. Governmental or other interference in the market in an effort to maintain prices at a predetermined level. This may involve subsidies, purchases, and/or other devices. Cf. *resale price maintenance agreements.*

price-offer curve (applied to labor). Using a map of *indifference curves* for a worker, with work (income) on the *y* axis and leisure on the *x* axis, a fan of straight lines from any given point on the *x* axis to points on the *y* axis will show different wage rates. An indifference curve on the map shows the various combinations of work (income) with leisure which will yield equal satisfaction to the worker. The points of tangency of the wage-rate lines to the indifference curves trace out the price-offer curve. This curve shows that as the wage rate rises in its earlier stages the worker desires more hours of work but as the wage rate continues to rise the worker ultimately shifts to less hours of work. Any other good could be substituted on the *x* axis to get the price-offer curve for that good.

PRICE-OFFER CURVE

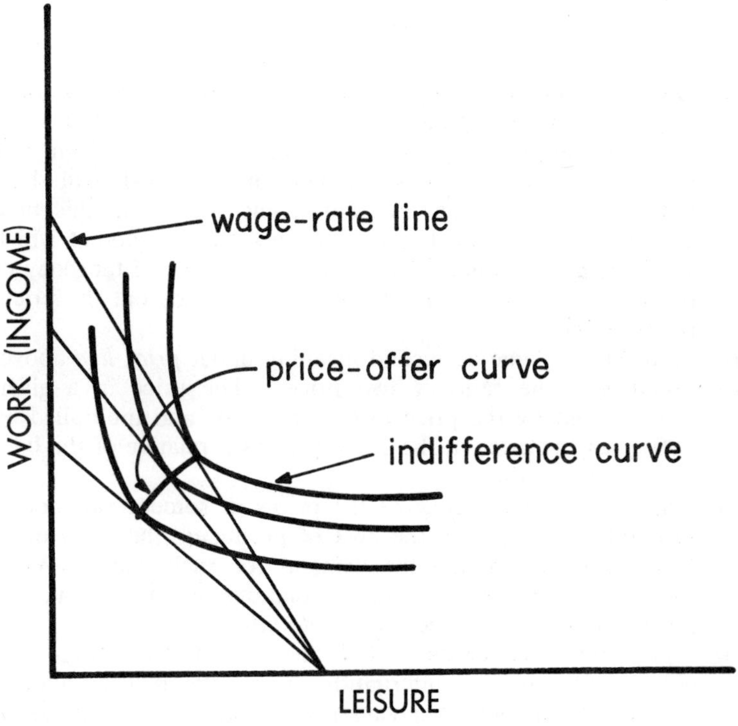

Figure 44.

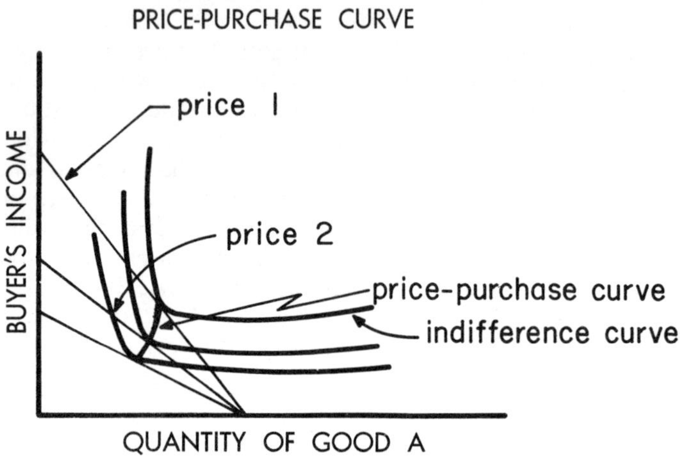

Figure 45.

price-purchase curve. Using a map of *indifference curves* for a buyer of good *A*, with quantity of *A* on the *x* axis and income of the buyer on the *y* axis, a fan of straight lines from any given point on the *x* axis to points on the *y* axis will show different prices for *A*. An indifference curve on this map shows the various combinations of income and good *A* which yield the buyer equal satisfaction. The points of tangency of the price lines to the indifference curves trace out the price-purchase curve.

price-ratio line. Same as second meaning under *price line* above.

price relative. The ratio of two prices. The price in a given year divided by the price in the base year and multiplied by 100 gives the price in the given year as a relative of the base year price of 100.

price rigidity. The tendency of the prices of some goods not to respond to changes in the cost of producing the good or in conditions determining the demand for such goods. When the rigidity of price in such situations is intentional, the phenonenon is described as an *administered price*.

price specie-flow mechanism. The theory that when trade and gold are free to move internationally in settlement of balances of trade, a country receiving gold because of an excess of exports over imports will find its price level rising because of the increase in its money supply. As a result the country will experience less exports. Conversely, because of higher prices at home its imports will grow. This will require the export of gold and the price level of imports will rise enough to produce equilibrium of trade. Opposite events occur in the country from which the gold was first shipped.

price spread. See *spread.*

price support. Various programs designed to maintain a price at a given level, such as subsidies or purchasing for storage.

price war. Such a severe lowering of price by one seller which other sellers must follow that some of the sellers would be financially ruined if the price war continued over a long period of time.

pricing, types of. See the following specific terms:

average cost pricing
basing point pricing
delivered pricing
full cost pricing
job pricing
marginal cost pricing
mill base pricing
target pricing
zone pricing

pricing out of the market. Colloquial term for a price set so high as to result in a very small number of sales.

prima facie. Latin for "at first sight." In law, such evidence as will carry the verdict in favor of one party if nothing is presented in rebuttal is called a prima facie case or prima facie evidence.

primage. In marine transportation, a premium formerly paid ship's officers for safe transportation of cargo. Presently there are few such premiums and they accrue to the ship's owners.

primary bank reserve. The total of *legal reserves* plus *working reserves.* This total is shown on bank statements with the title "cash and due from banks."

primary beneficiary. In life insurance, the person who is to receive the proceeds of the policy if alive at the time of the death of the insured. If the primary beneficiary predeceases the insured, the contingent beneficiary named in the policy takes the proceeds.

primary boycott. The labor or other group conducting the boycott merely refrains from dealing with the offending employer or manufacturer and directly persuades prospective customers to do likewise. Cf. *secondary boycott.*

primary deposit. Deposits arising from cash or cash items left with a bank. Cf. *derivative deposit.*

primary earnings. In accounting, the actual and unadjusted earnings per share. Cf. *fully diluted earnings.*

primary market. In finance, the market where the initial sale by the issuer of securities occurs. Cf. *secondary market.*

primary power. In public utilities, the power available at all times except during emergency mechanical failures. Cf. *secondary power.*

primary reserve. See *primary bank reserve.*

prime bill. A bill of exchange which is considered an excellent credit risk.

prime cost. (1) In economics, the English term for *variable cost.* (2) In accounting, the raw material and direct labor costs of a manufactured product.

prime rate. In banking, the rate of interest charged the most credit-worthy customers for short term loans.

principal. (1) The person who designates another as his *agent.* (2) The capital sum as distinguished from interest or profits.

priority. See *absolute priority* and *relative priority.*

prior preferred stock. A preferred stock which has priority over other preferred stock.

private bank. (1) An unincorporated bank (individual or partnership) engaged in deposit and credit operations. (2) Any bank except the central bank. In this sense, the term is typically of English and European use.

private brand. Same as *house brand.*

private carrier. Used in two senses: (1) All carriers not common carriers (thus including *contract carriers*). (2) Carriers excluding common and contract, that is carriers not holding themselves out to the public and not usually for hire. Distinguish *common carrier, contract carrier* and *industrial carrier.*

privateering. Operations in wartime conducted under a *letter of marque and reprisal* against shipping of an enemy country with the privateer having the right to retain captured property.

private debt. In national income accounting, total corporate debt less duplicating corporate debt owed by one part of an economic system to another.

private placement. Same as *direct placement.*

private property. (1) Any system which permits individuals to own and accumulate real and personal property, particularly the means of production. (2) More narrowly, the right of exclusive ownership of real and personal property for consumption.

private warehouse. Any warehouse not holding itself out as renting to the public.

privilege. In the stock market, the term for an option contract.

See *call, put, spread, straddle.*

privity. The mutual or successive relationship to the same rights in property between owners establishes privity of such owners.

privity of contract. The relationship between two parties to a *contract.*

privity of estate. The relationship between landlord and tenant or those having title in common to any property.

privity of possession. The relationship between successive occupants of property where the later occupant obtains his right from the prior.

probability. The quantity between 0 and 1 (conventional limits) that states what fraction of trials (repetitions) produce a given result.

probability curve. See *normal curve, Poisson curve.*

probability distribution. The likelihood of each of all of the possible outcomes in a situation. Customarily the total probability is set equal to 1. Thus each outcome will carry a probability stated as a fraction or decimal.

probability of ruin. The probability that one person can withstand a series of losses or adverse events. This probability depends on three factors: (1) the likelihood of winning (the "odds"), (2) the amount placed at risk in each gamble, and (3) the resources available to the gambler. If the "odds" of winning are equal to the odds of losing, the probability of ruin is $1 - R/(R + W)$, where W is the amount of winnings the gambler seeks to achieve if the amount placed at risk each time is constant, and R is the resources of the gambler. If the odds are not even, the probability of ruin is

$$\frac{(q/p)^R \; [1 - (q/p)^W]}{1 - (q/p)^{R+W}}$$

where p represents the probability of winning and q cr $(1 - p)$ the probability of losing.

probability sample. Any type of *random sample.*

probability theory. The study of random or chance phenomena by the use of mathematical models through analysis of a long sequence of observations which approach a stable pattern. Cf. *conditional probability, expected value.*

probable error. The range (plus and minus from the mean of the measure) within which there is one chance in two that the particular statistical measure (such as the arithmetic mean) of a sample will fall when drawn from a universe. The probable error is 0.6745 times the *standard deviation* of the particular distribution involved if it is normal. Cf. *standard error*.

probate court. In law, a court with jurisdiction over wills and inheritance from those dying intestate. Usually this court also has jurisdiction over *guardians* and their *wards*.

probate of a will. Establishing through proof the validity of a will in a competent court.

procedendo. In law, a writ by a higher court directing a lower court to proceed to final determination in a case where the grounds for bringing the case before the higher court cannot be established at the present time.

process. In law, a written document issued by a court.

processing tax. A tax levied on the manufacturing or processing of a certain article. Incorporated in the first *Agricultural Adjustment Act* which was declared unconstitutional although this type of tax is not in itself unconstitutional.

process method of cost accounting. A system of accumulating manufacturing costs by process (or by department or *cost center*). These accumulated costs are allocated on some averaging basis to the units of the product flowing through the process. This system is usable where there is mass production of homogeneous units as opposed to the production of individual or special jobs. Cf. *job method of cost accounting*.

producers' cooperative. An association of producers or workmen to pool capital and resources for marketing as a group the goods or services produced by the individual members of the cooperative.

producer's goods. Goods which satisfy human wants indirectly, not being wanted for consumption but for the sake of creating goods which will satisfy human wants directly. They include raw materials, machinery, and factories.

producers' surplus. The difference between the market price at which a producer sells and the respective lower supply prices at which he would be willing to offer lesser amounts of the particular commodity. Cf. *consumer's surplus*.

product contour or curve. Same as *iso-product curve*.

product cost. A cost so closely identified with the product that it can be inventoried, that is, included in the cost of inventory.

product differentiation. Any difference, real or imaginary, in two or more very similar goods or services which may result in a preference for one over the other even though their prices are identical, or even though the one may be priced higher than the other. Advertising, reputation for quality, or even personality of seller or selling firms may result in such differentiation by the buyer.

product homogeneity. The situation in which a given product of one producer is considered in the minds of buyers to be identical with the same type of product of other producers.

production. The creation of things or services which are directly or indirectly capable of satisfying human wants.

production bonus. A wage system combining the *piecework* system with the *day-rate* system so that workers are paid a minimum wage for minimum output and piece rates above the minimum output.

production coefficient. The production coefficient of a given factor of production is the quantity of that factor necessary to produce one unit of product; the assumption can be made that the quantity of the factor is fixed or that it is variable and this will result respectively in a linear or curvilinear relation.

production contour or curve. Same as *iso-product curve.*

production for use. An expression used to mean a system of production where profits would be disregarded and goods would be produced for use only. A euphemism for socialism.

production function. A statement of production as an equation involving the factors of production such that for any given combination of factors there is only one amount of product but for one amount of product there are usually many possible combinations of factors.

production loan. A loan, the proceeds of which are used for the purpose of producing goods or services.

production ray. With quantity of *factor of production* A on one axis and quantity of factor of production B on the other axis and when the proportions in which the factors can be used to produce a given product cannot be altered, a straight line from the original traces the path of output expansion. The slope of the line indicates the ratio in which the factors are used. Constant returns is not implied by the fact that the line (ray) is straight. If another process of making the same product from the same factors is available and this process also uses the factors in fixed proportion, another straight line can be drawn from the origin but of different slope if the proportion of the factors is different from the first process.

production revenue contour. If selling costs are put on one axis and output prices on the other axis, an *indifference curve* will trace all combinations of selling costs and output prices which will yield a seller a given production revenue. There will be a different curve (circular in shape and concentric) for each total production revenue, and one point at the center of the concentric curves giving the one combination of price and

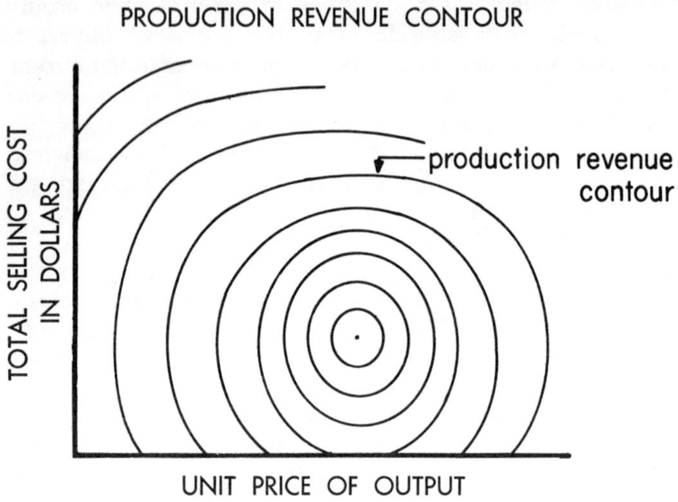

Figure 46.

selling cost yielding the maximum production revenue. Cf. *sales contour, sales line.*

production schedule. A tabular arrangement showing the product resulting from varying combinations of the different factors of production. From the schedule can be determined the best combination of factors for each quantity of product once the prices per unit are set for each *factor of production.*

production transformation. The use of one asset in the processes of production to increase other assets owned. Cf. *market transformation.*

production unit method of depreciation. Taking the initial cost of a capital asset, deducting the expected salvage value at the time it is discarded, and spreading the difference on the basis of actual units produced in a period as a per cent of total number of units which the asset will produce in its expected life. Cf. *unit cost method of depreciation.*

productivity. The amount of product turned out by a worker (or unit of another factor of production) per unit of time.

product liability insurance. Insurance protecting the manufacturer against claims made by purchasers of his product for defects in the product for which the law imposes liability on the manufacturer.

product line. A group of products related to each other, such as different models or types.

product mix. The ratios of different products made by one process or producer to the total output. Changes in these ratios are called changes in the product mix.

product moment. In correlation analysis, the sum of the products of the deviations of the values of the independent variable from its arithmetic mean times the deviations of the values of the dependent variable from its arithmetic mean.

produit net. The "net product" of extractive industries (mining, fishing, agriculture, etc.). A term common to the *Physiocrats.*

professional speculators. Those who devote all or a substantial part of their time and effort to trading in commodities and/or securities with the expectation of profiting from changes in prices.

profit. (1) In accounting, *net profit* or *gross profit* (see those terms). (2) In economics, the remainder after all factors of production have been fully compensated. It is the compensation for uncertainty (pure or competitive profit), or for monopoly (monopoly profit or rent), or a windfall.

profit, types of. See the following specific terms:

book profit	*operating profit*
gross profit	*paper profit*
net profit	*undistributed profits (tax)*
normal profit	

profitability accounting. Same as *responsibility accounting.*

profitability index. In capital budgeting, the ratio of the *net present value* of a project to the cost of the project. Puts different-sized projects on a comparable basis.

profit-and-loss account. In this account are recorded transfer entries from all the income and expense accounts. The balance of the profit-and-loss account closes into the surplus account of a corporation or the capital account in a single proprietorship or partnership.

profit-and-loss statement. A statement summarizing the income and expense of any organization to show net profit or loss for the fiscal period involved.

profit a prendre. In law, the right to take soil, gravel, minerals, and the like, from land.

profit break-even point. Assuming a plant organized for a given ideal volume of output, units of output are put on one axis and total dollars on the other axis. The profit break-even point is the intersection of the total income curve (including accruals) and the total cost curve (including accruals).

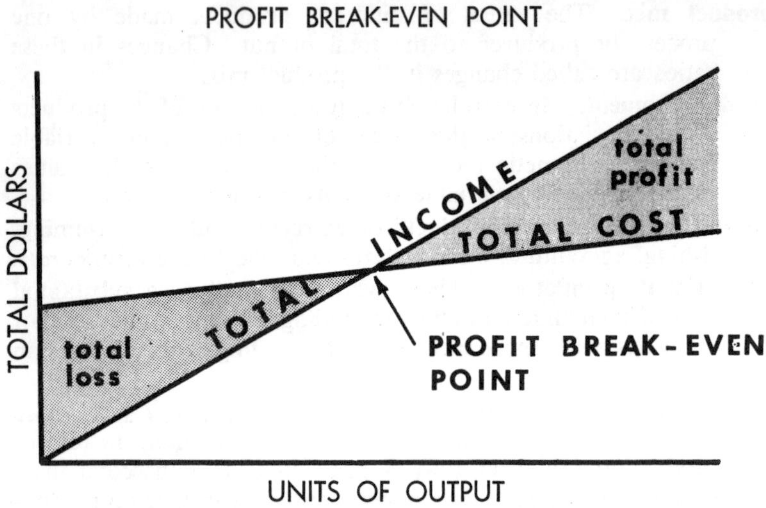

Figure 47.

profit center. Division of a firm into various centers of activity to facilitate accounting and analysis of the profit performance of each center.

profit contribution. The difference between sales and *variable costs.* By definition this is the same as *net profits* plus *fixed costs.*

profit insurance. Same as *use and occupancy insurance.*

profit sharing. A principle of distributing income whereby the workmen in a firm receive, in addition to their regular wages, a share in the profits of the concern which would ordinarily go to the owners. Cf. *qualified pension, profit sharing and stock bonus plans.*

profit-sharing bond. Same as *participating bond.*

profit taking. In the stock market, the sudden selling by a large group of speculators to realize profits they have.

pro forma. Latin for "for the sake of form." Used to describe accounting, financial, and other statements or conclusions based upon assumed or anticipated facts.

pro forma budget. Same as *project budget.*

programmed cost. In a classification of all costs into programmed, *standby,* and *variable,* programmed costs are those whose results are difficult to measure and largely discretionary, e.g., advertising and research. Cf. *standby costs* and *variable costs.*

progressive tax. (1) A tax levied at an increasing rate of taxation against income or property such that the rate increases as the *tax base* increases. (2) A tax whose effect is to take an increasingly larger percentage of *income.*

prohibition. In law, a writ issued by a higher court directing a lower court to cease its activity, usually on the ground that the lower court has no jurisdiction or is proceeding in contravention of law.

project budget. A budget separate from the general budget of a business and containing estimates for a contemplated activity such as a new product.

projection. In statistics, an estimate of future quantities based upon the extension of present relationships but which may also incorporate expected changes in such relationships.

proletariat. Workers who own no capital goods and are entirely dependent upon wages. Originally used by Marx in the theory of communism but now in general use. Cf. *bourgeois.*

promissory note. A written promise to pay a stated amount. The note may be negotiable or not depending on whether it meets the requirements of being *negotiable.*

promoter. One who initiates an enterprise and carries it through the initial stages before turning it over to the actual managers. The promoter may continue as a manager.

promotional elasticity. See *elasticity, promotional.*

proof of loss. In insurance, the sworn statement of the insured setting forth an itemized statement of the loss suffered, circumstances, and insurance covering the claim.

propensity to consume (average). The ratio between consumption and income (for an individual or a country). Cf. *marginal propensity to consume.*

propensity to invest (average). The ratio between new capital formation and *national income.* Cf. *marginal propensity to invest.*

propensity to save (average). The ratio between the income not spent on consumption and *national income,* or in the case of an individual, the ratio of income not spent on consumption to income. Cf. *marginal propensity to save.*

pro. per. Abbreviation for *propria persona.*

property. Used in several senses: (1) material things and rights subject to ownership, (2) the right to own, use, or enjoy the services of material things and rights.

property, types of. See the following specific terms:

intangible personal property *personal property*

private property *real property*
public property *tangible personal property*

property tax. A tax levied on property as the base. Traditionally such taxes have been proportional, i.e., at a uniform rate per unit of value.

proportion, the. The ratio of notes and gold and silver coin held by the banking department of the Bank of England (the reserve) to its deposit liabilities.

proportional rate. In transportation, a rate to be used only as a factor in making a *combination through rate,* e.g., a rate from New York to Chicago for traffic going beyond Chicago. Cf. *basing rate.*

proportional tax. (1) A uniform rate of taxation applied against the base of all income or property regardless of their amount. Real estate taxes are an example. (2) A tax whose effect is to take the same percentage of income.

propria persona. Latin for "in his own person." In law, a person is entitled to conduct his own suit personally and need not be represented by an attorney.

proprietary company. The parent or *holding company.*

pro rata. Latin for "in proportion." E.g., in insolvency, the debtor's assets are distributed pro rata to the amount of the claims of creditors of equal standing.

pro rata distribution clause. In fire insurance, the clause providing that the amount of insurance covering a multiple-building situation shall apply as a maximum for each building in that proportion of the face value which the value of each building bears to the total value of all the buildings covered.

pro rata liability clause. In insurance, a clause providing that where more than one *policy* covers the loss, the limit of liability under the policy will be the ratio of the face amount of the policy to the total face amount of all policies covering the loss.

pro rata rate. In insurance, the adjustment of the *premium* upon cancellation by pro rating on a strict time basis and not using a higher rate for the shorter period. Cf. *short rate.*

prospectus. A statement issued by a corporation at the time that securities are offered. The prospectus gives the details of the various issues of the corporation and other financial data such as comparative balance sheets and operating statements.

prosperity (also expansion or peak). The period of a business cycle when production is highest. Maximum employment, high wages, and optimism are prevalent.

protection and indemnity clause or insurance. In insurance, a clause in a *marine insurance* policy (or a policy providing such coverage when the basic marine insurance policy has no such clause) extending the type of risks covered.

protectionism. The policy of controlling imports and/or exports in an effort to achieve a specific objective. For example, a country may throw up tariff walls and other controls in an effort to get an "infant" industry started within the country or to promote expansion of an industry vital to defense.

protective covenants. In finance, provisions in a loan arrangement designed to reduce the risk of the lender such as restrictions against increase in officers' salaries and dividends.

protective tariff. A tariff levied on imports to protect producers at home against foreign competition. It helps to diversify the industries of a country, but it raises the cost of production and the cost of living. Cf. *revenue tariff.*

protest. A certificate of protest is a written statement that a negotiable instrument has been presented by a notary for acceptance or payment and has been dishonored. It is necessary to protest only foreign instruments. (Foreign means out-of-state, not out of country.)

proxy. A written authorization by a stockholder designating another person to vote for him. Where more than one proxy has been signed, the one with the latest date cancels all others by implication except that a proxy given by the seller to the buyer of stock after the record date for the particular meeting is irrevocable.

prudent investment cost theory of rate making. In utility and railroad rate making, the prudent investment cost is the amount which a prudent investor would have paid at the time of devotion to public use, but never more than the amount paid by the present owner of the property. On this base the rate of return is computed. Cf. *cost of capital, fair return on fair value, investment cost, original cost,* and *reproduction cost theories of rate making.*

prudent man rule. The rule that permits a trustee to step outside the *legal list* for investment of trust assets provided the trustee acts prudently. Most prudent man rules limit the percentage of trust assets permitted outside the legal list.

psychic income. The amount of personal gratification a good or service gives the owner or receiver. There is no standard for measuring it.

psychological theory of the cycle. Emphasis is placed in this theory on waves of optimism or pessimism as causing the business cycle through the consequent buying or hoarding. Many causes are recognized as possible reasons for the optimism or pessimism.

public corporation. (1) A corporation whose controlling stock is owned by a unit of government. (2) A corporation whose stock is partly owned by the public. Cf. *close corporation.*

public credit. The capacity of political units to acquire funds in return for their promise to pay. Represented by government, municipal, and other public agencies' bonds and notes.

public debt. The total debt of the governmental units of a country, including that of the central or national government and that of the state or local governments. Cf. *national debt.*

public domain. (1) After expiration of a copyright or patent the ideas involved are in the public domain and may be exploited by anyone. (2) Land owned by the government.

public finance. An area of economics devoted to the study of the taxing, borrowing, collection, appropriation, and disbursement of monies for governmental purposes.

publicity. Any form of nonpersonal presentation of goods, services, or ideas to a group, including *advertising.*

public liability insurance. Insurance designed to protect against losses caused by personal conduct, property, or agents of a person. The insured is indemnified for claims (liability) for which he is legally accountable. This type of insurance excludes liability for auto damage, workman's compensation and similarly clearly defined categories for which other insurance is available.

public monopoly. A product or service which is by law reserved to the government as producer, e.g., in the U.S., the postal service and in some countries, railroads.

public property. (1) The material things owned by public authority and over which some governmental agency usually exercises control. (2) Also property over which citizens generally have some rights.

public service commission. A state agency authorized to regulate public utilities and transportation utilities as to rates, service schedules, extensions of service, and many other aspects of their business.

public utilities. A group of industries given monopoly status by the state to furnish public necessities. Their prices and other practices have long been subject to regulation by state or federal commissions. Chief among these industries are electric, gas, telephone, telegraph, water, warehouses, and local transportation. The railroads, truck, bus, and air lines are sometimes included in the term and sometimes classed separately.

public warehouse. Any warehouse that holds itself out as renting to the public. Subject to government regulation as to rates, being a public utility.

PUHCA Public Utility Holding Company Act. Passed by Congress in 1935 to regulate public utility holding companies. For the principal provisions see *death sentence.*

puisne judge. A lower or associate judge as contrasted to the chief judge.

pump priming. The theory that money incomes can be increased in a depression mostly through government expenditures, on the assumption that a given expenditure by the government will induce additional expenditures through turnover of the money. If, however, the psychological reaction of the people to the process is fear, the exactly opposite result may occur: a lesser *velocity of circulation.*

punitive damages. Damages awarded in a lawsuit over and above actual damages suffered, to make an example of the offending party. Punitive damages are allowed when conduct is malicious or reckless.

purchase and leaseback. Same as *sale and leaseback.*

purchase group. In security underwriting, the group of investment banking firms that buys an entire issue of securities from the issuing company, each member of the group buying a stated amount. The part each member of the group cannot sell is then turned over to a syndicate manager who sells the remaining securities to the other members of the purchase group or to the members of the *selling group.* Cf. *competitive bidding.*

purchase method of accounting. That method of accounting for a *merger* in which any difference between the merger terms and the book value of the acquired company is accounted for as good will on the asset side of the balance sheet and as *acquired surplus* on the liability side. The *earned surplus* of the acquired company is added to the *capital surplus* of the acquiring company. Cf. *pooling of interests.*

purchase money mortgage. The reconveyance of property by the purchaser to a third party or to the seller at the time of purchase to secure the payment of the balance of the purchase price.

purchase order. A business form sent by the buyer to the seller indicating the kind and quantity of merchandise desired and often setting out the price from a catalog or price list. Cf. *acknowledgement.*

purchasing agent (middleman). An *agent middleman,* not to be confused with the purchasing official of a company, who acts only for buyers. Distinguished from the merchandise broker in that the purchasing agent acts continuously for his principal.

purchasing power of money. Refers to the value of money in buying goods. The purchasing power of money varies inversely with the general price level.

purchasing power parity theory. A theory to explain the rate of exchange between currencies not on a metallic standard. According to the theory, a rate of exchange will be established which equates the domestic purchasing power of the two currencies.

purchasing power risk. In investments, used in contradistinction to *financial risk* and *interest rate risk* to refer to the risk that the price level may move thus affecting the market value of bonds, for example, relative to common stocks.

pure competition. Used in two senses: (1) In a general sense, the market situation in which no individual buyers or sellers are large enough to influence the market. (2) In economic theory, the market situation in which (a) buyers are completely indifferent as to which seller they purchase from so

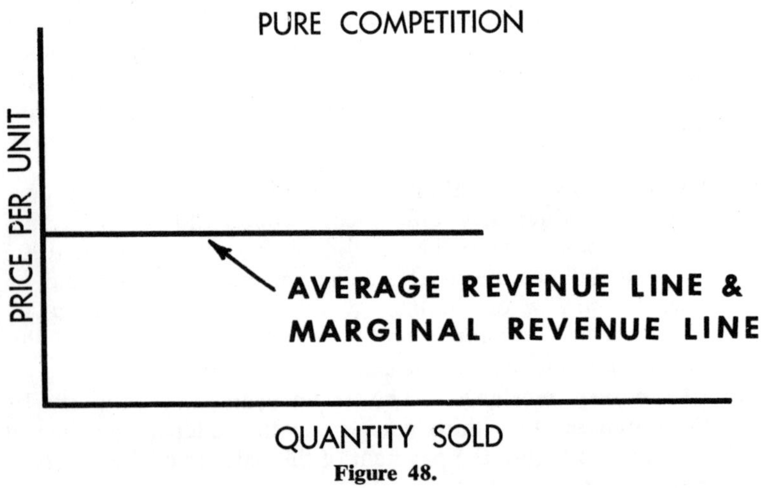

Figure 48.

long as prices are the same, and (b) the amount which each seller offers is so small relative to the total that he cannot influence the market. When used in the second sense, competition can be pure but imperfect. Cf. *perfect competition, imperfect competition.*

pure economics. The theoretical study of economics, that is, the study of economic data and principles under certain assumptions.

pure premium. In insurance, that part of the *premium* estimated to cover losses but not including expenses or profits.

purposive sample. Selection of a sample as any segment of the universe known to have the same average for one characteristic as the universe has, and assuming that in other characteristics (to be studied) it is likewise representative and that the unknown status of the universe as to these characteristics can be established from the sample. Cf. *area sample, quota sample, random sample, stratified sample, systematic sample.*

push money. Extra compensation paid by a manufacturer or distributor to the sales personnel of a *retail store* for extra effort in promoting particular goods.

put. An option permitting its holder to sell a certain commodity at a fixed price for a stated quantity and within a stated period. Such a right is purchased for a fee paid the one who agrees to accept the goods if they are offered. The buyer of this right to sell expects the price of the commodity to fall so that he can deliver the commodity (the put) at a profit. If the price rises, the option need not be exercised. The reverse transaction is a *call.*

putting out system. The English term for the *domestic system.*

PWA Public Works Administration. Started with the *National Industrial Recovery Act* which administered the spending of several billion dollars appropriated for public works during the 1930's.

pyramiding. (1) In finance, the narrowing of the amount of capital needed to control a business through the use of a number of *holding companies,* making use of the principle that ownership of 50% of the voting stock of a corporation gives control. (2) In the stock market, an increase of holdings of a particular stock financed out of the margin created by a rise in the price of shares already owned. (3) See *tax pyramiding.*

quadratic mean. This value is obtained by squaring all the values of the items in a series, then adding these squares and dividing this total by the number of items, and then extracting the square root of this result.

quadratic programming. Analogous to *linear programming* except that the *objective function* (that which will be maximized or minimized) is quadratic rather than linear. The constraints are linear.

qualified acceptance. (1) With reference to a bill of exchange, a variation of the terms by the acceptor. The holder can then treat the bill as dishonored. (2) With regard to contracts, a qualified acceptance is no acceptance but a counter offer.

qualified indorsement. Words of indorsement indicating that the indorser does not agree to the full liability of an indorser. The most common words so used are "without recourse." However, this does not free such an indorser completely from liability. He is still liable for the other warranties listed under *indorsement* but is freed of the warranty that the instrument will be paid at maturity.

qualified pension, profit sharing and stock bonus plans. Plans meeting the requirements of section 401 of the Internal Revenue Code so that employer contributions are deductible for income tax purposes.

qualified report. In accounting, a report by a certified public accountant not containing the usual statements but qualified, e.g., by a statement that some transactions were not verified.

qualified stock option plan. A plan for the issuance of *stock options* to key employees of a corporation. The plan must qualify under section 422 of the Internal Revenue Code in order for employees to gain the benefit of *capital gains tax* rates when they exercise the option, hold the shares for six months and sell. Prior to Jan. 1, 1964, such a plan was called a restricted stock option plan under section 424 of the Internal Revenue Code.

quality assurance. A broader term than *quality control.* Thus includes all activities beyond sampling and probability study of tests designed to assure maintenance of quality.

quality control. A statistical technique based on probability and sampling to determine to a given level of confidence whether stated variables in the universe have exceeded stated limits of the sample being met. Cf. *quality assurance.*

quantity discount. A discount allowed on the principle that larger quantities involve lower costs. For example, $10/dozen with 10% discount for a gross.

quantity theory of money. A theory that the price level is determined by the quantity of money in circulation and the velocity of circulation of that money. The leading statement is *PT = MV, Fisher's equation,* where *P* is the general price level, *T* is the volume of transactions, *M* is the quantity of money and *V* is the velocity of money. Cf. *commodity theory of money.*

quantity variance. In accounting, the standard price for a resource times the difference between the quantity actually used and the standard quantity allowed to make a given number of units of product.

quantum meruit. Latin for "what he has deserved." Where there is no contract price stated for goods or services and no gift was intended, the party furnishing the goods or services can recover on a quantum meruit basis, i.e., the reasonable value of the goods or services that were accepted.

quartile. The item dividing a *frequency distribution* into 4 groups equal in number. There are three quartile points with the second quartile marking the midpoint or median.

quartile deviation. A measure of dispersion which is determined by the difference between the values of the first and third quartile points divided by 2: $Q.D. = (Q_3 - Q_1)/2$. Also called semi-interquartile range.

quasi contract. A legal doctrine dealing with situations in which there is no contract between the parties (either express or implied in fact). There are well defined categories to which the doctrine applies much as if these were a contract. For example, money paid to a party under mistake can be recovered on quasi-contractual grounds.

quasi-public corporation. A corporaton whose stock is owned by private persons and corporations but which is run by public representatives, such as the Federal Reserve System.

quasi rent. The yield on an investment in capital goods (sunk cost) can be viewed as quasi rent. If there is no alternative use, the total yield, and if there is an alternative use, the yield over the alternative is called quasi-rent. The capital good will not be a determinant of the price of the product since it will continue to be used as long as the price is greater than the average variable cost. Thus any return on such goods is similar to a rent.

queuing theory. The analysis of waiting lines and waiting times. Two measurable quantities form the basis of analysis: (1) the arrival rate and (2) the service rate or departure rate. These measurements are then converted to probability distributions for mathematical analysis.

questionnaire. An orderly arrangement of questions submitted to one or more persons for answering. Cf. *schedule.*

quia timet. Latin for "because he fears." In law, a writ or bill in equity seeking protection against anticipated injury.

quick asset. Cash, marketable securities, accounts receivable, or other asset which can be immediately converted into cash with a minimum loss. Inventories are normally excluded.

quick asset ratio. The ratio of cash, accounts receivable, and marketable securities to *current liabilities.* Also called *acid test.*

quickie strike. Same as *wildcat strike.*

quid pro quo. Latin for "one thing for another." In law, a common term referring to the fact that a contract requires mutual consideration.

quiet title, action to. A legal remedy by which the party who believes himself to be the owner can clear up defects in his title to the land.

quitclaim deed. A deed in which the grantor (party giving the deed) signs away whatever rights he may have in the property involved but makes no guaranty what rights, if any, he has. Cf. *warranty deed.*

quorum. The number of persons legally necessary (in person or by proxy, as the case may be) in order to conduct a valid meeting, e.g., of stockholders or a board of directors.

quota agreement. An agreement between members of a cartel assigning each firm a fixed proportion of the total production of the cartel. Cf. *export quotas, import quotas.*

quota buying. Similar to *buying to minimum inventory* but requires less supervision. The best reorder size is determined and this is divided into anticipated annual sales to get the number of times per year for reordering. Cf. *order buying, buying to minimum inventory.*

quota sample. The separation of an aggregate into groups on the basis of a common characteristic, such as age or sex, and the formation of a sample by selecting from each group the same proportion of the sample as that group bears to the total aggregate. Cf. *area sample, purposive sample, random sample, stratified sample, systematic sample.*

quota share reinsurance. In insurance, a *reinsurance* contract providing that there will be reinsurance of a quota amount or percentage of all insurance falling within the terms of the agreement.

quotations. The current published price of any commodity or security. Often two prices are given: (1) the price asked by sellers, (2) the price offered by buyers. Cf. *bid* and *ask*.

quo warranto. Latin for "by what authority." A suit to test the authority of a person in office or of a corporation to its franchise or charter.

rack jobber. A wholesaler who services racks in supermarket stores.

rack rent. An excessively high rent, that is rent which equals the profit on what is produced on the rented property.

radius clause. A clause in an employment contract under which the employee agrees not to leave the employer and join a competing employer in a given area within a specified period.

railroad bond. (1) An arrangement under which transportation between *bonded warehouses* can take place in bonded railroad cars. (2) The usual bond or security, but issued by a railroad.

railroads, Class I. A classification used by the Interstate Commerce Commission to include those railroads having annual operating revenues in excess of $3,000,000. **Class II.** Those railroads with annual operating revenues less than $3,000,000.

railroad subrogation waiver clause. In insurance, a clause providing that the release by the insured of a railroad from liability as a condition for getting services will not void the insured's right to recover under the policy.

random error. An error (deviation of an observed value from a true value) which is not in any sense biased and hence the distribution of items has a mean or other equally acceptable measure of central location at zero or some other true central point. Cf. *sampling error, standard error, systematic error.*

random numbers. A sequence of numbers such that there is no relation to each other anywhere in the sequence, thus all numbers have an equal chance of occurring at any point in the sequence.

random sample. Selection of a limited number of observations from a universe by chance. Efforts to attain random selection are carried out by using a prepared table of random numbers or selection of items at stated intervals. Cf. *area sample, purposive sample, quota sample, stratified sample, systematic sample.*

range. (1) The total dispersion of a frequency distribution. The highest value minus the lowest value of the distribution. (2) In real estate law, a width of six miles running north and south in the United States as established by U.S. survey and used as a basis for land title descriptions.

rank correlation. The degree of concordance between the rankings of two statistical series.

ratchet effect. Using the analogy of an automobile jack, the ratchet effect in income analysis refers to the establishing of successive plateaus as income increases with the expectation that it will not slip back. Thus, as applied particularly to the *consumption function,* the concept that a change in the absolute level of income is associated with a change in the *marginal propensity to consume.*

rate. The charge per unit for goods or services.

rate base. The "base" is the total investment on which the "rate" of return allowed to a public utility is computed. The "total investment" is determined under different theories, e.g., *fair return on fair value, original cost, investment cost, prudent investment cost, reproduction new cost.* The rate base may be established by evaluation of the asset side of the balance sheet or by consideration of the liability side, the latter being the *cost of capital theory.*

rate basis. The formula of the specific factors which control the construction of a rate.

rate discrimination. Charging different rates for the same service furnished two or more customers or classes of commodities. Also, charging different rates for different services where the rate differences are not supported by differences in the costs of furnishing the service.

rate-making line. A transportation line which controls the making of rates between points because of geographical location.

rate-making, rule of. In transportation, the rule enacted by Congress and presently requiring recognition of three factors in rate making: (1) what the traffic will bear, (2) what the service costs are and (3) what the carrier needs to maintain plant and operations.

rate making, theories of. See the following specific terms:

cost of capital theory of rate making
fair return on fair value theory of rate making
investment cost theory of rate making
original cost theory of rate making
prudent investment cost theory of rate making
reproduction new cost theory of rate making

rate of return (in capital budgeting). That rate which makes the discounted cash receipts of an investment just equal to the discounted cash outlays but assuming capital is free of cost.

rate of return (in public utilities). (1) That rate, allowed by the regulatory body or actually earned, which the after-income-tax earnings of a *public utility* are of the *rate base* of that *utility*.

rate (public utilities), types of. See the following specific terms:

block meter rate	*Hopkinson rate*
demand rate	*meter rate*
fixture rate	*step-meter rate*
flat rate	*Wright rate*

rate scale. A table of rates graduated according to distance or zones.

rate (transportation), types of. See the following specific terms:

all-commodity rate	*export rate*
alternative rate	*group rate*
any-quantity rate	*import rate*
basing rate	*joint rate*
basing-point rate	*joint combination rate*
blanket rate	*joint through rate*
breaking-point rate	*local rate*
bridge rate	*mixed carload rate*
class rate	*paper rate*
column rate	*proportional rate*
combination rate	*released rate*
combination through rate	*short rate*
commodity rate	*standard rate*
cut-back rate	*through rate*
differential rate	*transit rate*

rate war. Cutthroat competition between two or more carriers in an effort to attract freight by cutting rates. Now exists only in unregulated services. A *price war* in transportation.

ratification. (1) A general legal doctrine concerning the approval or acceptance by a party of the responsibility for or benefits from an act after it is done. Most commonly occurs in the field of principal and agent where ratification constitutes the affirmance by the principal of an act done by an agent without authority. Ratification dates back to the date of the act. Ratification may be expressed or implied. (2) The approval of treaties between countries to make them binding. In the United States such authority of approval rests in the U.S. Senate.

rating (in insurance), types of. See the following specific terms:

experience rating
manual rating
merit rating
retrospective rating
schedule rating

rating bureau. In insurance, an agency which collects experience on risks in an area and establishes rates. The agency may be formed by a group of insurers or be under close control by the state.

ratio analysis. In finance, the use of various ratios (such as asset turnover) for comparison with the ratios of the same firm earlier in time or with those ratios of other firms to establish the progress or deterioration of a firm as to liquidity, profitability, and other aspects.

ratio, types of. See the following specific terms:

acid test ratio
asset turnover ratio
benefit-cost ratio
bond ratio
capital ratio
capital-deposit ratio
capital-output ratio
capital turnover ratio
cash position ratio
cash to daily purchases ratio
common stock ratio
concentration ratio
coverage ratio
current ratio
debt coverage ratio
deposit ratio
deposit-capital ratio
expense ratio
fixed charge coverage ratio
gross plant turnover
gross profit ratio
inventory turnover ratio
invested capital turnover
loss ratio
market ratio
merchandise turnover ratio
mint ratio
operating ratio
plant (or fixed asset) turnover ratio
preferred stock ratio
price-earnings ratio
quick asset ratio
raw material turnover ratio
receivables turnover ratio
reserve ratio
return ratio
risk ratio
specialization ratio
tangible asset turnover
total asset turnover ratio
transportation ratio
von Neumann ratio
working capital turnover
work in process turnover ratio
yield ratio

ratio chart. A graph designed to show relative rather than absolute changes. The most common type is the semi-log chart for time series scaled logarithmically on the *y* axis and arithmetically on the *x* axis. A straight line on this graph shows a constant rate of change. See Figure 34, page 261.

rationalization. A term used, especially as applied to Germany after World War I, to describe a conscious and determined effort to obtain the economies which vertical and horizontal combinations have to offer. This may be achieved by market sharing, quotas and similar devices.

rationing. Any arrangement, usually under governmental regulation, limiting the quantity of product which can be purchased by a given class of buyers.

rationing of exchange. Governmental control of foreign exchange through the forced surrender of exchange by exporters for domestic currency at the government rate, and the subsequent allocation of such exchange to importers according to a government ration schedule.

raw material turnover. The amount of goods going into process during a period divided by the average raw material inventory.

REA Rural Electrification Administration. The REA was created in the Department of Agriculture in 1935. Its chief duty is to make loans to finance the cost of putting electricity and telephones into rural areas.

reaction curve or function. In the theory of *duopoly,* the reaction curve is the locus of all the points of maximum profit for each firm for each corresponding quantity of a good that its rival may produce.

readiness-to-serve costs. In public utilities, the costs incident to the maintenance of facilities in order to be able to serve on demand by the public. Identical with overhead costs in public utilities.

Reading rule. In insurance, where a blanket policy covers two items also insured by two specific policies one on each item, the blanket insurance is apportioned between the two items in the proportion of the values of the items insured by it, and then the usual contribution applies between the blanket policy and each specific policy in the ratio of the face values. Cf. *Cromie, Kinne,* and *Page* rules for this general situation.

real accounts. Accounts whose balances carry over from one period to the next and appear on the balance sheet. These include asset accounts and related valuation reserves, liability accounts and net worth accounts. Cf. *nominal account.*

real balance effect. Same as *Pigou effect.*

real bills doctrine. The principle that if only "real" bills (i.e., bills growing out of trade transactions) are discounted, the expansion of bank money will be in proportion to the needs of trade. Expansion and contraction would thus be automatic. Cf. *banking school principle.*

real chattels. See *chattels, real.*

real costs. (1) Costs measured in dollars of constant purchasing power or adjusted by some index serving the same purpose. Cf. *nominal cost.* (2) Costs which involve effort or sacrifice.

real estate. An interest in land or things attached to land with the intention of not being moved.

real estate mortgage bonds. The bonds of a corporation (and sometimes of an individual) which are secured by a mortgage upon its real property.

real estate tax. A tax on land, buildings, and improvements on land. Cf. *property tax.*

real income. (1) Money income measured in terms of purchasing power. (2) Commodities and services which a person receives in kind plus what can be purchased with his monetary income. Cf. *income in kind.*

real interest rate. The nominal interest rate (the interest rate actually found in the market) corrected for changes in the value of money.

realization. (1) The disposal of assets for cash. Cf. *liquidate.* (2) In income taxation, the tax is not levied until the income is "realized," i.e., the income-yielding process has reached a point where the law considers the income definite enough to tax.

realization account. An account established to summarize and adjust the accounts of a business being liquidated. The account reflects the item by item realization of the assets through reduction to cash or application to the reduction of liabilities.

realized investment. The total of *intended investment* plus *unintended investment.* This total will always equal *ex post savings.*

real national income. The *national income* measured in terms of unchanging purchasing power. Usually measured by dividing *national income* in current dollars by a *price index.*

real product. *Gross national product* stated in terms of money with constant purchasing power. Usually measured by dividing *gross national product* in current dollars by a *price index.*

real property. Essentially, land and rights to land and improvements to land. Included within the meaning of "land" for this purpose are buildings and permanent improvements to the land. Certain rights to land (for example, easements and short term leases) are sometimes put in a separate subclass under the term "chattels real." Contrasted with personal property which is the term for movable property of all kinds.

real time. See *on-line, real-time.*

realty. Same as *real property.*

real unconsumption theory. That type which emphasizes "real" factors such as income maldistribution as the origin of underconsumption. Cf. *monetary underconsumption theory.*

real wages. The amount of goods and services which one can buy with his money wages at any given time. Cf. *money wages.*

rebate. The paying back of some part of the charges that have been made for a service or commodity.

recapitalization. A voluntary readjustment of the bonds and stocks of a corporation. For example, replacing debentures with mortgage bonds or replacing part of the common stock by an issue of second preferred stock. Does not imply financial embarrassment of the corporation. Cf. *reorganization.*

recapitalization surplus. The surplus resulting upon a *recapitalization,* which usually arises from reduction in the par value of stocks and the exchange of bonds for securities of lesser value.

recapture clause. (1) A clause in the Esch-Cummins Act of 1920 allowing railroads to retain one-half of earnings in excess of what the act defined as a fair return on the value of capital assets, and requiring the payment of the other half to the government for application to weaker railroads. The term has since been generalized to describe any public utility statute or franchise of similar pattern. (2) In contracts generally, any provision for redetermination of rates or charges in the event experience under the contract is more favorable than anticipated.

receipt. A written acknowledgment that something has been received.

receivable. A shortened term for *account receivable.*

receivables turnover. See *accounts receivable turnover.* Cf. *collection period.*

receiver. See *receivership.*

receiver's certificate. A short-term note issued by a receiver, after approval by the court that appointed the receiver, for the purpose of carrying out orderly liquidation or reorganization. This certificate has first priority on the assets not otherwise mortgaged.

receivership. A legal proceeding involving the appointment by a court of a person (the receiver) to administer the affairs of a person or firm unable to meet its debts as they mature. The receiver administers matters until a decision is made to reorganize or to liquidate. If the decision, by court or by owners, is to liquidate, the receiver carries out the liquidation, although his title is changed to trustee in bankruptcy.

recession. A mild form of depression. See *business cycle.*

reciprocal. In statistics, 1 divided by a number gives the reciprocal of the number. Cf. *complement.*

reciprocal buying. Any arrangement under which a seller of one product or service buys another product or service from one of his customers.

reciprocal demand. The first country's demand for the second country's product measured in terms of the first country's product. The concept was first developed by Mill in his "Equation of International Demand" to determine the actual ratio at which goods are traded. It will depend upon the elasticity of each country's demand (and supply) for the other country's product. Cf. *comparative advantage.*

reciprocal demurrage. A demurrage system which assesses shippers for car detention and charges carriers for failure to furnish cars as ordered. Cf. *average agreement demurrage.*

reciprocal exchange. In insurance, an unincorporated association writing insurance for its own members.

reciprocal insurance. An insurance plan administered by a reciprocal exchange rather than an insurance company. Under the plan each insured is also an insurer of the others covered by the plan.

reciprocal laws. Laws that provide that state A will extend to the citizens and corporations of state B the same rights as the laws of state B extend to citizens and corporations of state A. Tax and insurance laws frequently have such provisions.

reciprocal trade agreement. An executive agreement between countries providing for interchange of goods at mutually lowered tariffs or other advantageous terms. The United States Reciprocal Trade Agreements Act was passed in 1934 and has since been renewed.

reciprocity principle. Granting concessions in return for concessions you will receive. Or the mutual placement of business by one firm with another in return for receiving business from the other firm.

reclamation. (1) In banking, the reclaiming or correcting of negotiable paper whose face amount was incorrectly recorded in the clearing house. (2) Restoring or activating an idle natural resource.

recognizance. In law, an obligation entered into by a person before a court to do a specified act, such as making an appearance on a set day. The recognizance may or may not be supported by a bail bond. Distinguish from a release of a person under bond.

reconciliation. (1) An accounting statement "reconciling" a bank statement of a depositor's account with the books of account of the depositor. Items on the bank statement but not on the books (e.g., bank charges), and items on the books but not on the bank statement (e.g., outstanding checks) are arranged in a statement to verify the bank balance against the books. (2) Any accounting statement showing the consistency of two other accounting statements or accounts.

reconsignment. In transportation, any change, other than a change in route, made before arrival of goods at the destination when the change is made under conditions permitted by rules of the carrier.

record date. In corporation matters, the date established by the board of directors as the closing time to establish the "record" of stockholders (those shown on the books as stockowners) to receive a dividend, have voting rights for a given meeting, or some other benefit.

recording acts. All states have statutes governing the recording of real estate documents and to some extent for personal property mortgages. These statutes provide that an innocent purchaser is bound only by the title as disclosed by the record. Unrecorded documents of which he has no knowledge do not bind him. For example, if a buyer purchases a piece of real estate against which there is an unrecorded mortgage of which he has no knowledge, the buyer avoids the mortgage.

recoupment. In modern times, the equivalent of a counterclaim. More technically, the right to deduct from one party's claim for a debt a claim of the opposite party growing out of the same matter. Distinguish an *offset* which arises out of any matter between the same persons.

recourse. (1) The right of the holder of a negotiable document to collect from parties who previously held the document if the party primarily obligated to pay on the document does not pay it. (2) The right of the purchaser of *accounts receivable* to look to the seller for a deficiency in any account. This right exists only if it is specifically agreed upon.

recovery. The period following a depression in which business improves. See *business cycle*.

recruitment ratio. The ratio of the number of recruits to be discovered and appraised to fill one job opening.

recurring cost. The expenses of a business which keep on recurring, such as wages, raw materials, etc.

recursive system. A system in which a causal chain of events is established on the assumption that only one endogenous variable at a time is the *dependent variable*. An illustration is the *cobweb theorem*. See figures 9, 10 and 11, pages 75 and 76.

reddendum clause. In real estate law, that clause in a *deed* reserving something to the grantor.

redeemable bond. Same as *callable bond*.

redeemable preferred stock. Same as *callable preferred stock*.

redemption. (1) A legal doctrine most commonly applied in the field of mortgages. After a *foreclosure* there is a right in the party foreclosed to redeem that property within a certain time by coming forward with the payments due. This is called a right of redemption or equity of redemption. (2) The payment of cash by the borrower or issuer for bank notes or securities.

redemption price. The price at which a corporation may at its option require the surrender of a bond before maturity or a preferred stock providing the security is issued pursuant to such a right.

"red herring." In finance, an advance copy of the statement (prospectus) to be filed with the Securities and Exchange Commission preceding an issue of securities. The copy is marked in red ink, "not a solicitation, for information only."

rediscount. The resale of a promissory note or bill of exchange by one who has bought such a document. Particularly used with reference to the sale by member banks to Federal Reserve Banks of *commercial paper*. The rediscount process involves the payment by the seller of a charge (the rediscount) in advance much the same as a discount. Cf. *advance*.

rediscount rate. The rate of discount applied when commercial paper is resold, as in the case of member banks transferring their loans to Federal Reserve Banks.

redraft. A new *bill of exchange* drawn by the holder of a *protested* bill on any of those liable on the defaulted bill.

reduced form equation. In *econometrics,* the equation(s) resulting from a reduction of the size of a model, namely, by reducing the number of equations in the model or system. Such reduction is effected by eliminating equations of equilibrium (identities) and equations which fix the value of exogenous variables. The reduced form equation(s) are thus stated in terms of exogenous variables whose values can be established by least squares methods and these values substituted in the original form equations to establish the parameters (coefficients) of the original equations. Cf. *adjustment equation, behavioral equation, definitional equation, final equation, restraint equation,* and *structural equation.*

redundancy. In operations research, the relative degree of structure in a sequence of outcomes. This is 1 — (the observed measure of inherent order of a series of outcomes divided by the maximum value possible for the measure of inherent order of a series of outcomes). The measure of inherent order of a sequence of outcomes is *entropy,* for which the symbol *H* is used.

re-exchange. The charge by the drawer of a *redraft* for his expense due to the default on the original draft.

re-export. Exporting commodities in the same form in which they were imported. The storage of such commodities is one of the functions of a *free port.*

referee. A person appointed by a court of equity to investigate and report to the court, usually about a complicated factual matter.

refinancing. Replacing an existing financial structure of bonds or stocks with a new one, usually at a lower rate of interest or dividend.

reflation. The process of managing currency for the purpose of restoring a previous price level.

reflexivity. A relationship is reflexive if it holds between a thing and itself. For example, in the case of real numbers if we can use an = (equal) sign between any two items, they are said to be reflexive.

reformation of a contract. In law, a court of *equity* or with equity powers may issue a decree changing a contract to conform to the true intention of the parties where the contract as signed does not do so. The proof of the true intention in such a case must be clear.

refund annuity. An annuity policy which provides that upon death of the annuitant the difference between the purchase price of the annuity and the total of payments to the annuitant will be paid in a lump sum or in continuing periodic payments to the person designated by the annuitant. Cf. *cash refund annuity*.

refunding. (1) In finance, the replacement of an outstanding issue or issues of bonds by a new issue either at or before maturity. Usual purposes are the extension of the loan period or the reduction of the interest rate. (2) In general, the repayment of all or part of money paid previously.

refunding bonds. Bonds used to replace existing bonds.

refunding mortgage bonds. Any mortgage bond issue which replaces an existing bond issue or issues. Sometimes the term is abused to describe the funding of short term debt under a high sounding title.

register. Any book recording transactions, stock ownership lists, ships and their movements, or similar facts.

registered bond. A bond entered on the books of the issuing corporation or of its transfer agent in the name of the purchaser, whose name also appears on the face of the bonds. Either principal alone or both principal and interest may be registered.

registered check. A *check* written by a bank teller against funds advanced by the person seeking the check. A special register and numbering system is used. Not to be confused with a *certified check*.

registered coupon bond. A bond that is registered as to the owner but whose attached interest coupons are payable to bearer.

registered representative. In the stock market, the modern term for a *customer's man,* i.e., an employee of an exchange member who deals with the public.

registered tonnage (vessel). In marine transportation, the total cubic footage of ship divided by 100, on the assumption that 100 cubic feet is equal to one ton. Cf. *dead-weight tonnage (vessel), gross tonnage (vessel), net tonnage (vessel).*

register of deeds. An office, usually one in each county of a state, where documents affecting the title to land are recorded. The same office often is designated for recording chattel mortgages and other documents affecting security rights in personal property.

register ton. A unit of measurement in marine transportation. The volume of 100 cubic feet of space.

registration statement. The statement required by the Securities

Act of 1933 to be filed with the *SEC* in the case of securities (some exceptions) sold in interstate commerce or through the mails. The registration statement must contain complete information about the issue and the issuer. A condensed form of this statement (called the *prospectus),* is made available to the investor. If the statement is not satisfactory, a *stop order* may be issued. Some state laws now require registration statements.

registry. The listing of a ship under the law of the country whose flag is flown and without regard to the citizenship of the ship's owners. Foreign registry offers less stringent requirements than U.S. registry.

regression analysis. The development of average relationships between variables by means of the *least squares method* or *correlation.*

regression coefficient. The coefficient associated with an independent variable when a line of average relationship (*regression line*) has been fitted to the observed values of a dependent variable and one or more independent variables. The regression coefficient is called "gross" when it considers the relationship of the dependent variable and only one independent variable and *"net"* when it considers the effect of other (more than one) independent variables.

regression line. Any line which describes an average relationship between two or more variables. Usually the line is developed by the *least squares method* or *correlation.*

regressive supply. The market situation in which quantity offered increases as price decreases. Farm production tends to do this.

regressive tax. (1) A tax against income or property where the rate of taxation diminishes with increases in the base (income or property). The rate of diminution may be constant, increasing or decreasing. (2) A tax whose effect is to take a decreasing percentage of income. Eg., the cigarette tax. The general sales tax is usually called regressive because it takes a larger percentage of the income of low income families in spite of the fact that the rates are proportional.

regret criterion. In a situation of uncertainty, where the probabilities of various eventualities (states of nature) are unknown, the basis of decision should be the minimization of regret with regret measured by the difference between each payoff assumed actually received and the payoff that one could have received if one had known the state of nature that was going to occur. Also called *minimax.* Cf. *Laplace cri-*

terion, maximin, and *optimism criterion.*

regular way delivery. On the stock market, delivery and payment are to be made on the fourth business day after a transaction except that for government bonds, the following business day is used. Cf. *cash basis delivery* and *delayed delivery.*

regulatory taxation. The use of taxation not only for purposes of public revenue but to control by restricting economic development along any given line. Cf. *incentive taxation.*

rehypothecation. In the stock market, the repledging of a security by a broker or realer to whom the security has been pledged. Technically not a repledge because possession is not surrendered but rather the right to order sale on default is given.

Reichsbank. German for "imperial bank." The central bank of Germany which receives and disburses state funds.

Reilly's law. The proposition that two cities attract retail trade from an intermediate point in the vicinity of the breaking point (the 50% point, where each has equal influence) approximately in direct proportion to the population of the two cities, and in inverse proportion to the square of the distance from these two cities to the intermediate town. An empirical statement based on considerable research, not valid where there is a great difference between populations.

reinstatement. In insurance, (1) the restoring of a policy holder to his position before suspension or cancellation of the policy, (2) bringing the amount of the policy back to the original amount after a loss has been paid. Without this latter step, the policy remains reduced in amount by each loss paid.

reinsurance. The dividing of a risk too large for one insurance company by transferring part of the risk to another company by agreement which varies as to the terms applicable to the risk transferred.

reinsurance, types of. See the following specific terms:

catastrophe reinsurance
excess reinsurance
faculative reinsurance
quota share reinsurance
share reinsurance
stop-loss reinsurance
surplus reinsurance

reinsurance treaty. The agreement between insurance companies covering *reinsurance* by one insurance company (the reinsurer) of all or part of the risks of another insurance company (the reinsured, i.e., the insurance company which first assumed the risk).

reinsured. The insurance company (the insurer) whose losses will be born in whole or in part by another insurance company (the reinsurer) pursuant to an agreement.

reinsurer. The insurance company assuming part or all of the losses of another insurance company (the insurer) under an agreement.

REIT. Real Estate Investment Trust. A *trust* or *limited partnership* which invests in real estate for the purpose of taking accelerated depreciation as allowable losses for income tax purposes in current years. Later the properties will be sold for capital gains which are taxed at a lower rate. The device of trust or limited partnership facilitates the sale of units of ownership as small as $5,000.

rejoinder. See *pleadings.*

relation, the. An English term for the ratio between net increase in consumption and the net investment induced by the net increase in consumption. Cf. *acceleration principle.*

relative average deviation. The *average deviation* divided by the *median.*

relative income hypothesis. (1) The argument that the level of consumption is largely a function of one's peer group. (2) The argument that current consumption is related to the ratio of previous peak income to present income. Identified with Duesenberry. Cf. *absolute income hypothesis, life-cycle income hypothesis, past income hypothesis,* and *permanent income hypothesis.*

relative priority. A principle of reorganization under which each group of creditors and stockholders, based on seniority, survives the reorganization but the losses of each group are inversely proportional to its seniority. For example, if there are $500,000 in assets, $500,000 in bonds, $500,000 in common stock and $500,000 in preferred stock, the reorganization might give the bondholders 75 cents on the dollar, the preferred stockholders 20 cents on the dollar, and the common 5 cents on the dollar. Cf. *absolute priority.*

relative quartile deviation. The *quartile deviation* divided by the median. Or, the difference between the first and third quartile points divided by the sum of these two points. Also called *coefficient of dispersion* and *coefficient of quartile deviation.*

relatives index number. See *average of relatives index number.*

relative skewness. The difference between the *mean* and the *mode,* divided by the *standard deviation.* Also called *coefficient of skewness.*

relative standard deviation. The *standard deviation* divided by the *arithmetic mean.* Also called *coefficient of variation.*

release. A written document terminating an obligation or liability, or what may be thought to be such. It is a contract and thus must conform to all the requirements of a contract if it is to be binding.

released rate. With respect to a commodity varying greatly in value, a released rate is an agreement by the shipper to set a limit to the value of the shipment in return for a concession in the rate. Now illegal under the Interstate Commerce Act except for baggage, special livestock, and specific exemptions by the Commission.

release of judgment. Same as *satisfaction of judgment.*

release of lien. Same as *satisfaction of lien.*

release of mortgage. Same as *satisfaction of mortgage.*

relevant cost. The cost figure required in a specific application such as income tax computation.

reliability. In statistics, the degree to which repetition of the same test will produce the same results. Distinguish *validity.*

reliction. The addition to a piece of land by the withdrawal of a river or sea.

remainder. A future interest in land in a party other than the grantor. A period of time must elapse between the present and the time when the remainder man comes into possession. Ordinarily the interest in between is a life estate. Cf. *reversion.*

remainderman. The one owning the *remainder* of an interest in property after (in point of time) preceding interests.

remargining. Where securities have been purchased "on *margin*," a subsequent change in the market prices of the securities will change the ratio of the margin to the new prices of the securities, and the process of restoring the original margin ratio is remargining. Cf. *margin call.*

remittance slip. An identification slip accompanying a remittance.

remittitur. The order issued by a court of appeals sending the case back to a lower court after the lower court's decision has been reversed or modified.

remonitization. Used in two senses: (1) "legal" remonitization occurs when a country passes a law removing one type of money from its legal tender list, (2) "factual" remonitization occurs when the price of the precious metal falls below the mint price and metal which had been melted down from its coined state is returned to money use. Also applicable to non-metallic forms of money.

removal bond. A customs bond given for possible duties by one removing imported goods from a warehouse for processing for export.

rendu price. An import *delivered` price.* The price of imported goods including all charges for tariff and freight.

renegotiation. Contracts by the government for war supplies during World War II contained a "renegotiation" clause as required by statute. Under the clause the profits of a contractor were examined after completion of the contract and subject to reduction to a level consistent with the efficiency and risk in performance of the contract.

renewable term life insurance. A form of life insurance under which the annual premium is level during each term. At the beginning of the new term the premium rises in accordance with the age attained. The renewal at the end of each term is automatic and without medical examination.

rent. The amount paid for the use of land or some other factor of production.

rent, types of. See the following specific terms:

contingent rent
dead rent
economic rent
ground rent
rack rent

rental rate. Same as *flat rate.*

rentes. French interest-bearing bonds without maturity date. Cf. *consol.*

rentier. Originally, one who derived the bulk of his income from the renting of land. More generally used to describe one whose income is largely derived from the investment of previously acquired wealth.

reopening clause. A provision in a labor contract permitting the renegotiation of limited parts of the contract prior to its expiration if stated conditions materialize.

reorganization. The legal readjustment of bonds and stocks of a corporation, usually eliminating some of the securities which have become worthless because the value of the firm's assets has fallen. Cf. *recapitalization.*

reorganization bond. Same as *adjustment bond.*

reorganization surplus. See *acquired surplus.*

reparations. As commonly used, this refers to money, goods, or services paid by one nation to another as compensation for damages incurred in war. It was applied to the sums which Germany was required by treaty to pay to France and other nations for the damages caused in the first world war.

repatriation. In business, the repurchase of securities of a domestically operating company from foreign security holders.

replacement cost. The cost of restoring property lost or damaged to its condition before the destruction. Also the cost of replacing even though no actual loss has occurred.

replacement insurance. Insurance providing that a loss will be covered for the replacement of the property new. Hence the difference between the depreciated value of the lost property and replacement cost will be paid, but only if the property is actually replaced.

replevin. A legal remedy by which one party can have the sheriff take specific property from another party pending a decision as to who has the right to possess it. The party thus getting possession must post a bond. The party from whom the property was replevied can in some states get it back by a counter action in replevin plus a bond. The action does not decide who owns the property, but merely who has the right to possession.

replevin bond. See *replevin.*

replication. In legal procedure, the reply by a *plaintiff* in a law suit to the *defendant's* answer.

reply. See *pleadings.*

reporting pay. Payment made to workers for reporting to work when there is no work available and the worker was not given advance notice not to report.

reporting policy. In insurance, a policy covering fluctuating stocks of goods which must be reported at stated intervals for adjustment of the premium.

representative firm. A theoretical device invented by Marshall for economic analysis. He defines it as "a firm that has its fair share of those *internal* and *external economies* which appertain to the aggregate scale of production in the industry to which it belongs." *Not* an "average" firm in the statistical sense.

representative money. Paper money containing a certification that the government issuing it holds a standard amount of precious metal as reserve. Frequently the reserve metal can be called for by the holder if he so desires.

repressed inflation. The situation where there is limited control of prices and wages accompanied by an increase in money demand for goods relative to the supply of goods after the economy is at full employment.

reprieve. The suspension of a criminal sentence for a period of time. Not a pardon (which cancels a sentence) and not a commutation (which reduces a sentence).

reprisal. See *letter of marque and reprisal.*

reproduction new cost theory of rate making. In public utility and transportation rate making, reproduction new cost is the current cost of reproducing the present facilities less accrued depreciation. On this base the rate of return is computed. Cf. *cost of capital, fair return on fair value, investment cost, original cost,* and *prudent investment theories of rate making.*

repudiation. The refusal to perform the whole or any part of a contractual obligation.

repurchase agreement. In finance, the sale of securities, usually government bills, to an investor with excess temporary funds subject to the agreement of the seller to buy back from the investor after an agreed period.

required bank reserve. The amount which a member bank is required to have on deposit with the Federal Reserve Bank or in vault cash. This amount is presently 4% of *time deposits* and for *country banks* 12% of *demand deposits* and for *reserve city banks* 16.5% of demand deposits. Cf. *legal reserve.*

requirements contract. Same as *full requirements contract.*

res adjudicata or res judicata. The legal doctrine that once a legal question is decided on the merits by a court of competent jurisdiction, it cannot again be reexamined except for a timely appeal from the decision of a court, or a later claim of fraud, mistake or new evidence.

resale price maintenance agreement. An agreement exacted by the seller from the buyer to the effect that the buyer will not resell at less than a stated minimum price. Sometimes the additional requirement is expressly stated that each succeeding buyer must agree likewise. In many states the resale price is binding upon all vendors after due publication of such an agreement with one or more buyers. Cf. *fair trade practice acts.*

rescind. In law, to revoke an action or agreement. This can always be done by consent of all parties. It can be done despite the objection of one party only when the rules of law permit.

rescript. A duplicate of a document.

reservation price. The price below which sellers will refrain from selling at the present time. Often based on the belief that prices in the future will rise, or other considerations resting on the amount of goods presently on hand.

reserve bank credit. Credit extended to member banks by the Federal Reserve Bank through rediscounting member bank loans, purchasing acceptances, or direct loans on various security. In addition, all deposits made by a member bank qualify.

reserve city bank. In the Federal Reserve System, a member bank located in a reserve city. The list of reserve cities changes from time to time, but it is not limited to cities where Federal Reserve Banks exist. See *Federal Reserve System.*

reserve ratio. In banking, the ratio of the balance of a member bank at the Federal Reserve Bank plus vault cash to the demand deposits of the member bank is the primary reserve ratio. The secondary reserve ratio is the ratio of government securities held by a bank to its demand deposits. There is also the time deposit reserve ratio: the ratio of the balance held at the Federal Reserve Bank plus vault cash against time deposits.

reserved surplus. Same as *appropriated surplus.*

reserves. (1) A name common to certain amounts that are taken periodically from profits and set aside for specific purposes. (2) *bank reserves.* (3) In insurance, the present value of the liability under a policy. Cf. *contingency reserve, depletion reserve, depreciation reserve, funded reserve, hidden reserve, initial reserve, legal reserve, liability reserve, mean reserve, surplus reserve, terminal reserve, valuation reserve.*

reserve value. In life insurance, the present value of accumulations of a policy. Deducting the *surrender charge* from this reserve gives the *cash surrender value.* Cf. *initial reserve, mean reserve, terminal reserve.*

res gestae. Latin for "the things done." In law, statements or acts made under the pressure of the situation so that there is little likelihood of lying. Such matter constitutes an exception to the *hearsay* rule which bars testimony by a witness as to statements made by another offered to prove the truth of what is stated.

residence. In law, one may have many residences but only one domicile. The legal definition of what is a residence varies according to the question involved. Thus who is a resident may vary for questions of auto driver's license or of taxation. The status may define the term in each case. Cf. *domicile.*

residual theory of wages. A generalization that labor is the residual claimant to the product of industry after all capital costs have been paid. Cf. *bargaining theory of wages, lump of labor theory of wages, marginal productivity of wages, subsistence theory of wages, wage fund theory of wages.*

residual value. The market value of an asset after the lapse of a period of time.

residuary legacy. A provision in a will leaving all property not otherwise disposed of in the will to one called the residuary legatee. Cf. *demonstrative legacy, general legacy, lapsed legacy,* and *specific legacy.*

residuary legatee. One who participates in that part of the estate of a deceased person not otherwise disposed of by the will.

res inter alios acta. Latin for "acts done between others." In law, the rule barring admission into evidence of declarations or other acts of those who are mere strangers to each other.

res ipsa loquitur. Latin for "the matter speaks for itself." In law, a doctrine that in certain situations (usually negligence cases), mere proof of what happened establishes a presumption sufficient to carry the case unless evidence to the contrary is produced.

res judicata. See *res adjudicata.*

respondeat superior. Latin for "the principal should be looked to (liable)." In law, the rule that a principal or master is liable for the acts of his agent or servant done in the furtherance of the principal's business.

respondent. (1) The *defendant* in an *equity* suit. (2) The party who contends against the appellant of an *appeal.*

respondentia. A combination of money-lending on the security of the cargo of a ship and insurance of that cargo so that if the cargo of the ship is lost, the lender cannot recover the money lent. Cf. *bottomry.*

responsibility accounting. Organizing accounting by centers of responsibility for management to permit analysis of performance against plans for revenues and costs for each center. Cf. *profit center.*

resting order. In trading, an instruction to buy or sell at a figure away from the current level.

restitution. In law, the body of rules governing the situations other than contract or tort in which rights and duties arise with reference to restoring a person to his original position. Thus the law of lost goods falls into this category.

rest-of-the-world sector. See *sector accounts.*

restoration premium. In insurance, the *premium* charged to restore the policy to its original *face* amount after a loss is paid. No such premium is due when the policy has an *automatic reinstatement clause.*

restraint equation. In *econometrics,* an equation stating technological or institutional limitations such as a production function or tax laws. Cf. *adjustment equation, behavioral equation, definitional equation, final equation, reduced form equation,* and *structural equation.*

restraint of trade. Under the *Sherman Antitrust Act* of 1890 two classifications of illegal conduct were established: (1) restraint of trade and (2) monopoly or conspiring to monopolize. Restraint of trade has since been interpreted to refer to any practices tending to limit the freedom of business activities. In the Standard Oil case of 1911, the Supreme Court attempted a limitation on this rule preventing only "unreasonable restraints of trade." Cf. *rule of reason.*

restricted stock option plan. The older (pre-1964) term for *qualified stock option plan.*

restrictive indorsement. In effect this indorsement stops negotiability by restricting what can be done with the instrument. For example "pay Smith only" or "for deposit only to the account of . . ."

resulting trust. A trust arising from the conduct and implied intention of persons. E.g., if A pays the money for a purchase but the document of transfer shows B's name, a resulting trust in favor of A arises.

retailer. One who sells to the ultimate consumer. He may sell to institutions but most of his sales are to individuals and usually in small lots.

retail gravitation law. Same as *Reilly's law.*

retail method of inventory. A method of approximating the inventory by records kept at retail prices. The cost value of the inventory is determined by applying to the inventory at retail a percentage which is the complement of the average rate of gross profit (original mark-up plus additional mark-up minus mark-downs).

retail store. An establishment selling merchandise directly to personal, household, and farm users.

retail store, types of. See the following specific terms:

chain store	*limited-line store*
department store	*specialty store*
general merchandise store	*variety store*

retained earnings. (1) *Net profit* for the period less dividends paid. (2) In the sense of accumulated retained earnings, same as *earned surplus.*

retainer. The fee paid to a professional person to engage his services.

retention policy. In insurance, a policy in which the *insured* agrees to bear (retains) part of the losses suffered and the *insurer* pays the other part. Such policies carry lower premium rates than apply when there is no retention.

retention rate. The ratio of *retained earnings* to total earnings of a given period.

retirement annuity. An annuity policy in which payments to the annuitant commence at some date after the purchase date. If death of the annuitant occurs in this interval or surrender is desired, an agreed amount is refunded to the annuitant's estate. Cf. *deferred annuity.*

retirement income insurance. Life insurance payable on the death of the insured before a stated age with a provision for a *life annuity* if the insured reaches that age.

retirement method of depreciation. An older system formerly used by railroads and public utilities under which many smaller unit assets were dealt with by charging the entire replacement amounts each year as depreciation on the ground that the rate of replacement was relatively stable from year to year.

retroactive restoration. Restoration of a *surety bond* or an *insurance policy* to the original *face value* after a loss has been paid so as to cover (1) prior losses which may be discovered after the first loss and (2) future losses.

retrocession. In insurance, the *reinsurance* of a risk by a *reinsurer* with still another insurance company.

retrocessionaire. In insurance, the insurance company accepting a *retrocession (reinsurance* from a *reinsurer).*

retrospective rating. In workmen's compensation insurance and some other types of insurance, a method for adjusting the initial premium on the basis of the losses during the period of insurance, but subject to maximum and minimum limitations on the new determination of premium. Cf. *experience rating, manual rating, merit rating, schedule rating.*

return on investment. (1) The annual income from an investment divided by the amount of the investment. (2) The average annual income from an investment over its life divided by the cost of the investment.

return premium. In insurance, the amount due the insured upon a cancellation of the policy, a reduction of the *face value* of the policy, or a reduction in rates. Cf. *pro rata rate* and *short rate.*

return ratio. In capital budgeting, the ratio of (1) the difference between the expected return (in dollars) from a proposed investment and the proposed investment (in dollars) divided by (2) the proposed investment in dollars.

returns to scale. Comparing the returns of an enterprise (if all factors of production are proportionately increased or decreased) to the scale of operations. Cf. *constant costs, increasing costs, decreasing costs.* Distinguish *diminishing marginal productivity, law of,* which is concerned with varying the proportions of the factors.

revalorization. The process of restoring the former value of the monetary unit.

revaluation. (1) Same as *revalorization.* (2) In general, bringing book values of an asset into line with market values.

revenue. The cash received in a period as distinguished from income which includes noncash items as well as items for which payment was received in an earlier period, and items earned in this period but not yet paid for.

revenue bond. A bond which is to be paid from the revenues of a specific project such as a stadium.

revenue sharing. The collection of taxes by one unit of government (such as the federal government) and distribution of part of these taxes to other units of government (such as states and cities) but without compliance requirements as to expenditure of the funds such as attach to *grants-in-aid.*

revenue tariff. A tariff or duty laid on imported goods to bring in revenue and not to protect any industries. Cf. *protective tariff.*

reverse split. The issuance of one share of stock in exchange for a number of shares of stock now outstanding. Cf. *stock split.*

reversing entry. See *adjusting entry.*

reversion. The interest remaining (either expressly or by implication) in a party giving a grant of real estate. It arises because the party granting has not given away the entire future use of the property. Cf *remainder.*

reversionary annuity. Same as *survivorship annuity.*

revival. See *business cycle.*

revocable credit. A credit which can, before the date it expires, be canceled, revoked, or withdrawn without the consent of the person in whose favor the credit is given. Used principally in foreign trade and travel. Also called credit line.

revocable letter of credit. A *letter of credit* which can be canceled at any time.

revolving credit. A credit established by a bank (or business house) permitting a borrower (or customer) to make new withdrawals (or purchases of goods) equal to payments made on prior accounts.

revolving fund. A fund from which withdrawals are made either as loans or as disbursements with the obligation of repaying the fund (with or without interest) to keep the fund intact.

revolving letter of credit. A *letter of credit* that renews itself as credit is drawn against it.

RFC Reconstruction Finance Corporation. Created by Congress in 1932 at President Hoover's urgent demand to bring back prosperity by loaning to corporations temporarily embarrassed. The loss ratio on loans has been low, and during World War II RFC was converted into a war loan agency.

Ricardian theory of rent. An explanation of differences in land rent as reflecting the differing levels of productivity of land over no-rent or marginal land.

Ricardo effect. The Ricardo effect is so called because it is assumed in the Ricardian proposition that a rise in real wages will encourage capitalists to substitute machinery for labor.

rider. (1) In insurance, a form attached to a policy adding special provisions to the regular terms of the policy. (2) In government, an unrelated addition to a legislative bill.

ridge line. An *isoquant* (see Figure 29, page 235) in two dimensions (each of which is an input) projected from the third dimensional "hill" of output. The contours or ridges of this hill are called ridge lines.

rights offering. The issuance of new shares by distributing *stock rights* to existing stockholders.

right of action. In law, a claim enforceable by a court. Same as *cause of action.*

right of representation. See *per stirpes.*

right of way. (1) As applied to a railroad or utility it means a narrow strip of land on which tracks, pipes, lines, etc., are laid. Cf. *easement.* (2) The legal right to proceed, as at a road crossing where two cars meet.

right-to-work laws. Provisions in state statutes or constitutions outlawing the closed shop clause in labor contracts, under which an employee must first become a union member before being employed. Variously extended to include outlawing the union shop, under which an employee must join a union after entering employment.

rights. See *stock rights.*

ringing out. In the commodities market, the practice of periodically settling outstanding futures contracts before they mature. Often this is done through a third party.

riparian rights. The rights of an owner whose land abuts water to land under the water. The rights are different from state to state and often depend on whether the waters are a river, lake, or ocean. Cf. *littoral rights.*

risk. The chance or possibility of gain or loss. (1) Risk may be economic, moral, physical, etc. In finance, risk is classified as *business risk, financial risk, market risk, money rate (interest rate) risk*, and *purchasing power risk.* (2) See *probability of ruin* for the likelihood of surviving a consecutive series of adverse events. (3) Risk is frequently measured by the *standard deviation*; the greater the standard deviation (or variability) of a series, the greater the risk.

risk index. The ratio of the present value interest factor for a riskless cash flow to the present value interest factor for the risky flow.

risk premium. The excess earnings of an investment with a variable return over an asset with a certain return.

risk ratio. In banking, the ratio of the total risk assets to total capital accounts. Risk assets may be defined as all assets less cash (and due from other banks) and government bonds. Cf. *deposit ratio.*

Robert's rules of order. See *parliamentary law.*

Robinson-Patman Act. An amendment in 1936 to the *Clayton Act.* The principle of the amendment is to declare illegal the charging of different prices to different buyers unless the price differences are "justified" by cost differences, with the burden of proof resting upon the vendor or unless the vendor has lowered his price to meet already existing competition in the area.

Rochdale plan. The consumer cooperative plan begun in Rochdale, England, in 1844, with capital contributed by members but only one vote to each person regardless of capital contributed. Return on capital was limited to the *legal rate,* with sales at prevailing market prices and surplus retained as reserve or distributed to members according to their purchases. Cf. *consumers' cooperatives.*

R.O.G. Receipts of goods. In figuring discounts, R.O.G. means that computation is made from date of receipt of goods (R.O.G.) rather than date of shipment or invoice. Cf. *E.O.M.*

ROI Abbreviation for "return on investment."

roll-back. Colloquial term for governmental action requiring the adoption of an earlier and lower price as the maximum price to be permitted.

rolling stock. In transportation, movable property, such as trucks freight and passenger cars, and locomotives.

root-mean-square deviation. Same as *standard deviation.*

rotating shift. The arrangement of a working schedule so that employees interchange working hours, e.g., the graveyard shift may alternate with the swing shift every other month.

roundabout production. The process by which goods are produced in order to produce other goods which in turn are used to produce consumer goods. It is not implied that an inefficient method is to be used.

round lot. The term applied to the unit of trading on the New York Stock Exchange, namely, 100 shares in the case of stock and $1000 par value in the case of bonds, except for some special instances.

round turn or trip. A term in the stock or commodity market referring to the purchase and resale of the same lot. Usually used in calculating the change in the market price needed before a profit results since commission is payable both on the purchase and the resale.

Rowan premium plan. An incentive wage plan under which the employee receives a minimum wage for all work up to the standard output and thereafter his wage plus a percentage thereof determined by the ratio of time saved to time allowed for the task. Cf. *Bedaux, Emerson, Gantt, Halsey, Merrick* and *Taylor plans.*

royalties. The price paid for the leasing of mineral or other land in the form of a price per unit of product taken out of the land. Also applied to the return paid to authors of books, songs, or moving pictures, or to the holders of patents.

RRB Railroad Retirement Board. The RRB, established in 1935, administers a retirement system for the payment of annuities and pensions to aged and disabled railroad employees and a correlated unemployment insurance system.

"rubber check." A worthless check that "bounces back" to the indorsers.

rule against perpetuities. In law, the common-law rule that a future interest in land must vest within the time period of lives in being at the time the interest is created, plus 21 years. The term "vest" means that the person to enjoy the interest must be identified within this time period and any conditions attached to the taking of an interest must have been resolved. Any attempted interests beyond the period are void. In deciding whether the rule has been violated, determination is made as of the time of the creation of the interest, and invalidity is established by showing the mere possibility that the rule would be violated. Thus, a gift to the widow of my youngest son after a gift to my son for his life is void. The woman might not be identifiable within the period (assuming my youngest son is not yet born). Cf. *rule against suspension of the power of alienation* and *rule against unreasonable accumulations.*

rule against suspension of the power of alienation. As an alternate to or supplement to the *rule against perpetuities,* some states by statute have a rule limiting the period during which the power to deal with land can be suspended in order to avoid the social problems involved with the nonsaleability of land. This rule can be simply avoided by giving the grantee the power to sell the land and imposing the control on the proceeds of the sale. Cf. *rule against perpetuities* and *rule against unreasonable accumulations.*

rule against unreasonable accumulations. As part of the pattern of control involving the *rule against perpetuities* and the *rule against suspension of the power of alienation*, many states impose a limit on the period of time during which a *trust* can be directed to accumulate its income without making a distribution to beneficiaries. Such legislation began with the *Thelusson Act* in England designed to deal with a large estate containing accumulation provisions which might have resulted in total acquisition of English property by that estate within a finite time.

rule in Shelley's case. In real estate law, a common-law rule that when there is a conveyance to a grantee of a *freehold estate* and later in the same grant an interest is created to this grantee's heirs, the entire fee has been granted to him and any other interests created are void.

rule nisi. See *decree nisi.*

rule of capture. A common-law rule that a well owner obtains title to all oil raised through his well regardless of its original location under the property of his neighbors.

rule of reason. A rule of interpretation announced in the Standard Oil case (1911) by the U.S. Supreme Court in interpreting the *Sherman Antitrust Act* provision forbidding every combination in restraint of trade. The majority of the court interpreted this to permit "reasonable" restraints.

run. (1) In banking, the sudden withdrawal of deposits from a bank due to fear. (2) In production, a continuous period of manufacturing.

running with the land. Considered part of the ownership or title of land. An *easement appurtenant* (over another's land) runs with the land which enjoys that easement.

s Abbreviation for solidus, Latin for shilling, a unit of English money. There are twenty shillings to the pound.

sabotage. Deliberate conduct damaging machinery, destroying raw materials, or turning out defective work.

sacrifice tax theory. A tax theory which argues that taxes should be so levied that the burden of a tax causes equal sacrifice to all taxpayers. Cf. *ability to pay, benefit* and *diffusion tax theories.*

saddle point. In game theory, an equilibrium situation in which there is a coincidence of the *maximin* strategy of one player with the *minimax* strategy of the other player. Such a coincidence need not exist. The term "saddle point" evolved because the geometric representation of the strategies of the two players in three dimensions shows a shape approximately like a saddle, with the saddle point in the pit of the saddle.

safe deposit privilege. A plan by which customers rent compartments in a vault to keep valuable documents and possessions.

safety factor. (1) In finance, the ratio of interest on funded debt to net income before taxes but after such interest has been deducted. (2) A numerical multiplier of the forecast error to determine the level of a safety stock to reduce outages.

safety fund system. A system of bank insurance used in New York in the 19th century. The state treasurer held the fund derived from payments of three per cent of each bank's capital stock. The fund guaranteed the bank notes issued by bank members of the system.

safety stock. The amount of inventory required to avoid a *stock out* to a given level of probability. Cf. *anticipation stock, cycle stock, lot-size stock.*

salary. (1) In business usage, salary refers to a fixed monthly rate of pay; wages to an hourly rate. (2) In economics, "wages" includes all forms of compensation including salaries.

sale. The transfer of *title* to property. It is not necessary to transfer the right to *possession* at the same time title passes. Also distinguish between a contract to sell and a sale. The former is merely an agreement to transfer title at a later date. For example, I may contract to sell something which I do not now have or which is not now in existence. The difference is important in determining who has the risk of loss. In general and unless otherwise agreed, risk of loss rests where title is.

sales, types of. See the following specific terms:

bulk sale
conditional sale
forced sale
installment (buying)
sale and lease back
sale on approval
sale or return
short sale
wash sale

sale and lease back. A sale of an asset to a vendee who immediately leases back to the vendor. The usual objectives are (1) to free cash in the amount of the purchase price for other uses by the vendor, (2) for benefits not otherwise available such as deduction by the vendor of the full value of the property for income tax purposes as rental payments over a period of time shorter than would be in depreciation where the base period is the allowable depreciable life. The rental payments total the purchase price plus interest less an estimated salvage value.

sale for the account. On the stock exchange, a sale of stock contemplating future delivery.

sale on approval. A contract under which title does not pass to the buyer until he indicates his approval (or fails to disapprove within a stated time). Unless otherwise specified, risk of loss stays with the seller until approval is indicated. Distinguish *conditional sale, consignment,* and *sale or return.*

sale or return. A contract under which there is a sale and title immediately passes to the buyer who has the right to revest title in the seller by returning the goods. The buyer takes risk of loss, however, while the goods are in his hands. Distinguish *conditional sale, consignment, sale on approval.*

sales budget. An estimate of the probable dollar sales and probable expenses of selling and publicity for a specified period.

sales charge. The initial charge made by some investment companies to cover the commission paid to salesmen and other initial costs of opening an account.

sales contour. If selling costs are put on one axis and output prices on the other axis, an *indifference curve* will trace all combinations of selling costs and output prices which will enable a seller to dispose of a given quantity of output. There will be a different curve for each quantity of output. Cf. *production revenue contour, sales line.* See Figure 49.

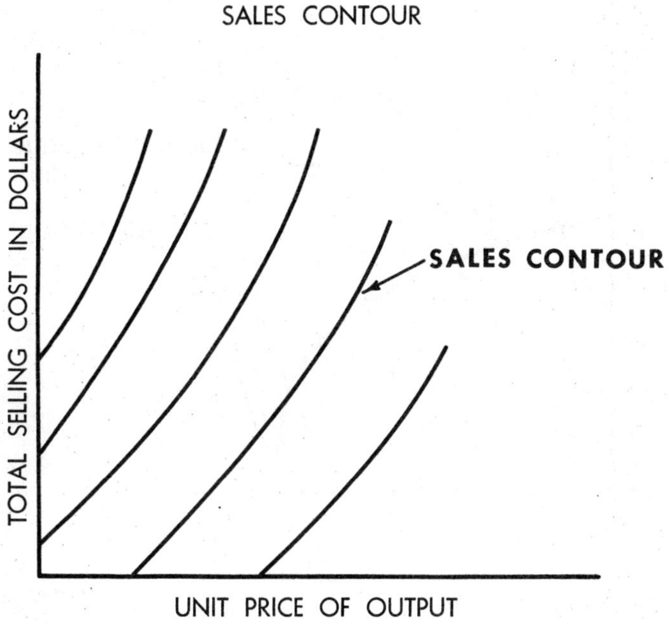

Figure 49.

sales curve. Same as *demand curve.*

sales finance company. A company whose principal business is purchasing the *accounts receivable* of other businesses at a discount. Usually there is recourse by the sales finance company against the seller of the goods if the buyer defaults on payments.

sales line. In economic theory, if selling costs are put on one axis, and output prices on the other axis, one indifference curve *(sales contour)* will trace all combinations of price and selling cost enabling a seller to sell a given quantity of output. Another indifference curve *(production revenue contour)* will trace all combinations of price and selling cost yielding the seller a given production revenue. The "sales line" traces the points of tangency of the sales contours and the production revenue contours. Thus a point on this line gives the best price and selling cost combination to use in selling a given output, and the line itself gives the path for increasing or decreasing output most efficiently.

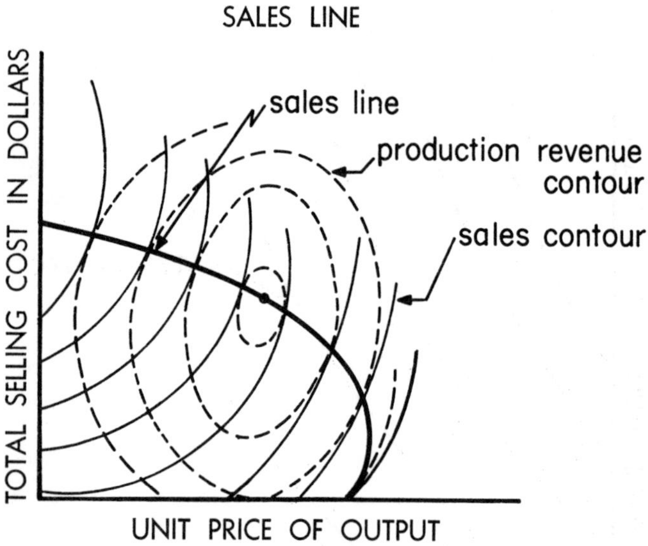

Figure 50.

sales potential. The possible sales of a commodity or a service in a given area or market within a specified period.

sales-purchase curve. With price on the *Y* axis and quantity purchased on the positive side of the *X* axis and quantity sold on the negative side of the *X* axis, the sales-purchase curve traces the quantities that an individual is able to buy or sell at various prices. On the negative side of the *X* axis the area under the curve is a set of all attainable positions, but points above the curve are unattainable. On the positive side of the *X* axis, the area under the curve is a set of points unattainable, but over the curve the points are attainable. The sales-purchase curve will be horizontal in a *perfect market,* ascending in an *imperfect market,* and descending in a *pluperfect market.*

sales quota. A figure in dollars or units of sales for a specified period for use in supervision of selling efforts.

sales schedule. Same as *demand schedule.*

sales tax. A tax levied upon a good at the time of sale. Sales taxes may be (1) on specific commodities, such as liquor, gasoline, and tobacco, (2) on all retail sales, (3) on all sales (see *turnover tax*).

sample. (1) In statistics, a limited or finite number of items of data selected from a universe or population. The accuracy of the mean of a *random sample* increases inversely to the square root of the size of the sample. Cf. *probability sample, purposive sample, quota sample, random sample, stratified sample, systematic sample.* (2) In marketing, one or more units of a product given free (or sold at a price far below market) in order to induce prospective buyers to give it a trial, or to enable them to determine its characteristics by inspection or analysis.

sample reliability. The reliability of the arithmetic mean of a sample can be judged by dividing the estimated standard deviation of the items in the universe by the square root of the number of cases in the sample. The estimate of the *standard deviation* of items in the universe, in turn, can be had by multiplying the standard deviation of the sample by $n/(n - 1)$ where n is the number of cases in the sample.

sampling. In statistics and research, a sampling is an approximation of the nature or magnitude of some characteristics of a universe arrived at through actual measurement of some of the individual units or elements of that universe, called a sample, which may be chosen at random or by other methods.

sampling error. That part of the difference between a population value and an estimate of such value (when a random sample is taken) arising from the fact of sampling. The sampling error of the mean of a random sample varies inversely with the square root of the number of items in the sample and is distinct from errors due to imperfect selection, biased response, observational errors, etc. Cf. *random error, standard error, systematic error.*

Samuelson-Stolper effect. The proposition that under *free trade* (no tariffs on imports) goods may serve as a partial substitute for immigration of labor into a labor-scarce economy (such as the United States) and hence that *real wages* might fall under free trade (the relative and absolute share of labor might go down although real *national product* would go up under free trade in such a situation).

Samuelson substitution theorem. In *input-output analysis,* the proposition that even where variation of input proportions is possible, it will never be advantageous to vary input proportions when there is constant *returns to scale,* only one scarce input, and no joint products.

Sanborn map. In fire insurance, a map locating the risks in large cities with the insurance carried on the different locations.

sandwich lease. When land is leased to a *lessee,* who in turn releases the land to another (the relessee), the first lease is called a sandwich lease.

satisfaction of judgment. A document stating payment has been received and signed by a *judgment creditor* and filed in the same court or courts where the judgment is docketed.

satisfaction of lien. A document signed by a *lien holder* releasing from his claim property which had been subjected to a lien either by operation of law or by a document signed by the debtor.

satisfaction of mortgage. A document signed by the mortgagee acknowledging payment of the loan and releasing the described property. The document is executed as a deed (witnessed and notarized) for recording in the *register of deeds.*

satisfice. As opposed to maximization as a criterion, satisficing seeks only the attainment of at least a minimum level.

Savage criterion. Same as *regret criterion.*

saver's surplus. The difference between the amount of interest which savers actually get and the amount of interest for which they would have been willing to lend if the demand for loans (quantity demanded) had been less is a saver's surplus. Cf. *consumer's surplus.*

saving. (1) Popularly, the amount which an individual withdraws from current income for investment. More scientifically, the difference between income and consumption (Keynes), or disposable income of the present day (earned income of yesterday) minus consumption expenditure of the present day (Robertson). Under the last definition, investment can be greater than saving because money can be spent from sources other than today's income. (2) More precisely, *saving* is a flow during a period, whereas *savings* is the stock as of a certain point in time.

saving ratio. The ratio of saving to output, usually denoted by the symbol α.

savings. The stock of unconsumed income at a certain point in time as distinguished from *saving,* which is a flow, or the difference between *income* and *consumption* during a particular period.

savings and loan association. The modern term for a *building and loan association.*

Savings and Loan Insurance Corporation, Federal. A corporation created in 1934 to insure the shares in the federal savings and loan associations and the shares of such building and loan associations as applied and qualified. Shareholders are insured up to $20,000 for each individual account. This insurance does not guarantee payment of an account on demand but rather the sufficiency of the assets to cover the accounts.

savings bank. A bank which accepts small deposits for long terms and pays a rate of interest on these deposits, but does no checking business. The deposits are invested in high grade securities. Savings banks may be mutual or stock banks. Usually *commercial banks* maintain a savings department.

savings turnover ratio. A measure of savings activity used by savings institutions. The ratio is savings received during a period divided by total savings at the beginning of the period.

savings withdrawal ratio. A measure to compare inflow and outflow of savings. The ratio is savings received in a period divided by savings withdrawn in that period.

Say's law of markets. Formulated by Jean Baptiste Say (1767–1832), a French economist, the law holds that aggregate demand price of output as a whole is equal to its aggregate supply price for all volumes of output. It emphasizes that there can never be general overproduction because every supply generates equivalent demand. The law assumes that *liquidity preferences* do not change.

scab. A slang term for strikebreaker. A person who seeks employment in a shop at a time when a strike is going on.

scale effect. The effect on the size of output of each firm in an industry caused by a change in the price of a factor of input or by a change in the price of the product. There is also a substitution effect which involves the recombination of the factors to use more of the factor which is made relatively cheap by the price change.

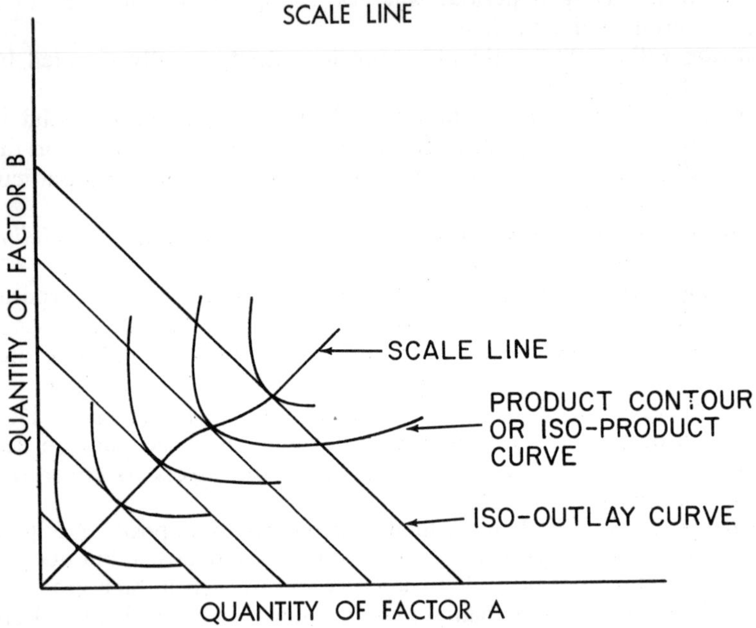

Figure 51.

scale line. In economic theory, if quantities of one factor of production are put on one axis and quantities of another factor are put on the other axis, one indifference curve *(iso-outlay curve)* traces all combinations of the two factors which can be purchased for the same amount of money. Another indifference curve *(iso-product curve)* traces all combinations of the two factors which yield the same quantity of product. The scale line traces the points of tangency of the iso-outlay curves and the iso-product curves. Thus a point on this line gives the cheapest combination of the factors for each given quantity of output, and the line itself traces the path for increasing or decreasing output most efficiently.

scalp. On the stock exchange, a *short* transaction made in contemplation of closing out at a profit.

scarce currency. In international finance, the term "scarce currency" is used to describe the situation where the demand for a particular country's currency threatens to exhaust the available supply at the usual rates of exchange. When a currency becomes "scarce" in the *International Monetary Fund,* members of the fund are authorized to introduce exchange restrictions against that country.

scatter diagram. In statistics, a graph with one variable measured on the *x* axis and the other variable measured on the *y* axis and each item of a distribution plotted on this graph. If there is a relationship between the two variables the points plotted will tend to follow a diagonal line.

schedule. (1) Any orderly arrangement of information. (2) In economic analysis, the tabular arrangement of prices and quantities or other data.

schedule bond. A *fidelity bond* naming the persons whose proper performance of duties is covered rather than stating the offices covered regardless of who holds the office. Cf. *position bond.*

scheduled property. The property covered by a *valued policy,* namely, the list of property covered, together with the agreed value of each item.

schedule policy. In insurance, a policy which covers under separate insuring agreements in one policy several hazards which are frequently handled under separate polices. Cf. *all-risk insurance.*

schedule rating. In insurance, the variation of the manual rate (see manual rating) by corrections for stated factors increasing or decreasing the risk involved but not including the risk history of the particular insured. E.g., a 5% premium reduction for a sprinkler system which reduces fire risk. Cf. *experience rating, manual rating, merit rating, retrospective rating.*

science. (1) Any organized body of knowledge of general significance. (2) A body of knowledge dealing with phenomena having such constant relation that there can be generalizations known as laws. (3) In a narrow sense, used to denote only the natural sciences.

scienter. The word refers to knowledge on the part of one who has made false representations. There is a dispute in the law as to whether representations must involve scienter in order to impose liability on the misrepresenting party.

scrip or script. A written claim which is issued instead of money or shares of stock which will be paid later to redeem the scrip. For example, "scrip" money during the bank holiday of 1933, which was a claim to money at a later date. Cf. *scrip dividend.*

scrip or script dividend. A dividend paid by *scrip* and not by cash or stock. The scrip may itself have a maturity date or not and may bear interest or not.

scire facias. Latin for "you may cause to know." In law, an order of a court directing a recognition of a public record unless reason can be shown to the contrary. Thus, this writ is used to revive an unexecuted judgment or to investigate the compliance of a corporation with its charter.

Scitovsky double criterion. In *welfare economics,* a change in the economy is an improvement only if (1) those who gain evaluate their gains at a higher figure than the value which the losers set on their losses (the *Kaldor criterion*) and if, at the same time, the return move from the new position to the old position will not result in those who gain evaluating their gains at a higher figure than the value at which the losers set their losses (reverse *Kaldor criterion*). Cf. *Bergson criterion, Kaldor criterion,* and *Paretian optimality.*

SCS Soil Conservation Service. The SCS was created in 1935 to aid in eliminating soil erosion and some flood control.

SDR. Special drawing rights. A device of the *International Monetary Fund* to enable countries to convert excess U.S. dollar balances held by them.

seal. In law, any mark written or printed in addition to the signature which a party desires to adopt as a seal. Hence the frequently used "L.S." printed on forms. In many states the presence or absence of a seal still has important consequences. For example, the statute of limitations on a sealed document may be twice as long as on an unsealed document.

sealed bid. An offer to perform a contract submitted together with the offers of others in sealed envelopes. The person or government requesting the offers opens the envelopes simultaneously and awards the contract to the responsible bidder who quotes the lowest price for the specified materials or work. The essence of the system lies in the fact that if each bidder is in ignorance of other prices being quoted at the time he is quoting, the lowest possible price will be elicited. Cf. *open bid.*

seasonal index. An index of the seasonal pattern of a business. Applied to monthly figures, various systems of arriving at an average figure for each month are used (e.g., *link relative,* ratio of data to moving average, ratio of data to trend). The average figure for each of the twelve months is totaled and divided by twelve to get the average of the year. The average of each month is then divided by this average of the year and the result is the seasonal index. Analogous calculations can be made for other time intervals.

seasonal tolerance clause. A labor contract clause permitting seasonal overtime without liability for overtime rates of pay.

seasonal variation. The fluctuation in any series of economic data during a year which recurs consistently from one year to the next. Ordinary methods of measuring such variations are simple average, *link relative,* ratio of data to moving average, and ratio of data to trend.

SEC Securities and Exchange Commission. A federal agency created in 1934 to administer the *Securities Act of 1933* and the *Securities Exchange Act of 1934.* The commission also administers the *Public Utility Holding Company Act of 1935,* the *Investment Company Act* of 1940, and the *Trust Indenture Act* of 1939.

secondary bank reserve. High grade securities which are readily convertible into money.

secondary boycott. The labor group conducting such a boycott strikes against its own employer to force him to cease business with another "offending" employer. Declared illegal by the *Taft-Hartley Amendment* to *National Labor Relations Act.* Cf. *primary boycott* and *hot cargo.*

secondary deposit. Same as *derivative deposit.*

secondary distribution. In finance, the sale of a large block of stock on a stock exchange by a holder (not the corporation) after the close of business for the day. Only the seller pays a commission. Cf. *exchange distribution.*

secondary evidence rule. In law, the rule admitting copies (or other secondary evidence) when sufficient explanation is offered as to why the original (or other primary evidence) is not available. Cf. *best evidence rule.*

secondary market. In finance, the market where resale occurs of securities already issued. Cf. *primary market.*

secondary offering. The sale of a block of securities by a large stockholder.

secondary picketing. A form of picketing in which an establishment not involved in the labor dispute is picketed by employees of another establishment which is so involved because of the relationship between the establishments with the hope that the establishment not in the dispute will put pressure on the establishment that is.

secondary power. In public utilities, power that can be interrupted at the decision of the producer within terms set down by contract with the customer. Cf. *primary power.*

secondary reserve. See *secondary bank reserve.*

secondary strike. A strike which spreads to firms furnishing goods to the business where the principal strike is in effect. Distinguished from a *sympathetic* strike which is a more general term applying to situations where there is no real dispute between the second employer and his employees.

sectional tariff. In transportation, a tariff made in sections, with each section containing different rates between the same points with provisions for alternative application.

sector accounts. The division of the economy of a country into four areas: business, government, personal, and rest-of-the world, for the purpose of examining the flows between the sectors. The rest-of-the world sector includes the import-export and capital flows to and from foreign countries.

secular stagnation theory. The theory is not concerned with problems of the business cycle but with the view that the economy has reached "maturity": the frontier is gone, the rate of population increase is declining, important discoveries are lacking, etc. Hence long periods of depression and only short interludes of prosperity are to be expected except as this is changed by government policy.

secular trends. Used in connection with the business cycle and meaning the average course that would be followed by economic activities over a period of several cycles. The trend may be calculated by fitting a line by the *least squares method* to the *deseasonalized* data.

secured creditor. One whose claim against a debtor has been secured by the pledge of property or a lien. Cf. *unsecured creditor.*

secured loan. A promise to pay by a person, corporation, or government and against the promise are pledged specific assets usually by means of a mortgage.

securities. A collective name for all kinds of written instruments in the form of mortgages, bonds, stocks, bills of exchange, bills of lading, dock warrants, warehouse receipts, certificates of ownership, acceptances, etc.

Securities Act of 1933. Federal legislation providing for registration of securities offered for sale to the public in interstate commerce or through the mails. The purpose of registration is to furnish complete and accurate information to investors. The commission has authority to stop issues until proper information is furnished.

Securities Exchange Act of 1934. This act provides for the regulation of securities exchanges and over-the-counter trading through the Securities and Exchange Commission. Also provides for publication of information regarding the condition of corporations whose securities are listed on an exchange.

security holding company. Same as *holding company.*

security issue tax. A tax levied upon the initial issuance of stock by a corporation. Both federal and state governments levy such a tax.

security market. The places for sale and purchase of stocks and bonds: on the organized exchange (see *stock exchange*) and in the unorganized market. Cf. *over the counter market.*

seigniorage. The profit which a government makes on the coinage of money. At one time princes and kings made nice profits from money coinage. Practically all modern governments forego this.

seizin. The possession of premises under claim of ownership of a freehold estate (i.e., an estate for life or greater).

selective selling. The policy of selling to a limited number of accounts in any geographical area.

self-generating theory of cycle. See *endogenous theory of business cycle.*

self-insurance. The practice of establishing a reserve fund to meet losses rather than covering the losses by an insurance policy. The term may be loosely used to refer to the same situation even if no reserve fund is set up.

self-liquidating. An investment or loan for a purpose that is expected to yield a return sufficient to retire the loan and interest.

sell down. The offering of a large block of securities by a large stockholder. Hence a *secondary offering.*

seller's lien. Same as *vendor's lien.*

sellers' market. A condition of the market in which there is a scarcity of goods available and hence sellers can dictate conditions of sale or set a higher price. Cf. *buyers' market.*

sellers' monopoly. The market situation in which a single seller or group is able to dictate the price at which a commodity will be sold. More accurately referred to as *monopoly* or *oligopoly.*

sellers' surplus. The difference between what the seller received in the market and any lower price for which he would have been willing to sell.

selling against the box. The practice (typically by a large stockholder who desires to shield his selling of his shares) of *selling short* and delivering borrowed certificates rather than the shares the seller holds in his strong box.

selling agent. An agent middleman who acts continuously for his principal with complete responsibility for selling the entire output of the principal's plant and wide discretion as to sale prices. He may take possession and may perform the credit and collection function. Distinguish *manufacturer's agent.*

selling group. In finance, the group working for underwriters of a stock or bond issue in selling to customers. The selling group ordinarily act as agents and can turn back any stock remaining unsold. Cf. *purchase group.*

selling short. The agreement to deliver at a future date a security or commodity which the seller does not own, but which he hopes to buy later at a lower price. Cf. *buying long.*

semiaverages method of fitting a straight line. The division of data into two equal groups (the upper half and the lower half) with the *arithmetic mean* to be established for each group. Then a straight line through these two means will give an approximation of a linear *regression line.* Cf. *least squares method.*

semidurable goods. *Goods* which have a normal life in use from six months to three years.

semi-interquartile range. Same as *quartile deviation.*

semilogarithmic chart. A graph in which one axis is scaled in logarithms and the other axis is scaled arithmetically (with natural numbers). See Figure 34, page 261.

semiskilled labor. Frequently defined as work for which some training of less than one year is required. Work requiring more training than that is usually called skilled labor.

semitontine system. An insurance policy provision providing a surrender value if a policy lapses prior to a dividend distribution.

semivariable cost. A cost which is fixed if output does not exceed a certain range but will change outside that range.

seniority. Giving sole or primary consideration in promotions, vacancies, layoffs, etc., to employees in the order of their length of service with that employer. The policy may be voluntary on the part of the employer or may be provided for in a labor contract with a union. Many variations of the policy exist, e.g., an employee may have *double seniority:* (1) seniority within his own department and (2) seniority throughout the plant.

senior lien. An interest in property having priority over other interests as to payment; not necessarily an interest which has existed longer than others.

sensitivity analysis. The study of the effect of small changes in a variable upon the final outcome.

separation of powers. The powers of the U.S. government are divided among three branches: (1) the executive (the President, cabinet, commissions, etc.), (2) the legislative (Congress: the Senate and the House of Representatives), (3) the judiciary (the U.S. Supreme Court and inferior federal courts).

separation rate. In personnel management, the ratio of the number of employees terminating work during the month to the average working force in the month. Separations are broken down into three categories: quit, discharge, and layoff, and a separate rate for each category is computed in a parallel manner.

sequence analysis. The study of the casual connection of the economic events of one period with the economic events of the succeeding period or periods.

sequential analysis. A sampling method in which a terminal decision depends not on the size of the sample as in conventional sampling but on the values of successive observations. As each item is tested, a decision is made on the basis of the observed values up to that point as to whether to continue sampling or to terminate. For this purpose, the observed values at each point are compared with a precalculated range and frequency determining acceptance or rejection.

sequestration. In law, a *writ* installing representatives of a court to compel performance of a court order.

serial bonds. A serial bond issue consists of a number of bonds issued at the same time but with different maturity dates (serially due), usually with interest rates varying for the different maturity dates. Distinguish *series bonds.*

serial correlation. The situation in which two different time series are correlated when the values of one series are lagged (by a fixed time interval) with the values of the other series. Cf. *autocorrelation.*

series bonds. Groups of bonds (e.g., Series A, Series B) issued usually at different times and with different maturities but under the authority of the same indenture. Distinguish *serial bond.*

service function. In inventory analysis, the relation of *safety factor* to service level, thus the fraction of quantity demanded that is met from inventory.

service lease. Same as *operating lease.*

servo system. A system in which output is fed back into an earlier stage of the system to help determine future input.

setoff. In general, the right of the defendant in a law suit to "setoff" (deduct) any claims which he has against the plaintiff. This subject is covered by statutes which differ from state to state. For example, in one state the defendant may be able to set off only *liquidated* claims, in another state he may be permitted to set off any claim. Cf. *counterclaim.*

settlement options. In *life insurance,* the right of the beneficiary to select among alternatives upon the death of the insured or on maturity of an endowment policy: (1) lump-sum cash payment, (2) leaving the proceeds to earn interest, (3) instalment payments over a fixed period, (4) periodic payments for the life of the beneficiary, or (5) periodic payments for the life of the beneficiary with a minimum number of payments guaranteed. The right of the beneficiary to make such a selection may be restricted by the insured person.

settlor. The one who creates a trust.

severable contract. A contract whose performance is divisible into parts particularly as regards the price for each part.

severance pay. Same as *dismissal pay.*

severance tax. A tax imposed on the privilege of removing or using natural resources.

shadow price. (1) The *opportunity cost* implied by a given resource allocation. Used in evaluating an investment project, the shadow price is the contribution of a factor to the economy which is lost when it is removed from its present use to use in the project being analyzed. (2) In *linear programming,* shadow prices are the values that must be assigned to a unit of capacity in each of the departments in order to maximize the value of the output. Hence, a shadow price is the economic value per unit of a scarce resource in a particular production situation.

shape-up. The practice in shipping trades under which the employer selects work crews from men reporting for work.

sharecropping. An agricultural system found particularly in the southern United States under which the landlord furnishes land and equipment, and the tenant pays the landlord a percentage of the crops by way of rent.

share elasticity. The ratio of (1) the change in the percentage of a market that a particular producer has to (2) the change in the percentage that the price differential between the producer's price schedule and the price schedules of his competitors is to the price schedules of his competitors.

shareholder or stockholder. The owner of a stock certificate, a part owner of the corporation.

share reinsurance. *Reinsurance* in which the *reinsured* participates on a share basis with the reinsurer in any losses. Cf. *surplus reinsurance.*

shares. See *stock.*

sharing the market. Any scheme by which sellers limit their individual efforts to given parts of the total market for a product or service, e.g., the "sharing" may be on a geographical basis.

shaving (a note.) (1) Discounting a noninterest-bearing time note at a rate much higher than the legal one. (2) In finance, paying an extra charge to get an extension of time to pay for or deliver a security.

Shelley's case. See *rule in Shelley's case.*

sheriff's deed. In law, a deed executed by a sheriff pursuant to the *judgment* of a court as in the case of a *foreclosure* where the deed would read to the highest bidder confirmed by the court.

sheriff's sale. A public sale of *real estate* or *personal property* conducted by a sheriff pursuant to the order of a court. The highest bidder prevails subject to court approval of the price. Cf. *upset price.*

Sherman Antitrust Act. Passed by Congress in 1890 with the purpose of barring acts or contracts "in restraint of trade" or "tending to monopoly." Provides for recovery of treble damages upon conviction. Amended by *Clayton Act, Robinson-Patman Act, Miller-Tydings Act, Webb-Pomerene Act.* Cf. *rule of reason.*

Sherman Silver Purchase Act. Passed by Congress in 1890, requiring the Secretary of the Treasury to purchase 4½ million ounces of silver monthly and issue in payment Treasury Notes redeemable in gold or silver. Repealed in 1893.

shift differential. Same as *shift premium.*

shifting of taxation. See *tax incidence.*

shift (in industry), types of. See the following specific terms:

graveyard shift	*split shift*
rotating shift	*swing shift*

shift premium. An additional payment made to workers who work outside the normal working hours of the daytime. Distinguish from *overtime.* The shift premium is due regardless of the number of hours worked; overtime is due only for work in excess of a stipulated number of hours. Both may be applicable at the same time. Also called shift differential.

shift variable. In *econometrics,* a variable introduced into a model for the purpose of causing a shift in a function (such as a supply curve) so that another function (such as a demand curve) can be identified. Thus the shift variable should be such as to affect one function but not the other function. Cf. *endogenous variable, exogenous variable, instrumental variable, jointly dependent variable, predetermined variable.*

shilling. A unit of English money. There are twenty shillings to the *pound.* Shilling is abbreviated s.

shinplaster. Colloquial term for worthless currency or promissory notes.

shock and error model. In *econometrics,* a system of equations containing random disturbances of specific variables and errors in the specific equations.

shock model. In *econometrics,* a system of equations containing random disturbances of the variables in contrast to a system wherein the variables are subject to errors of observation.

shock term. In *econometrics*, same as *disturbance term.*

shop book rule. In law, a rule making shop books admissible in evidence without the testimony of the person who made the actual entry but on the testimony of the person in charge of the books, provided the entries were made in the regular course of business.

shopping goods. Consumers' goods which the customer, before buying, usually compares as to quality, price, style, etc., i.e., the customer shops around. Cf. *convenience goods, fashion goods, impulse goods, point of purchase goods, specialty goods.*

shop steward. A union representative who handles union matters within a given department of a company.

short. See *selling short.*

short covering. The purchase of a security or commodity by a trader who has earlier gone short, i.e., sold at an agreed price for future delivery. Short covering thus constitutes taking the profit or accepting a loss in an effort to avoid further loss.

short line. A selection from a vendor's complete assortment so that a store buyer may save time in inspection.

short rate. In insurance, the charge made for insurance cancelled before the expiration of the term of the policy. The rate is somewhat higher for this period than would be the proportion of the premium based on time elapsed. Cf. *pro rata rate.*

short run. A general term in economic theory. The period of time during which *some* of the costs of a particular firm are fixed and cannot be changed substantially, such as the plant size. Cf. *long run.*

short run cost. In the short run there are some *fixed costs* and hence both the *average cost curve* and *marginal cost curve* (see Figure 2, page 27) have more curvature than in the long run where all resources are variable.

short run equilibrium. See *equilibrium of firm or industry, (partial) short run.*

short sale. See *selling short.*

short ton. 2,000 pounds. Cf. *long ton.*

SIC. Standard Industrial Classification—the industry and product classification numbering system used by the U.S. Census. Cf. *SITC.*

sight bill. Same as *demand bill.*

sight draft. A check or draft drawn on a bank, commercial house, or debtor which demands payment immediately upon presentation.

sigma. (1) The capital Greek letter, Σ, denotes the sum of a number of items. (2) The small Greek letter, σ denotes the *standard deviation.*

silent or sleeping partner. Colloquially, any partner who does not actively participate in the business. He has the same liability as an active partner unless he qualifies himself as a limited partner in a *limited partnership.*

silver certificates. Paper money backed by silver in the United States Treasury and redeemable in silver. Issued since 1878.

silver dollar. Coined since 1792, containing 371¼ grains of silver (77.34% of an ounce) and 41¼ grains of alloy. Total weight is 412½ grains. Based on the Spanish dollar.

Silver Purchase Act of 1934. Authorized and directed the Secretary of the Treasury to purchase silver at home and abroad until the proportion of silver in the combined stocks of gold and silver of the United States is one-fourth of the total monetary value of such stocks or until the price of silver is $1.29½ an ounce. No time limit is set for the achievement of a three-to-one ratio between gold and silver.

silver standard. That monetary system under which money is convertible into silver at a specified rate and vice versa and free shipment of silver internationally is permitted.
Cf. *monetary standard, types of.*

simple arbitrage. *Abitrage* achieved by using only three markets Cf. *compound arbitrage.*

simple average. (1) An average in which the individual items are not weighted. Cf. *weighted average.* (2) In *marine insurance,* same as *particular average.*

simple correlation. The *correlation* of two variables.

simple interest. Calculation of interest such that no interest is computed on interest past due.

simplex method in linear programming. Starting with any feasible solution and then examining the solutions on either side to see if improvement can be made. If so, moving to the new solution point in the direction indicated by previous improvement and examining the next possible solution. This is continued until no further improvement is possible.

simulation. A technique for building models that reproduce part or all of the output of a behavioral system; a model in which time is a variable. Various objectives may be pursued, such as optimizing a controlled variable (queuing theory), exploring the paths by which stability is attained or estimating the values of unknowns where the outcome in known and some of the variables are controlled.

simulation model. A model involving a time dimension so that the results of a preceding period can be incorporated in the new period.

simultaneous equations. A system of equations such that the same value for each variable will satisfy each equation.

single liability. The situation in which the stockholder is liable for the corporation's losses only to the extent of his investment.

single premium life insurance. Life insurance for which the premium is paid once.

single schedule tariff. A tariff which has the same rate for a commodity regardless of the country of origin.

single tax. A proposal by Henry George that the government appropriate all of the unearned increment of land by means of a tax, and that this tax alone would yield revenues large enough so that the government could abolish all other taxes.

sinking fund. (1) In general accounting, segregated assets which are being accumulated for a specific purpose. (2) In governmental accounting, a fund established to accumulate resources for the retirement of bonds, but not for the payment of interest which is handled through the *general fund* or a special revenue fund.

sinking fund bond. A bond to be paid from a sinking fund, that is, from segregated assets gradually accumulated for that purpose.

sinking fund method of depreciation. Taking the initial cost of a capital asset, deducting the expected salvage value at the time it is expected to be discarded and spreading the difference in equal installments per unit of time over the estimated life of the asset, but with recognition of interest on the amount of depreciation to be earned from a fund actually established, thus reducing the net charge for each period by the interest to be earned with the interest deduction computed as either (a) the interest on the annual charge which will bring the charge to full amount at maturity or (b) the interest this year on all prior charges.

SITC. Standard International Trade Classification—the industry and product classification numbering system used by the United Nations. Cf. *SIC.*

sit-down strike. A work stoppage in which the worker refuses to leave the company's premises.

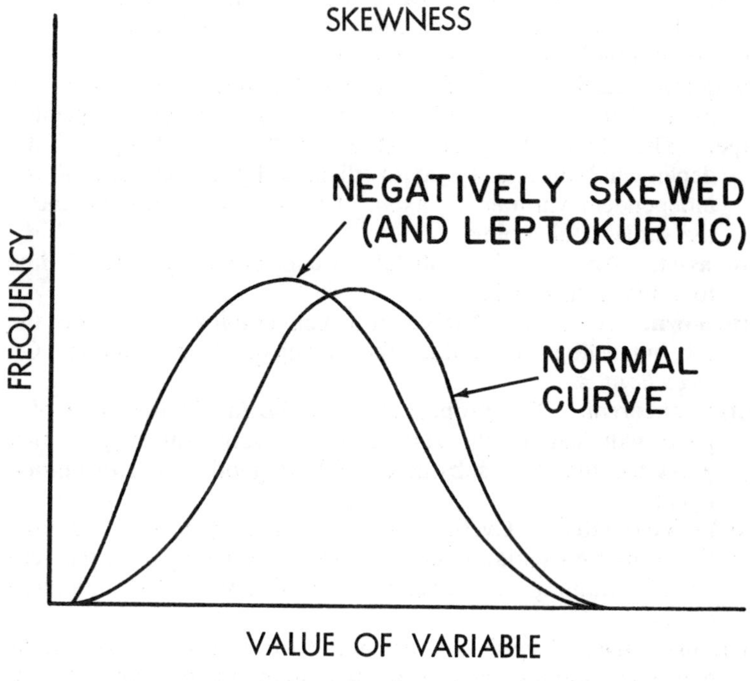

Figure 52.

skewness. The degree to which a frequency curve lacks symmetry. There is skewness when the mean, median, and mode are not identical in value. The most common measure of skewness is the difference between the arithmetic mean and the mode, and for a relative measure, dividing this result by the *standard deviation.* Mathematically, skewness is the fourth moment around the *arithmetic mean.*

skilled labor. Work which requires training or apprenticeship before one is able successfully to pursue it, e.g., the die sinker. The line separating skilled and semi-skilled labor is often set at one year's training required to qualify.

slack variable. A variable added to an inequation in order to be able to state the inequation as an equation. Thus if $2X + 4Y \leq 100$, this can be stated as $2X + 4Y + Z = 100$, where Z is defined as taking up any "slack" needed to eliminate the possibility that the left-hand side of the equation has a value less than 100.

slander. A spoken untruth which damages the reputation of the party about whom the statement is untrue. Cf. *libel.*

sleeping partner. Same as *silent partner.*

sliding-scale tariff. A tariff in which the duty varies with the price of the goods, whether the duty is ad valorem or specific.

slope. The slope of a curve at a point is the change of the dependent variable (y axis) divided by the change of the independent variable (x axis). The slope of a straight line is the same at all points.

slow asset. An asset that will take a considerable period of time to convert into cash.

slow-down. A form of strike in which employees stay on the job but deliberately reduce their efficiency in production. Cf. *stretchout.*

Slutsky theorem. The proposition that the fall in the price of a good will lead to the substitution of some quantity of that good for the near substitutes of that good. Cf. *substitution effect.*

Slutsky-Yule effect. Cyclical behavior in a series (even though the resulting oscillation is nonexistent) resulting from the very act of summing or averaging successive values of a random series.

small loan acts. Legislation providing for licensing personal finance companies and setting maximum interest rates (often as high as 3% per month) for loans under $1,000.

Smith-Connally Act. A federal law of 1943 enacted as a war measure justifying government seizure of plants affected by a labor dispute and forbidding strikes unless 30 days notice was given. Government seizure, control of wages and prices were part of an integrated program.

smoothing constant. In *exponential smoothing*, the fraction of the difference between the actual result and the forecasted result that is then added to the previously smoothed value to get the new smoothed value.

SMSA. Standard Metropolitan Statistical Area—a geographical area including the trading area around a city (more than the limits of a city) used by the U.S. Census as a reporting unit.

Smyth v. Ames Rule. This case, decided in 1898 by the U.S. Supreme Court, established the principle that public utilities are to have rates so set that they yield a "fair return on the fair value of the property devoted to public service." This rule was overthrown as far as the constitutional limit is concerned by the Hope case in 1944, establishing the principle that rates are to be so set that the end result fairly balances the interests of the consumer and the investor.

social insurance. Insurance made compulsory by the government for workers in the United States against the risks of unemployment, industrial accidents and old age.

socialism. An economic system which would have the government or guilds of workers own and operate all means of production thus restricting, if not entirely eliminating, private enterprise. Many varieties of socialism exist. Sometimes the term is used also to include communism as a type of socialism. Cf. *Fabian socialism, guild socialism.*

social marginal product. The net contribution of a marginal unit or project to the national product.

social sciences. The study of human beings as members of a group. The social sciences are much less developed in their generalizations than the biological or physical sciences. The ordinarily accepted classification is: political economy (economics), political science (government), sociology, and history. Other sciences have social aspects, e.g., anthropology and ethnology.

Social Security Act. Passed by Congress in 1935. There are two separate principles: (1) a tax paid by the employer and a tax paid by the employee on a limited amount of annual wages earned in employment specified by the law, and (2) a benefit program for the aged, disabled, widows and children, etc., which is not entirely dependent upon whether any tax was paid by the beneficiary. The act includes not only the old age provisions, but aids to the states for administering unemployment insurance.

social welfare function. In *welfare economics,* an *indifference map* showing the relative values placed on two or more social values.

sociology. Two meanings: (1) The most general of all the social sciences. It has the same relation to the special social sciences, as economics and politics, that biology has to botany and zoology. It concerns itself with the origin and development, the structure and functions, of all forms of human association. (2) More narrowly, the social science which deals with social relations not already covered by the "older" social sciences such as economics and politics, particularly such problems as family relations, poverty, criminology, etc.

soft goods. Nondurable consumers' goods. Cf. *hard goods.*

soft market. A condition in which the market prices are falling or the relative number of buyers is decreasing.

soft money. (1) Paper money as opposed to metallic money, the latter being called "hard money." (2) Sometimes, money with no stability in purchasing power or international exchange.

sole proprietorship. The simplest form of business organization in which one individual owns and controls the enterprise. All the personal assets of the individual are subject to the indebtedness of the business.

solidarism. A doctrine of mutual dependence emphasizing that each individual has economically justifiable obligations to less fortunate individuals.

solvency. This term is used in two different primary meanings: (1) An enterprise is solvent when it is able to meet its obligations as they become due. This is the "equity" sense. (2) An enterprise is solvent when the total of its assets exceed the total of its liabilities. This is the "bankruptcy" sense.

source and application of funds statement. A statement of the sources of funds of a business and the uses or applications of such funds during any given period between two points in time. Sources of funds are (1) increases in liabilities, (2) increases in net worth, and (3) decreases in assets. Applications of funds are (1) decreases in liabilities, (2) decreases in net worth, and (3) increases in assets.

span of control. In management, the maximum number of subordinates or functions that can be handled effectively.

special agent. An agent whose powers to act for his principal are limited.

special appearance. The appearance of a party in court solely for the purpose of denying the court's jurisdiction over him, usually on the ground of defective service of papers or that the proceeding is in an improper court.

special assessment. A payment imposed when the special benefit of a government service results in an increase in the value of the land, such as the widening of a narrow street.

special assessment bond. In municipal finance, a bond secured by the pledge of the assessments against specific property. The assessments may be limited to a specific number of annual assessments for a fixed amount or unlimited as to the rate or amount of tax that may be levied against the benefited property.

special assessment fund. In governmental accounting, a fund established to account for financing improvements or services from special charges levied against the properties or persons benefited.

special deposit. A deposit in which the depositor avoids creating a creditor-debtor relationship and creates a *bailment*. The principal benefit would occur in bankruptcy when the special deposit is held separate from the general deposits and thus in a preferred status.

special indorsement. The payee or indorsee by prior indorsement placing the name of the person to whom the instrument is to be transferred after the words "pay to the order of . . ." and signing his name under this form. Also called indorsement in full.

special issue. In law, a pleading creates a special issue (as opposed to the general issue) when it denies only a particular allegation but one without which the plaintiff cannot prevail.

specialist. In finance, a member of the stock exchange who handles for other brokers, orders with limits above or below the current market price, and who may deal for his own account. The specialist usually confines himself to one or a few issues.

special offering. On the N.Y. Stock Exchange, the offering of a block of securities during the regular trading session at a fixed price with no commission payable except by a seller. Cf. *secondary offering.*

specialization ratio. As used in the census, the percentage of the output of those firms classified as an industry that is confined to one product area. Cf. *concentration ratio* and *coverage ratio.*

specialty. In law, a promise under seal to pay money.

specialty goods. Those particular consumers' goods on which the buyer characteristically insists and for which he is willing to make a special purchasing effort. Cf. *convenience goods, fashion goods, impulse goods, point of purchase goods, shopping goods.*

specialty store. A retail store which makes its appeal on the basis of a restricted class or classes of goods for which the buyer is willing to make a special purchasing effort, e.g., a shoe store, a men's wear store, etc.

special verdict. In law, a verdict which makes separate findings on a number of the issues in a case as well as a final finding for one party or the other. The special verdict must be consistent in all its parts or it will be set aside by the court. Cf. *general verdict.*

special warranty deed. A *warranty deed* in which the grantor states he will defend the *grantee* only against acts of himself and persons claiming under himself. Actually this is little more than a *quitclaim deed.*

specie. Coin, usually gold or silver. Hard money.

specification. A detailed statement by the purchaser of the quality of material, processes and methods of production, dimensions and tolerances, and physical tests which must be met by the product to be manufactured by the seller. The specification often is accompanied by detailed engineering drawings called blueprints.

specification problem. In *econometrics*, the problem of stating the variables to be included in the analysis and the function or relationship of those variables.

specific commodity sales tax. In effect, the same as an *excise tax.* Examples are the taxes on gasoline, drugs, etc.

specific deposit. A deposit made for a specific purpose, for example, bond coupons deposited for collection purpose only. Not a *general deposit.* The bank becomes only the agent or bailee of the depositor and not the debtor. The distinction is important in the case of bankruptcy or failure to follow instructions.

specific duty. Same as *specific tariff.*

specific legacy. A provision in a *will* leaving specific property to the person named. If this property is disposed of by the testator before he dies, the legacy is adeemed (cf. *ademption*) and the person receives nothing. Cf. *demonstrative legacy, lapsed legacy, general legacy,* and *residuary legacy.*

specific performance. The right to have a contract specifically enforced, i.e., according to its terms rather than the mere recovery of damages. The right exists where damages are an inadequate remedy. Where personal services are involved, the court will not order specific performance of the services, but may issue an injunction preventing the performance of such services for others.

specific tariff. A tariff based on the number of units, weight, or other specific measure but not value. Cf. *ad valorem tariff.*

spectral analysis. Determination of the probability that hypothesized cycles exist in data by fitting sine or cosine functions in a manner analogous to the fitting of a straight line in *regression.*

speculation. The buying or selling of goods or securities in the hope of making a profit from the change in price.

speculative demand for money. The demand for money originating with the belief that future prices will fall (or future interest rates rise) and hence it will be profitable to delay purchases and investments. Cf. *precautionary demand for money, transactions demand for money.*

speculative market. An organized exchange where speculative buying and selling regularly occur.

speed-up. An increase in the rate of production without an increase in compensation.

spendthrift trust. A trust whose terms bar creditors from reaching the income or principal of the beneficiary.

spin-off. The distribution by a parent corporation of the controlling stock in a subsidiary corporation to the stockholders of the parent corporation. Cf. *split-off.*

split. See *stock split.*

split-income. The federal income tax provision that the incomes of a married couple may be considered as earned one-half by the husband and one-half by the wife where a joint return is filed. The tax on one-half is then computed and multiplied by two. This has the effect of reducing the total tax in all cases except the lowest bracket.

split inventory appraisal. In public utilities, splitting a utility system into two or more parts to reflect construction in high or low cost times, and applying the costs of production of each cost era to the part of the plant constructed during that era in order to arrive at a value for the whole.

split-off. The exchange of stock by the shareholders of a parent (controlling) corporation in return for stock in a subsidiary corporation. Cf. *spin-off.*

split order. On the stock market, an order to a broker to buy or sell partly at one price or time and partly at another.

split shift. The arrangement of an employee's work schedule so that the working day is broken up by periods during which the employee is not working.

split-up. The surrender by the shareholders of a parent (controlling) corporation of all their stock in the parent in return for stock in a subsidiary corporation and the subsequent dissolution of the parent corporation.

spot delivery. Immediate delivery.

spot market. Same as *cash market*.

spot price. The price for a good deliverable immediately.

spot stock. A stock of goods shipped by a producer to a public warehouse as his property with the intention of disposing of the goods to a distinct market.

spot trading. Cash sales for immediate delivery. Contrasted to *futures trading*.

spread. (1) In general, the difference between total cost of production and selling price to consumers. In this sense, the mark up. (2) In underwriting, the difference between the buying price of the underwriter and selling price to the public. (3) On exchanges, the difference between present spot or cash prices and present prices for future delivery. (4) On exchanges, a combination of a *call* and a *put*, so that the purchaser of the spread may at his option demand delivery from or make delivery to the seller of the spread. The *put* and the *call* are for different prices. If they are for the same price, it would be a *straddle*. (5) The difference between *ask* and *bid* prices.

spurious correlation. The correlation of two or more series, each of which is a ratio. Thus, correlating per capita consumption of a good against per capita income instead of a *multiple correlation* of consumption of a good, population, and income. The answer resulting from the two methods will be different.

squatter's right: The right to land acquired by one who has continuously occupied the land without recognition of the rights of the owner for the period required by law to establish *adverse possession*. The period set by law is twenty years in most states.

stabilization. In general, intervention to prevent fluctuations. (1) In economics, intervention by government to stabilize the price level, employment, exchange rates or other areas. (2) In finance, buying or selling of a security in order to hold its price steady particularly during the time of selling of securities by an underwriter.

stabilization fund. See *exchange stabilization fund*.

stabilized bond. A bond whose principal and interest are adjusted to price level changes by an index to allow for changes in purchasing power.

stabilized dollar. Same as *compensated dollar*.

stable equilibrium. In economics, a condition which once achieved will continue indefinitely unless there is a change in some noneconomic condition. Changes in economic conditions will be followed by re-establishment of the original equilibrium. Cf. *dynamic equilibrium, equilibrium of firm or industry (partial) long run, equilibrium of firm or industry (partial) short run, expectational equilibrium, general equilibrium (under monopoly or monopolistic competition), general equilibrium (under pure competition), intermediate equilibrium, market equilibrium, normal equilibrium, partial equilibrium, static equilibrium,* and *unstable equilibrium.*

stable model. A model in which there is a tendency to return to the initial condition after a disturbance has been introduced. Cf. *unstable model.*

staff position. A place in the "staff" organization, non-operating personnel in the sense that they do not work directly on the production but give specialized, technical, or professional assistance to "line" members. Distinguish *line position.*

stagnation. The situation in which per capita real income is constant or declining.

stagnation thesis. The proposition that American per capita real income of the decade of the 1930's would not rise in the future because of (1) a declining rate of population growth, (2) the disappearance of the geographic frontier, (3) the growth of the absolute volume of savings, and (4) the tendency of new techniques of production to be capital-saving rather than capital-using.

standard absorption costing. The cost of a finished unit is calculated as the sum of labor, material and manufacturing overhead, each taken at a standard cost rather than actual cost. Deviations of standard from actual costs are collected in variance accounts. Cf. *standard direct costing.*

standard cost method of inventory. Valuing manufactured goods on the basis of predetermined standards set for the materials, direct labor, and manufacturing overhead. These standards are separately determined for each product by analysis of prior records with adjustment for changed conditions. The differences between costs so determined (called standard costs) and the actual costs are collected in variance accounts.

standard deviation. The standard deviation is symbolized by the small Greek letter sigma (σ), and is the square root of the sum of the squares of the deviations of the items in a series from the arithmetic mean, divided by the number of items, or $\sigma = \sqrt{\frac{\Sigma x^2}{N}}$ where x is the deviation of the items from the arithmetic mean and N is the number of items.

standard deviation of universe (estimated from sample). The estimate of the standard deviation of the universe is the product of the standard deviation of the sample times the expression $\sqrt{n/(n-1)}$ where n is the number of cases in the sample.

standard direct costing. The cost of a finished unit is calculated as the sum of labor and material taken at standard cost rather than actual costs. Manufacturing overhead, however, is included at actual cost. Cf. *standard absorption costing.*

standard error. The term applied to various statistical measures (such as the arithmetic mean) which gives the range within which (plus or minus from the mean of the measure) the measure will fall two times out of three when samples are drawn from a universe following the *normal curve.* The standard error depends upon the size of the sample and the dispersion in the universe. For the arithmetic mean, the standard error equals the *standard deviation* of the universe divided by the square root of the number of items in the sample. Cf. *probable error, random error, sampling error, systematic error.*

standard error of estimate. The quadratic mean of the deviations of observed values from a regression line. Hence it is the *standard deviation* measured from the line of regression rather than the arithmetic mean. The standard error of estimate itself follows the normal table if there is a normal distribution. Then there is a 2 out of 3 chance that an observation will fall within the computed value plus or minus the standard error of estimate.

A common formula for this is $\sigma_y \sqrt{1 - r^2}$ where r is the coefficient of correlation and σ_y is the standard deviation of the variable whose error is being estimated in the case of a *correlation* study.

An alternate formula is the square root of the ratio of (1) the sum of the squares of the deviations of the actual values of the variable from the computed values of the variable divided by (2) the number of values of the variable.

To adjust for *degrees of freedom* where the sample is small the standard error of estimate is the square root of quotient: (1) the sum of the squares of the deviations of the observed values from the fitted line, divided by (2) the number of observations less the number of constants in the regression equation (the number of absolute terms and coefficients of independent variables).

standard error of regression coefficient. The standard error of the regression of a sample is $S_y/S_x\sqrt{n}$ where S_y is the standard error of estimate of the sample, S_x is the standard deviation of the variable whose regression coefficient is involved, and n is the number of items in the sample.

standard error of the mean. See *standard error.*

standard fire policy. Many states provide that fire insurance must be written in the form of policy set out in the statutes. This is called the standard fire policy. In many states an attempt to deviate from this form by the insurer gives the insured the benefit of the standard form or the actual policy language used, whichever is more favorable to the insured.

standard-gamble method. The central idea is that if a decision-maker faces a series of choices among which he must select, and if he indicates his preferences for the results of the choices by weighting, then by use of the probabilities which attach to each choice, it is possible to select that choice which will maximize the value of the expected outcome for the particular decision-maker since the value of each expected outcome is the product of its probability times its preference rating.

standard grade. A grade sanctioned by government or common usage.

standardization. The establishing of widely accepted and unvarying standards (limits within which dimensions, volume, weight, age, etc. are held) in the production of merchandise.

standard loss clause. Same as *mortgage loss clause.*

standard money. The money or unit of money on which a particular country's monetary system is based.

"standard of life" line. Same as *income consumption curve.*

standard of living. The necessities, comforts, and luxuries which a given social or economic group regards as essential for its well-being.

standard parts. The design of parts for a product so that the same part may be used in many products, thus reducing the investment in inventory of parts needed and the investment in manufacturing facilities.

standard rate. In transportation, a rate established by direct routes from one point to another in relation to which rates via other routes between the same points are established.

standard stock. Same as *base stock.*

standby cost. In a classification of all costs into *programmed,* standby, and *variable,* standby costs are those that would be continued when an operation is temporarily shut down. Cf. *programmed cost* and *variable cost.*

standby line of credit. A *line of credit* which guarantees funds will be available when needed as opposed to an *open line* which can be cancelled by the creditor.

standby underwriting. The purchase pursuant to agreement by investment banking firms of the unsold portion of an issue offered by the issuing company directly to its own security holders or some other restricted group.

standstill agreements. The term used in international economics with reference to external debt payment to describe the agreement of creditors to permit temporary freezing of their credits. Cf. *moratorium.*

stare decisis. The legal doctrine that principles of cases already decided will be applied to a new case. Departure from previously applied principles are called overrulings.

state bank. A bank which receives its charter from the government of the state in which it is located. It may join the Federal Reserve System and the Federal Deposit Insurance Corporation provided it qualifies under the law and regulations.

stated value. In the case of no par shares of stock of a corporation, the stated value of a share is the dollar amount per share set aside by resolution of the board of directors or by the charter as capital and therefore unavailable for dividends until the stated value is reduced. Cf. *par value.*

static budget. A budget reflecting only one level of volume. Cf. *flexible budget.*

static equilibrium. Equilibrium such that population and its composition, stocks of capital and its composition, consumption and its composition, prices, the quantity of money, and other economic variables are constant. Cf. *dynamic equilibrium.* But static equilibrium can also be defined as simply abstracting from the time dimension. In this sense, the definitions given of *neutral equilibrium, stable equilibrium,* and *unstable equilibrium* would all satisfy static equilibrium. Still other definitions exist. Cf. *dynamic equilibrium, equilibrium of firm or industry (partial) long run, equilibrium of firm or industry (partial) short run, expectational equilibrium, general equilibrium (under monopoly or monopolistic competition), general equilibrium (under pure competition), intermediate equilibrium, market equilibrium, normal equilibrium, partial equilibrium, stable equilibrium,* and *unstable equilibrium.*

static model. In *econometrics*, a model in which no explicit consideration is given to time as a variable. Cf. *dynamic model.*

statics. In economic theory, the consideration of economic situations without regard to changes over time. Cf. *dynamics, comparative statics.*

stationary distribution. A *frequency* or *probability distribution* describing the occurrence of a particular event over a period of time in which the *parameters* of the distribution remain constant (e.g. the *mean* and *standard deviation*). Hence there is no seasonal or secular trend in the distribution.

stationary state. In economic theory, an economy in which economic factors are assumed not to change independently but only as the result of an assumed change in one of the factors. In particular, population is constant in numbers and composition, the rates of production and consumption of commodities are constant, prices are constant and there is no net saving or capital accumulation.

station-order car. In transportation, a car loaded by a shipper with less-than-carload lots destined to different points along the same route and loaded in the order of destinations. There is no handling at the terminal points by the carrier.

statism. Same as *controlled economy.*

statistic. A value computed from a sample; often misused in the plural as a synonym for figures or numbers.

statistical inference. That group of techniques centered in probability; thus the *normal* and other distributions, the chi-square test, etc. used in sampling and hypothesis testing.

statute law. A rule governing the conduct of persons established by the legislature and stated in a code.

statute of frauds. Originally enacted in England in 1677 and now enforced in all our states substantially as passed in England. It should be called a statute requiring written evidence in the proof of certain classes of contracts where the opposite party insists on that sort of proof. Contracts most commonly falling in this class are contracts covering: (1) real estate, (2) guarantees, (3) mutual promises to marry, (4) executor's contracts, (5) contracts requiring more than a year to perform, and (6) contracts for more than a specified amount (usually from $50 to $500) unless there is part performance.

statutes at large. In law, the statutes or laws as actually passed by the legislature; distinguished from the collection of laws appearing in compilations.

statutes of limitations. Laws which make rights legally unenforceable after a certain number of years on the ground that the party waited too long. The length of time that a right can endure varies in the statutes dependent upon the type of right it is.

statutory merger. A merger or combination of two businesses pursuant to the statute of the state of incorporation under which one company survives and the other is absorbed. If a new company replaces the two merging companies, this is called a *consolidation.*

stay of execution. In law, the delay in putting a judgment into effect pending an appeal. The mere taking of an appeal does not work a stay of execution, which may be granted by the lower court subject to conditions such as the posting of a bond.

steady state model. The condition of a system in which behavior has settled down so that the operating characteristics can be described by a *stationary distribution.* Distinguish *transient state model.*

step-by-step financing. Any system, particularly leases, by which a firm enters a temporary commitment contemporaneously with acquiring an asset rather than making financial commitments in advance of acquiring the asset.

step meter rate. In public utilities, a constant charge per unit of service within a step or range of quantity, with another rate applicable to the next range, and so on.

step-rate premium insurance. Life insurance providing for a premium that may increase or decrease periodically during the life of the policy.

step rate schedule. In public utilities, a form of the *block meter rate system.* The price is uniform for each unit of service but the uniform price is reduced as the buyer's purchases increase. At the point where the price changes there is a short range of "free" service. For example, 7¢/100 for 100 or less units, 6¢/100 for 0 to 200 units, etc. Cf. *block meter rate.*

sterilizing gold. A country "sterilizes" gold when its central monetary authority purchases the gold coming into the country but to prevent the rise in prices which would occur under the ordinary workings of the gold standard, the monetary authority refuses to let the gold increase its monetary circulation. Specifically, in the U.S., the purchase of gold by the Treasury but refusal to issue gold certificates covering the gold.

sterling area. An association of countries involving trade preferences between the members and pooling of their holdings of certain currencies, particularly American dollars, for maximum mutual benefit. The group was formed in 1939 upon the opening of World War II and included Egypt, Eire, Iceland, Iran, and the entire British Empire with the dominions (except Canada), all under British leadership.

sterling bloc. Those countries whose trade is heavily with England and whose monetary program and currencies were kept at parity with the English pound through monetary reserves deposited in London. The bloc included the Scandinavian countries, Uruguay, Bolivia, the countries of the British Empire, and to an extent Argentina and Japan. The bloc came into existence when England left the gold standard in 1931 and the bloc was replaced by the *sterling area* in 1939.

steward. Same as *union steward.*

"sticky" prices. Prices which do not change readily. The opposite is flexible prices.

stipulation. In law, an agreement either in writing or orally in open court by the parties as to some or all the facts to obviate the necessity of proving the facts.

stochastic. In statistics, a variation that is random as opposed to determined or biased.

stochastic model. A model using random variables. Cf. *nonstochastic model.*

stochastic process. A process involving some degree of assurance, but not certainty, in knowing what the outcome will be.

stock. (1) The certificates of ownership interests in a corporation. (2) The capital acquired through the sale of shares by a corporation. (3) An accumulation of raw materials, semifinished goods or goods ready for sale.

stock (corporation), types of. See the following specific terms:

active stock
assented stock
assessable stock
authorized stock
barometer stock
blank stock
bonus stock
callable preferred stock
capital stock
class A & B stock
classified common stock
common stock
convertible stock
cumulative preferred stock
debenture stock
dollar stock
donated stock
founder's stock
full paid stock
full stock
growth stock
guaranteed stock
guaranty stock
half stock

inactive stock
interim stock
letter stock
listed stock
nonassessable stock
noncumulative preferred stock
nonvoting stock
no par stock
paid up stock
par stock
participating preferred stock
penny stock
performance stock
preference stock
preferred stock
premium stock
prior preferred stock
redeemable preferred stock
treasury stock
unissued stock
unlisted stock
voting stock
watered stock

stock (inventory), types of. See the following specific terms:

anticipation stock
available stock
base stock
cycle stock
floor stock
line-balancing stock
lot-size stock
normal stock
safety stock
standard stock

stockbroker. An agent who buys or sells stocks and bonds.

stock certificate. Written evidence of the ownership of one or more shares of the capital stock of a corporation.

stock dividend. Distributing stock of a corporation as a dividend on other stock of the same corporation. If the dividend is common stock declared on common stock, the only result other than to reduce the value of each share of common and to maintain the proportionate interest of each stockholder is to transfer part of surplus to the stock account. Distinguish *stock split*.

stock exchange. (1) A place where stocks and bonds are bought and sold through brokers under definite rules and at regular hours. (2) The organization constituting the exchange.

stockholders. The holders of stock, the owners or proprietors of the corporate enterprise. Also called shareholders.

stock insurance company. An insurance company with stockholders who get the profit or suffer the loss of the insurance business rather than having the gain or loss distributed among the people insured. Cf. *mutual company insurance*.

stock jobber. An English term for *commission broker*. In England, the stock jobber sells to the public and buys from a *floor trader*.

stock repurchase agreement. An agreement by a corporation at the time the stock is issued to repurchase the stock on demand.

Particularly used in the utility field for sales to employees or customers. Also used as an incentive which allows employees to own the stock during the period of employment but requires them to resell the stock to the employer upon termination of employment.

stock option. The right to purchase shares of a corporation upon set conditions. The term "stock option" is used when the right is issued other than pro rata to all existing shareholders. When so issued to existing stockholders, the option is called a *"stock right."* Cf. *qualified stock option plan performance stock.*

stock out. The situation in which inventory has been exhausted before orders on hand are completed.

stock right. A right to purchase stock issued pro rata to existing shareholders. Sometimes issued on a "when, as, and if" basis; that is, the holder can buy the stock when it is issued, on such basis or of such kind as is issued, and if it is issued. The theoretical value of a New York right (the right that goes with one existing share) is determined by the following formula *before* the ex rights date:

$$\frac{\text{market price} - \text{subscription price}}{\text{number of rights needed to buy one share} + 1}$$

After the ex rights date drop the "1" from the formula. A Philadelphia right is the right to buy one share of the new issue and is worth the value of a New York right times the number of such rights needed to buy one new share.

stock split. The issuance of a number of shares for each share of stock now outstanding. The purpose of a stock split is to reduce the market price per share in order to make for wider trading and a larger price for the same ownership. Cf. *reverse split.*

stock split-down. Same as *reverse split.*

stock subscription. An agreement to purchase the stock of a corporation *from* the corporation:

stock transfer tax. A tax on the sale or transfer (by gift, for example) of shares of stock based on the market value at the time of transfer. Presently such a tax is levied by the federal government and by the states of Florida, New York, South Carolina and Texas.

stock warrant. In finance, an option to purchase stock from the issuer at a fixed price for a stated period. When the period is less than 30 days, the option is called a *stock right.*

stop-loss order. In finance, an order to buy (or sell) when the market price of the security is at or above (at or below in the case of selling) a stated figure called the "stop price."

stop-loss reinsurance. *Excess reinsurance* against all loss after the total of losses (or loss ratio) of an insurer's line of insurance reaches a stated figure.

stop order. An order by the Securities and Exchange Commission or a state securities agency stopping the issuance of securities until a satisfactory *registration statement* has been filed.

stoppage in transit rights. The right of an unpaid seller to repossess goods while they are in the hands of the carrier if the buyer goes insolvent.

stop payment order. An order by a depositor to his bank not to pay an issued check.

stop price. See *stop-loss order.*

store. (1) A place in which goods are sold at retail. In Great Britain known as a "shop." (2) A supply of goods stored.

store, types of. See the following specific terms:

chain store	*unit store*
department store	*variety store*
specialty store	*voluntary chain store*

store credit. Same as *book credit.*

store-door delivery. Where the public carrier picks up goods at the store and delivers them at the door of the buyer. A common feature of truck service, but only lately of railroads.

straddle. A combination of a *call* and a *put* permitting the call and the put to be exercised at the same price (if both for the same goods), which is approximately the market price. Also used generally to refer to a call in one commodity and a put in another. Cf. *spread.*

straight bill of lading. A nonnegotiable bill of lading, providing for delivery of merchandise by a carrier to the person named in the bill. Cf. *order bill of lading.*

straight letter of credit. A *letter of credit* in which the issuer (e.g., a bank) recognizes only the person named (e.g., an exporter) as authorized to draw drafts under the letter for advances to the named person for whose benefit the letter is issued.

straight life annuity. See *life annuity.*

straight life insurance. Same as *whole life insurance.*

straight-line method of depreciation. Taking the initial cost of a capital asset, deducting the expected salvage value at the time it is expected to be discarded, and spreading the difference in equal installments per unit of time over an estimated life of the asset.

straight-line rate. (1) A rate that is directly proportional to the quantity of service consumed. (2) A rate that is the same for each unit.

straight mortgage. A mortgage under which the borrower is obligated to pay interest during the term of the mortgage with the full amount of the principal to become due at the end of the mortgage term.

straight time. Distinguished from *piecework* and *overtime*. Straight time consists of the normal number of hours of work per day or per week, to which the standard rate of pay is applied.

stratified sample. Using known characteristics of the universe to guide the selection of a sample. (1) Division of the universe into groups (strata) each containing the known characteristic. (2) Selection of the percentage of items for the sample from each group which that group bears in the universe. Or if different sample sizes are taken from each strata, then weighting the results in the proportion that the group bears to the universe. Cf. *area sample, purposive sample, quota sample, random sample, systematic sample.*

street certificate. A stock certificate with a blank indorsement by an owner whose signature is guaranteed so that the stock can be transferred by delivery without the formality of transfer on the books of the corporation.

street name. The name of a broker or bank appearing on a corporate security with blank endorsement by the broker or bank. The security can then be transferred merely by delivery since the endorsement is well-known. Street name is used for convenience or to shield identity of the true owner.

street price. In securities trading, the price for a stock delivered outside the stock exchange process.

stretch-out. An increase in quantity of work required of an employee without a proportional increase in pay. Cf. *slow-down.*

strike. A cessation of work on the part of the employees for the purpose of enforcing certain demands usually concerning the terms of their continued employment. The strikers intend to hold on to their jobs while fighting for their goal.

strike, types of. See the following specific terms:

direct strike	*jurisdictional strike*
economic strike	*quickie strike*
general strike	*secondary strike*

sit-down strike *wildcat strike*
sympathetic strike

strike-breaking. The hiring of workers to take the place of strikers.

strike suit. In corporation finance, a term used to designate a law suit by a minority stockholder whose main purpose is to be bought out (at a high price) by the management in order to get rid of his objections.

striking a jury. In law, the process of elimination of prospective jurors from the panel to establish the actual jury.

striking price. With respect to a *stock warrant*, the exercise price at which the holder can call for stock.

structural equation. In *econometrics,* an equation stating the relationship between variables in an economic system. Such an equation may be a *definitional equation* or a *behavioral equation.* Cf. *adjustment equation, definitional equation, final equation, reduced form equation,* and *restraint equation.*

SUB Supplementary unemployment benefits. Amounts provided in a labor contract as additions to the *unemployment compensation* provided by law.

subcontract. A contract by which one who has agreed to perform work for another arranges with a new party for the actual performance of all or a part of the work. The party who originally contracted to do the work remains liable for its performance unless specifically released by the party for whom the work is to be done.

sublease. A lease of premises to another granted by one who himself holds the premises by lease.

submarginal land. Land which does not even pay the cost of cultivation.

suboptimization. When there is more than one objective and such objectives are interdependent, the optimization of one objective may result in a lower degree of possible realization of the other objectives which are then suboptimized.

subordinated bonds or debentures. *Bonds* or *debentures* which yield priority in liquidation to other (senior) debt of a corporation. Usually such bonds or debentures are not subordinate to general creditors but only to debt owed to a financial institution.

suboutcome. A conclusion established by analysis of a few factors when isolated from the total environment.

subpoena. A court order commanding the appearance of a person in court to testify as a witness. Unexcused failure to attend as ordered results in a contempt of court for which the penalty is a fine or imprisonment or both.

subpoena duces tecum. A *subpoena* (court order) directing the witness to bring with him certain named papers or objects.

subrogation. A legal doctrine entitling a third party to be substituted for one of the original parties to a transaction. Most commonly occurs in the field of insurance where the insurer has a right of subrogation upon paying the claim and may assert the rights of the insured. Also in the law of suretyship, where the surety has a right of subrogation upon making good for his principal.

subscribed capital. The total *capital stock* contracted for. When paid for, it becomes *paid-in capital.*

subscription contract. (1) A contract for the purchase of stock from a corporation issuing its own stock. (2) Colloquially, any agreement to purchase by a buyer.

subscription right. Same as *stock right.*

subsidiary account. An account providing the detail for a *controlling account.*

subsidiary coins. Coins of less than $1.00.

subsidiary company. A corporation controlled by another corporatio through sufficient voting stock.

subsidiary ledger. A ledger which supports a general ledger control account and contains in detail all the information which is represented by a total figure in the general ledger control account, e.g., customers' ledger, creditors' ledger, expense ledger, capital stock ledger.

subsidy. A sum of money granted by the state to assist in the establishment or support of an enterprise or program which is considered to be of some advantage to the public.

subsistence theory of wages. The theory of some classical economists (England, 1775–1840) that wages would in the long run tend to be at the level just sufficient for the working population to maintain and reproduce itself. By this was not meant the minimum physical standard of life but rather the level of wage below which families would reduce the number of children. Cf. *bargaining theory of wages, lump of labor theory of wages, marginal productivity theory of wages, residual theory of wages, wage fund theory of wages.*

substantive law. The legal rules concerning rights and duties, as opposed to adjective law which pertains to the procedures of the law.

substitutional goods. A relationship between two or more commodities such that commodity X is substitutive for commodity Y in the customer's budget if an increase in the supply of X lowers the marginal utility of Y in terms of money (i.e., the marginal rate of substitution for money decreases). Cf. *complementary goods.*

substitution effect. (1) The effect of a change in the price of a commodity upon the demand schedule for that commodity resulting from a change in the price of that good relative to other goods. Cf. *income effect.* (2) In production, the effect of a change in the price of one factor of production upon the combination of factors used because of the substitution of factors which follows.

subvention. A grant or subsidy.

succession. In law, the passage of personal property on death is called succession as distinct from the passage of real estate which is called inheritance.

succession tax. The generic term covering all forms of *estate* and *inheritance* taxes. Taxes associated with the transfer of property on the death of a person.

Suffolk bank system. A Massachusetts plan started in 1837, under which participating banks agreed to accept only the notes of such out-of-town banks as maintained a sufficient redemption account in the system. This held the notes of participating banks at par.

sui juris. Latin for "of his own right." Used to describe one who is legally competent to act.

summarizing entry. An entry in journal form written below the footings in a columnar journal showing the debits and credits to be equal.

summary account. In accounting, same as *closing account.*

summons. An order of a court to appear at a stated time and place to defend in a law suit. Unexcused failure to attend results in a decision by default against the absent party.

sum-of-the-years-digits method of depreciation. Taking the initial cost of a capital asset, deducting the expected salvage value at the time it is expected to be discarded, and spreading the difference over the life of the asset, deducting each year that fraction of this difference determined in the following way: Add the numbers of the number of years of life of the asset (thus for an asset of 4 years life, add 1, 2, 3, and 4 to get 10) and use each of these numbers as the numerator of fractions whose denominator is the sum of the digits (thus 1/10, 2/10, 3/10, 4/10). The fractions are then used in reverse order (the first year's depreciation would be 4/10).

sumptuary law. A law designed to prevent the consumption of goods considered harmful to the health or welfare of society.

sunk cost. Once an investment is made and cannot be altered it is called a sunk cost.

sunspot theory. A theory of the business cycle arguing that sunspot activity affects the weather which in turn affects agriculture and this in turn affects the entire economy.

supercession. *Obsolescence* is sometimes divided by accountants into two elements: (1) supercession: changes in the art producing more efficient machines and methods, (2) inadequacy: changes in the scale of operation causing redesigning, etc.

supernumerary income. Same as *discretionary income.*

supersedeas. In law, a writ staying the proceedings. Originally an order by a court of equity to a court of law. Now used by an appellate court in emergency situations.

superseniority. Special seniority rights given to some workers in order to prefer them over other employees. For example, placing union officers at the head of the seniority list during their term of office.

supplementary costs. Same as *fixed costs.*

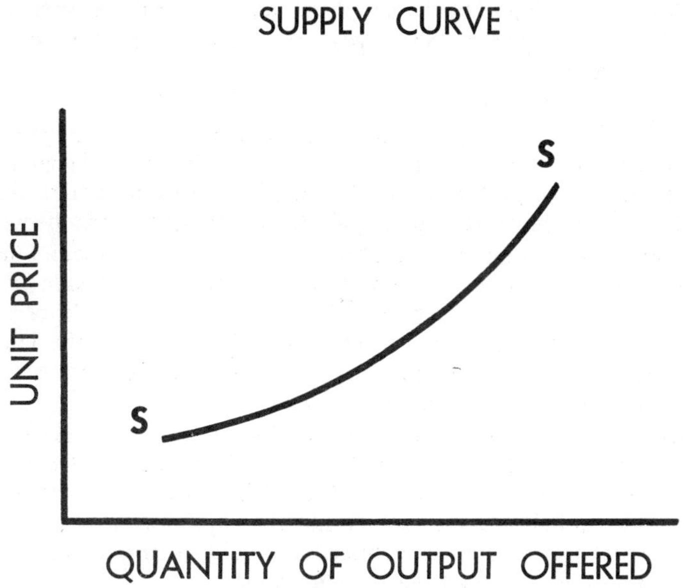

Figure 53.

supply. (1) The amount of a good that sellers are ready to sell at each specified price in a given market at a given time. Also called supply schedule. (2) Sometimes used to mean quantity forthcoming at one specified price.

supply curve. A graphical presentation of supply with dollars on the vertical axis and quantity of product on the horizontal axis. Then the curve connecting the different quantities of product that sellers will offer at different prices is a supply curve. See Figure 53 on preceding page.

supply schedule. A tabular arrangement showing the quantities of product that sellers will offer at different prices.

supply space. In anti-trust law, a concept that competition is affected not only by merging of two firms producing the same product but by mergers where the same resources such as similar marketing channels of two firms occupy the same "supply space."

support price. Used particularly in connection with the U.S. Department of Agriculture's program to maintain prices for farm produce. The support price for a particular commodity is a percentage of the *parity price* for that commodity.

suppressed inflation. The situation where prices and wages are controlled by law, and there is an increase in money demand for goods relative to the supply of goods after the economy is at full employment. Shortages are adjusted then by rationing or priorities.

supra protest. See *payment supra protest*.

surety bond. A written promise by an insurer (the surety) to reimburse the party named in the bond (the insured) against the failure of performance of obligations or duties undertaken by another party (the principal) for the benefit of the insured.

suretyship. A three-party relationship in which the principal and the surety each binds himself to perform on one side of a contract with a third party who is on the other side of the contract. As between the surety and the principal, the latter is primarily bound to perform, and only one performance is contemplated. Cf. *guarantee, indemnity*.

surplus. (1) In a financial statement the excess of assets over creditor liabilities and capital stock. When accumulated from profits it is called earned surplus. If from other sources, it is called capital surplus. Sometimes the capital surplus account is broken down into categories, e.g., paid-in surplus, revaluation surplus, etc. (2) See *surplus value*.

surplus, types of. See the following specific terms:

acquired surplus	*donated surplus*
appraised surplus	*earned surplus*
appreciation surplus	*paid-in surplus*
appropriated surplus	*producer's surplus*
capital surplus	*recapitalization surplus*
consumer's surplus	*reorganization surplus*
divisible surplus	*reserved surplus*

surplus reinsurance. *Reinsurance* by the *reinsurer* of losses above a stated amount (which is born by the *insurer),* with the reinsurer participating in such losses on a share basis. Cf. *share reinsurance.*

surplus reserve. An amount of surplus or net worth set up as a reserve to indicate it is considered not available for withdrawal in dividends.

surplus value. (1) In speaking of the distribution under Marxian theory of the revenue of an enterprise, all the amounts paid except payments to labor are called surplus value. (2) In economics other than Marxian theory, (a) any payment to a *factor of production* in excess of what is needed to draw it into production, or (b) the excess of what a consumer would be willing to pay for a good over what the market price is, and this is called *consumer's surplus,* or (c) the excess which a producer gets when selling a good at market price over what he would be willing to sell for if the price were at the lowest point at which he would sell, and this is called *producer's surplus.*

surrender charge. Used primarily in insurance, but also in general finance, the charge exacted for unscheduled termination of insurance or some financial arrangement.

surrender value. In life insurance it consists of the amount of money which the insurance company will pay to the policyholder upon surrender of his policy before death.

surrogate. In law, a deputy or division of the court of *equity.* Frequently, this title is applied to a *probate court.*

surtax. A tax levied in addition to another tax (the latter usually called the normal tax). The surtax is often graduated or progressive whereas the normal tax is often proportional.

survey agent. Same as *application agent.*

survivorship annuity. An annuity which provides for payments to a beneficiary after the death of the annuitant. There are different types, e.g., *cash refund.*

survivor technique. On the premise that the more efficient firms survive, a study of the growth or decline of various sized firms in an industry will yield a cost input pattern tracing the *economy of scale* of an industry.

suspense account. An account containing items whose final resolution is doubtful.

sweated industries. Industries in which wages are low and hours are long. See *sweating system.*

sweating system. A term used to describe a method of treating employees by taking advantage of their necessities to force them to the limit of their endurance and ability for the lowest possible wage.

Swedish budget. A governmental budget which is balanced over a period of years rather than for each particular year.

swing service. In transportation, the collection of cars from various assembly points and movement to terminal concentration points.

swing shift. (1) The usual term for the eight-hour shift beginning about four o'clock in the afternoon and running to midnight. (2) Originally the schedule of hours in a company operating continuously seven days a week, in which the hours and days of work vary each week on a three-week cycle to cover time allowed regular shifts as time off. Cf. *day shift, graveyard shift.*

switch trade. On a commodity exchange, if a broker cannot execute an order for a particular month but executes it for another month and reports the trade executed as ordered, it is a switch trade and the broker is liable to his principal for any profit so made.

symmetallism. A monetary standard under which a government buys and sells gold and silver in fixed proportions in order to maintain the weighted average price of gold and silver constant.

symmetry. A relationship is symmetric if in relating one thing to another, the second similarly relates to the first as is true of "is married to" in a monogamous society.

sympathetic strike. When workers with no direct grievance against their own employers go on a strike in order to support the strike of some allied union. E.g., if steam fitters, sheet metal workers, and other building trade craftsmen with no grievance of their own join in a strike to help the plumbers who are striking for a wage increase.

syndicalism. From "syndicate," meaning "union." An economic system which would place the control of all industries in the hands of the workers of each specific firm or industry.

syndicate. (1) Any combination of persons (individuals or corporations) to achieve a common business purpose. Acts directed to this purpose impose unlimited liability on each of the participants. (2) Especially used to describe those united in the sale of a particular stock or bond issue. Cf. *divided syndicate, undivided syndicate.*

synergism. Particularly in *mergers*, the concept that the combination of two companies may produce more earnings or less risk than the total of the two separate companies. Similarly for combination of other economic parts such as *product lines.*

systematic error. (1) In statistics, an error that is in some sense biased as distinguished from a *random error.* Thus the distribution of items has a mean or other acceptable measure located away from zero. Cf. *random error, standard error.* (2) In personnel management, the measure of difference (or error) by individual raters of individual traits from the mean of all raters. The formula sums the deviations of each rater (observing the signs) from the mean and divides by the number of persons rated.

systematic risk. The tendency of the return and price of an investment to move with the general market. Hence, *nondiversifiable risk.* Cf. *unsystematic risk.*

systematic sample. Arranging a population in some objective order and then taking every nth item. Cf. *area sample, purpose sample, quota sample, random sample, stratified sample.*

TAB Tax anticipation bill. Same as tax anticipation certificate except sold at a discount and bears no interest.

tableau economique. A flow-chart presentation of the flow of income, used by many members of the *physiocrat school.* Income-receiving groups are divided into 3 categories: (1) the productive class (agriculture and mining), (2) the owning class (property owners), and (3) the sterile class (merchants, manufacturers and servants). The distribution of the income created by the first class to the other two classes is shown as well as the return of this income to the first class through purchases of its output, the produit net.

tacking. In law, the addition of a more recent claim to an earlier one to lengthen the period claimed under *adverse possession.* Also used in other areas of law.

Taft-Hartley Act of 1947. An amendment to *National Labor Relations Act of 1935* based on the theory of equalizing the bargaining power of management with that of labor. Principal provisions: (1) specification of unfair labor practices by labor, (2) granting individual workers the right to prosecute for unfair labor practices by union or company officials, (3) anti-Communist provisions, (4) restriction of the closed shop, (5) prohibition of *secondary boycott*. Cf. *hot cargo*.

take-home pay. The actual amount of wages which the worker receives after all deductions, including taxes.

tale quale. Latin for "in such shape as it is." Used in commodity transactions.

talisman. A juror summoned to fill out a jury when the regular panel is exhausted.

tangible asset. (1) In law and taxation, an asset that has physical, material substance. (2) In accounting and finance in a broader sense to include securities, notes, and claims but not good-will, patents, copyrights, trade-marks, secret processes, and like items, which are considered intangibles.

tangible assets turnover. *Net sales* divided by *tangible assets.*

tangible net worth. The *net wotrh* of a business excluding such assets as good will and patents in calculating.

tangible personal property. Movable wealth, such as household furniture, farm machinery, automobiles, farm animals, jewelry, etc.

tap line. In transportation, a railroad covering a short distance, usually owned by the industries which it serves and "tapping" the main line of a carrier.

tare weight. The weight of a container and the material for packing, or the weight of a vehicle exclusive of contents.

target pricing. A policy of pricing products so as to earn a "target" rate of return on the capital invested in the production and sale of the goods.

tariff. (1) A customs duty or tax laid on goods as they enter (or leave) a country. The United States Constitution forbids duties on exports and all duties on commerce between states. Tariff duties are either specific, i.e., according to the number or bulk of the items, or ad valorem, i.e., according to the value of the goods. (2) A schedule of transportation rates and rules affecting the application of rates for specific schedules. Cf. *rates,* e.g., for class tariff, cf. *class rates*.

tariff, types of. See the following specific terms:

ad valorem tariff *anti-dumping tariff*

compensating tariff
compound tariff
countervailing tariff
differential tariff
flexible tariff
mixed tariff
multiple tariff
preferential tariff
protective tariff
revenue tariff
sectional tariff
specific tariff

tariff rate. In insurance, the rate established by a *rating bureau.*

tariff war. The use of tariffs to further the competitive position of a country particularly in response to similar conduct by another country.

tax. A compulsory payment to the government to defray the expenses which it has incurred in performing services for the common benefit. Three characteristics are present in a tax: (1) compulsion, (2) apportionment without close reference to individual benefit, (3) use of the proceeds for the public welfare.

tax, types of. See the following specific terms:

ad valorem tax
apportioned tax
capital gains tax
capital stock tax
capitation tax
classified tax
consumption tax
death tax
degressive tax
direct tax
double tax
estate tax
excess profits tax
excise tax
forward shifting tax
general property tax
general sales tax
gift tax
graded tax
graduated tax
gross receipts tax
head tax
hidden tax
income tax
indirect tax
indirect business tax
indirect tax
inheritance tax
in lieu tax
nuisance tax
payroll tax
poll tax
presumptive tax
processing tax
progressive tax
property tax
real estate tax
regressive tax
sales tax
security issue tax
severance tax
single tax
social security tax
specific commodity sales tax
stock transfer tax
succession tax
surtax
transfer tax
turnover tax
undistributed profits tax
use tax
withholding tax
yield tax

tax abatement. The reduction of a tax because the tax was improperly levied or because of a legislative directive.

tax amortization. Cf. *tax capitalization.*

tax anticipation certificate. Certificates bearing interest, bought by the people from the government, to be held to maturity and applied to tax payment.

tax anticipation note. Same as *tax anticipation certificate.*

tax anticipation warrant. Same as *tax anticipation certificate.*

tax assessment. The valuation placed upon property in order to levy a tax on it is called the assessed valuation. Applying the tax rate to this valuation produces the tax.

tax assessor. A public official who assesses property values, i.e., places an official valuation on wealth or property rights for the purpose of levying a tax against them, or establishes taxable income in the case of the income tax.

taxation of costs. In law, the determination of the amount of costs to which the prevailing party in a lawsuit is entitled.

tax avoidance. A legal method of avoiding a tax. Distinguish *tax evasion* which is illegal avoidance.

tax base. The value or unit to which the tax rate is applied to determine the tax due. In property taxes, the base is the assessed valuation. In income tax, the base is net taxable income.

tax bond. Same as *tax anticipation certificate.*

tax capitalization. To the extent that a tax is not shifted, it can be capitalized at an assumed rate of interest by dividing the tax (or change in tax) by the rate of interest and subtracting this amount from the value of the asset before the tax change. Most commonly done with the property tax.

tax carryback and carryover. A provision which is often in American corporation income and excess profits taxes to the effect that losses (or in the case of an excess profits tax, unused credits) can be carried over to apply against a preceding or following year's income. The effect is to level income over the years for tax purposes.

tax commission. An administrative body administering a tax. With respect to property taxes the principal functions are: (1) to equalize local assessments throughout the state, (2) to assess certain classes of corporate property, and (3) to supervise the original assessment if it is being made by local officials. Similar functions are performed with respect to income taxes.

Tax Court of the U.S. A special Federal court which hears appeals from the decisions of the Bureau of Internal Revenue about almost all federal taxes (except tariffs). Formerly called the U.S. Board of Tax Appeals. Appeals from this court go to the U.S. Court of Appeals.

tax credit. Same as *tax offset.*

tax deed. In the event of a taxpayer's default in the payment of real estate taxes, a tax warrant covering the right to collect the taxes is sold. After a stated time period, the holder of the tax warrant can apply for a tax deed from the taxing governmental unit granting ownership of the real estate to the holder of the tax warrant upon surrender of the tax warrant.

tax effect. Technically speaking the tax effect is the result in *output* change caused by the tax change. The result in *price* change is called incidence.

tax equivalent. The payment by a municipally (or federally) owned utility made to other units of government in lieu of taxes because of tax exemption of the governmentally owned utility.

tax evasion. An illegal method of avoiding a tax. Distinguish *tax avoidance.*

tax exemption. (1) Total exemption or freedom from tax such as is granted educational, charitable, religious, and similar non-profit organizations. (2) Partial exemption or freedom from tax such as the $600 exemption per person in the federal income tax.

tax-exempt securities. The interest on the securities of state and local governments is presently exempt from federal income tax. *Capital gains* on such securities are not so exempt. However, when such securities are initially sold at a discount, such discount is considered tax free interest.

tax farming. A practice dating from ancient times of the sale by the government of its tax claims to private individuals who either pay the government less than the face of the claims or exact more than the face of the claim from the taxpayer.

tax-free exchange. Such an exchange of one good for another as is recognized by the income tax law to involve no present recognition for tax purposes. The new good assumes the tax basis of the old good. As soon as some money (the "boot") is involved in the transaction there is at least partial recognition of taxability.

tax haven corporation. Any corporation used to avoid or reduce income taxes, particularly, a foreign corporation whose income may not be taxed to its U.S. stockholders until paid over to them as dividends.

tax impact. The immediate obligation of a tax or the immediate effect of the tax.

tax incidence. (1) In general, the final resting place of a tax after all shifting has occurred. (2) Technically speaking, the tax incidence is the *price* change resulting from a tax change. The *output* change resulting from a tax change is the tax effect.

tax levy. (1) In law, the formal order for tax payment upon the assessed base. (2) In property taxes, the determination of the total revenue which is to be realized by the tax.

tax limit. A constitutional or statutory limit placed on the kind of tax or maximum tax rate that a political subdivision can impose.

tax loophole. An obvious discrimination or exemption from tax.

tax offset. The tax offset is a form of tax cancellation or exemption. A tax is levied, but it is remitted in whole or in part usually on the basis of another tax paid.

tax pyramiding. The situation in which a tax imposed on one is added to his cost and the customary mark-up is applied to this total. Thus a *mark-up* is taken on the tax.

tax rate. The ratio of the tax to the tax base. The rate to be applied to the assessed value to determine the amount of tax.

tax roll. A list of taxpayers with a statement opposite each name of the total assessment and the amount of tax due on this assessment.

tax sale. The selling of the taxpayer's property to collect delinquent taxes from the proceeds of the sale.

tax selling. In the stock market, the phenomenon of deliberate selling of securities which have been held six months or more and presently have a lower market value than their cost (or other basis) to the taxpayer for the purpose of offsetting this capital loss against other capital gains and thus reducing income tax liability.

tax sharing. The situation in which one political unit (often a state) levies and collects a tax whose proceeds are then shared in part with other political units (such as counties or cities) under a formula set by statute.

tax shield. In *capital budgeting*, some expenditures that are deductible for income tax purposes (such as start-up costs for a new plant) are recognized as reducing (shielding against) income taxes that otherwise would be due. Depreciation acts similarly.

tax shifting. The process of passing the tax from the one who pays the tax to a person forward such as to the one who buys or uses the taxed article or service, e.g., adding the gasoline tax to the price of the gasoline or the admissions tax to the price of admissions. A tax may also be shifted backward to the producer of the taxed good in the form of a lower revenue after taxes for the product or service purchased. Distinguish *tax effect.*

tax, theories of. See the following specific terms:

ability to pay tax theory	*diffusion tax theory*
benefit tax theory	*sacrifice tax theory*

tax title. The ownership of property by purchase from the government which has gotten it by foreclosure from a defaulting taxpayer.

tax warrant. In the event of a taxpayer's default in the payment of real estate taxes, a tax warrant covering the right to collect the taxes is sold on a bidding basis. In this way, the governmental unit increases its immediate collections. Ultimately the unpaid holder of the tax warrants can get a *tax deed* to the property whose taxes are delinquent.

Taylor differential piece rate plan. An incentive wage plan providing a lower piece rate for substandard work and a higher piece rate for work beyond the standard. Cf. *Bedaux, Emerson, Gantt, Halsey, Merrick,* and *Rowan plans.*

Taylorism. Named after F. W. Taylor, a term applied to the scientific management of labor. For example, efficient machinery and plant layout, time and motion studies, etc.

"t" curve. The adaptation of the *Gaussian curve* or *normal distribution* to small samples. A method through the use of degrees of freedom for determination of the significance of a difference between two averages. For example, splitting a sample into men and women, computing their separate averages, and from the number in the sample determining the probability that the difference in averages is significant or due to chance. Cf. *Gibrat distribution, log normal distribution, normal distribution, Pareto distribution, Poisson distribution,* and *Yule distribution.* See *t value.*

team track. In transportation, a track on which cars are placed for use by the public in loading and unloading when the shipper lacks his own spur.

technocracy. A term devised in the 1930's for the argument that the benefits of labor-saving inventions were not passed on to consumers and insufficient purchasing power resulted.

technological unemployment. Unemployment caused by a change or accumulation of changes in methods of production.

temporary admission. A system of admitting goods to a country for later export, and under specified conditions no duty is applied.

temporary injunction. A court order restraining conduct until a hearing can be had on whether the injunction should be made permanent. One seeking a temporary injunction must usually furnish a bond to cover any damage that might result if it appears at the hearing that he is not entitled to the injunction.

tenancy (as to duration). A lease or right to occupy (1) for years: i.e., for a definite period of time, e.g., 2 years 5 months; (2) at will: i.e., terminable at any time by the landlord; (3) at sufferance: i.e., where the tenant holds over after a lease expires; or (4) for life: i.e., the right to occupy for one's life.

tenancy by the entirety. Ownership as husband and wife. In most states today, equated by statute to *joint tenancy*.

tenancy in common. Ownership by two or more people of property in common with the interest of the one dying passing to his heirs and not to his cotenants. Cf. *joint tenancy*.

tender. In law, the offer of: money in payment or delivery of a deed or goods. In the event tender is unjustiably refused, a mortgage is discharged and interest ceases from that date in the case of a loan.

tender offer. In finance, an offer to purchase shares made by one company direct to the stockholders of another company, with a view to acquiring control of the second company. Used in an effort to go around the management of the second company which is resisting acquisition.

tenement. In law, anything of permanent nature with regard to land or its income. Cf. *hereditaments*.

tenendum clause. In real estate law, a clause in a *deed* no longer having meaning but originally describing the tenure by which the land was held.

ten-forty. A U.S. government bond redeemable at the option of the U.S. after ten years and payable after forty years. Cf. *five-twenty*.

tenor. In finance, the period of time between inception and maturity of an obligation.

term bond. A bond of an issue in which all the bonds have a single maturity. Cf. *serial bond*.

terminal bond. A bond issued to finance the construction of a rail, truck, or air terminal.

terminal reserve. The reserve of an insurance policy at the end of the policy year. Cf. *initial reserve, mean reserve.*

terminal wage. Same as *dismissal pay.*

termination of offer. An offer can be ended by acceptance, counteroffer, expiration of time, insanity, or death of the offeror or offeree, refusal to accept, or revocation of the offer.

term insurance. Insurance which runs for a stated period of time (the term). Most frequently applied to that type of life insurance which runs for a fixed period only rather than until death. Term insurance has no cash surrender value.

term loan. A loan to a business for a term, usually one to ten years, and usually repayable in installments.

term of court. In law, a court sits for a number of terms or periods per year. Important because of the rule restricting the judge as to changing the judgment after the term in which it was entered, except for statutory reasons.

terms of trade. The relation of export and import prices. Terms of trade become most favorable if the prices of imported goods fall in relation to prices of exported goods. This is also called the barter terms of trade. The "double factoral terms of trade" is the ratio between the quantities of the productive factors in the two countries necessary to produce quantities of product of equal value in foreign trade.

testament. Same as *will.*

testamentary capacity. In law, the ability of a person to make a will. This requires the minimum statutory age and sufficient mental capacity to know one's property and to judge the various alternative dispositions available.

testamentary trust. A trust created by a decedent in his will. Cf. *inter vivos trust.*

testator. A person who has died leaving a will.

t.f. Till-forbid. In advertising, an instruction to continue placing an advertisement in each issue of a publication until countermanded.

Theil's statistic. A test of the goodness of fit of a forecast to the actual value. Computed as $U^2 = \Sigma(P-A)^2/\Sigma A^2$ in which P is the predicted percentage change from the prior actual and A is the actual percentage change from the prior actual value. U can vary from zero for a perfect forecast to 1 and more for a poor forecast.

Thelusson Act. See *rule against unreasonable accumulations.*

thin corporation. In income taxes, a thin corporation is one with little equity relative to debt in an effort to take out as deductible interest what is really a dividend where the debt and equity are held in the same proportion by each individual holder.

thin market. Same as *narrow market.*

third market. In securities, the purchase and sale of securities listed on a stock exchange without routing the transaction through the exchange. Called "off board" trading.

third-party beneficiary. See *beneficiary.*

three-D policy. A surety and fidelity insurance policy covering losses due to dishonesty, disappearance and destruction.

three-position promotion plan. A personnel system such that the worker is learning a higher level job while doing his present job, and teaching another worker on a lower level the job from which he himself was promoted.

threshold worker. A worker with no job experience.

through bill of lading. A *bill of lading* for a shipment to be handled by more than one carrier en route to its destination.

through rate. In transportation, the rate applicable from the point of origin to the destination of freight. It may be either a *joint rate* or a combination of two or more rates.

tied loan. Used particularly with reference to a foreign loan whose proceeds are to be applied to purchases in the lending country.

tie-in sale. See *tying contract.*

tight money. Same as *dear money.*

time-adjusted rate of return. That rate of discount which equates the *present value* of expected cash inflows from a project to the present value of expected cash outflows of that project.

time and motion study. A study of the operations performed on a given job and the timing of each operation. Used for two purposes: (1) to improve the way the job is done, or (2) to establish a standard amount of work per hour in connection with a *piecework* system of wages.

time bargain. In finance, a firm contract to deliver securities at a set future date. Not an option.

time bill. A bill of exchange payable at a future date rather than immediately.

time deposit. A bank deposit which is subject to at least thirty days notice before withdrawal. Thirty days notice is the dividing line between time and demand deposits used by the Federal Reserve System.

time draft. A draft that is payable a certain number of days after sight or after date. Thirty, sixty, ninety days are common time limits.

TIME INDIFFERENCE CURVE

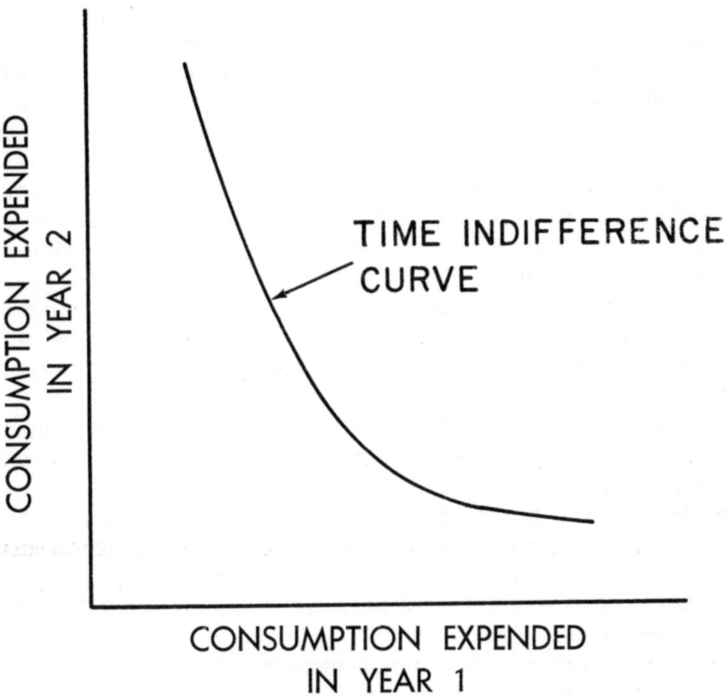

Figure 54.

time indifference curve. Using an *indifference map* with consumption expenditure in year 1 on the x axis and consumption expenditure in year 2 on the y axis, a time indifference curve traces all the combinations of consumption expenditures in the two years that give equal satisfaction. The slope of the time indifference curve is the rate of time substitution.

time loan. A loan for a stated period of time. Distinguish *call loan.*

time preference theory of interest. An explanation of interest as the price people are willing to pay for immediate possession of goods as opposed to future possession. Cf. *abstinence theory of interest, agio theory of interest, liquidity preference theory of interest, loanable funds theory of interest,* and *marginal productivity theory of interest.*

time reversal test. In statistics, a method of testing the mathematical validity of an index number. The base period data are changed in identification to the later period and the later period's data are treated as the base period's. Then if the index number computed for the former base period is multiplied by the index number originally computed and the result is unity, the test is met. The simple aggregate index number, the geometric average of relatives, and the ideal index number meet this test. Cf. *factor reversal test.*

time series. Data with time as the independent variable and some other factor as the dependent variable, as contrasted to a *frequency distribution* in which data is presented without regard to the time factor.

time series analysis. The study of *time series* in order to project the trend. Typically seasonal and cyclical patterns are removed, leaving the trend and random effects. Cf. *cross section data.*

time series data. Observations of the values of economic variables over a series of successive time intervals. Cf. *cross section data.*

times interest and preferred dividend earned. A common measure of the "earnings protection" which preferred stock has. The figure is computed by dividing the net earnings per year (after taxes) by the sum of the interest and preferred dividend requirements.

times interest earned. A common measure of the "earnings protection" which a bond has. (1) The number of times the interest requirement of a business was earned in a period and hence a measure of the degree of safety enjoyed by the owner of the debt. Computed as the amount available to pay interest to all creditors divided by the interest requirements of all debts with equal or prior standing. (2) An alternate method (called the "prior deductions" basis) is available where there are debts with priority. This is to take the total amount available for all interest charges, deduct the interest charges of debts having priority, and divide the remainder by the interest requirements of the junior debt to get the times interest earned for the junior debt. The first method is preferred.

In addition to these two methods, each method can use either (1) the amount available to pay interest before income taxes or (2) the amount available to pay interest after income taxes. As long as interest is deductible in determining income taxes, the former is the preferred method.

times preferred dividend earned. A common measure of "earnings protection" which preferred stock has. The figure is computed by dividing the net earnings per year (after taxes, interest, and any prior dividends) by the preferred dividend requirements of that issue for that year. Cf. (1) as to bonds, *times interest earned,* (2) as to common stock, *earnings per share.*

time wages or time work. Wages paid by the hour, day, week, month, or year.

title. Evidence of ownership of anything of value. Property and rights of great social importance require written evidence of title, such as a deed to land, or a stock certificate for ownership in a corporation.

title insurance. See *guaranty of title.*

TNEC Temporary National Economic Committee. A committee created by Congress in 1938 to study monopoly and concentration of economic power. The extensive publications of the results of hearings by this committee constitute important references.

to arrive price. In foreign trade, the price quoted by a seller for goods already in transit.

token money. Coins circulating at a value above the metal in the coin, such as cents, nickles, and dimes in the United States.

token payment. (1) Same as *earnest money.* (2) The payment of a small part of a debt.

tolerance. The limit in variance of size or quality permitted in a specification for a product.

ton mile. In transportation, a unit of measurement: one ton moved one mile.

tonnage. See *dead weight tonnage, gross tonnage, net tonnage.*

tontine. Any scheme in which payments are made by a large number of persons with eventual distribution to those who survive after a time interval.

Torrens system. A system used in some states for the issuance of title certificates (covering the ownership of land) by the state instead of the *guaranty of title* by a title insurance company. Cf. *guaranty of title.*

tort. An injury to the person, property, or right of another not arising out of a contract. In order for legal liability to follow, the injury must have violated the legal duty owed to another. Examples of torts are: slander, libel, assault, trespass on the property of another, etc. Cf. *business tort.*

tortfeasor. In law, a person who has committed a *tort.*

total asset turnover. The ratio obtained by dividing total assets into sales but more correctly, dividing total *operating assets* into sales since funds devoted to outside investments do not affect sales but produce an independent income.

total cost curve. With total costs on the *y* axis and quantity of output produced on the *x* axis, the total cost curve starts at the origin and traces the total costs of producing different quantities of output. The curve will start on the *y* axis above the origin by the amount of *fixed costs* and proceed as a straight line at an angle upward if variable unit costs are constant but ultimately the slope will increase as the maximum efficiency volume is passed for a given plant.

totalitarian. Refers to governments in which state control has been extended to practically every phase of human existence.

total outlay curve. Same as *budget line.*

total output curve. Holding some *factors of production* fixed (such as plant size) and permitting one or more factors of production to vary in physical units (such as labor and materials), the total output curve traces the quantities of output in physical units that result as the number of units of the variable factor are varied. With units of output on the *y* axis and units of the variable factor on the *x* axis, the total output curve will rise at a faster rate, reach a maximum, and then descend because of, first, the less efficient use, then efficient use, and finally inefficient use of the fixed factor.

total revenue curve. With total revenue on the *y* axis and quantity of units of the good sold on the *x* axis, the total revenue starts at the origin and traces the total receipts from different quantities of the good sold. If the price received per unit sold is constant, the total revenue curve will be a straight line starting at the origin and rising at an angle. If the price received for successively larger quantities is lower, the curve will taper away from the *y* axis.

total unit cost. Same as *average cost.*

Totten trust. A *trust* of a savings account created simply by the deposit of money for the benefit of another. Named Totten after the New York court decision holding such action sufficient to constitute a *trust.*

township. In surveys of U.S. public lands, an approximately square area of land consisting of 36 sections with each section containing 640 acres.

trackage right. A right obtained by one carrier to operate its trains over the tracks of another carrier.

tract book. A book containing *plats* of the land parcels in given areas.

trade acceptance. A *trade bill* which has been signed by the buyer to show his obligation to make payment as stated in the bill of exchange.

trade association. An association of dealers or manufacturers engaged in a particular trade for interchange of information, establishment of standards, and other activities of common interest to the members. The Writing Paper Manufacturers' Association was the first. Chambers of Commerce are in a sense trade associations although more general in character.

trade bill. A *bill of exchange* drawn by the seller of goods on the buyer and covering payment of the goods.

trade credit. Same as *book credit.*

trade cycle. The English term for *business cycle.*

trade discounts. Discounts allowed a middleman from the list price (the price the producer wants the ultimate customer to pay) to cover the middleman's margin (his costs plus his profit).

trade dollar. A special silver coin minted by the United States from 1873 to 1885 with more silver content than the standard silver dollar and intended for trade with the Orient.

trade-mark. A distinctive device or imprint used by a person to identify his products. Trade-marks can be registered under U.S. law and also in many individual states. In the U.S., the first person to use a trade-mark in a given area (geographical or product-wise) normally has the exclusive right to it regardless of who first registers it. Canadian and Latin-American law usually give exclusive right to the first registrant.

trader. One who buys or sells for his own account for a short-term profit.

trade terms. The conditions governing the sale of property such as the time payment is due, any discounts for prepayment, when risk of loss passes from seller to buyer, the point at which ownership passes, who pays the freight, etc.

trade union. (1) Generally used in the same sense as labor union. (2) More narrowly, used in the same sense as craft union.

trading area. The physical area from which trade is drawn to a retail store or retail shopping district, or to a wholesaling establishment or wholesaling center.

trading difference. In finance, the fraction of a point in price charged for shares bought or sold in *odd lots.*

trading down. The action by a merchandiser in buying and selling cheaper goods in an effort to increase volume.

trading limit. (1) Prices above or below which trading is not permitted during any one day. (2) The maximum quantity of commodity futures which may be purchased or sold by one person or on any one trading day. Both are fixed by the Commodity Exchange Commission.

trading on margin. See *margin.*

trading on the equity. See *leverage factor.*

trading up. The action by a merchandiser in handling goods of higher price and quality in an effort to increase the profit margin.

train mile. In transportation, a unit of measurement: the movement of one train of cars one mile. Cf. *car mile.*

tramp steamer. A ship not operating on a regular route but whose ports of call are determined by what cargo it picks up from one port to the next.

transactions demand for money. The demand for money originating with the need for cash balances to carry on the day-to-day volume of business. Cf. *precautionary demand for money, speculative demand for money.*

transactions equation. See *Fisher equation.*

transactions tax. A tax on turnover; a sales tax on both retail and wholesale sales.

transaction velocity of money. The ratio of the total of all money transactions in a time period to the quantity of money. Distinguish *income velocity of money.*

transferability. The ability to transfer ownership or title. Distinguish from *negotiability.* Transferability can be restricted by so stating in a contract. The usual word is nonassignable. Negotiability can also be restricted by stating *nonnegotiable.* This does not prevent transfer by assignment but cuts off the benefits of negotiability which include the transferee's legal right to deny certain defenses such as fraudulent inducement.

transfer agent. The one designated to keep the record of stocks and bonds of a corporation. Often the original of this record is not kept by the corporation but by an independent specialist in these matters such as a bank, trust company or other agent.

transfer book. See *closing of transfer book.*

transfer income. Income received without service rendered by the person receiving it. The major transfer incomes are old age pensions, unemployment relief, and social security. Government bond interest gets special treatment under this term.

transfer in contemplation of death. To prevent avoidance of death taxes by transfers when death is likely, the rule of transfer in contemplation of death taxes such a transfer as if it were made at death.

transfer journal. A book kept by a corporation to show stock certificates issued, transferred, and cancelled.

transfer payments. Large payments of an abnormal character by one country to another, e.g., reparation payments, which involve no increase in output.

transfer price. The price charged by one unit of a business when it supplies a product or service to another part of that business.

transfer tax. See *stock transfer tax.*

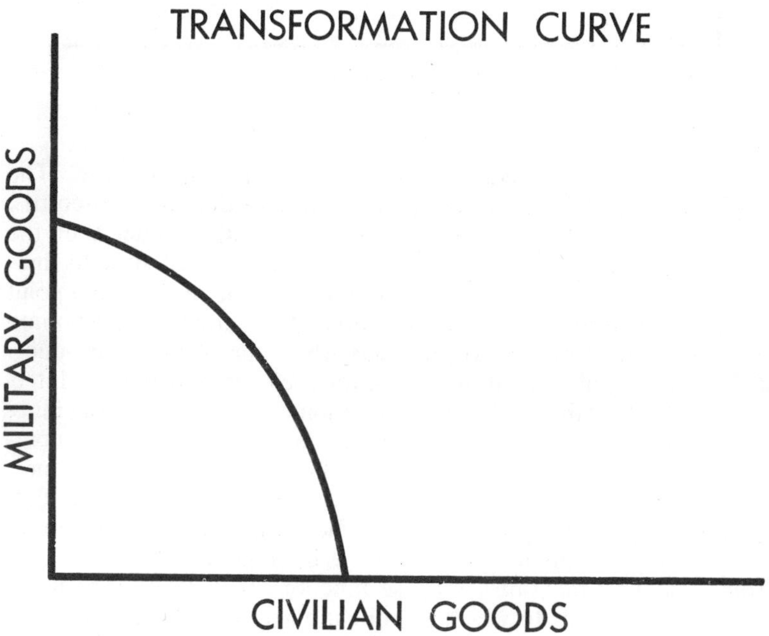

Figure 55.

transformation curve. (1) As applied to an economy, using a graph with military goods on the y axis and civilian goods on the x axis, the transformation curve traces all the combinations

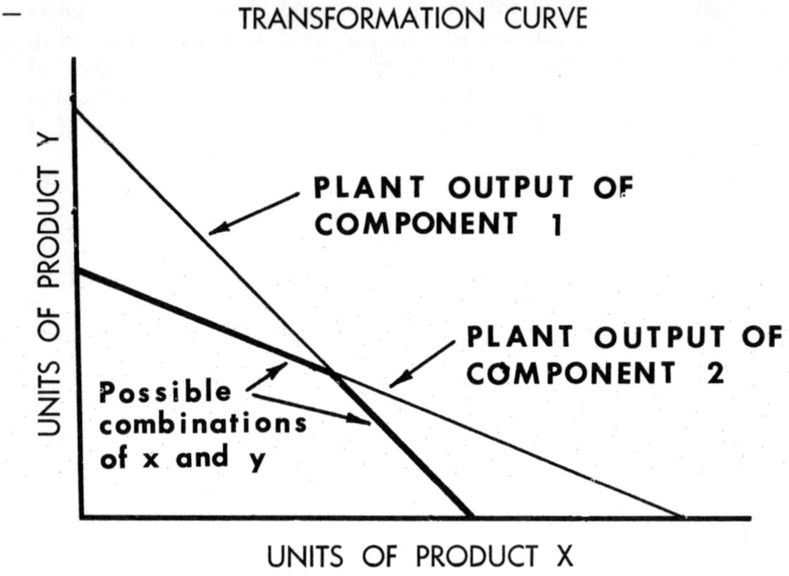

Figure 56.

of both types of goods which the economy can produce. The curve is concave to the origin because of diminishing returns. (2) As applied to a firm, using a graph with product *X* on the *x* axis and product *Y* on the *y* axis, a series of straight lines (not parallel to each other) from a point on one axis to a point on the other axis will each trace the output of a common component of the two products which the plant can produce. The several straight lines (one for each component) will intersect each other. The transformation curve, following the inner boundary created by the intersections, traces the various combinations of the two products which the plant can produce. As this boundary is followed, each kink in it marks a shift from one component as the factor limiting production to another component acting as a limiting factor.

transformation functions. Those functions that define the attainable positions to which a firm can move in terms of the structure of its assets, liabilities, and other variables. There are two kinds of transformation functions: *market functions* and *production functions*.

transient state model. The condition of a system in which behavior has not yet settled down so that the operating characteristics are changing and cannot be described by a *stationary dis-*

tribution. Distinguish *steady state model.*

transit items. Checks and other items payable in cash outside the city of the bank which receives them from its depositor.

transitivity. The situation in which, if $a = b$ and $b = c$, a will also equal c. For this condition to exist, both of the prior statements must be in the same dimension, e.g., length measured linearly.

transit number. The identification of a bank on its checks under the national numerical system. The number has three parts, the first, designating the location of the bank, the second the bank's name and the third (below the line) the Federal Reserve district and area within the district. These numbers facilitate routing out-of-town checks.

transitory action. In law, a matter which can be tried anywhere that jurisdiction can be obtained over the person of the defendant. Contract and tort actions are transitory but real estate actions must be brought in the county of the real estate, probate must occur in the county of domicile, and in a few other cases the action is not transitory.

transit privilege. A privilege extended to shippers by railroads which permits commodities to be stopped in transit for storing, processing, or finishing, and still receive a through rate.

transit rate. In transportation, a rate restricted to traffic which has been or will be processed between origin and destination.

transplacement. An error caused by moving all digits to the right or left of the proper columns without changing the order of the digits. Cf. *transposition.*

transportation ratio. In railroads, the ratio of transportation expense to operating revenues. Transportation expense includes the cost of moving trains (but not depreciation, repairs, and maintenance).

transposition. An error caused by interchanging of digits. Cf. *transplacement.*

transshipment. (1) In transportation, the transfer of goods from one carrier to another. (2) In marketing, the shipment by a dealer to another outside his regular territory.

trap car. A car placed on the shipper's siding, into which are loaded less than carload shipments. These shipments are reloaded into the other cars at the terminal of the carrier at the point of origin.

traveler's check. A check payable on sight. Used to facilitate cashing the check by eliminating any question whether there are sufficient funds on deposit to clear the check, and offering the one accepting the check an opportunity to verify a countersignature against an authentic signature.

traveler's letter of credit. A *letter of credit* addressed to correspondent banks. The traveler then calls on any of the named banks, identifies himself with a signature card from the issuing bank, and draws credit.

Treasury bill. An obligation of the United States Treasury with a maturity date less than one year from date of issue and bearing no interest but sold at a discount. Distinguished from a *certificate of indebtedness,* which likewise is of a maturity of one year or less but bears interest.

Treasury bonds. Used in three senses: (1) issued bonds which have been reacquired by the corporation from the bondholders, (2) bonds issued by U.S. Treasury, (3) authorized but unsold bonds still in the "treasury" of the corporation.

Treasury certificate. An obligation of the United States Treasury usually with one year maturity and paying interest on a coupon basis.

Treasury note. An obligation of the United States Treasury with maturity one to five years from date of issue.

treasury stock. (1) Issued stock which has been reacquired by the corporation from stockholders. (2) Less commonly, authorized but unissued stock which is still in the "treasury" of the corporation.

Treasury warrant. An order on the U.S. Treasury in ordinary bank check form. It is the instrument by which all treasury disbursements are made.

trend. (1) Same as *regression line.* (2) Same as *secular trend.*

trespass. Violating the real estate rights of another person. An action at law can be had to recover the damages which result.

trial balance. A list of all acounts which have balances in the ledger to verify the equality of the debit and credit sides of the ledger. A trial balance does not verify the correctness of accounts since many errors can be made and the trial balance still show equality of debits and credits.

trial balance, adjusted. The *trial balance* that would be obtained if prepared immediately after the *adjusting entries* are posted. It is also obtained by the trial balance columns with the adjustment columns on the *working papers.*

trial balance, post-closing. A *trial balance* of the ledger after the *adjusting* and *closing entries* have been posted.

triangular trade. A pattern of trade between three countries. The usual example in American trade is taken from the eighteenth century when America exported rum to Africa for slaves who were transported to the West Indies and traded for sugar which was brought back to America for rum manufacture, and the renewal of the cycle.

trough. See *business cycle.*

trover and conversion. A type of action at common law to recover damages for personal property wrongfully appropriated.

truck wholesaler. A wholesaler who does no storage but functions between the producer's platform and the retailer.

true bill. In law, the verdict of a *grand jury* that there is sufficient evidence to warrant a trial.

trunk lines. The railroads operating in the territory between Chicago or St. Louis and the Atlantic Coast. The most important are the Penn Central, Erie, and Baltimore & Ohio (B. & O.).

trust. (1) A trust, as the term was originally used in corporate history, meant a combination of corporations in which the stock of the constituent corporations was assigned to a board of trustees in order to create unified business control over the corporations. A trust was not a corporation; it was a combination of corporations. While trusts of the type here described have disappeared, having been declared illegal where the corporations are in the same type of business, the term "trust" has survived and popularly is applied to any large scale business or corporation which is a monopoly or has a tendency toward it. (2) In law, a device which puts legal title and control of property in the hands of one party (the trustee) for the benefit of another party (the beneficiary).

trust, types of. See the following specific terms:

circular trust
constructive trust
discretionary trust
dry trust
fixed investment trust
fixed trust
general management trust
horizontal trust
inter vivos trust
Massachusetts trust
passive trust
precatory trust
resulting trust
spendthrift trust
testamentary trust
vertical trust
voting trust

trust and agency fund. In governmental accounting, a fund established to account for assets held by the government as trustee or agent, e.g., the government is trustee of a fund bequeathed to it under a will for loaning for stated purposes, but agent of a fund to account for taxes collected for other governmental units.

trust certificate. A shortened term for *equipment trust certificate.*

trust company. A corporation organized primarily to act as trustee for estates, to act as guardian of minors, and as custodian of property held in trust. Also to buy and sell securities for customers, advise them in regard to investments, and in creating estates.

trust deed. The document creating a *trust.* Same as *trust indenture.*

trustee. The person to whom property is conveyed to be administered for the benefit of another, called the beneficiary, pursuant to the terms of the conveyance.

trustee in bankruptcy. The person or persons appointed by the court to liquidate the assets of a bankrupt or to supervise reorganization, although the one performing the latter function is usually called a receiver.

trust fund. The assets held by a trustee for a beneficiary.

trust indenture. The written document containing the terms and conditions binding the trustee and his conduct. The document is signed by the person or persons establishing the trust (called the settlor) and by the trustee.

Trust Indenture Act. Passed by Congress in 1939, this law regulates some of the terms and conditions of trust arrangements in connection with corporate security issues.

trust receipt. A relatively recent financing device, the trust receipt is a document indicating that the entruster has advanced money to the trustee for the purchase of goods with the trustee to hold the goods in trust until the debt is paid. This is a better device than the conditional sale because the law of trusts hems in the trustee much more than the law of sales protects the seller.

turn. A shortened form of *turnover.*

turnover. Generally, the number of times that a cycle takes place in a given unit of time. For example, an inventory turnover of 5/year means that, with inventory at a stable figure throughout the year, five times the inventory is sold in a year.

turnover, types of. See the following specific terms:

accounts receivable turnover
asset turnover
capital or investment turnover
finished goods turnover
gross plant turnover
inventory turnover
invested capital turnover
labor turnover
merchandise turnover
operating asset turnover
plant (or fixed assets) turnover
raw material turnover
receivables turnover

tangible assets turnover *work in process turnover*
working capital turnover

turnover ratios. See *turnover, types of.*

turnover tax. A sales tax levied on every transaction whether wholesale or retail.

turnpikes. Improved roads for the use of which a toll is commonly charged.

TVA Tennessee Valley Authority. A government corporation operating water control properties in the watershed of the Tennessee River for national defense, navigation, and for the development of hydroelectric power for agriculture and industry in the Tennessee Valley.

t value. In cases of a small sample (less than 30) the distribution of frequencies of a statistic such as the *arithmetic mean* of the sample must take account of *degrees of freedom.* The *t* curve tracing such a distribution is symmetrical but the dispersion is greater than that of the *normal distribution.* The dispersion is greatest when the degree of freedom is 1, and the dispersion approaches that of the normal curve as the degrees of freedom increase.

In application, a significance ratio is computed for comparison with a table showing the value at which the ratio exceeds the value of that ratio that might occur from chance at a given level of probability, such as 99 per cent.

Thus the significance ratio for determining the probability that the *arithmetic mean* of a sample with a value of 590 comes from a universe having a mean of 575 is (590 — 575) divided by the standard deviation of the mean of the universe. This ratio is then compared to a table showing the critical values for this ratio for different degrees of freedom (the number of items in the sample less one) and at different levels of probability. The *t* value in *correlation* analysis is the *regression coefficient* divided by the *standard deviation* of the regression coefficient.

twisting. (1) In insurance, persuading a policy holder to drop one policy and take another for the purpose of the additional commission received by the agent. (2) In finance, shifting from long-term debt to short-term or vice versa to take advantage of interest rate changes which affect either long-term or short-term more than proportionately.

two-bin system of inventory. A type of *fixed order system* in which inventory is carried in two bins and a replenishment order is issued when the first bin is empty. When this order is received the second bin is refilled and the excess put into the first (or working) bin.

two-dollar broker. A member of the stock exchange who handles transactions for another member. Until 1919, the rate was $2 per 100 shares. Hence the term. Same as *contract broker*.

two-name paper. Any document, such as an indorsed check or an accepted bill of exchange, where two persons are liable for payment. Usually one is primarily liable and the other secondarily (after the first has defaulted).

two-part tariff. A practice in which the buyer pays two prices for a joint product consisting of a fixed and variable component. The fixed component is independent of degree of utilization and the variable changes with use, e.g., an installation charge and a variable charge for use.

two stage least squares. In *econometrics*, a method of dealing with an *overidentified model* in which one or more *endogenous variables* appear on the right-hand side of the estimating equation. Estimates of such a right-hand side endogenous variable are first made by a *regression* of the *exogenous variables* on this endogenous variable. Then these estimates of the right-hand side endogenous variable are used in the original estimating equation for the second regression to establish the relation of the dependent variable to the independent variables.

tying contract. An agreement by a party buying or leasing a particular product that as a condition of his contract (1) the buyer will not buy or lease from another in the same business, or agreeing that (2) the buyer will buy or lease associated products of the same seller or lessor. Certain practices of this type have been declared illegal under the *Clayton Act*.

ultimate facts. In law, the vital facts put in issue as distinguished from the evidentiary facts designed to establish the ultimate facts.

ultra vires. Latin for "beyond the powers." Generally used to describe an act by a corporation or its agent which is beyond the powers set out in the *articles of incorporation*.

unaccrued. Used particularly with reference to income resulting when payments are received but not yet due as in the case of one receiving a rent payment before the due date. To the one making the payment this is *prepaid expense*.

unadjusted rate of return method (in capital budgeting). Same as *accounting method of return.*

unassociated variance. The sum of the squares of that part of the deviation of a variable from its arithmetic mean represented by the distance from a line of *least squares* to the actual values of the variable divided by the number of items. Cf. *associated variance* and *variance.* (See Figure 1, page 22.)

unassociated variation. The *unassociated variance* times the number of items. Hence, the sum of the squares of that part of the deviation of a variable from its *arithmetic mean* represented by the distance from a line of *least squares* to the actual values of the variable. Cf. *associated variation* and *variation.*

uncertainty. See *noninsurable risk.*

unconfirmed letter of credit. A *letter of credit* for which a credit has been established but on which the advising bank does not guarantee payment.

underabsorbed overhead. Same as *underapplied overhead.*

underapplied overhead. In accounting, the excess of overhead incurred over overhead applied or recognized in an accounting rate.

under bond. Storage of goods in a warehouse (licensed or owned by the government) until released by payment of an excise tax or duty or for re-export.

undercapitalized. A business with insufficient ownership funds for the scale of operations it is carrying on.

underconsumption theory of the business cycle. A term used in explaining the depression of the business cycle as the result of a failure of consumption to keep pace with the growth in savings. This failure is stated to arise either from too unequal a distribution of incomes or from an inherent tendency to save more than can be profitably invested. Cf. *monetary unnderconsumption theory, real underconsumption theory.*

underdetermined system. In *econometrics,* a system of equations (even though *consistent* and *independent*) such that the number of variables is greater than the number of equations and hence in the final equation (after elimination of all the other variables possible), more than one variable is left. Therefore, there are an infinite number of solutions. Cf. *just determined system* and *overdetermined system.*

underemployment equilibrium. See *Keynesian economics.*

underidentified model. See *underdetermined system.*

underinsurance. Insurance for less than the value of the goods or the amount of the risk. Cf. *coinsurance, self-insurance.*

underlying bonds. That bond issue, in the case of a company with several bond issues, which stands prior as to income (or security).

underlying mortgage. A mortgage prior in claim to another mortgage, e.g., when speaking of second mortgage, the first mortgage is the underlying mortgage.

underlying policy. Same as *master policy.*

underpricing. The policy common in the public offering of securities. As an incentive to the prospective buyer, the underwriter (or issuer) of new securities either as to (1) an issue already publicly held or (2) an issue of a company being offered to the public for the first time, deliberately seeks to offer the issue at a discount of up to 10 per cent below the underwriter's estimate of the probable price at the time of issuance.

under protest. A payment made under compulsion with the payor using these words to negative any implication from the act of payment that he is waiving whatever rights he may have.

undertaking. In law, an engagement by one party guaranteeing some performance. Thus a bond guaranteeing payment of costs on appeal signed by bondsmen.

under the rule. In the stock market, the purchase or sale of securities by an officer of the exchange to complete the transaction of a delinquent trader.

underwriter. (1) Any person, banker, or syndicate that guarantees to furnish a definite sum of money by a definite date to a business or government in return for an issue of bonds or stock. (2) In insurance, the one assuming a risk in return for the payment of a premium is an underwriter.

underwriting profit. In insurance, that part of the profit of an *insurer* that represents *earned premiums* less losses and expenses and hence excludes profits or earnings on investments.

underwriting spread. See *spread.*

underwriting syndicate. A combination of underwriters joined together in a joint venture to undertake the resale of securities which are to be purchased from the corporation issuing the securities (or from an intermediary). The syndicate operates under a contract setting out the terms of their responsibilities.

undifferentiated oligopoly. The situation in which a product is sold by only a few but the product is standardized (such as steel). Cf. *differentiated oligopoly.*

undistributed profits. Those profits retained by business and not paid out as dividends.

undistributed profits tax. A tax designed to supplement the income tax. By holding profits in a corporation and not paying dividends, stockholders can delay the income tax that would personally be due if dividends were paid. Also by letting such earnings accrue stockholders can get the earnings out by selling part of their stock and paying only a capital gains tax. Hence section 535 of the Internal Revenue Code imposes a heavy tax on earnings kept in a corporation without a good business reason. This section was known from 1936 to 1954 as section 102 and is still frequently so described.

undivided right. The right of one person in property owned jointly by several persons. Each person has a right to his stated proportion of the total property and no exclusive right to any particular part of the property.

undivided syndicate. In finance, the absence of a limitation in an *underwriting* agreement upon the number of shares for which each underwriter is liable and hence each underwriter is liable for his proportion of any shares on which other underwriters default.

unearned charges. The term describing obligations incurred but not covered by earnings, e.g., bond interest incurred during a loss period.

unearned discount. In accounting, interest in the form of a discount already collected but not yet earned.

unearned income. (1) In accounting, income received in advance of the accounting period to which it is allocable. (2) In some forms of income taxation a preferential treatment is given to earned income defined as income from services performed and all other income is considered unearned for this purpose.

unearned increment. An increase in the value of property for which society and not the individual is considered responsible. A good example is the increased value of urban land because of a city's growth. Cf. *single tax.*

unearned premium. In insurance, that part of a *premium* which is allocable to the part of the *policy* period which has not yet expired.

unearned premium reserve. The *reserve* established on the account books of an insurer in the amount of *unearned premiums.*

unemployment. A condition in which men are willing and able to work but cannot find employment at the going wage rate. Applied by analogy to other idle resources.

unemployment, types of. See the following specfiic terms:

cyclical unemployment *frictional unemployment*
disguised unemployment *technological unemployment*

unemployment compensation. Payments made to workers who are unemployed and meet the requirements of the law involved to qualify for such payments. The requirements usually are: (1) that the worker be not unemployed voluntarily, (2) that the worker have worked in employment that is "covered" by the law, (3) that the worker be willing and able to take employment offered him, and (4) that an initial period (the "waiting period") of unemployment have elapsed before compensation is due. In effect in every state of the Union since July 1, 1937.

unemployment insurance. Insurance premiums collected by the state and federal governments from which *unemployment compensation* is paid. Technically these premiums are taxes.

unexpired cost. In accounting, a cost properly carried forward to future periods as an asset measure.

unexplained variance. Same as *unassociated variance.*

unfair competition. At common law, unfair competition was restricted to meaning misrepresentation. Hence the new term "unfair methods of competition" was devised by Congress in 1914 to deal with monopoly-producing activities in the Federal Trade Commission Act.

unfair labor practice. Originally, conduct by an employer in violation of the provisions of *NLRA,* National Labor Relations act of 1935, or of a state labor relations act. Under the *Taft-Hartley Act of 1947* unions can also be guilty of unfair labor practices.

unfair labor practice strike. A strike to correct *unfair labor practices.* Distinguish *economic strike.*

unfair list. A list of employers said to be unfair to labor. Used as a weapon by union labor. Cf. *fair list, black list.*

unfair methods of competition. The term includes all methods by which trade is restrained and monopoly encouraged and originates in the Federal Trade Commission Act of 1914. Some states also have laws on the subject but there is no uniformity in them.

unfair trade practice acts. Approximately half of the states have passed such laws barring retailers and/or wholesalers from selling merchandise for less than invoice cost, or in some instances for less than cost plus a stipulated percentage mark-up (e.g., in Wisconsin, 6 to 8% on certain merchandise). Cf. *price floor laws, fair trade practice acts.*

unfavorable balance of trade. A theory of *mercantilism* that an unfavorable balance of trade is to be avoided. The balance is unfavorable when the money total of imports exceeds the money total of exports.

unfunded debt. (1) The indebtedness of a business or government which lacks formal evidence such as a bond. (2) Usually the line is drawn that unfunded debt is all debt due within one year. Cf. *floating debt.*

unified bond. Same as *consolidated bond.*

uniform commercial code. See *uniform laws.*

uniform delivered price. A pricing system under which a product is sold at the same price and delivered anywhere within a given area without additional charge for the delivery.

uniform laws. To encourage uniformity particularly with regard to laws affecting interstate commerce, a national commission has drafted legislation for adoption by the states. The most important uniform laws cover negotiable instruments, sales, partnerships, warehouse receipts, and bills of lading. Only the law covering negotiable instruments has been adopted by all 50 states. Recently the uniform commercial code consolidates a number of the earlier uniform laws such as negotiable instruments, sales and conditional sales.

unilateral contract. A contract in which complete performance is given by one party at the time of contract in return for a promise by the other party.

unilateral mistake. In law, a mistake by one party to a contract. Cf. *bilateral mistake.*

unimodal. A *frequency distribution* with a single *mode.*

unintended investment. The addition to *intended investment* in inventories arising because businessmen anticipated a higher sales volume than actually resulted.

union. The term is ordinarily used to describe an organization of workers for the purpose of obtaining higher wages, shorter hours, and better working conditions. It can be used in a broader sense to refer to any uniting of workers for any objective.

union, types of. See the following specific terms:

closed union
company union
craft union
dual union
federal labor local union
horizontal union
independent union
industrial union
international union
open union
trade union
vertical union

union certification. The issuance of a decision by the Natonal Labor Relations Board (or a similar state agency) that a union has qualified under the law as the representative of employees. The principal requirement for certification is a majority vote by the employees selecting the union for their bargaining unit.

union label. A label indicating that a product was made by union labor.

union loss clause. Same as *mortgage loss clause.*

union security clauses. The general term applied to clauses in a labor contract which are designed to give the union security. The most common clauses falling in this category are: (1) *maintenance of membership,* (2) *closed shop,* (3) *union shop.*

union shop. A business firm in which a nonunion worker may be hired but after a stated period must become a member of the union in order to continue work. Cf. *agency shop, closed shop, open shop, preferential shop.*

union steward. A union officer or representative.

unissued stock. The amount of authorized stock which a corporation has not yet sold.

unit bank. A bank with only one place of business.

unit billing. A system used by some railroads in which papers for local freight traffic are made out at the point of origin instead of the point of destination.

unit cost (average). Total costs divided by the number of units of output.

unit-cost method of depreciation. To *sinking fund depreciation* is added interest on the asset and estimated cost of operation of the asset, including repairs and maintenance, and the combined charges are distributed on the basis of the number of units produced in a period as a percent of total units expected to be produced over the expected life of the asset. Cf. *production unit cost method of depreciation.*

United States Court of Customs and Patent Appeals. The federal appellate court handling questions arising under customs and patent laws. Patent infringement suits may also be brought in the federal district courts.

United States rule. A rule first established by the U.S. Supreme Court that partial payments of delinquent interest-bearing debts are to be applied first to the retirement of past due interest and then to principal. Cf. *merchant's rule.*

unit-of-production method of depreciation. Same as *unit cost method of depreciation.*

unit store. (1) A mercantile establishment which has only one place of business. (2) One unit of a group of stores.

univariate analysis. The analysis of values of one variable, e.g., determination of the *standard deviation.* Cf. *bivariate analysis* and *multivariate analysis.*

universe. In statistics, the entire body of possible data. Used particularly to distinguish between *all* the data and a sample taken from all the data.

unlawful detainer. A common-law remedy by which the landlord can have a tenant evicted when the tenant has overstayed his term or has broken the terms of his lease. Cf. *ejectment.*

unlimited liability. The right of creditors to attach and seize any assets of a debtor to the extent of the indebtedness held against a business. A characteristic of the partnership and the individual proprietorship.

unlimited tax bond. In municipal finance, a bond secured by the pledge of taxes which may be levied at an unlimited rate and in an unlimited amount.

unlisted security. A security which is not traded on a recognized stock exchange is referred to as unlisted.

unlisted trading. Trading in securities not fully listed on a stock exchange. Although they appear on the board, the stocks do not meet listing requirements. This unlisted privilege is limited to stock which had the right prior to 1934 (the date of the Securities Exchange Act). The term is also applied to trading on the regional exchanges in stocks listed there.

unproductive labor. (1) Expenditure of human energy on the production of something which has no economic value. (2) Also in a comparative sense when labor is wasted or used inefficiently. (3) Sometimes used to refer to work that does not involve a material product.

unsatisfied judgment fund. In several states, the fund maintained from taxes for the purpose of satisfying judgments held by persons injured in automobile accidents who have been unable to collect the judgment because of lack of insurance or financial responsibility of the party against whom judgment was entered.

unsecured creditor. A lender whose loan or debt is not secured by any collateral or mortgage. Cf. *secured creditor.*

unskilled labor. Work for which very little training or skill is required. Labor is defined as skilled when a training period of at least one year is required.

unstable equilibrium. In economics, a condition which once achieved will continue indefinitely unless one of the variables (economic or noneconomic) is altered, and then the system will not return to the original equilibrium and will not come to rest unless there is further alteration of a variable. Cf. *dynamic equilibrium, equilibrium of firm or industry (partial) long run, equilibrium of firm or industry (partial) short run, expectational equilibrium, general equilibrium (under monopoly or monopolistic competition), general equilibrium (under pure competition), intermediate equilibrium, market equilibrium, momentary equilibrium, neutral equilibrium, normal equilibrium, partial equilibrium, stable equilibrium,* and *static equilibrium.*

unstable model. A model in which the introduction of a disturbance will result in amplification of the consequences of the disturbance. Cf. *stable model.*

unsystematic risk. The absence of correlation of the return and price of an investment with the general market. Hence *diversifiable risk.* Cf. *systematic risk.*

unvalued stock. A rare term for *no par stock.*

upset price. A provision in most foreclosure laws providing that what is being sold must bring more than a minimum amount established by the court or it cannot be sold. A guard against collusion by the debtor with others to defeat his creditor. Also protects the debtor from a creditor who is interested in bidding in at a very low price.

upstream loan. A holding company with poor credit using its subsidiaries as a source of funds. Such lending by the subsidiary to a parent will not appear on a consolidated statement of the parent and the subsidiaries.

urbanization. The movement of people from small communities concerned chiefly or solely with agriculture to larger communities whose activities are primarily centered in trade, government, manufacturing, or allied interests.

usage variance. Same as *quantity variance.*

usance. The period of time allowed by law or commercial practice for the payment of a bill of exchange.

use and occupancy insurance. Protection against loss after fire (during the period of reconstruction) of the net profits from the use of destroyed property and practically all the necessarily continuing expenses. The principal exclusions from coverage are direct labor, materials and variable costs.

use plan. A pricing scheme (provided the product is capable of several uses with each use commanding a different price) giving the producer an average or blended price for his whole output. This is the average of the different prices received by the distributor when he in turn sells or uses. For example, milk used for fluid, butter, cheese, and ice cream purposes. Cf. *base surplus plan.*

user cost. The difference between the value of an asset when it is not used and when it is used, after allowing for capital maintenance. Thus the amount by which the discounted future earnings of the asset have been reduced by use.

USES United States Employment Service. A part of the U.S. Federal Security Agency supervising a nationwide network of free employment offices administered by the states with federal funds.

use tax. This tax is merely a device to protect the sales tax from wholesale evasion. A state having a sales tax places a similar tax on the use of all articles on which no sales tax has been paid so that people are not encouraged to go out of the state to make tax-free purchases which they can then bring home.

use value. The value placed on a good or service, not for its possible exchange, but for its usefulness to the individual directly.

usurious rate of interest. The maximum rate of interest which the law allows. Not to be confused with the *legal rate of interest* which is the rate applied by law when there is no agreement by the parties as to the rate of interest.

usury. Interest in excess of the maximum rate allowed by law and therefore illegal. Cf. *legal rate of interest.*

utility. (1) The ability of a material good or a service to satisfy human wants. (2) Colloquially for "public utility."

utility fund. In governmental accounting, a fund established to account for self-supporting enterprises rendering services primarily to the public. Distinguish *working capital fund.*

utility, place. That part of utility arising from the fact that a good or service is in proper place for use.

utility, possession. That part of utility arising from the fact that the good or service is in the possession of the one who will use it.

utility, time. That part of utility arising from the fact that a good or service is available at the time it is wanted.

utilization factor in public utilities. The ratio of the peak load to the installed capacity of a plant or system. Cf. *capacity factor, diversity factor, load factor.*

utopia. An imaginary place where political and economic arrangements are approximately correct. Used by Sir Thomas More in 1516 to describe such a state in a book entitled "Utopia."

vacancy ratio. The percentage of available housing units fit for occupancy but unoccupied. Cf. *occupancy ratio.*

vacation pay. (1) Payment to an employee for working hours spent on vacation; (2) payment to an employee in lieu of the regular vacation time.

validity. In statistics, the degree to which a test measures the object which it is intended to measure. Distinguish *reliability.*

valorization scheme. Direct government or cartel intervention in world markets to maintain the price of a product. A famous instance was the Brazilian valorization scheme for coffee.

valuation reserve. An amount deducted from an asset to indicate by estimate that the market value of the asset is less than the full amount of the asset (for example, an account receivable), or in the case of a liability to indicate the estimate that the liability may be greater (for example, income taxes) than stated on the books.

value. The utility of a good weighted by its price. Also the quantity of one good that is exchangeable for the quantity of another good.

value, types of. See the following specific terms:

cash surrender value
commissioner's value
convention value
exchange value
market value
net present value
no par value
par value
stated value
surrender value
use value

value added. The difference between the purchase price of raw materials or finished parts and the sale price of the product. If depreciation and indirect business taxes are deducted from this difference the value added for all output is national income.

value date. In banking, the date on which a deposit is recognized as effective due to the time needed for collection of checks.

valued policy. In insurance, a policy which sets an agreed value on each item of property in the event of total loss. Cf. *nonvalued policy.*

valued policy law. A state statute requiring insurance companies to pay the *face value* of the policy in the event of total loss unless a *coinsurance clause* is operable to reduce this amount.

value of money. Its purchasing power. The amount of goods and services it will buy at any given time.

value of service principle. In railroad and utility rate making, "charging what the traffic will bear" by establishing the rate at the upper limit of what the great bulk of buyers is thought to be willing to pay. Cf. *cost of service principle.*

value of the marginal product. Identical with *marginal revenue product* in a competitive market. In a noncompetitive market, the value of the marginal product (marginal product times previous market price) is larger than marginal revenue product by the amount that price must be lowered to move the marginal product, reckoning the loss in price on all prior units as a deduction from the value of the marginal product.

variable. A magnitude whose value changes are quantitatively measurable rather than only quantitatively distinguishable. Cf. *attribute.*

continuous variable
dependent variable
discrete variable
dummy variable
endogenous variable
exogenous variable
independent variable
instrumental variable
jointly dependent variable
predetermined variable
shift variable

variable annuity. An annuity contract providing for the investment of the purchase price in equity securities to provide a degree of protection against the changing value of the dollar downward. Accordingly the payments which the annuitant will receive vary from time to time.

variable budget. Same as *flexible budget.*

variable costing. Same as *direct costing.*

variable costs. Those expenses of a business or industry that vary with the amount of business done or the volume of goods produced.

variable markup pricing. Same as *flexible markup pricing* and *cost-plus pricing.*

variable proportions, law of. Same as *diminishing marginal productivity, law of.*

variable-ratio plan. An investment plan under which funds are divided at a time considered normal into two equal parts: a stock fund to purchase diversified common stocks and a cash fund to be held in liquid form. When prices rise, shares are sold to maintain the ratio of the stock fund value and the cash fund, and vice versa when prices fall. This assumes fluctuations about a normal which may periodically be readjusted to take a long term trend into account. Cf. *constant-dollar plan, constant ratio plan, dollar averaging.*

variance. The square of the *standard deviation* of a number of items. Hence, the sum of the squares of the deviations of the observed values from the *arithmetic mean* of the observed values divided by the number of items. Cf. *associated variance* and *unassociated variance.* (See Figure 1, page 22.)

variance account. In the *standard cost method of inventory* the difference between actual cost of production and standard costs of production is set up in a separate account where such variances are to be recorded. Typically, the standard cost is separately established for a product as to materials, direct labor, and manufacturing overhead. The account may further be broken down for the several causes of variation: e.g., in the case of materials: price, quantity, mix, etc.

variance analysis. The separation of total variance (the sum of the squares of deviations of observed data from their *arithmetic mean* divided by the number of items) into components associated with the several sources of such variance on the basis of classification of the observations.

variation. The *variance* times the number of items. Hence, the sum of the squares of the deviations of the observed values from the *arithmetic* mean. Variation (total) is divided into *associated variation* and *unassociated variation.*

variety store. A retail store handling a wide assortment of goods of low unit price, e.g., a 5¢ to $1.00 store.

Veblenian school. One of the schools of *institutional economics.* Emphasis is placed on a sociological treatment, e.g., in terms of a *leisure class* which engages in *conspicuous consumption.*

velocity of circulation. The average number of times in a year which a dollar serves as income (the income velocity) or an expenditure (the transactions velocity).

vendee. The buyer of property.

vendor. The seller of property.

vendor's lien. The right of an unpaid seller to withhold possession of property until he is paid unless the agreement specifically requires the transfer of possession at a date in advance of the date for payment.

venire. The name of a writ by which a jury is summoned.

venireman. A jury member who has been summoned by a *venire* as opposed to a talesman, who is selected by the court from bystanders.

venue. Even though the court may have jurisdiction over the persons involved and the subject matter, the case must still be brought in the proper court geographically considered. The concept arises from the common-law rule that the case must be tried where the events occurred.

verdict. See *general verdict* and *special verdict.*

vertical combination. A combination which unites under one ownership a number of plants that are engaged in successive processes or stages of production and marketing. Distinguish *circular combination, horizontal combination.*

vertical trust. Same as *vertical combination.*

vertical union. Same as *industrial union.*

vested. (1) A legal term to identify a right of immediate enjoyment or a right to future enjoyment which cannot be altered without the consent of the party having the right. (2) In real estate law, the term is used more technically to describe a future interest in land that has been finalized by the determination of what individual is to take the property and the accomplishment of any conditions attached to the interest.

vested remainder. In law, an interest in property to commence in enjoyment at some time in the future but with the person who is to enjoy it determined at present and no condition attached to the interest. Cf. *contingent remainder.*

vestibule training. Training of an employee by the employer in his own school before actual shop experience.

vice propre. French, meaning "inherent vice."

visible items of foreign trade. The merchandise, specie, and other "visible" items entering foreign trade. Distinguish *invisible items of foreign trade.*

vis major. Latin, meaning "superior force." In law, an *act of God.*

vocational groups. A system of economic organization involving self-government within groups of employers and employees in similar industries.

voidable contract. An agreement or promise between two parties in which one party has the right to decide whether he will go ahead with the contract or whether he will consider the contract as void. E.g., an infant has this right of election on all contracts made with him except those for necessities.

void contract. An effort to enter an agreement or promise which is contrary to law or public policy as interpreted by the courts. No contract ever exists, the court merely declaring this fact when it calls a contract void.

voir dire. In law, a preliminary examination to determine whether a witness or juryman has an interest in the case.

volume of trade. The amount of goods bought and sold during a certain time, usually a year. Sometimes also used in business to mean the dollar volume of trade.

voluntary bankruptcy. Bankruptcy proceedings begun by the petition of a debtor who seeks to wind up his affairs.

voluntary chain store. One of a group of retailers each of whom owns and operates his own store but is associated voluntarily for cooperative buying, advertising, and/or other functions.

voluntary conveyance. In law, a transfer of property without consideration.

voluntary plan. In *insurance,* same as *level charge plan.*

von Neumann-Morgenstern utility index. The use of individual preferences enabling the analyst to determine which of several alternatives is preferable when the alternatives have objective probabilities and selection will be made on the basis of these probabilities weighted by the preferences of the individual in the form of a maximum expected payoff. Cf. *cardinal utility theory* and *ordinal utility theory.*

von Neumann ratio. The ratio of the mean-square successive difference to the *variance.* Denoted by the symbol *K.* The mean-square successive difference is the sum of the squares of the successive differences in the observations of a series divided by the number of observations less one. The ratio *(K)* is used to test for *autocorrelation* by comparing *K* for a particular series with the critical values of *K* (at given levels of probability and for the given number of observations). If *K* is less than one critical value, positive autocorrelation exists; and if *K* is greater than the other critical value, negative autocorrelation exists. An alternate method of testing for autocorrelation is the *Durbin-Watson test.*

voting. In corporations, voting may be of three types (depending on the law, articles and by-laws): (1) common law voting: one vote to each person regardless of number of shares held, (2) cumulative voting: applicable to the election of directors, permitting the individual to cumulate all his votes for one candidate or to spread them as he sees fit (for example, if nine directors are to be elected and one share of voting stock is held, the nine votes can be cast all for one candidate or divided), (3) ordinary voting: one vote for each share of voting stock with all directors to be elected one at a time.

voting stock. Stock which gives the right to the holder to vote at corporate meetings. As to various methods of voting, see *voting.*

voting trust. A legal device by which the owners of voting stock (usually the common stock) assign the shares for a definite period of time to a group known as voting trustees and receive in return certificates of beneficial interest in the trust. Designed to concentrate control of a corporation and improve continuity of policy.

voucher. A form used for internal control of payments and prepared at the time an obligation is incurred. The form shows the correct accounting entry to be made and provides for authorization of payment by signature of one or more officers.

voucher check. The attached stub of a check or other device which contains information as to the purpose of the payment.

voucher register. A book of original entry in which information is accumulated as to cash payments.

wage. The price paid to those who render any kind of service. Usually based on the hour, day, week. In economics, all types of compensation for services are wages.

wage, types of. See the following specific terms:

guaranteed annual wage
incentive wage
minimum wage
money wage
piece wage
real wage
time wage

wage ceiling. The top wage payable per hour to a given class of workmen. Used by the government in wartime to curb inflation.

wage differential. Any difference in wages paid to workers for the *same* work is called a wage differential. E.g., a wage differential based on the sex of the worker or based on the geographical area.

wage fund theory of wages. A generalization that on the demand side wages are determined by a fund allocated in advance by the entrepreneur in his production plans or determined by the capital funds in existence at any one time. Cf. *bargaining theory of wages, lump of labor theory of wages, marginal productivity theory of wages, residual theory of wages, subsistence theory of wages.*

wage-price spiral. The process of interaction between wage increases and price increases, with an increase in one leading to an increase in the other, this in turn to another increase in the first, and so on.

Wages and Hours Act. See *Fair Labor Standards Act.*

wages of management. The wages or salary which the manager of a business could earn if he hired out to another employer.

wage stabilization. A program for keeping wages at a pre-determined level.

wage theories. See the following specific terms:

bargaining theory of wages
lump of wages theory of wages
marginal productivity theory of wages
residual theory of wages
subsistence theory of wages
wage fund theory of wages

waggon jobber. Same as *truck wholesaler.*

Wagner Act. See *NLRA* National Labor Relations Act.

Wagner's law. The hypothesis by the nineteenth century German economist that as real income increases, the ratio of expenditures on public or social goods increases relative to private goods.

waiver. A general legal doctrine concerning the voluntary abandonment by a person of some or all of his rights. Such an abandonment may be implied from conduct. Thus a *lien* on property is lost when possession is voluntarily surrendered.

waiver clause. In insurance, a policy provision that either the insurer or the insured may act as he thinks needed to minimize the loss without prejudice to any rights under the policy.

waiver of premium clause. See *disability premium waiver insurance.*

walkout. The only difference between a strike and a walkout is that in a walkout the workers leave work which they have already begun. Could be called a strike on short notice.

Wall Street. A short narrow street in lower New York City. It is the chief financial center of the United States and has become synonymous with financial interests and money markets.

Walras' law. In *general equilibrium* analysis, quantities of goods demanded and supplied are stated in terms of price as one of the *independent variables.* But the price of money in such a system is equal to unity (a constant). There might therefore be one more equation than there are unknown variables in the system. Hence the proposition that the price of money is not an equation but an identity since anyone demanding a quantity of goods is by definition offering in exchange an equal amount of money (and conversely for supply) is Walras' law.

Walrasian model. A system in which all economic variables are considered endogenous and all the variables not included are noneconomic, such as technology conditions or psychological demand factors.

Walsh-Healy Act. A federal law in 1936 providing that workers employed on government contracts over $10,000 be paid the prevailing minimum wage, prohibiting employment of males under 16 and females under 18, and requiring time-and-one half for work over 8 hours a day or 40 hours a week. Cf. *Bacon-Davis Act.*

ward. In law a person who is under the control of a *guardian.*

warehouse receipt. A document issued by a warehouse for goods stored. The document may be in *negotiable* form or not. Transfer of the ownership of the goods in the warehouse can be done by indorsement and delivery of the warehouse receipt by the seller to the buyer.

warehouse, types of. See the following specific terms:

bonded warehouse	*private warehouse*
field warehouse	*public warehouse*

warehousing loan. A loan made on inventory held in warehouses. Cf. *field warehousing loan.*

war-profits tax. A tax on profits arising from war efforts. A distinction exists between this and excess profits taxation which reaches high profits whatever their cause.

warrant. (1) In governmental accounting, a draft upon the treasurer for the immediate payment of money, or in some cases payable only out of certain revenues when and if received. (2) In law, the document used in criminal proceedings to authorize an arrest. (3) In finance, a long-term option to buy another security (usually common stock) at a stated price.

warranted rate of growth. That rate of growth of *national income* which will keep *planned savings* and *planned investment* equal. See explanation under *Harrod-Domar model.* Cf. *actual rate of growth* and *natural rate of growth.*

warranty. An undertaking by one party that certain facts are true. It may be either express or implied, and most commonly occurs in a sale or in insurance. Cf. *implied warranty.*

warranty deed. A deed in which the grantor (the party selling) warrants or guarantees certain matters, for example, a warranty that the grantee (the person buying) will enjoy peaceful ownership and that if he does not, the grantor will bear the expense of defending title. Cf. *quit-claim deed.*

wash sale. A fictitious stock sale by two or more brokers in order to create a market price for a security or for tax evasion. It may also consist of two or more outside operators who match their orders for purchase and sale so that a seeming market activity is given to stock. Illegal and prohibited by law and by the exchanges. In the case of taxes, a repurchase within 30 days at a loss is classed as a wash sale and the loss will not be recognized for income tax purposes.

waste. The legal term for damage done by a person to real estate.

wasting asset. An asset which is consumed in its use. Timber, gas, oil, mineral, and similar holdings are called wasting assets.

watered stock. The situation in which a corporation issues more stock than the true value of its assets. The purpose may be to hide heavy earnings or to give promoters a profit.

water rights. In law, the rights of owners of adjacent land and of the public to waters such as rivers and lakes.

waybill. A document made out by the carrier at the point of origin which shows the point of origin, destination, route, consignor, consignee, description of shipment, and freight charge. Not to be confused with a *bill of lading* which is a document of title to the shipment.

wealth. (1) Ordinarily, anything useful and owned by human beings. (2) The term is also used in special senses, e.g., the national wealth (the total resources of a country).

weather theory of the cycle. This theory emphasizes that weather is the primary determinant of variations in agricultural output. In an economy where agriculture is dominant, the theory argues that the conditions in agriculture are transmitted to the rest of that economy.

Webb-Pomerene Act of 1918. An act of Congress permitting American firms to combine for purposes of export and exempting such an association from the *Sherman Antitrust Act* providing no injury is done to an individual American exporter.

week order. On the stock exchange, an order to buy or sell which automatically expires if it cannot be executed during the coming week.

weighted average. An average in which weights are assigned to the items to be averaged. Thus an item assigned a double weight is multiplied by two. In computing the average, the sum of the weighted items is divided by the sum of the weights rather than by the number of items as in an unweighted mean.

welfare clause. The clause in the U.S. Constitution authorizing the federal government to provide for the "general welfare." For a long period (to 1936–37) the clause was held by the courts to authorize nothing except what was specifically otherwise authorized in the Constitution. Now a broader definition prevails. Cf. *implied powers.*

welfare economics. A theoretical system of economics which analyzes economic data in terms of maximizing human welfare of the greatest number and not merely maximizing the profits of the entrepreneur. Cf. *mixed economy.*

Wheeler-Lea Act. An amendment in 1938 of the Federal Trade Commission Act of 1914, especially regarding (1) the definition of unfair acts or practices in commerce and (2) false or misleading advertising of foods, drugs, therapeutic devices, and cosmetics.

when issued. The practice of trading in securities on the new basis, as in the case of *stock splits,* as soon as the new basis is authorized but before the new shares are actually issued.

white list. A list of employees who are considered by employers to be satisfactory because they do not agitate on labor questions. Cf. *black list.*

whole coverage. Same as *full coverage.*

whole life insurance. Also called ordinary or straight life insurance. Life insurance in which the insured pays a flat premium as long as he lives, but not beyond the age of 96 (100 under the *CSO* table). It is in effect an *endowment insurance* at that age.

wholesaler. A merchant middleman who sells to other middlemen, industrial or commercial users but who does not sell in significant amounts to ultimate consumers.

Wicksell effect. The proposition that the rate of interest is smaller than the *value* of the marginal net product of money capital because money capital is used to purchase both real capital goods and labor. The transfer of labor from direct to indirect use causes an increase in wages which absorbs part of the money capital and causes real saving to be smaller than monetary saving. This effect is counterbalanced by the fall in the rate of interest releasing some money capital hitherto used for interest payments and now available to purchase real capital. This is sometimes abbreviated to: the Wicksell effect is the unproductive absorption of an increase in capital (or the deviation of the rate of interest from the marginal net product of money capital).

widening of capital. Increasing the quantity of capital employed through increasing the volume of goods produced but without changing the ratio of the amount of capital employed to a given quantity of goods. Cf. *deepening of capital.*

wildcat bank. A name applied to banks located in the wilds. Inaccessible places were selected by the promoters of these banks so that holders of their notes could not present them for redemption. Eventually this term was applied to all unstable banks.

wildcat money. Bank notes issued by *wildcat banks.*

wildcat strike. A strike which has not been called pursuant to the procedure specified in the constitution of the union or a contract entered by a union.

will. A document by which a person at his death bequeathes his property to others. The document is valid only if made by a person of legal age, sound mind, without coercion, and signed in the presence of witnesses. The legally required number of witnesses varies in different states.

windfall gain or loss. A gain or loss which is involuntary and not foreseen. Often results from an unforeseen change in price of goods.

window dressing. The practice of executing transactions shortly before the end of an accounting period to change artificially the items in the accounting statements of the period.

wire transfer. An order to pay money transmitted by telegraph or cable to secure immediate transfer.

with average. In *marine insurance,* a policy covering all *particular average* losses or all such losses over an agreed minimum.

with exchange. In banking, the phrase means that the collection charge of a *bill of exchange* is due from the payor together with the *face* of the bill.

withholding tax. A method of collecting estimated income taxes as the income is earned rather than delaying payment until the end of the year. The tax is collected by deductions from payments due the taxpayer from employers.

without prejudice. A legal term indicating that an action, such as an offer to settle, is made without any admissions or waivers by the action.

without recourse. Indorsement of an instrument with these words eliminates the liability of the indorser on the instrument for nonpayment in case the check or draft is not paid, but does not eliminate the liability for the other warranties made by an indorser. See *indorsement.*

w.i., when issued. A term used to designate stock not yet issued but one in which dealings are carried on. Stock sold "w.i." is deliverable in the future.

workable competition. (1) The situation in which there are a number of noncolluding firms in each market area, no one firm occupies a large part of the market, and new firms can enter the market on terms approximately equal to the terms enjoyed by existing firms. (2) The situation in which no net social gain can be found as the result of any change that might be proposed in the competitive situation of an industry.

working capital. Total *current assets.* Cf. *working capital (net).*

working capital fund. In governmental accounting, a fund established to account for internal service activities rendered to a government's own departments.

working capital (net). Used in two senses: (1) in accounting, the difference between current assets and current liabilities, (2) in public utilities, the amount of cash required by a business to carry on operation.

working capital turnover. The ratio of sales to current assets.

working papers. The tabular papers used by an accountant in preparing the balance sheet, profit and loss, and other financial statements. These papers summarize the balances in the various subaccounts, make adjustments, and include computations such as inventory valuation.

working reserve (bank). Working reserves for a bank consist of cash items in process of collection and demand deposits with other individual banks, but not deposits with the Federal Reserve Bank.

work in process. Inventory on which work has been begun but not finished. Excludes raw materials and purchased parts on which no work has been done.

work in process turnover. The amount of *work in process* transferred to finished products during a period divided by the average work in process inventory of that period.

workmen's compensation insurance. Insurance which protects employers against their liability for accidents to employees, the amount due the workman being stipulated by the workmen's compensation law of the given states. Compulsory in many states.

workmen's compensation laws. Laws designed to compel employers to assume financial liability in case of accidents which happen to employees during their employment. The basic principle is that the consumer should pay for this cost of production. The common law which is replaced by workmen's compensation had three doctrines that often prevented recovery by a workman: (1) *assumption of the risk* peculiar to his employment, (2) *fellow servant* responsibility, (3) *contributory negligence* of the worker himself.

workout loan. A loan granted to a borrower in a distressed financial condition pursuant to a plan to "work out" of the difficulty. Accordingly many restrictions are imposed to assure the achievement of the purpose.

work permit. See *agency shop.*

World Bank. See *International Bank for Reconstruction and Development.*

Wright demand rate. In public utilities, a rate emphasizing load factor (ratio of average use to peak use). Many specific forms of this rate have been developed.

writ. A written order of a court directing a court officer to perform an act such as seizing property.

writs, types of. See the following specific terms:

assistance
attachment
ejectment
error
execution
fieri facias
habeas corpus
injunction
mandamus
ne exeat
procedendo
prohibition
quia timet
quo warranto
remittitur
replevin
scire facias
sequestration
supercedeas
venire

writing up or writing down. Increasing (or decreasing) the value at which assets are shown in the accounts, usually on the ground that there has been an increase or decrease in the market value of the asset.

writ of assistance. In law, a writ of a court directing the sheriff to evict the *defendant* from real estate and to place the *plaintiff* in possession.

writ of error. In law, a *writ* (1) directing the judges of a court to examine the record leading to the *judgment* in a case or (2) directing a lower court to send the record to an appellate court for review. The first is called a writ of error coram nobis. Cf. *writ of certiorari.*

yardstick rates. Rates of one business used as a criterion for the basic regulation of rates charged by other companies. Originated with the TVA which set a standard with which charges of other utilities are compared.

year-end dividend. An extra dividend paid at the end of the fiscal year in addition to the regular dividend.

yellow-dog contract. A contract of employment providing that the employee will not join a labor organization. Now illegal under the National Labor Relations Act and as early as the Norris-LaGuardia Act of 1932.

yield. In the case of stock, the ratio of dividends per share in dollars to purchase price per share in dollars.

yield curve. In finance, with time to maturity plotted on the x axis and interest rate on the y axis, the curve tracing the variation in interest rate for a given security (or given quality of security).

yield (gross). In the case of bonds, the ratio of interest in dollars to purchase price. Cf. *yield to maturity.*

yield method (in capital budgeting). The determination of that rate which will equate the cash flows (periodic cash) received from an investment with the cash flows laid out for an investment. Cf. *accounting method, present value method.*

yield tax. A tax on the harvested or realized amount, e.g., a tax on the value of trees cut and at the time of cutting.

yield test. In insurance, the determination of the *yield* of corporate bonds held by an insurer to establish the valuation rule to apply. Corporate bonds yielding more than 1.5% over U.S. government bonds of the same maturity are valued at market price; those with a differential less than 1.5% are valued on an amortization basis.

yield to maturity. The calculated return of a bond, giving effect to (1) the dollars received in annual interest payments, (2) the amortization of the difference between the purchase price and the redemption value, and (3) the number of years to maturity.

A simple approximation formula is $Y = \frac{100-P}{T} + {}^{I}\!/_{P}$

where P = price paid or current price
T = years to maturity
I = face rate of interest in dollars per year

Cf. *annual return* and *current yield.*

York-Antwerp rules. In *marine insurance,* the rules applicable in most countries to settling a *general average* loss involving a number of interested parties, such as the ship owners, the cargo owners, and the owners of related interests.

Young plan. The plan advanced in 1929 by Owen Young to supersede the *Dawes plan* by reducing German reparations and making a definite schedule for such payments, as well as removing most controls over the German economy.

Yule distribution. A statement of the size distribution of firms combining *Gibrat's law of proportionate effect* for firms above a minimum size and an assumption of a constant birth rate for new firms. Specifically, if $f(s)ds$ is the probability density of firms of size s, then the Yule distribution is $f(s) = KB(s,r + 1)$ where r is a *parameter,* K is a normalizing constant and $B(s,r + 1)$ is the beta function of s and $(r + 1)$ Cf. *Gibrat distribution, log-normal distribution, normal distribution, Pareto distribution, Poisson distribution, t distribution.*

zero-sum game. A game played by a number of persons with the winner (or winners) receiving all the stakes of the loser (or losers); such that the algebraic sum of gains and losses is zero.

Zollverein. German for *customs union.* An association of countries to eliminate (or reduce) tariffs between countries that are members of the association and sometimes to adopt uniform tariffs regarding nonmembers. Cf. *Benelux.*

zone freight rate. One freight rate applicable to shipments from any of the points in one area or zone to any of the points in another.

zone pricing. A pricing system under which the seller divides the market into a number of zones, quoting different prices in different zones. Originally a compromise between *f.o.b.* under which the seller pays all the freight and *c.f.* under which the buyer pays all freight. The term now extends beyond the freight question. Cf. *basing point system, delivered price, f.o.b. pricing,* and *mill base system.*

zone rate. In public utilities, a rate system under which territory served is divided into zones usually following cost differences between the areas, and the rates are made uniform within a zone for service but different as between zones.

zoning laws. Ordinances or laws passed by cities and towns restricting certain sections of land in their use, e.g., residential, business, industrial, etc.